Antidiscrimination Law and Social Equality

Antidiscrimination Law and Social Equality

ANDREW KOPPELMAN

Yale University Press   New Haven and London

Designed by Sonia L. Scanlon.
Set in Minion type by Rainsford Type,
Danbury, Connecticut.
Printed in the United States of America by
BookCrafters, Inc., Chelsea, Michigan.

Library of Congress Cataloging-in-Publication Data

Koppelman, Andrew.
Antidiscrimination law and social equality /
Andrew Koppelman.
p.   cm.
Includes bibliographical references and index.
ISBN 0-300-06482-9 (cloth : alk. paper)
1. Equality—United States.
2. Discrimination—Law and legislation—
United States.   I. Title.
JC575.K65   1996
323.42'0973—dc20   95-42471
CIP

A catalogue record for this book is available
from the British Library.

The paper in this book meets the guidelines
for permanence and durability of the Committee
on Production Guidelines for Book Longevity
of the Council on Library Resources.

10 9 8 7 6 5 4 3 2 1

To my mother and to the memory of my father

Contents

Acknowledgments

My claim of sole authorship on the title page is a bit of an exaggeration; I couldn't have done this alone. This book began as a doctoral dissertation in the Yale Political Science Department, where Bruce Ackerman, Rogers M. Smith, and Steven Smith were as fine a group of supervisors as a student could hope for. All read multiple drafts with unflagging attention and graciously endured my incessant visits to their offices. The entire manuscript was also read by James W. Bailey, Shelley Burtt, John DiIulio, Samuel Issacharoff, Rogan Kersh, Madeline Morris, and Harry Wellington, each of whom offered helpful comments. For comments on individual chapters, thanks to Akhil Amar, Lawrie Balfour, John Boswell, George Chauncey, Henry Cohen, Peter DeMarneffe, Richard Epstein, Robert P. George, Robert Goodin, Amy Gutmann, James Hackney, Hendrik Hartog, Janet Halley, Jennifer Hochschild, Kenneth Karst, Arthur Kuflik, Marianne Engelman Lado, Sylvia Law, Brenda Lyshaug, Tim Lytton, David Mayhew, Richard Mohr, Walter Murphy, Russell Nieli, Thomas Pogge, Marc Poirier, Eva Saks, Frederick Schauer, Ian Shapiro, Joseph Sommer, Jonathan Stein, Cass Sunstein, Jim Tourtelott, and Steven Winter. Parts of the manuscript also received helpful comments at the Princeton Politics, Ethics, and Public Affairs Workshop and the Northeastern University School of Law Faculty Colloquium.

Everyone with whom I've had so much as a casual conversation about this subject in the past seven or eight years has sharpened my understanding of these issues. In this regard I am particularly grateful to my undergraduate and graduate students at Princeton, and (in addition to all those already mentioned) to Oliver Avens, Peter Berkowitz, Micaela DiLeonardo, Alan Dillingham, Wayne Edisis, Owen Fiss, Melvin Gilbert, Gregory Herek, Rick Hills, Carla Ingersoll, George Kateb, George Koppelman, Kitty Koppelman, Margaret Koppelman, Nancy Koppelman, Ruby Koppelman, John Kornfeld, Joan Lefford, Dan Lucich, Conrad Lynn, Catharine MacKinnon, Doug Reed, Alan Ryan, Raj Seshu, Jim Whitman, Evan Wolfson, Jim Wooten, and Ron Zucker.

James W. Bailey and Matthew Viglione also offered insightful comments and valuable research assistance.

Valerie Quinn not only has been a thoughtful interlocutor, a willing sounding board, a careful reader, and my best friend but she has cheerfully borne her first years of married life with a husband whose mind was often elsewhere. My son, Miles, made a crucial contribution by learning to entertain himself for hours while his father, sitting a few feet away, remained obliviously focused on this work.

Portions of this book have appeared in earlier form in the *New York University Law Review* and the *Yale Law Journal.*

Financial support was provided by the Center for the Study of Law, Economics, and Public Policy, Yale Law School; the National Endowment for the Humanities; the Princeton University Committee on Research in the Humanities and Social Sciences; and the Program in Ethics and the Professions, Harvard University.

Antidiscrimination Law and Social Equality

Introduction

Many and perhaps most Americans readily endorse the following propositions. (1) Part of what defines a free society is that it is none of the government's business what citizens believe and that the shaping of citizens' beliefs is not a legitimate task of a liberal state. (2) Racism, sexism, and similar ideologies are so evil and destructive of the proper workings of a free society that the state should do whatever it can to eradicate them.

The two propositions are, of course, contradictory, and ever since the Civil War antidiscrimination law has attempted to devise some accommodation between them. The approach first taken was to weaken the second principle in order to accommodate the first. This move is perhaps clearest in *Plessy v. Ferguson,* the 1896 decision in which the Fourteenth Amendment was held to permit a law that required racial segregation. The Supreme Court declared that "[t]he object of the amendment was undoubtedly to enforce the absolute equality of the two races before the law, but in the nature of things it could not have been intended to abolish distinctions based upon color, or to enforce social, as distinguished from political equality. . . ."[1] This distinction between social and political equality, and the exclusion of the former from antidiscrimination concerns, was taken for granted by the sole dissenter as well: "Every true man has pride of race," wrote Justice John M. Harlan, "and under appropriate circumstances when the rights of others, his equals before the law, are not to be affected, it is his privilege to express such pride and to take such action based upon it as to him seems proper."[2]

---

1. *Plessy v. Ferguson,* 163 U.S. 538, 544 (1896); cf. pp. 551–52. The Fourteenth Amendment provides, in pertinent part: "No State shall . . . deny to any person within its jurisdiction the equal protection of the laws."

2. *Plessy,* p. 554 (Harlan, J., dissenting). For Harlan's denial that integration implies social equality, see p. 561. In the examples that Harlan gives of situations in which whites and blacks might reasonably wish to travel together, the black is the employed servant of the white (see p. 553). Many of the Fourteenth Amendment's framers also believed in this distinction between social and political equality. See Raoul Berger, *Government by Judiciary: The Transformation of the Fourteenth Amendment* (Cambridge: Harvard University Press, 1977), pp. 169–76.

In recent years, the distinction between social and political equality that all the justices apparently took for granted in *Plessy* has been widely questioned, and many judicial and academic discussions of antidiscrimination envisage instead an increasingly ambitious project of cultural transformation. The growing tendency is to weaken the first of the two contradictory propositions in order to accommodate the second. This movement arguably began with *Brown v. Board of Education*, the case that effectively overruled *Plessy* by declaring that government-imposed segregation was unconstitutional. As Alexander Bickel observed, *Brown* relied on the argument "that the detrimental consequences of school segregation were heightened—merely heightened—when segregation had the sanction of law."[3] The movement for social equality was accelerated by the Civil Rights Act of 1964, which involved massive governmental intrusion into private economic choices. It also could be seen in the critique of societal racism that the civil rights movement of the 1960s made a part of ordinary political discourse. Today this project of cultural transformation is reflected in a broad range of demands that are made in the name of antidiscrimination. Traditional controversies over de facto school and housing segregation, school busing, and affirmative action have not abated, and they have been joined by new debates over discriminatory acts previously regarded as outside the reach of law, such as those by private clubs. There is now enormous sensitivity to the often subtle racial messages conveyed by everything from movies to school curricula. Some now call for the legal suppression of racist speech. It is frequently argued that American culture is pervasively racist and that therefore not only the condition of blacks but the consciousness of whites needs to be transformed.

The extension of antidiscrimination concerns from race to sex reaches even deeper into the workings of civil society. When sex discrimination in employment was outlawed in the 1960s, few imagined that sexual-equality concerns would become relevant to discussions of divorce, abortion, rape, pornography, or prostitution. New issues of sexual equality have also arisen in employment law itself, including sexual harassment, pregnancy leave, and comparable worth. It is now widely recognized that inequality in the workplace reinforces and is reinforced by inequality in the home, where women are disproportionately saddled with the unpaid tasks of housework and child care.

---

3. Alexander Bickel, *The Supreme Court and the Idea of Progress* (New Haven: Yale University Press, 1978), pp. 119–20.

Some feminists argue that the inferior social status of women has its roots in patterns of early childhood socialization that teach girls to take pleasure in their own subordination, and that these patterns, too, need to be changed.

Finally, there is pressure to extend antidiscrimination protection to other groups, most controversially to lesbians and gay men, who are asking not only for protection against discrimination but also for legal recognition of their right to marry and raise children. These demands are far more modest than those being made on behalf of blacks and women, since they involve only the equality before the law that was denied to blacks in *Plessy*. Nonetheless, they elicit vociferous resistance, for they would tend to change social mores, increasing the likelihood that eventually homosexuality would be regarded as in no way inferior to heterosexuality. It is the *social* equality of gays that opponents of gay rights are primarily concerned to resist.

These movements for social equality increasingly involve friction not only with conservative concerns for the preservation of traditionally valued institutions but also with such core liberal goals as freedom of speech, freedom of association, and freedom of religion. The question arises whether this broadening of antidiscrimination's ambitions is justified—more specifically, whether it rests on a legitimate inference from past cases whose proper resolution is already settled. Reasoning by analogy, the standard intellectual tool of lawyers, is a particularly attractive approach to this controversy,[4] because discourse on antidiscrimination law today, for all the division it reflects, rests on a solid consensus. Those as far apart as Jesse Jackson and William Bradford Reynolds agree that slavery was wrong; that theories of racial inferiority were wrong; that *Plessy v. Ferguson* was wrong; that *Brown v. Board of Education* was correct; that the civil rights acts of the 1960s, which outlawed private discrimination in employment and housing, are good laws; that sex discrimination is wrong for the same reasons that race discrimination is wrong.[5]

The disagreements have to do most fundamentally with what principles underlie these agreed-upon cases.[6] What is the evil that antidiscrimination law

---

4. On the strengths and weaknesses of this mode of reasoning, see Cass R. Sunstein, "On Analogical Reasoning," 106 *Harv. L. Rev.* 741 (1993).

5. Libertarians such as Richard Epstein take a different line, arguing, for example, that law should not coerce people to enter transactions they do not wish to enter. Part of my task in this book will be to answer the libertarians and to show that the consensus view is correct.

6. There are also tactical disagreements about how to achieve agreed-upon goals, such as the reduction of racially motivated violence, but these are beyond the scope of this book.

seeks to remedy? Is it simply a failure of impartiality on the part of government? Or is it a broader societal problem? If the latter, precisely what is the problem and why is it something that society is obligated to address?

Put baldly, the original formulation exemplified by both opinions in *Plessy* held that while the white majority had a duty to govern without racial partiality, it had no duty to stop being racist. Today many people feel that there is such a duty, and that it extends beyond racism to forbid prejudice against women and gays. Thus, for example, it is thought that the same considerations that made segregated schools wrong also make it wrong to tell certain jokes, even if (perhaps especially if) no one in the company in which they are told is likely to be offended. This book will defend the modern view. The government's efforts at institutional restructuring and the ordinary citizens' stigmatization of racism and other invidious beliefs are best understood as parts of a single project. Because there is now intense controversy over attempts to reshape culture in the name of antidiscrimination, it has become important to clarify what that project is and to what extent it is justified.

The project I am describing is one that already engages the many Americans who are persuaded that there are unconscious racist, sexist, and homophobic connotations to many meanings and practices they once took for granted, and who are working toward change. The state, too, is often engaged in such a transformative project. It is careful *not to encourage* racism, as when it (and here "it" sometimes means the judiciary) resists political demands for laws that disadvantage blacks, and it *discourages* racism, without directly relying on its coercive power, when it refuses to enforce racially restrictive covenants, or when it registers interracial marriages. Sometimes, however, the state uses coercion in order to transform citizens' racial consciousness. Schools are desegregated against parents' wishes, and part of the justification offered for this is that desegregation will produce less racism among children. Similar justifications have been given for the compulsory desegregation of the workplace, or of housing. The potential of antidiscrimination law to function as an overt instrument of cultural transformation has become more apparent in the context of sex discrimination law: the recently developed law of sexual harassment is forcing a significant shift in the mores of the workplace, even to the point of inducing some employers to adopt programs to reeducate their workers. Predictably, this transformative project calls forth resistance. Disagreement over this widespread effort to reshape culture has become one of the enduring sore points of contemporary American politics. Political theory, however, has been strangely silent about the foundations of a politics of cultural meaning. There has been an explosion of valuable work that *presupposes* a project of cultural transformation, but little has been written that *defends* that project.[7] This book is, in part, an effort to fill that gap.

There are worthy liberal traditions, deeply rooted in American culture, that regard with suspicion any attempt by government to transform the citizens' beliefs and preferences. Yet unless such a reshaping is deemed appropriate at least in some cases, many well-settled practices of antidiscrimination law cannot be justified. For example, antidiscrimination law restricts employers' ability to make race or sex a qualification for a job. The courts insist on this restriction even when employers' desire to discriminate reflects customers' preferences, and even for jobs whose whole point is to elicit certain customer reactions.[8] Thus, *Diaz v. Pan American World Airways, Inc.*[9] held that an airline could not justify its practice of hiring only female cabin attendants, even though female attendants had higher performance ratings than male attendants, female attendants seemed better able to reassure passengers who were anxious about flying, and both male and female passengers preferred female attendants. The provision of the Civil Rights Act of 1964 permitting sex discrimination where sex was a "bona fide occupational qualification" for the job, the court held, only applied "when the *essence* of the business operation would be undermined by not hiring members of one sex exclusively."[10] This was not the case here:

> The primary function of an airline is to transport passengers safely from one point to another. While a pleasant environment, enhanced by the obvious cosmetic effect that female stewardesses provide as well as, according to the findings of the trial court, their apparent ability to perform the non-mechanical functions of the job in a more effective manner than most men, may all be important, they are tangential to the essence of the business involved. No one has suggested that having male stewards will so seriously affect the operation of an airline as to jeopardize or even

7. A notable exception is Iris Marion Young's *Justice and the Politics of Difference* (Princeton: Princeton University Press, 1990), which I discuss in Chapter 2. Young argues, as I do, that social equality is a goal of social justice. See, e.g., p. 173.

8. See Alan Wertheimer, "Jobs, Qualifications, and Preferences," 94 *Ethics* 99 (1983).

9. 442 F.2d 385 (5th Cir. 1971).

10. Ibid., p. 388, emphasis in original.

minimize its ability to provide safe transportation from one place to another.[11]

Richard Epstein observes that this argument contains an error familiar to students of contract law. "Contracts do not have 'essences.' They have multiple terms and dimensions, and sensible contracting requires parties to make trade-offs at the margin of these many distinct dimensions. The choice that customers make between airlines depends not only on safety (a factor that may differ by only a tiny degree among the major carriers) but also on price, schedule, ground service, food, and of course in-flight service." Even if consumer demand is perfectly inelastic, so that the antidiscrimination rule will not cost airlines any business, "the social loss is measured by the decline in net consumer satisfaction." The *Diaz* case, Epstein argues, is a step toward tyranny: "[t]he statute tells a firm that it cannot provide its customers with the service they want and instead tells the customers to like the services that are provided."[12]

This argument cannot be easily dismissed. Samuel Issacharoff argues that "[w]here the imposition of antidiscrimination norms results in no loss of firm competitiveness vis-à-vis other firms, there is no other obvious reason why 'net consumer satisfaction' should override a societal determination to open up opportunities across a number of fields for persons of nontraditional races or sexes within that field."[13] But every job has qualifications that exclude certain classes of persons from competing for those jobs: most of us are too short to be professional basketball players and too tall to be professional jockeys. Should customer preferences also be ignored in this context in order to open up opportunities for persons of nontraditional heights within those fields? If not, why are race and sex different? Epstein is right that "very powerful justifications have to be found for one group to announce that another group's preferences just do not matter and they will be forced to do business with others on terms they find disadvantageous."[14] Even acknowledging that preferences are malleable, some justification is necessary when government goes into the business of deliberately shaping them. A showing that cultural

11. Ibid.

12. Richard A. Epstein, *Forbidden Grounds: The Case Against Employment Discrimination Laws* (Cambridge: Harvard University Press, 1992), p. 302, 303, 305.

13. Samuel Issacharoff, "Contractual Liberties in Discriminatory Markets," 70 *Tex. L. Rev.* 1219, 1244 (1992) (review of Epstein, *Forbidden Grounds*).

14. Epstein, *Forbidden Grounds*, p. 305.

reconstruction is a legitimate goal of the law is necessary in order to justify, not only novel and radical proposals, but rules of antidiscrimination law that have been around for decades. (Discarding those rules, on the other hand, would have ramifications well beyond the airline case. Epstein's position would equally justify employment discrimination against blacks whenever this reflects customers' racist preferences.) The theory that I will develop in this book is therefore important, not only for the controversial positions that I shall defend, but also for the justification of commitments that most Americans, liberal and conservative alike, already share.

A word about the position from which you are being addressed is in order. I am a white male, heterosexually inclined and married, securely employed, and comfortably above the poverty level—in short, a beneficiary of the system of privilege that this book discusses. My primary audience is people like me (though the topic is obviously of interest to others as well). My inquiry here might be stated to this primary audience as follows: Now that overt racism has been stigmatized and largely eliminated from political and legal decision making, what are our remaining obligations to the groups that those like us have traditionally oppressed, and whose oppression continues to benefit us? My claim is that we cannot do justice to these groups unless we change our very patterns of cultural expression and unconscious thinking.[15] At the least, we must become aware of these patterns, so that we can prevent them from influencing our behavior and avoid passing them on to our children. And this project of cultural transformation is one in which the state is appropriately enlisted where it can be helpful.

This book, then, will try to show why the elimination of racism and similarly invidious beliefs is an appropriate undertaking, both for citizens in general and for the state in particular. The question of *how* this is to be accomplished is a much larger and more complicated issue, and is beyond the scope of this book. I will, however, say how the conception I am defending *can* support certain measures, such as preferential treatment, given certain empirical premises that I find plausible but cannot fully defend here. My goal is to build a bridge between two well-developed discourses, antidiscrimination law and po-

---

15. Because the inquiry focuses on the pathologies of the dominant culture, this book is silent about what, if anything, "really" constitutes black identity, or female identity, or lesbian identity, or gay identity. My inquiry is focused on the false, unjustifiably stigmatizing meanings that are typically attached to these statuses. My interest is in sickness rather than health, illusion rather than reality.

litical philosophy, that have had surprisingly little contact given the centrality of issues of race, sex, and sexuality in American politics.

What I shall call "the antidiscrimination project" seeks to reconstruct social reality to eliminate or marginalize the shared meanings, practices, and institutions that unjustifiably single out certain groups of citizens for stigma and disadvantage. I apologize for this clumsy and somewhat misleading term, which I use for want of a better one. Iris Marion Young has observed that discrimination is not the only or even the primary wrong that is inflicted on oppressed groups such as blacks and women.

> If one focuses on discrimination as the primary wrong groups suffer, then the more profound wrongs of exploitation, marginalization, powerlessness, cultural imperialism, and violence that we still suffer go undiscussed and unaddressed. One misses how the weight of society's institutions and people's assumptions, habits, and behavior toward others are directed at reproducing the material and ideological conditions that make life easier for, provide greater real opportunities to, and establish the priority of the point of view of white heterosexual men.[16]

I nonetheless use the term "antidiscrimination project" because it plainly indicates that area of social practice concerned with remedying the disadvantages of blacks, women, and other unjustly stigmatized groups.[17] "The equality project" or "the anti-oppression project" would be too broad, because inequality and oppression both sometimes take forms that are not directly traceable to the entrenched, taken-for-granted social meanings of race, sex, or sexuality. "The civil rights project" would be too narrow, because the aim of the project is to transform culture, not just legal entitlements, and to end those unjust private practices—the most notorious of which is discrimination—that exacerbate the disadvantages of these groups.

16. Young, *Justice and the Politics of Difference*, pp. 196–97.

17. I have focused here on blacks, women, and gays. I argue in Chapters 3 and 4 that a group is an appropriate beneficiary of this kind of project of cultural reconstruction if it has been disadvantaged in the same way as blacks and for similarly unacceptable reasons. There are, of course, other groups whose claims are worthy of consideration: ethnic groups such as Hispanics and Asians, and other groups such as the aged or the physically less able. I take up the cases I do in order to help fix ideas, not because the cases I do not take up are undeserving of attention. This book does not purport to offer an exhaustive list of the forms of cultural oppression. It will, I hope, provide the tools to think about other cases as well as those I specifically address.

This project is worth undertaking for three reasons. First, the government cannot attain the level of impartiality among citizens that justice and democracy require so long as racism and similarly invidious beliefs remain pervasive in the culture from which governmental decision makers are drawn. Second, every human being has a need to be recognized as a valued member of society; justification is required whenever such recognition is withheld, and no such justification is possible for the prejudices at issue here. Third, the extreme material disadvantages that some citizens suffer, and that no one should have to endure, are reinforced and perpetuated by these prejudices.

Stigmatized social status and the concomitant withholding of respect are in a sense the central evil the project seeks to remedy, since it is the source of the poison that contaminates, and renders unfair the outcomes of, public and private decision making. Stigma and insult are familiar parts of the daily experience of many in our society who are, for example, black, female, or gay. (It is compounded for those who belong to more than one of these categories.) The message of their inferiority is ubiquitous and constant, often received from people who do not even realize they are communicating it. The other injuries that concern the antidiscrimination project are bound up with this one. It is because some classes of people are stigmatized and regarded as inferior that government decision making fails to give due regard to their interests; the disproportionate poverty of women and blacks signifies their stigmatized social status.

In the paradigmatic case of blacks, the ultimate goal of antidiscrimination law is to eliminate not merely racial inequality but racism itself. The Fourteenth Amendment prohibits the state from using its power to promote racism and other beliefs that unfairly stigmatize some classes of people. Antidiscrimination statutes prohibit private actors from distributing valued goods such as jobs and housing in accordance with them. Both of these legal mechanisms are best understood as part of this larger project of cultural transformation.

I am *not* claiming that American culture is monolithically racist and sexist. Fifty years ago, prevailing attitudes were far worse than they are now. Although much remains to be done, the progress that has been made is remarkable. Racism and sexism are endemic in American culture, but they coexist (uneasily) with liberal and egalitarian traditions that are very much at odds with them. The tension between these competing values has been a source of political dispute for centuries, with participants often attempting (sometimes successfully) to enlist the assistance of the state.[18] The question this book seeks to address is whether such state involvement in the reshaping of culture is justified, and if so, what the limits of such legitimate involvement are.

The antidiscrimination project represents a claim of enormous moral power: the demand that society recognize the human worth of all its members, that no person arbitrarily be despised or devalued. Yet as soon as we begin to try to carry it out, we find ourselves in collision with other moral considerations, equally powerful, that demand that the project be a limited one: social order, efficiency, communal solidarity, individual liberty. As Isaiah Berlin has observed, because "the ends of men are many, and not all of them are in principle compatible with each other . . . the possibility of conflict—and of tragedy—can never wholly be eliminated from human life, either personal or social. The necessity of choosing between absolute claims is then an inescapable characteristic of the human condition."[19] The project's scope is limited, paradoxically, by the very magnitude of the evil it seeks to combat. For the meanings, practices, and institutions that stigmatize unjustly are the same meanings, practices, and institutions that constitute our culture. And because this is so, to carry out the project from above would require the totalitarian smashing and reshaping of that culture. We have already seen what fruit such efforts have borne in this century. The project can be accomplished only with the willing participation of the citizens. And they are entitled to decide to what degree they will devote themselves to it, for the demands the project makes on them are tempered by other imperatives equally absolute.

Even acknowledging that it would be terrible if government were to pursue the antidiscrimination project single-mindedly, we must also acknowledge how terrible it would be if government did not pursue it at all. In the present political climate, when it has become fashionable to denounce the project's transformative ambitions as "the cult of political correctness," the latter seems the more pressing danger. No formula can dictate how to resolve conflicts among values when they arise. The formulation of the antidiscrimination project I am setting forth here is useful because it permits the people doing the balancing to understand as fully as possible the values they must weigh against one another. The philosophical case for the values that compete with the

18. See Rogers M. Smith, "Beyond Tocqueville, Myrdal, and Hartz: The Multiple Traditions in America," 87 *Am. Pol. Sci. Rev.* 549 (1993).

19. Isaiah Berlin, "Two Concepts of Liberty," in *Four Essays on Liberty* (Oxford: Oxford University Press, 1969), p. 169.

antidiscrimination project are well understood, but there remains considerable confusion about what evil antidiscrimination law seeks to address. Unless decision makers understand what the antidiscrimination project is and why it is important, they are unlikely to strike the correct balance between it and other values.

This is primarily an essay in philosophy rather than law. While the argument implies a theory of the Civil War amendments,[20] I do not pretend that such a theory is adequately developed here. The purpose of this book is not to show that these principles are embodied in any existing constitutional provision, statute, or set of legal precedents. The theorists of antidiscrimination law on whom I draw have all made that claim. If at least one of them is right, and if, as I claim, they all converge in supporting the antidiscrimination project as I conceive it, then my conclusions have legal implications. I shall state these where they arise. I do not, however, give much attention to the text and history of the Fourteenth Amendment or its place within the structure of the Constitution as a whole. That work has been capably done by others.

Rather, my aim here is to formulate the principles that ought to guide a society in which some are unjustly stigmatized. Political philosophy is usually addressed to some state actor: courts, legislatures, the framers of constitutions. This book is addressed not only to them but also to the people at large. It obviously matters which side the government is on. Both Jim Crow laws and civil rights statutes have, in their time, helped shape popular culture, and this book will explore when and why it is appropriate for laws to do this. But the obligations I am exploring attach primarily to citizens, not government. I shall examine Supreme Court decisions, among other sources, but I shall do this because the Court is an unusually influential participant in the debate about the philosophical basis of antidiscrimination law, and the ideas that appear in its opinions are usually held by a significant part of the citizenry.

The first four chapters argue that the shift in antidiscrimination discourse toward a project of cultural transformation is, indeed, demanded by powerful and persuasive moral principles. The last two chapters consider the limits of that project. Chapters 1 and 2 critically survey the leading theories of antidiscrimination law, and show that all are implicitly committed to the antidiscrim-

---

20. The Thirteenth Amendment, outlawing slavery, the Fourteenth, guaranteeing due process and the equal protection of the laws, and the Fifteenth, prohibiting denial of the vote on account of race, were all passed in the immediate aftermath of the Civil War.

ination project as I have described it. Chapters 3 and 4 defend the extension of the project toward promoting the social equality of women and gays. Chapter 5 examines contemporary liberal theory in order to see how it adjudicates conflicts between civil liberties and the commitment to eradicating racism, sexism, and heterosexism. Finally, Chapter 6 takes up the controversy over hate speech and pornography, in which the tension between the antidiscrimination project and other liberal commitments is especially clear.

1

Process-Based Theories

What, precisely, is the evil that antidiscrimination law seeks to remedy? I begin with this question, because if the evil is local or of modest scale, then measures to remedy it may be correspondingly confined. If the evil is broad and pervasive, then the effort to end it must be a correspondingly broad and ambitious project.

In these first two chapters, I will argue for the latter view. My method will be dialectical: I will describe the major theories of antidiscrimination law that have been set forth and subject them to critical examination. Although I find weaknesses in each of the theories, each also has a valid core, and my aim is a synthesis that preserves and builds upon the best in all of them. Each theory insightfully describes one moment of a larger process by which the inferior status of certain groups is socially produced and reproduced. It is this process of cultural construction, I conclude, that antidiscrimination law seeks to change.

The evil that antidiscrimination law seeks to remedy is most typically understood by analogy with or as instantiated by the segregated schools that the Supreme Court declared unconstitutional in *Brown v. Board of Education*.[1] Antidiscrimination law, it is said, prohibits discriminations of that sort. But what does that mean? What was wrong with segregated schools?

The gravamen of *Brown* was that segregated schools violated the equal protection clause of the Fourteenth Amendment, which provides that "No State shall . . . deny to any person within its jurisdiction the equal protection of the laws." The historical record shows that the amendment was intended, at the very least, to make clear the power of Congress to nullify the notorious Black Codes, which were enacted by the Southern states immediately after the Civil

1. 347 U.S. 483 (1954).

13

War in an attempt to restore slavery to the greatest extent consistent with formal emancipation.[2] This does not exhaust the amendment's reach, however. There is much evidence that the framers intended a broad guarantee of equality, and one of the most persuasive pieces of this evidence is the sweeping language of the equal protection clause itself.

This clause has been the site of much of the disputation, and most of the philosophizing, about the meaning of antidiscrimination law. There is general agreement that impermissible discrimination is the kind that, if practiced by government, would violate this constitutional provision. Antidiscrimination law reaches private action because some private actors are held to the same obligation not to discriminate that government has (whatever that obligation may be). But as Owen Fiss has observed, no content can be found in the equal protection clause without the aid of some kind of interpretive theory:

> The words—no state shall "deny to any person within its jurisdiction the equal protection of the laws"—do not state an intelligible rule of decision. In that sense the text has no meaning. The Clause contains the word "equal" and thereby gives constitutional status to the ideal of equality, but that ideal is capable of a wide range of meanings. This ambiguity has created the need for a mediating principle.[3]

The ambiguity of the equal protection clause has forced its interpreters to devise more specific conceptions of equality, and to argue that the text should be read as enacting one such specific conception. Because the clause's language (and, as it happens, its legislative history) provides so little guidance, the search for such a conception has perforce been as much a moral as a legal inquiry. Since the language is vague enough to be consistent with many different conceptions of equality, interpreters have tended to ask themselves which of these conceptions is most attractive in itself. The provision's vagueness has forced lawyers to become philosophers. Here I leave to one side the question of whether this is an appropriate or desirable way for lawyers to proceed. The

2. For a brief account of the Black Codes, see Eric Foner, *Reconstruction: America's Unfinished Revolution* (New York: Harper & Row, 1988), pp. 199–210; on the intent of the framers of the Fourteenth Amendment, see William E. Nelson, *The Fourteenth Amendment: From Political Principle to Judicial Doctrine* (Cambridge and London: Harvard University Press, 1988).

3. Owen Fiss, "Groups and the Equal Protection Clause," in Marshall Cohen, Thomas Nagel, and Thomas Scanlon, eds., *Equality and Preferential Treatment* (Princeton: Princeton University Press, 1977), p. 85.

fact is that, by so proceeding, different legal theorists have come up with different conceptions of equality, each of which has something important to teach us. Since lawyers have had to become philosophers, I propose here to read them as philosophers, examining the mediating principles that have been offered, by the Supreme Court and its commentators, to give meaning to the equal protection clause.

The Court's own justifications for its interpretations of the equal protection clause are too thin, fragmentary, and inconsistently followed in its decisions to be properly called a "theory." To begin with, the Court has interpreted the equal protection clause as prohibiting arbitrary discrimination, or treating similar things dissimilarly. Without more, this produces a very deferential standard of judicial review. "The general rule is that legislation is presumed to be valid and will be sustained if the classification drawn by the statute is rationally related to a legitimate state interest."[4] Because this stress on mere rationality threatens to transform the clause into a minor protection against legislative carelessness,[5] the clause has been given teeth in cases where the challenged classification is based on race: "[A]ll legal restrictions which challenge the civil rights of a single racial group are immediately suspect."[6] When legislation employs such classifications, "these laws are subjected to strict scrutiny and will be sustained only if they are suitably tailored to serve a compelling state interest."[7] This second, higher level of scrutiny has been justified with the explanation that race is "so seldom relevant to the achievement of any legitimate interest that laws grounded in such considerations are deemed to reflect prejudice and antipathy—a view that those in the burdened class are not as worthy and deserving as others."[8] Almost no legislation has been able to satisfy that test, whereas almost any legislation can meet the "minimal scrutiny" that asks whether the statute is rationally related to a legitimate state interest.[9] In the 1970s, the Court devised a third, intermediate level of scrutiny:

4. *City of Cleburne v. Cleburne Living Center,* 473 U.S. 432, 440 (1985).

5. And perhaps not even against that, since any statute's terms suggest a purpose that the statute rationally serves. See Robert F. Nagel, Note, "Legislative Purpose, Rationality, and Equal Protection," 82 *Yale L. J.* 123 (1972).

6. *Korematsu v. United States,* 323 U.S. 214, 216 (1944).

7. *Cleburne,* at 440.

8. Ibid.

9. See Gerald Gunther, "The Supreme Court, 1971 Term—Foreword: In Search of Evolving Doctrine on a Changing Court: A Model for a Newer Equal Protection," 86 *Harv. L. Rev.* 1, 8 (1972).

classifications based on sex[10] or illegitimacy[11] are what has been infelicitously called "quasi-suspect"; they "will survive equal protection scrutiny to the extent they are substantially related to a legitimate state interest."[12] The Court has not, however, explained how it has determined whether a given type of classification is suspect or quasi-suspect.[13] Moreover, commentators have noted that the insistence on close fit between means and end, varying in strictness with the level of scrutiny, has only an indirect relation to the evils of racial oppression against which the clause was originally enacted.[14] As for cases in which a law does not overtly employ a suspect classification, but disproportionately harms blacks, the Court has said that there is no constitutional violation unless the legislators were motivated by discriminatory intent.[15] Rather than offering a theory of the amendment to explain why intent was an appropriate standard, however, the Court has said only that it was apprehensive about the consequences of one alternative rule.[16]

Because the Court has been so cryptic, commentators have sought to do what the Court has not by explaining more explicitly the principle or principles that define impermissible discrimination. Some of these writers think that the law is primarily concerned with a flawed *process* of decision making, whereas others focus on the *results* of discrimination, though different thinkers stress different results. I will address the work of the former in this chapter and of the latter in the next. I believe both approaches are ultimately inadequate,

10. *Craig v. Boren*, 429 U.S. 190 (1976).

11. *Mathews v. Lucas*, 427 U.S. 495 (1976).

12. *Mills v. Habluetzel*, 456 U.S. 91, 99 (1982).

13. See Judith A. Baer, *Equality Under the Constitution: Reclaiming the Fourteenth Amendment* (Ithaca and London: Cornell University Press, 1983), pp. 260–64.

14. See Fiss, "Groups and the Equal Protection Clause," pp. 84–123.

15. *Hunter v. Underwood*, 471 U.S. 222, 227–28 (1985); *Personnel Adm'r v. Feeney*, 442 U.S. 256, 272 (1979); *Village of Arlington Heights v. Metropolitan Dev. Housing Corp.*, 429 U.S. 252, 265 (1977); *Washington v. Davis*, 426 U.S. 229, 246–48 (1976).

16. "A rule that a statute designed to serve neutral ends is nevertheless invalid, absent compelling justification, if in practice it benefits or burdens one race more than another would be far reaching and would raise serious questions about, and perhaps invalidate, a whole range of tax, welfare, public service, regulatory, and licensing statutes that may be more burdensome to the poor and to the average black than to the more affluent white." *Washington v. Davis*, at 248. This ignores the possibility of any intermediate principle between these two extremes, such as a shift in the burden of proof. See Paul Brest, "The Supreme Court, 1975 Term—Foreword: In Defense of the Antidiscrimination Principle," 90 *Harv. L. Rev.* 1, 29 (1976); Theodore Eisenberg, "Disproportionate Impact and Illicit Motive: Theories of Constitutional Adjudication," 52 *N.Y.U. L. Rev.* 36, 46–47 (1977).

even taken purely on their own terms, because they fail to map sufficiently the evil they seek to remedy. The aspirations of each theorist can only be realized in the context of a larger transformative project—one that seeks to eliminate from ordinary social life the meanings, practices, and institutions that unjustifiably stigmatize and disadvantage some groups.

Focusing on Process

The process-based understanding of equal protection builds on footnote four in *United States v. Carolene Products,* which declared that "prejudice against discrete and insular minorities may be a special condition, which tends seriously to curtail the operation of those political processes ordinarily to be relied upon to protect minorities, and which may call for a correspondingly more searching judicial inquiry."[17] The Court eventually developed this suggestion into doctrine: "[A]ll legal restrictions which curtail the civil rights of a single racial group are immediately suspect. That is not to say that all such restrictions are unconstitutional. It is to say that courts must subject them to more rigid scrutiny. Pressing public necessity may sometimes justify the existence of such restrictions; racial antagonism never can."[18] The settled doctrine today is that "the invidious quality of a law claimed to be racially discriminatory must ultimately be traced to a racially discriminatory purpose."[19] This view draws its power from the fact that the idea of equality does not entail the guarantee of any specific, substantive right. As John Hart Ely, the leading scholarly exponent of the process theory, puts it, "unconstitutionality in the distribution of benefits that are not themselves constitutionally required can intelligibly inhere only in the way the distribution was arrived at."[20]

Some commentators have objected that, because discriminatory intent is so hard to prove, the process theory in effect insulates most political decisions that disadvantage blacks from judicial review. David Strauss argues that the Court's adoption of the discriminatory intent requirement was an effort to tame the radical implications of the Fourteenth Amendment: "[O]f the several possible conceptions of discrimination, the Court chose the one that

17. 304 U.S. 144, 152 n. 4 (1938).

18. *Korematsu,* at 216.

19. *Washington v. Davis,* at 240.

20. John Hart Ely, *Democracy and Distrust* (Cambridge: Harvard University Press, 1980), p. 145.

appeared to be the most determinate and the least far-reaching."[21] In this chapter, however, I shall argue that even this conception requires an ambitious project of cultural transformation.

Ely's foundational premise, which he draws from the writings of Ronald Dworkin, is that the equal protection clause requires that citizens be treated with "equal concern and respect,"[22] and that the process that violates the Constitution is one in which the citizens are not so treated.[23] It will be convenient to begin by considering the argument as originally presented by Dworkin. While Dworkin is not often identified as a process theorist, we will see that he best articulates the conceptual foundation on which process theory relies.

Dworkin's Process Theory

According to Dworkin, any calculus for aggregating citizens' preferences that purports to treat each citizen equally, such as the calculus imagined by utilitarianism (which seeks to maximize citizens' welfare or the satisfaction of their

21. David Strauss, "Discriminatory Intent and the Taming of *Brown*," 56 *U. Chi. L. Rev.* 935, 939 (1989).

22. Ronald Dworkin, "Reverse Discrimination," in *Taking Rights Seriously* (Cambridge: Harvard University Press, 1978), pp. 226–28. Ely borrows the phrase from Dworkin; see *Democracy and Distrust*, p. 82. Dworkin makes equal concern and respect the fundamental principle not just of his theory of the amendment but of his larger philosophy of rights: "[O]ur intuitions about justice presuppose not only that people have rights but that one right among these is fundamental and even axiomatic. This most fundamental of rights is a distinct conception of equality, which I call the right to equal concern and respect." "Introduction," in *Taking Rights Seriously*, p. xii. Elaborating on what this means, Dworkin writes that government is obligated to treat those whom it governs "with concern, that is, as human beings who are capable of suffering and frustration, and respect, that is, as human beings who are capable of forming and acting on intelligent conceptions of how their lives should be lived." "What Rights Do We Have?," in *Taking Rights Seriously*, p. 272. The philosophical basis of this conception is not elaborated by Dworkin, who simply relies on the fact that it is widely held. "[F]ew citizens, and even fewer politicians, would now admit to political convictions that contradict the abstract principle of equal concern and respect." "Liberalism," in *A Matter of Principle* (Cambridge: Harvard University Press, 1985), p. 191.

Ely derives the principle from a duty of "virtual representation," *Democracy and Distrust*, pp. 82–87. This argument is discussed below.

23. Ely repeatedly stresses that his theory is concerned with process and not substance. Dworkin puts it this way less often, but when the issue arises he readily acknowledges that his theory is "in a sense, a 'process' or '*Carolene Products*' justification for [judicial] review." "The Forum of Principle," in *A Matter of Principle*, p. 66.

preferences), must consider only each citizen's *personal* preferences, defined as preferences for her own enjoyment of some goods or opportunities, and not any *external* preferences, defined as preferences she might have for the assignment of goods and opportunities to others.

> The distinction between personal and external preferences is of great importance for this reason. If a utilitarian argument counts external preferences along with personal preferences, then the egalitarian character of that argument is corrupted, because the chance that anyone's preferences have to succeed will then depend, not only on the demands that the personal preferences of others make on scarce resources, but on the respect or affection they have for him or for his way of life. If external preferences tip the balance, then the fact that a policy makes the community better off in a utilitarian sense would *not* provide a justification compatible with the right of those it disadvantages to be treated as equals.[24]

From this it follows that racist preferences must be excluded from the utilitarian calculus. If they are not, "[b]lacks will suffer, to a degree that depends upon the strength of the racist preference, from the fact that others think them less worthy of respect and concern."[25]

The right to equal concern and respect, Dworkin concludes, therefore can justify judicial review of democratically made decisions. The process theorists are characteristically troubled by Alexander Bickel's claims that "judicial review is a counter-majoritarian force in our system," and that "when the Supreme Court declares unconstitutional a legislative act or the action of an elected executive, it thwarts the will of the representatives of the actual people of the here and now; it exercises control, not in behalf of the prevailing majority, but against it."[26] Since Bickel, many constitutional theorists have seen their task as reconciling unpopular judicial decisions, such as *Brown v. Board of Education*, with Bickel's "counter-majoritarian difficulty." Dworkin's theory attempts to do this. The trumping of democratically reached decisions, he argues, is legitimate to the extent that these decisions are the expression of external preferences. It will, of course, ordinarily be impossible to determine

24. Dworkin, "Reverse Discrimination," in *Taking Rights Seriously,* p. 235.
25. Ibid.
26. Alexander Bickel, *The Least Dangerous Branch* (New Haven and London: Yale University Press, 2nd ed. 1986), pp. 16–17.

how many of the votes in a legislative decision were determined by personal preferences and how many were determined by external ones. "The liberal, therefore, needs a scheme of civil rights whose effect will be to determine those political decisions that are antecedently likely to reflect strong external preferences and to remove those decisions from majoritarian political institutions altogether."[27]

In order for this argument to be useful to us, it requires further refinement. Ely himself has objected that Dworkin's interpretation of utilitarianism will not, in general, work: "[I]n many ways the whole point of utilitarianism is to avoid picking and choosing among people's preferences (and the ways they arrived at them)—'push-pin is as good as poetry' and all that—and it is just that sort of picking and choosing that Dworkin is counseling."[28] If utilitarianism's goal is to maximize the amount of welfare or preference satisfaction in the world, then the failure to count certain kinds of preferences will hinder the realization of this goal.

Perhaps in response to this criticism, Dworkin has since recast his argument, so that it now focuses on the cognitive component of certain external preferences—a cognitive component that is inconsistent with the egalitarian commitment of utilitarianism.

> Utilitarianism must claim (as . . . any political theory must claim) truth for itself, and therefore must claim the falsity of any theory that contradicts it. It must itself occupy, that is, all the logical space that its content requires. But neutral utilitarianism claims (or, in any case, presupposes) that no one is, in principle, any more entitled to have any of his preferences fulfilled than anyone else is.[29]

Some preferences implicitly or explicitly deny what utilitarianism affirms.

> Suppose the community contains a Nazi, for example, whose set of preferences includes the preference that Aryans have more and Jews less of their preferences fulfilled just because of who they are. A neutral utilitarian cannot say that there is no reason in political morality for rejecting

---

27. Dworkin, "Liberalism," in *A Matter of Principle*, p. 197; see also idem, "What Rights Do We Have?," in *Taking Rights Seriously*, pp. 276–77.

28. John Hart Ely, "Professor Dworkin's External/Personal Preference Distinction," 1983 *Duke L. J.* 959, 978; for a similar objection, see H. L. A. Hart, "Between Utility and Rights," 79 *Colum. L. Rev.* 828, 842 (1979).

29. Dworkin, "Do We Have a Right to Pornography?," in *A Matter of Principle*, pp. 361–62.

or dishonoring that preference, for not dismissing it as just wrong, for not striving to fulfill it with all the dedication that officials devote to fulfilling any other sort of preference. For utilitarianism itself supplies such a reason: its most fundamental tenet is that people's preferences should be weighed on an equal basis in the same scales, that the Nazi theory of justice is profoundly wrong, and that officials should oppose the Nazi theory and strive to defeat rather than fulfill it. A neutral utilitarian is barred, for reasons of consistency, from taking the same politically neutral attitude toward the Nazi's political preference that he takes toward other sorts of preferences.[30]

This passage,[31] Ely observes, shows that Dworkin is selective in his hostility to external preferences. The kind of external preference that really cannot be permitted to infect the legislative process is "an external preference of the malign sort, involving a desire to deprive another person or group of an equal share of life's goods and opportunities."[32] It is legislation designed to gratify this kind of external preference, Ely concludes, that is constitutionally forbidden:

There is nothing wrong, either in utilitarian theory or in the context of the United States Constitution, with an individual constituent's gaining his satisfaction from the satisfaction of another or formulating his preferences on the basis of either a utilitarian balance or an ideal argument,

30. Ibid., p. 362. The argument has been independently developed, at greater length, by Robert E. Goodin, who makes clear the differences between it and Dworkin's original formulation. See his *Political Theory and Public Policy* (Chicago and London: University of Chicago Press, 1982), pp. 73–94, and his "Laundering Preferences," in Jon Elster and Aanund Hylland, eds., *Foundations of Social Choice Theory* (Cambridge: Cambridge University Press, 1986), pp. 85–86.

31. Actually, Ely ("Professor Dworkin's External/Personal Preference Distinction," p. 984) quotes an earlier, but not materially different, version of it. Ronald Dworkin, "Is There a Right to Pornography?," 1 *Oxford J. Leg. Stud.* 177, 203 (1981).

32. Ely, "Professor Dworkin's External/Personal Preference Distinction," p. 984. Hart, "Between Utility and Rights," p. 843, similarly notes that Dworkin's argument is that "a *particular kind* of external preference, one which denies liberty and is assumed to express contempt, fails to treat persons as equals. But this is a vice not of the mere externality of the preferences that have tipped the balance but of their content: that is, their liberty-denying and respect-denying content." Dworkin picked up on this suggestion, and (to my knowledge) made the Nazi argument for the first time, in his reply to Hart. See "A Reply by Ronald Dworkin," in Marshall Cohen, ed., *Ronald Dworkin and Contemporary Jurisprudence* (Totowa, N.J.: Rowman & Allanheld, 1984), pp. 283–85. This reply was later incorporated into the essay on pornography from which the quotations I use are drawn.

and certainly there is nothing wrong with a government official's taking preferences thus formed into full account in deciding what will most satisfy his constituency. What *does* violate the duty of equal representation that has informed our Constitution from the beginning, and undeniably animates the equal protection clause, is the counting of *one particular kind* of "external" preference, one rooted in a belief that certain racial or other groups simply deserve less of life's good things than the rest of us.[33]

This passage from Ely captures well what so many judges find attractive about a process-based theory of antidiscrimination law.[34] The reason certain preferences need to be excluded from the decision-making process is not because they are external, but because they are malign. Moreover, although Ely speaks of "malign external preferences,"[35] personal preferences can also be malign, in the sense that they are "rooted in a belief that certain racial or other groups simply deserve less of life's good things than the rest of us." As Dworkin's critics have observed, in a discriminatory society, whites, who are in the majority, "may have a perfectly natural personal preference for the status quo."[36] Dworkin's revised theory, however, is immune to this criticism. These whites are essentially asking that institutions be maintained that are designed to give their needs greater weight than the needs of blacks. This desire may be a personal preference, but it necessarily denies the equality that utilitarianism affirms.

The very grounds we have for accepting utilitarianism in the first place,

33. Ely, "Professor Dworkin's External/Personal Preference Distinction," p. 985 (emphases in original).

34. It is the conclusion that Dworkin's argument really leads to, though Ely has to state it for him. Dworkin appears to have modified his views to account for the criticism. The most recent, brief restatement of the argument, in *Law's Empire* (Cambridge: Belknap Press of Harvard University Press, 1986), no longer relies on the external/personal distinction. He still holds that "some preferences must be disregarded in any acceptable calculation of what makes the community better off on the whole," but he describes these uncountable preferences as "preferences that are rooted in some form of prejudice against one group" (Dworkin, *Law's Empire*, pp. 388, 384). He does not define "prejudice."

35. Ely, "Professor Dworkin's External/Personal Preference Distinction," pp. 985–86 n. 79.

36. Michel Rosenfeld, *Affirmative Action and Justice: A Philosophical and Constitutional Inquiry* (New Haven and London: Yale University Press, 1991), p. 108. See also James S. Liebman, "Desegregating Politics: 'All-Out' School Desegregation Explained," 90 *Colum. L. Rev.* 1463, 1536–37 (1990); Robert L. Simon, "Individual Rights and 'Benign' Discrimination," 90 *Ethics* 88, 93 (1979); George Sher, "Reverse Discrimination, the Future, and the Past," 90 *Ethics* 81, 83–84 (1979).

Dworkin argues, also require us to omit certain preferences from the utilitarian calculus. "Utilitarianism owes whatever appeal it has to its egalitarian cast. (Or, if that is too strong, would lose whatever appeal it has but for that cast.)"[37] A version of utilitarianism that regarded the welfare of certain persons as less valuable than the welfare of others would be a most unattractive one. But counting the personal preferences of whites for a racist regime corrupts utilitarianism in precisely that way. If the principle that everyone is entitled to equal concern and respect is a large part of one's reason for endorsing utilitarianism, then the version of utilitarianism that is endorsed must refuse to count those personal preferences. In Robert E. Goodin's pithy formulation, "We respect people's choices because we respect people, not the other way around."[38]

It may be misleading to characterize Dworkin as a process theorist, if this implies indifference to substantive goals. Similarly, it is unclear whether there is anything particularly utilitarian about his antidiscrimination theory. Will Kymlicka observes that the major weakness of utilitarianism is that it interprets the equal consideration to which persons are entitled "in terms of the aggregation of pre-existing preferences, whatever they are for, even if they invade the rights or commitments of others. But our intuitions tell us that equality should enter into the very formation of our preferences. Part of what it means to show equal consideration for others is taking into account what rightfully belongs to them in deciding on one's own goals in life."[39] Certain preferences are simply illegitimate. They are, as Ely puts it, malign. Their illegitimacy follows from, but does not necessarily depend upon, the correctness of utilitarianism as a moral theory. They are condemned by any philosophy that denies that race is an appropriate basis for treating different people with different degrees of concern and respect. Utilitarianism thus functions in Dworkin's argument as a placeholder for any philosophical view that contradicts racism. The same place in the argument might as easily be filled by liberalism, Christianity, or Marxism. The repudiation of racist decision making may thus be the object of what John Rawls has called "an overlapping consensus." Different persons will arrive at this conclusion on the basis of different comprehensive views, and each endorses it from her own point of view, but the object

37. Dworkin, "Do We Have a Right to Pornography?," in *A Matter of Principle*, p. 360.
38. Goodin, *Political Theory and Public Policy*, p. 80.
39. Will Kymlicka, *Contemporary Political Philosophy: An Introduction* (Oxford: Clarendon Press, 1990), p. 42.

of consensus is nonetheless a moral conception that is affirmed on moral grounds.[40]

Dworkin and Cultural Transformation

We have seen that Dworkin's argument condemns limitations on the opportunities of some that are the result of the malign preferences of others. Does Dworkin's theory thereby support a project of cultural transformation? I believe it does, because it reaches beyond government decision making. Dworkin writes that equal concern and respect entail "a right to political independence: the right that no one suffer disadvantage in the distribution of goods or opportunities on the ground that others think he should have less because of who he is or is not, or that others care less for him than they do for other people."[41] This formulation makes no reference to the identity of the entity doing the distributing. Government is not the only distributor of goods or opportunities; they are disbursed from loci scattered throughout society. Thus Dworkin can explain and justify civil rights statutes that prohibit discrimination by nongovernmental actors.

The duty of equal concern and respect, Dworkin thinks, applies only to public decision making. In our personal decisions, "we are not neutral and impartial, day to day, but committed and attached." This is not a moral failing, but a moral ideal. "We do not regret our personal commitment and partiality and engagement, or struggle to overcome these as signs of weakness. On the contrary we believe them human and appropriate. Only a zombie, we think, would be neutral about the good life in the decisions he made for others as well as himself, and only a monster would find no more demand in the pain of his child than in the cry of a stranger."[42] Nonetheless, some kinds of partiality in private decision making raise moral difficulties. Not all kinds of local attachment entail hostility toward or systematic devaluation of certain outgroups, and some attachments that do entail these things may nonetheless have no significant effect on the lives of those who are the objects of such

40. See John Rawls, *Political Liberalism* (New York: Columbia University Press, 1993), pp. 133–72, esp. pp. 147–48.

41. Dworkin, "Do We Have a Right to Pornography?," in *A Matter of Principle*, p. 364.

42. Ronald Dworkin, "Foundations of Liberal Equality," in Grethe B. Peterson, ed., *The Tanner Lectures on Human Values XI: 1990* (Salt Lake City: University of Utah Press, 1990), p. 14.

hostility or devaluation. But Dworkin argues that racism in the United States is not like that:

> American society is currently a racially conscious society; this is the inevitable and evident consequence of a history of slavery, repression, and prejudice. Black men and women, boys and girls, are not free to choose for themselves in what roles—or as members of what social groups—others will characterize them. They are black, and no other feature of personality or allegiance or ambition will so thoroughly influence how they will be perceived or treated by others, and the range and character of the lives that will be open to them.[43]

Dworkin further argues that "a political and economic system that allows prejudice to destroy some people's lives does not treat all members of the community with equal concern." For this reason, social resources should be distributed in a way calculated "to place victims [of prejudice] in a position as close as possible to that which they would occupy if prejudice did not exist." The argument here appears to be the same as that for why the state should not count, in its utilitarian calculus, white citizens' personal preferences for a racist status quo. By neutrally maintaining a market in which "people's bids . . . reflect contempt or dislike," the state is permitting malign preferences to determine people's life chances, just as it would if it allowed those preferences to influence its own decisions. In order to avoid this result, it must "protect people who are the objects of systematic prejudice from suffering any serious or pervasive disadvantage from that prejudice."[44]

Absent transformation of the culture that produces the prejudice, this goal cannot be attained. Law alone cannot prevent malign preferences from contaminating the distributive process in the private sector. The civil rights statutes only reach some private conduct, and that clumsily, with a high likelihood of error.[45] Moreover, there is a broad range of private decisions that are typ-

---

43. Dworkin, "Bakke's Case: Are Quotas Unfair?," in *A Matter of Principle*, p. 294.

44. Ronald Dworkin, "What is Equality? Part 3: The Place of Liberty," 73 *Iowa L. Rev.* 1, 36–37 (1987).

45. The likelihood of error in the application of the Civil Rights Act of 1964 is explored in some detail in Richard Epstein, *Forbidden Grounds: The Case Against Employment Discrimination Laws* (Cambridge and London: Harvard University Press, 1992), pp. 169–75, 222–25. Account must also be taken of the high economic and emotional costs of bringing antidiscrimination suits,

ically influenced by racial considerations, and that have major effects on the socioeconomic status of blacks, but that the state could not intervene in without massively intruding on individual autonomy—notably decisions about whom to marry.[46] As long as racist preferences themselves persist, the process by which goods are distributed will remain tainted. Dworkin's argument thus implies that process concerns may justify the state in seeking to reshape the preferences themselves. He acknowledges this when he writes that the purpose of affirmative action programs is to "decrease the degree to which whites think of blacks as a race rather than as people, and thus the degree to which blacks think of themselves that way," and that the goal of antidiscrimination law is nothing less than "reforming the racial consciousness of our society."[47]

Some doubt that all race-based personal preferences are malign in the sense of having a cognitive component that denies that blacks and whites are equally entitled to concern and respect. While personal aversions to blacks often arise from biases and stereotypes, Larry Alexander observes, they can "become relatively autonomous from their immoral origins and function for the discriminator no differently from aversions to spiders, snakes, and '40s big band music."[48] Joel Kovel distinguishes the "dominative" racist, who openly seeks to keep blacks down and will use force to do so, from the "aversive" racist, who consciously rejects racism but inwardly finds blacks distasteful and so "tries to ignore the existence of black people, tries to avoid contact with them, and at most to be polite, correct, and cold in whatever dealings are necessary between the races."[49] Aversive racism has become far more common than dominative racism. Alexander tentatively concludes that such racism is not

---

which means that a good deal of discrimination will remain undetected by the law. See Kristin Bumiller, *The Civil Rights Society: The Social Construction of Victims* (Baltimore and London: Johns Hopkins University Press, 1988), esp. pp. 26–30. The prohibition of housing discrimination has never been effective, and housing markets remain exceedingly segregated. See Douglas S. Massey and Nancy A. Denton, *American Apartheid: Segregation and the Making of the Underclass* (Cambridge and London: Harvard University Press, 1993). It is hard to imagine any remedy for this segregation that can succeed so long as whites are unwilling to live near blacks. See Nathan Glazer, "A Tale of Two Cities," *New Republic*, Aug. 2, 1993, pp. 39–41.

46. See Glenn C. Loury, "Why Should We Care About Group Inequality?", 5 *Soc. Phil. & Pol'y* 249, 258–59 (Aut. 1987).

47. Dworkin, "Bakke's Case: Are Quotas Unfair?," in *A Matter of Principle*, p. 295.

48. Larry Alexander, "What Makes Wrongful Discrimination Wrong? Biases, Preferences, Stereotypes, and Proxies," 141 *U. Pa. L. Rev.* 149, 193–94 (1992).

49. Joel Kovel, *White Racism: A Psychohistory* (New York: Columbia University Press, 1984), p. 54.

intrinsically immoral, because the aversive racist does not consciously hold that blacks are inferior to whites.[50]

Dworkin does not have a clear answer to Alexander's claim. Dworkin argues that inadmissible preferences include not only external preferences but also personal ones that would not exist but for the malign preferences. Thus,

> the associational preference of a white law student for white classmates . . . may be said to be a personal preference for an association with one kind of colleague rather than another. But it is a personal preference that is parasitic upon external preferences: except in very rare cases a white student prefers the company of other whites because he has racist, social, and political convictions, or because he has contempt for blacks as a group. If these associational preferences are counted in a utilitarian argument used to justify segregation, then the egalitarian character of the argument is destroyed just as if the underlying external preferences were counted directly.[51]

Alexander's argument, however, is that sometimes the preference of whites for association with other whites is *not* a consequence of the fact that those whites affirm what utilitarianism denies—that blacks are contemptible as a group. Without that cognitive element, it is not apparent why that preference should not count. Jazz and blues are artifacts of slavery and Jim Crow, and would not exist but for those institutions, but that obviously should not prevent a taste for those musical forms from being counted by the utilitarian.[52] Such a preference is not malign. It does not affirm what utilitarianism foundationally denies.

Alexander's claim is that this is true of some racism as well. Even if he is right, however (which is far from clear), it is quite unlikely to be true of *much* racism. The mindset Alexander describes is psychologically unstable: when one feels repelled by someone, one tends to rationalize this feeling by explaining it in terms of some objectively repulsive quality of that person. Even if one can coherently imagine a white person as regarding blacks with aversion while not devaluing or condemning them, whites' aversion to blacks is typically learned and held as part of a narrative in which black persons are implicitly

50. See Alexander, "What Makes Wrongful Discrimination Wrong?," p. 194. Alexander concludes that such preferences are contingently immoral, because of their aggregate effects.

51. Dworkin, "Reverse Discrimination," in *Taking Rights Seriously*, p. 236.

52. See Alexander, "What Makes Wrongful Discrimination Wrong?," pp. 178–79, 192–94.

understood as defective, substandard people. This cognitive component is present even where it is not explicit.

We earlier noted Kymlicka's view that considerations of equality ought to enter into the very formation of our preferences. We ought to form our plans and wants with due regard for the rights of others. Inadvertent harm may be immoral if the actor could have foreseen the harm and prevented it. Our moral obligations are not exhausted by the prohibition of malicious or deliberate harm; one also has an obligation to take care that one does not inadvertently harm others. If I back my car over a child, I cannot excuse myself by saying that I did not see her. I should have looked.[53] If certain otherwise innocent wants violate others' rights, then we are morally obligated to avoid developing such wants, or if we already have them, to rid ourselves of them. Aversive racism is such an illegitimate want. It carries connotations of insult, whether intended or not, because the aversive racist is unconsciously influenced by, and is transmitting, a cultural message of inferiority, the insulting character of which is well understood by its audience. A newspaper must not knowingly publish libelous advertisements, even though its motives for so doing—a desire for advertising revenue, say—are innocent of any desire to harm.[54] Under some circumstances, the messenger is responsible for the contents of the message. The obliviousness or indifference of whites to the injuries that their aversions inflict on blacks is itself racist. It is unlikely that these harms would be regarded so sanguinely if they were suffered by whites. Whether a decision-making process is contaminated by malign preferences can sometimes be determined by examining its effects, because unbiased decision makers will be reluctant to tolerate certain effects.

"Racism" is a protean word, capable of connoting a well-developed political or scientific ideology, a set of casually held beliefs, a norm, a gut reaction, or a thoughtless affect.[55] A dictionary struggles to take account of all of these, defining racism as "the assumption that psychocultural traits and capacities are determined by biological race and that races differ decisively from one another, which is usually coupled with a belief in the inherent superiority of

53. For a similar argument, see Iris Marion Young, *Justice and the Politics of Difference* (Princeton: Princeton University Press, 1990), pp. 148–51.

54. See, e.g., *New York Times v. Sullivan*, 376 U.S. 254 (1964).

55. See generally Kwame Anthony Appiah, "Racisms," in David Theo Goldberg, ed., *Anatomy of Racism* (Minneapolis: University of Minnesota Press, 1990), pp. 3–17.

a particular race and its right to domination over others."[56] Racism is of concern to the process theory, and more generally to the antidiscrimination project, because it is inconsistent with equal concern and respect. I therefore offer the following working definition of racism, which is what I will mean whenever I use the term: *the singling out of certain persons for diminished concern and respect on the basis of their race.* It should be clear from this definition that it is possible for racism to operate unconsciously. Paul Brest's brief account of the process theory notes that a large part of the problem of defective process is the tendency of decisions to reflect "racially selective sympathy and indifference," meaning "the unconscious failure to extend to a minority the same recognition of humanity, and hence the same sympathy and care, given as a matter of course to one's own group."[57] Unconscious racism can be even more insulting and destructive than the conscious kind. Richard Wasserstrom reports that before the end of segregation, "[a] lengthy account in a Southern newspaper about the high school band program in a certain city . . . emphasized especially the fact that it was a program in which *all high school students* in the city participated. Negro children neither were nor could be participants in the program. The article, however, saw no need to point this out. I submit that it neglected to do so not because everyone knew the fact, but because in a real sense the writer and the newspaper do not regard Negro high school students as children—persons, human beings—at all."[58] The newspaper writer may not have intended to insult the black children; he may simply not have thought of them at all. That is precisely the problem. Though greatly ameliorated since segregation, racism in the form of selective sympathy and indifference continues to pervade decision making.[59]

The argument against nongovernmental racism may be sharpened by restating it in terms of Michael Walzer's theory of distributive justice. Walzer holds that the meaning of different goods determines the appropriate principle

---

56. *Webster's Third New International Dictionary of the English Language* (Springfield, Mass.: G. & C. Merriam Co., 1976).

57. Brest, "In Defense of the Antidiscrimination Principle," pp. 7–8.

58. Richard Wasserstrom, "Rights, Human Rights and Racial Discrimination," in David Lyons, ed., *Rights* (Belmont, Calif.: Wadsworth, 1979), p. 57 (emphasis in original).

59. On the substantial improvement in white attitudes toward the political and social equality of blacks, see Howard Schuman, Charlotte Steeh, and Lawrence Bobo, *Racial Attitudes in America: Trends and Interpretations* (Cambridge and London: Harvard University Press, 1985), pp. 71–138.

for distribution of those goods. According to his theory of equality, "no citizen's standing in one sphere or with regard to one social good can be undercut by his standing in some other sphere, with regard to some other good." When one sphere's principles invade another sphere—for example, when an officeholder, who may indeed be the best qualified for the office she holds, parlays her position into access to superior medical care, access to better schools for her children, entrepreneurial activities, and so forth—the result is what Walzer calls "tyranny."[60]

The dominance of racial or sexual status appears to be tyranny in a double sense. First of all, such statuses ought not to be social goods at all. It is highly doubtful whether there should be any sphere in which one receives tangible or intangible advantages for being white or male or both. Second, it is still clearer that being white or male or both ought not to give one an advantage in the distribution of other social goods such as wealth, education, political power, and so forth. One of the central themes of *Spheres of Justice* is that money, more than any other social good, tends to enable tyranny with respect to other goods.[61] Race enables tyranny in similar ways.

The kind of argument Walzer makes has been criticized on the basis that a claim that social goods should only be distributed for "relevant reasons" presupposes "(1) that there is a social (and natural) essence to each human being included in which are his unique talents as well as his needs and desires; and (2) that citizens in a correctly organized society will freely distribute goods— income, power, praise, honor, and love—according to each individual's essential qualities." The trouble with Walzer's prescription is that it denies the value of "privacy understood as retreat from public scrutiny and recognition."[62] In order for others to give me precisely what I ought to have, there must be no gap between my true self and what others take me to be. It is doubtful whether such transparency is realizable or desirable.

Nonetheless, even if we are uncertain about the true bases of distributive justice, we can be confident that certain bases are wrong, and that race is among these. It is not the case that certain racial categories of people are intrinsically inferior and less deserving of concern and respect than others.

60. Michael Walzer, *Spheres of Justice: A Defense of Pluralism and Equality* (New York: Basic Books, 1983), p. 19.

61. See ibid., pp. 107–8.

62. Amy Gutmann, *Liberal Equality* (Cambridge: Cambridge University Press, 1980), pp. 115, 116.

However tenuous our understanding of distributive justice is, the area of certainty (in Rawls's terms, of overlapping consensus) is large enough to occupy the same conceptual space as, and so to contradict and exclude, racism. While we cannot know with certainty (or may reasonably disagree about) what every person ought to have, we can be confident that certain reasons are never relevant to the distribution of goods. If this is true, then the widespread use of those reasons in distributive decisions is an injustice.

The reason racism, more than other corrupting considerations, is of special concern to the process theorists is that it introduces a *principle* into the decision-making process that is inconsistent with, and tends to crowd out, the equal concern and respect to which citizens are entitled. What differentiates racism, whether conscious or unconscious, from other process defects, such as corruption and error, is that its aggregate effects are nonrandom and unidirectional, with the impact consistently falling on a single group. This is what makes it "tyranny" in Walzer's sense. It raises special concern for the same kinds of reasons that an invasion arouses more concern than ordinary crime: an invasion is not merely disorder but a rival kind of order. Similarly, racism not only deviates from appropriate principles of distribution but directly attacks and tends to displace them.

Thus we can answer Epstein's claim, discussed in the Introduction, that antidiscrimination law is an intolerable imposition on individual liberty because it interferes with people's private desires, such as white customers' preference for white clerks in a store. The justification for antidiscrimination law is that certain preferences are so malign that they contradict the whole point of counting preferences in the first place. We respect choices only because we respect people, and therefore we are justified in disregarding choices when such choices manifest and reinforce disrespect for people.

An Excursus on Reverse Discrimination

The much-debated issue of whether preferential treatment of blacks is a wise or good public policy is beyond the scope of this book. It is necessary for our purposes, however, to address the claim that such preferences are examples of the precise evil antidiscrimination law seeks to remedy. That claim is made in three ways: first, racial preferences are alleged to violate the rights of whites in precisely the same way that first-order discrimination violates the rights of blacks; second, racial preferences are alleged to be a manifestation of a decision-making process corrupted by racial factionalism; and third, racial preferences are alleged to increase the amount of prejudice against blacks and aggravate their material disadvantages. I look at the arguments for the first claim here, for the second later in this chapter, and for the third in Chapter 2.

The first claim holds, in essence, that racial preferences for blacks violate the Dworkinian rights of whites. An example can be found in *City of Richmond v. J. A. Croson Co.*: "To whatever racial group these citizens belong, their 'personal rights' to be treated with equal dignity and respect are implicated by a rigid rule erecting race as the sole criterion in an aspect of public decisionmaking."[63] The claim is that a defective process is one that takes race into account in the distribution of burdens and benefits. Discrimination against blacks does that; so does preferential treatment of blacks. The evil that antidiscrimination law seeks to eliminate, according to this theory, is unfairness to individuals: treatment of persons simply as representatives of groups is an indignity.[64] Dworkin thinks that reverse discrimination is unobjectionable, because the disadvantages of the whites who are discriminated against are not the result of unfair prejudice against them.[65] Robert Simon claims, however, that Dworkin's theory ought to condemn preferential treatment. "There is at least a prima facie incompatibility between equally respecting individuals as agents and dismissing an individual from consideration because of possession

63. 488 U.S. 469, 493 (1989) (plurality opinion by O'Connor, J., joined by White and Kennedy, JJ.).

64. "Such a selection process inevitably encourages us to stereotype our fellow human beings—to view their advancements, not as hard-won achievements, but as conferred benefits. It invites us to look upon people as possessors of racial characteristics, not as the unique individuals who they are. It submerges the vitality of personality under the deadening prejudgments of race." William Bradford Reynolds, "Individualism vs. Group Rights: The Legacy of *Brown*," 93 *Yale L.J.* 995, 1003 (1984). This line of reasoning is ubiquitous in the Supreme Court's arguments against racial preference. See *Croson*, p. 521 (Scalia, J., concurring) ("I share the view expressed by Alexander Bickel that ' . . . discrimination on the basis of race is illegal, immoral, unconstitutional, inherently wrong, and destructive of democratic society.") (quoting Alexander Bickel, *The Morality of Consent* [New Haven: Yale University Press, 1975], p. 133); *Croson*, p. 518 (Kennedy, J., concurring) ("The moral imperative of racial neutrality is the driving force of the Equal Protection Clause."); *Steelworkers v. Weber*, 443 U.S. 193, 228 n. 10 (1979) (Rehnquist, J., dissenting) ("Far from ironic, I find a prohibition on all preferential treatment based on race as elementary and fundamental as the principle that 'two wrongs do not make a right.' ").

65. See Dworkin, "Reverse Discrimination," in *Taking Rights Seriously*, pp. 223–39; idem, "Bakke's Case: Are Quotas Unfair?," in *A Matter of Principle*, pp. 293–331; and idem, *Law's Empire*, pp. 393–97.

of immutable physical characteristics. The former implies emphasis on an individual's character, choices, and capacities, while the latter excludes these as irrelevant."[66]

If, however, unfairness to individuals were the central concern of antidiscrimination law, it would be hard to explain why the law confines its protection to those discriminated against on the basis of race, color, religion, sex, or national origin. The unfairness of stereotyping seems endemic to *all* legislation, which, as Ely observes, generally takes the form of "a classification believed in statistical terms to be generally valid without leaving room for proof of individual deviation." Unfairness certainly is part of the evil with which antidiscrimination law is concerned, but it could not be the whole without attacking the idea of legislation itself. "[U]nbearable cost would result were the government obligated to create procedures for deciding every case on its individual merits."[67] The same is true of private decisions, such as those involving whom to hire for a job. The human mind simply cannot function without categorizing and stereotyping.

The color-blindness approach derives its appeal by seizing on one valid instance of the process theory's requirement that the legislator be impartial, fetishizing it, and forgetting its basis.[68] On closer scrutiny, the theory proves to be incoherent, because if carried to its logical conclusion it would do away with antidiscrimination law altogether—a result that even its proponents would concede to be absurd. David Strauss has shown that the prohibition of discrimination against blacks is not in tension with affirmative action, but is instead logically continuous with it. The complaint of racial factionalism aside, the principal arguments against affirmative action are that it can be economically irrational, impose significant social costs, and harm innocent victims. All these things are equally true of the antidiscrimination norm, which prohibits even economically efficient discrimination, and thus creates costs that usually fall upon innocent parties.[69]

Since neither legislatures nor individuals can function in the world without constantly (over)generalizing, the use of inaccurate generalizations cannot be the evil that antidiscrimination law seeks to eradicate. The injury to whites,

66. Simon, "Individual Rights and 'Benign' Discrimination," p. 96.
67. Ely, *Democracy and Distrust*, p. 155.
68. See Alan David Freeman, "Legitimizing Racial Discrimination Through Antidiscrimination Law: A Critical Review of Supreme Court Doctrine," 62 *Minn. L. Rev.* 1049, 1066 (1978).
69. David A. Strauss, "The Myth of Colorblindness," 1986 *Sup. Ct. Rev.* 99.

then, must be something other than inaccurate stereotyping, or being singled out to bear disproportionately the costs of racial equality.

The rights-based claim against racial preferences appears finally to depend on the notion that all persons have a right to equal consideration for the filling of any desired position. This can be shown by a thought experiment. A typical reverse-discrimination claim involves the fact that a certain proportion of competitively sought offices—jobs, or positions in an entering class —have been set aside for blacks. This, it is typically claimed, violates the rights of whites who are prevented from competing for those positions. Suppose, however, that instead of setting aside those positions, the legislature simply abolished them, shrinking the entering class of the medical school (or whatever the case may be) and devoting the money thus saved to some worthy purpose that benefited only blacks, such as a high school program on the historical evils of racism. The effect on the whites would be identical with that of racial set-asides: they would be prevented from competing for those positions, and those who would otherwise have filled the positions would disproportionately bear the cost of the effort to end racism. In this case, however, it is clear that no rights-based claim would be available to them. There are two differences between the two cases: first, the set-aside involves a racial classification; second, the set-aside involves jobs (or scarce opportunities for training for jobs), which can be the objects of meritocratic competition. If there is a *moral* difference between the two cases, it must lie in one of these differences. Is it in the racial classification itself? Strauss's argument shows that this cannot be so. Whatever is objectionable about racial classifications, *qua* classifications, is equally objectionable about other classifications that are widely used and tolerated. The whites' claim, then, is crucially dependent on the fact that *offices* are being created, and on the idea that they have a right to compete for those offices. We have returned to Walzer's argument that the meaning of certain goods determines the appropriate principle for distributing them. And, in fact, Walzer does oppose racial preference for this reason. Our thought experiment shows that Walzer's is the *only* plausible rights-based critique of racial preference. If that critique fails, then so does the rights-based case against preferences.

Walzer thinks that equal consideration as members of a community requires that all candidates for a position receive equal consideration on the basis of their qualifications. He specifically rejects Dworkin's claim that, because a black filling a job may help serve the societal interest in combating racism in a way that a white cannot, race itself may be a qualification.

> In our culture . . . careers are supposed to be open to talents; and people chosen for an office will want to be assured that they were chosen because they really do possess, to a greater degree than other candidates, the talents that the search committee thinks necessary to the office. The other candidates will want to be assured that their talents were seriously considered. And all the rest of us will want to know that both assurances are true.[70]

Thus, even though the decision to give preferential treatment to blacks may be uncontaminated by external preferences, it nonetheless violates the rights of the excluded whites. Walzer acknowledges the power of Dworkin's argument in cases of public expenditures, but claims that offices "cannot be distributed the way money can; they cut too close to the core of individuality and personal integrity. Once the community undertakes to distribute them, it must attend closely to their social meaning. And that requires equal consideration for all equally serious candidates."[71] It follows that a hiring process that takes race into account is equally bad whether whites or blacks are favored, and for the same reason: it departs from the norm of the career open to talents.

The trouble with this argument is that departures from that norm are openly tolerated in other contexts. Walzer himself acknowledges that "the policy of veteran's preference in civil service employment seems to have been widely accepted."[72] What does it reveal when a departure from "the career open to talents" stirs outrage and indignation only when blacks benefit from it? Patricia Williams provides a useful illustration:

> Sitting on university admission committees . . . I have seen black candidates who write on their applications comments such as, "Don't admit me if you have to lower your standards." I have never seen the same acutely self-conscious disavowals from students who are admitted because they meet some geographical criterion—such as living in Wyo-

---

70. Walzer, *Spheres of Justice*, pp. 152–53.

71. Ibid., p. 153.

72. Ibid., p. 154 n.; see also Robert K. Fullinwider, *The Reverse Discrimination Controversy: A Moral and Legal Analysis* (Totowa, N.J.: Rowman & Allanheld, 1980), pp. 47–48, 203.

ming, or France, or some other underrepresented area—or who are older re-entry students, or football heroes, or alumni children. I think this is so because these latter inclusionary categories are thought to indicate group life experiences . . . that "enrich" rather than "lower."[73]

That the deviation from "the career open to talents" to include blacks provokes resentment and guilt where these others do not is itself a datum that needs explaining.[74] As Randall Kennedy has noted, "What is so remarkable— and ominous—about the affirmative action debate is that so modest a reform calls forth such powerful resistance."[75]

If one recognizes that racism is part of the shared structure of meaning in the United States, this anomaly becomes more understandable. The singling out of affirmative action for special opprobrium, among all the deviations from "the career open to talents" that are institutionalized in this country, is best understood as one manifestation of "the unstated understanding by the mass of whites that they will accept large disparities in economic opportunity to other whites as long as they have a priority over blacks and other people of color for access to those opportunities."[76] The narrative of the lazy, undeserving, incompetent black eager to usurp the prerogatives of white men has been part of the mythos shared by American whites for so long that it slips easily, and probably unconsciously, into the background assumptions of many whites' moral reasoning.[77] In short, the norms that racial preference violates are, to a certain and perhaps decisive extent, racist ones.

73. Patricia J. Williams, "*Metro Broadcasting, Inc. v. FCC*: Regrouping in Singular Times," 104 *Harv. L. Rev.* 525, 542 (1990).

74. And this is one problem with the claim that affirmative action stigmatizes those it seeks to help, by implying that they are incapable of meeting ordinary standards of qualification: the color of those occupying the sought-after positions frequently affects observers' evaluation of their qualifications. If blacks will be stigmatized whether or not they are the beneficiaries of preferential treatment, then the stigma factor will at least in some cases be a wash rather than an argument against preferential treatment. See Margaret Jane Radin, "Affirmative Action Rhetoric," 8 *Soc. Phil. & Pol.* 130 (Spring 1991).

75. Randall Kennedy, "Persuasion and Distrust: A Comment on the Affirmative Action Debate," 99 *Harv. L. Rev.* 1327, 1334 (1986).

76. Derrick Bell, *Race, Racism and American Law* (3rd ed.; Boston: Little, Brown, 1992), p. 896.

77. Paul Sniderman and Thomas Piazza argue that "a number of whites dislike the idea of affirmative action so much and perceive it to be so unfair that they have come to dislike blacks as a consequence." Paul Sniderman and Thomas Piazza, *The Scar of Race* (Cambridge and London: Belknap Press of Harvard University Press, 1993), p. 8. They draw this conclusion on the basis of

Walzer thinks that social criticism is possible because "cultures are open to the possibility of contradiction (between principles and practices) as well as to . . . 'incoherence' (among everyday practices)."[78] This leaves out of account the possibility that principles themselves may contradict each other: that moral convictions about racial equality, for example, may conflict with other convictions about racial superiority that are no less deeply rooted in our culture.[79] The fact that deviations from "the career open to talents" are readily tolerated outside the racial context suggests that "the career open to talents," in itself, is not so powerful a moral principle in our culture as Walzer claims, and that it cannot do the work he tries to make it do unless it is supplemented by other cultural norms that are a good deal less attractive (and that Walzer obviously would repudiate).[80] The rights-based critique of racial preference is thus unpersuasive as an interpretation of process theory.

This is not to say, however, that white resentment of affirmative action programs should be ignored. It would be foolhardy to disregard any reaction, however misguided, against racial progress. If the reaction is strong and dan-

---

their "mere mention" survey experiment, which found that "merely asking whites to respond to the issue of affirmative action increases significantly the likelihood that they will perceive blacks as irresponsible and lazy" (p. 103). They argue that "whites' feelings toward blacks are a minor factor in promoting opposition to affirmative action" (p. 176; see also pp. 98–99). Rather, they claim, that opposition rests on values that have nothing to do with race: "Proposing to privilege some people rather than others, on the basis of a characteristic they were born with, violates a nearly universal norm of fairness" (p. 134). This reasoning takes no account of the possibility that the mention of affirmative action triggers the narrative of the undeserving black. They acknowledge that, in America, "A white will tend to acquire a negative characterization of blacks as irresponsible and unwilling to work hard before acquiring particular beliefs about whether blacks have, or have not, been unfairly treated" (p. 117). No account is taken of the hypothesis that this characterization is the source of the perceived unfairness of affirmative action, even though that hypothesis is just as consistent with their data as the one they advance.

78. Michael Walzer, *Interpretation and Social Criticism* (Cambridge and London: Harvard University Press, 1987), p. 29.

79. See Rogers M. Smith, "Beyond Tocqueville, Myrdal, and Hartz: The Multiple Traditions in America," 87 *Am. Pol. Sci. Rev.* 549 (Sept. 1993); Jennifer Hochschild, *The New American Dilemma: Liberal Democracy and School Desegregation* (New Haven and London: Yale University Press, 1984), pp. 1–12.

80. This illustrates Ian Shapiro's more general point, in his critique of Walzer, that "[t]o appeal to conventional meanings in a world where these are inevitably competing and conflicting will not resolve moral arguments without some additional premises that will allow for adjudication among these conflicting meanings." *Political Criticism* (Berkeley: University of California Press, 1990), p. 85.

gerous enough, it may even be prudent strategically to yield to it on the points on which it is most insistent.[81] There is wisdom in Walzer's conclusion that "the struggle against a racist past is more likely to be won if it is fought in ways that build on, rather than challenge, understandings of the social world shared by the great majority of Americans, black and white alike."[82] There must be limits to our deference to shared understandings, however, because some of these shared understandings are themselves racist. It is arguable that the compromise led by Booker T. Washington, who sought economic opportunity for blacks but did not insist too strenuously on voting rights, was prudent under the circumstances of the late nineteenth century.[83] Some whites then were as outraged and resentful at the thought of blacks voting as many whites are now at the thought of blacks receiving preferential treatment. Neither resentment seems to be rationally defensible or valid. It may be prudent to yield even to unjust demands when these are backed by sufficient force, and when defiance of them threatens a racial backlash that will make blacks even worse off than they already are. Considerations of prudence do not, however, turn injustice into justice.[84]

Ely's Process Theory

We noted that Dworkin's argument for excluding racist preferences from decision making was not necessarily linked to utilitarianism, but could be derived

---

81. This is the theme that runs through Thomas Byrne Edsall with Mary D. Edsall, *Chain Reaction: The Impact of Race, Rights, and Taxes on American Politics* (New York and London: W. W. Norton, 1992). Unfortunately, the Edsalls often imply without argument (what it must be comforting for some Democratic strategists to believe) that any measure that diminishes the Democrats' chances of winning the presidency by stirring white working-class resentment cannot be a measure that justice requires. See Adolph Reed Jr. and Julian Bond, "Equality: Why We Can't Wait," 253 *The Nation* 733 (Dec. 9, 1991) (discussing the Edsalls).

82. Walzer, *Spheres of Justice*, p. 154.

83. See Washington's address to the 1895 Atlanta Exposition, reprinted in Booker T. Washington, "Up From Slavery," in *Three Negro Classics* (New York: Avon, 1965), pp. 146–50.

84. This is emphasized by Bernard Boxill, who criticizes William Julius Wilson, Glenn Loury, and Shelby Steele for accepting, in different ways, that racial justice is not fully attainable in the contemporary United States. Boxill's analysis of these thinkers may be sound, but it does not follow that their arguments "must therefore be rejected or substantially altered." *Blacks and Social Justice* (Lanham, Maryland: Rowman & Littlefield, rev. ed. 1992), p. 227. If racism is so deeply entrenched that it will inevitably poison public policymaking, then that is a fact of life that must be taken into account, not ignored.

from any comprehensive philosophical view that denies that race is an appropriate basis for treating different people with different degrees of concern and respect. The democratic theory upon which Ely relies is one such philosophical view. The concept of malign preferences is crucial to making sense of Ely's theory.[85] Racist preferences must be excluded from the democratic decision-making process in Ely's theory for the same reason they must be excluded from the utilitarian calculus in Dworkin's theory: For both, allowing racism to influence the decision-making process would contradict the whole point of having that kind (democratic and utilitarian, respectively) of decision-making process.

Ely purports to offer a constitutional theory in which "the selection and accommodation of substantive values is left almost entirely to the political process," and in which judicial review is concerned solely with "what might capaciously be designated process writ large—with ensuring broad participation in the processes and distributions of government." Ely's answer to Bickel's countermajoritarian difficulty is to assign to the judiciary only that task with which the legislature cannot be trusted: "to keep the machinery of democratic government running as it should."[86] The basis of this concern about process is the theory of representative government, which requires

> not simply that the representative would not sever his interests from those of a majority of his constituency but also that he would not sever a majority coalition's interests from those of various minorities. Naturally that cannot mean that groups that constitute minorities of the population can never be treated less favorably than the rest, but it does preclude a refusal to *represent* them, the denial to minorities of what Professor Dworkin has called "equal concern and respect in the design and administration of the political institutions that govern them."[87]

It should be clear why malign preferences are condemned under Ely's theory. The citizens must all "be represented in the sense that their interests are not to be left out of account or valued negatively in the law-making process." So far, this is a persuasive argument. Unfortunately, the rest of Ely's account of antidiscrimination law is misleadingly incomplete, because he recognizes only

85. This is true even though the concept of malign preferences first appears in Ely's writing after his major book, *Democracy and Distrust,* is already in print.

86. Ely, *Democracy and Distrust,* pp. 87, 76, footnote omitted.

87. Ibid., p. 82, footnotes omitted.

two ways in which the legislative process can go wrong. First, legislation that disadvantages a minority may be motivated by "a simple desire to disadvantage the minority in question." Second, the legislation may reflect "prejudice," which is "a lens that distorts reality" inasmuch as it "blinds us to overlapping interests that in fact exist."[88]

Ely's view of the obligations of representative government is persuasive, but his psychology needs refinement. Malign preferences sometimes take the form of overt hostility, but even in the paradigmatic case of school segregation, they were subtler than this.[89] For example, the leading banker in Clarendon County, South Carolina, where the first of the *Brown* cases was filed, thought that the lower quality of the black schools was a matter of simple fairness: "after all, the banker noted, the white people paid the taxes and the white people were therefore entitled to the better schools."[90] When he said, "Yessir, we got good nigras in this county,"[91] he may have been sincere. It is not clear that he was "valuing their welfare negatively."[92] What is clear is that he valued their welfare *less* than the welfare of white children. Yet his beliefs fit Ely's own definition of malign preferences: he did "desire to deprive [blacks] of an equal share of life's goods and opportunities."[93]

The duty of representation is violated, not only when constituents' interests are "valued negatively," but also when they are "left out of account."[94] Recall Paul Brest's claim that a large part of the problem of defective process is the

88. Ibid., pp. 223 n. 33, 147, and 153.

89. See Strauss, "Discriminatory Intent and the Taming of *Brown*," pp. 962–64, discussing the astonishing statement in *Personnel Adm'r v. Feeney,* 442 U.S. 256, 279 (1979), that the Fourteenth Amendment is not violated unless a state action was taken " 'because of,' not merely 'in spite of,' its adverse effects upon an identifiable group."

90. Richard Kluger, *Simple Justice: The History of 'Brown v. Board of Education' and Black America's Struggle for Equality* (New York: Random House, 1976), p. 7. At best, Ely has correctly described some situations; the attitude of white Californians toward the Japanese-Americans with whom they competed economically before the latter were forcibly interned during World War II is an example. See Morton Grodzins, *Americans Betrayed: Politics and the Japanese Evacuation* (Chicago: University of Chicago Press, 1949), pp. 19–225.

91. Kluger, *Simple Justice,* p. 7.

92. Ely, *Democracy and Distrust,* p. 157.

93. Ely, "Professor Dworkin's External/Personal Preference Distinction," p. 984. The banker's invocation of proportional equality was, of course, disingenuous, since even the whites who were too poor to pay taxes got to go to the white schools.

94. Ely, *Democracy and Distrust,* p. 223 n. 33; cf. p. 151.

tendency of decisions to reflect racially selective sympathy and indifference. This suggests that Ely is too sanguine about the possibility of, for example, unconstitutional discrimination against the poor:

> [F]ailures to provide the poor with one or another good or service, insensitive as they may often seem to some of us, do not generally result from a sadistic desire to keep the miserable in their state of misery, or a stereotypical generalization about their characteristics, but rather from a reluctance to raise the taxes needed to support such expenditures—and at all events they will be susceptible to immediate translation into such constitutionally innocent terms.[95]

The possibility not considered is that the legislature values the well-being of the poor less than that of other citizens, and that this is why their interests are neglected in legislation. If that were the case—and it sounds like a plausible description of much of contemporary political reality—it would still violate the duty of representation.[96] In short, malign preferences take a broader variety of forms than Ely's account acknowledges.[97]

The only other kind of process failure Ely considers is "prejudice," by which he means "stereotyping." This is a matter less of malign preference than of error, but the error is of a kind that is the functional equivalent of a malign preference. While all legislation necessarily rests on generalizations, the legislative process is defective in cases "involving a generalization whose inci-

---

95. Ibid., p. 162. Ely has expressed some dissatisfaction with this passage. See his "Democracy and the Right to be Different," 56 *N.Y.U. L. Rev.* 397, 399 n. 5 (1981).

96. At one point, Ely seems to be conceding this. "For the representative to act on the basis of a naked desire—either his own or that of his constituents—that some minority simply be denied an equal share of life's goods and opportunities (Dworkin's terminology) is surely tantamount to valuing the welfare of that minority negatively (my terminology), and that, I argue at length, is a violation of the constitutionally imposed duty to 'represent' the entirety of one's constituency." "Professor Dworkin's External/Personal Preference Distinction," p. 985 n. 79. Even allowing for this capacious definition of "negative valuation," the illustration in the text shows that while he recognizes the possibility of non-malicious neglect in principle, he typically forgets it in application.

97. For a similar critique, see Stanley Conrad Fickle, "The Dawn's Early Light: The Contributions of John Hart Ely to Constitutional Theory," 56 *Ind. L. J.* 637, 655 (1981) (review of *Democracy and Distrust*). For another example of the limitations of Ely's psychology, see Andrew Koppelman, "Why Discrimination Against Lesbians and Gay Men is Sex Discrimination," 69 *N.Y.U. L. Rev.* 197, 281–84 (1994).

dence of counterexample is significantly higher than the legislative authority appears to have thought it was."[98] The problem derives, again, from the obligation to treat constituents with equal concern and respect. "[T]o disadvantage—in the perceived service of some overriding social goal—a thousand persons that a more individualized (but more costly) test or procedure would exclude, under the impression that only five hundred fit that description, is to deny the five hundred to whose existence you are oblivious *their* right to equal concern and respect, by valuing their welfare at zero."[99] This account overlooks the possibility that a stereotype may be normative rather than empirical, for example that women simply ought not to be as aggressive in their interactions as men, even in jobs that demand such aggressiveness.[100] A normative view of this sort may reflect selective sympathy and indifference—in this case, a desire (conscious or unconscious) to keep the most socially valued positions in male hands—but is not logically susceptible to empirical refutation. The cognitive and affective aspects of bias are not as distinct as Ely's account suggests.

Ely lays heavy stress on motive-based inquiry, arguing that what is suspected when a "suspect classification" is used is that an invidious motive is at work. Thus he seems to approve of the Court's holding that when a state action injures blacks but does not on the face of it discriminate against them, there is no constitutional violation unless discriminatory intent is proven.[101] But as Charles Lawrence III has argued, intent is a misleading indicator of defective process, because "the same process distortions will occur even when the racial prejudice is less apparent."[102] This is because racial prejudice—or what we have been calling inegalitarian external preference—is sometimes unconscious. Unconscious aversion toward blacks and devaluation of their interests deny blacks equal concern and respect as much as the wrongs that Ely describes, but these factors are missing from his account. What Ely has done for us, most importantly, is to give Dworkin's worry about malign external preferences a basis in democratic theory. It appears that democrats and utilitarians

98. Ely, *Democracy and Distrust*, p. 157.

99. Ibid., emphasis in original.

100. See, e.g., *Price Waterhouse v. Hopkins*, 490 U.S. 228 (1989).

101. Ely, *Democracy and Distrust*, p. 137 and n. 9, citing *Village of Arlington Heights v. Metropolitan Dev. Housing Corp.*, 429 U.S. 252 (1977).

102. Charles R. Lawrence III, "The Ego, the Id, and Equal Protection: Reckoning With Unconscious Racism," 39 *Stan. L. Rev.* 317, 347 (1987).

alike should strive to override political decisions predicated on malign preferences. Ely's account of how such preferences percolate through the decision-making process, however, is misleading and potentially pernicious insofar as it points to a part (and perhaps not the largest part) of the process defect and calls it the whole. Process theory's requirements are certainly violated by hatred and stereotyping, but other, unconscious aspects of racism are equally unacceptable.

Ely and Cultural Transformation

We have already seen that Dworkin's theory entails an ambitious project of cultural transformation. What about Ely's version of the process theory, which is concerned solely with government decision making? I believe that Ely's arguments, too, support such a project, because his requirement of government neutrality cannot be satisfied otherwise.

To see why this is so, consider *McCleskey v. Kemp,* in which a prisoner named Warren McCleskey challenged his death sentence by citing a massive study (the validity of which the Court did not dispute) showing that in Georgia, where the trial took place, murderers of whites were four times more likely to be sentenced to death than murderers of blacks. The Court rejected the challenge, because McCleskey had not shown that "the decision makers in *his* case acted with discriminatory purpose."[103] This reasoning egregiously disregards the requirements of process theory. McCleskey did show that more likely than not, had his victim not been white, he would not have been sentenced to death.[104] The decision-making process in Georgia death penalty cases is thoroughly infected by racism. It systematically undervalues the lives of blacks and overvalues the lives of whites. As Henry Louis Gates has observed, "the statistical regularity . . . in effect, functions like a rule; a rule governing judicial

103. 481 U.S. 279, 292 (1987), emphasis in original. For an argument that this application of the intent requirement was more stringent than that which the Court has required in other cases, such as jury venire selection, see Daniel R. Ortiz, "The Myth of Intent in Equal Protection," 41 *Stan. L. Rev.* 1105, 1142–49 (1989).

104. See *McCleskey,* 481 U.S. at 325 (Brennan, J., dissenting), 355 (Blackmun, J., dissenting). Henry Louis Gates has shown that the Court's reasoning implicitly relies on a premodern understanding of probability that is inconsistent with its purported acceptance of the validity of McCleskey's statistics. "Statistical Stigmata," in Drucilla Cornell, Michel Rosenfeld, and David Gray Carlson, eds., *Deconstruction and the Possibility of Justice* (New York and London: Routledge, 1992), pp. 330–45.

sentencing."[105] If considerations of race have been shown to have contaminated the decision-making process, that ought to be enough to satisfy the process theory.

It appears that McCleskey's argument was rejected not because of any weaknesses but rather for its too-potent strengths. The argument's implications frightened the Court: "McCleskey's claim, taken to its logical conclusion, throws into serious question the principles that underlie our entire criminal justice system. . . . [I]f we accepted McCleskey's claim that racial bias has impermissibly tainted the capital sentencing decision, we could soon be faced with similar claims as to other types of penalty."[106] This concern is arguably exaggerated, since greater safeguards are required in death penalty cases than in others.[107] But even if a remedy could be devised that was limited to death penalty cases—Randall Kennedy suggests "suspending executions pending the eradication of unjustified race-of-the-victim disparities"[108]—discrimination with respect to other types of penalty would remain a nagging problem. The demands of fair process are not confined to life-and-death decisions. The trouble is that civil order can be preserved even if the death penalty is dispensed with, conditionally or permanently,[109] but this is not true of the ordinary run of criminal penalties. It appears that the racial taint in their administration will not be cured until the day when the racial consciousness

105. Gates, "Statistical Stigmata," p. 335.

106. *McCleskey*, pp. 314–15. The Court noted (p. 315 n. 38) that "[s]tudies already exist that allegedly demonstrate a racial disparity in the length of prison sentences." For a review of the evidence of racism in the criminal justice system, see Stephanie Nickerson, Clara Mayo, and Althea Smith, "Racism in the Courtroom," in John F. Dovidio and Samuel L. Gaertner, eds., *Prejudice, Discrimination, and Racism* (Orlando: Academic Press, 1986), pp. 255–78.

107. See *McCleskey*, pp. 340 (Brennan, J., dissenting), 347–49 (Blackmun, J., dissenting), 366–67 (Stevens, J., dissenting). The problem of racial bias may also be more acute in death penalty cases, because "blacks (and women) are more likely to oppose the death penalty and thus to be excluded from capital juries." Robert A. Burt, "Disorder in the Court: The Death Penalty and the Constitution," 85 *Mich. L. Rev.* 1741, 1798 (1987).

108. Randall Kennedy, "*McCleskey v. Kemp*: Race, Capital Punishment, and the Supreme Court," 101 *Harv. L. Rev.* 1388, 1439 (1988). The state could also avoid discrimination by narrowing the class of death-eligible defendants to the most highly aggravated categories of cases, in which death sentences are consistently imposed without regard to race. See *McCleskey*, 481 U.S. at 367 (Stevens, J. dissenting); David C. Baldus, George Woodworth, and Charles A. Pulaski Jr., "Reflections on the 'Inevitability' of Racial Discrimination in Capital Sentencing and the 'Impossibility' of Its Prevention, Detection, and Correction," 51 *Wash. & Lee L. Rev.* 359, 397–98 (1994).

109. Cf. *McCleskey*, 481 U.S. at 367 (Stevens, J., dissenting).

of the ordinary juror or prosecutor is fundamentally altered.[110] It is, of course, beyond the capacities of the judiciary directly to accomplish that. The Court was right to worry about the implications of McCleskey's claim.[111] As Stephen Carter observes, "[i]t is unlikely that members of the jury that sentenced Mr. McCleskey got together and said to one another, 'Well, his victim was white, so he burns.' "[112] If racism can indeed affect the decision-making process unconsciously, then the demands imposed on the polity by the process theory

110. "Race is a fact of life and I'm not going to tell you that it's 100 percent gone, but I think the process is as fair as human endeavor can make it," Douglas Pullen, a Georgia district attorney, told the press. David Margolick, "In the Land of the Death Penalty, Accusations of Racial Bias," *N.Y. Times,* July 10, 1991, p. A12. Whether the process is as fair as human endeavor can make it depends, however, on whether human endeavor can change the significance of the fact of life that is race. Mr. Pullen may be correct that his own endeavors, alone and unaided, are incapable of making the process fairer. On the other hand, the study relied on by McCleskey found that "[t]he exercise of prosecutorial discretion is the principal source of the race-of-victim disparities observed in the system." David C. Baldus, George Woodworth, and Charles A. Pulaski Jr., *Equal Justice and the Death Penalty: A Legal and Empirical Analysis* (Boston: Northeastern University Press, 1990), p. 403. Moreover, Georgia itself has largely succeeded in eliminating discrimination on the basis of the race of the perpetrator, which was once pervasive in its criminal justice system. See Baldus, Woodworth, and Pulaski, "Reflections," pp. 396–97.

111. Justice Brennan rejected the majority's slippery-slope argument as suggesting "a fear of too much justice," *McCleskey,* 481 U.S. at 339. Because the massive study relied upon by McCleskey is "uniquely sophisticated," p. 341, and "not readily replicated through casual effort," p. 342, he argued, acceptance of it would "establish a remarkably stringent standard of statistical evidence unlikely to be satisfied with any frequency." P. 342. There are two ways of reading this argument. The first is that the evidence will not frequently be forthcoming because there is not much racism out there to be found. The implicit hypothesis is that racial discrimination taints the administration of the death penalty, but not other penalties. That sounds implausible on its face, and as noted above, the Court cited some evidence to the contrary. The second reading is that even if racism is rampant throughout the criminal justice system, there is no cause for alarm: Most of it will escape undetected, because the resources will not be forthcoming for the massive studies necessary to detect it. Such an argument itself suggests a fear of too much justice.

Justice Blackmun argued that even if a decision for McCleskey prompted further constitutional challenges, these would be welcome: "If a grant of relief to him were to lead to a closer examination of the effects of racial considerations throughout the criminal justice system, the system, and hence society, might benefit. Where no such factors come into play, the integrity of the system is enhanced. Where such considerations are shown to be significant, efforts can be made to eradicate their impermissible influence and to ensure the evenhanded application of criminal sanctions." Ibid., p. 365. But Blackmun does not consider the magnitude of the steps that would be required in order to "eradicate" the "impermissible influence" of racial prejudice.

112. Stephen L. Carter, "When Victims Happen To Be Black," 97 *Yale L. J.* 420, 442 (1988). Cf. Kennedy, "*McCleskey v. Kemp,*" p. 1420.

can only be satisfied by the transformation of the entire culture and the meanings it assigns to race.

One possible answer that process theory can offer (one more congenial to Ely than to Dworkin) is that impartiality is not required throughout society but only in the government decision-making process, which is amenable to judicial oversight. When government decisions are made that are contaminated by impermissible considerations, the judiciary can correct them. There is no need for sweeping social reforms.[113] This answer however still "requires the courts to do in practice exactly what it forbids them to do in theory.... To judge whether discriminatory intent made a difference, process theory requires the court to remake the government's decision without the impermissible motive and then to see whether the decision remains the same."[114] Since process theory aspires to an uncontaminated decision-making process that is, to the greatest extent possible, *democratic,* and in which the judiciary performs only those tasks for which it is well suited as an institution, this state of affairs must be deeply unsatisfactory in terms of that theory's most basic commitments. Those commitments provide reasons for bringing into being a world in which it is unnecessary for courts to make this kind of messy substantive judgment.

The solution of having the judiciary remake decisions may also be unsatisfactory to the process theorist on an even more fundamental level. There is no guarantee that the courts' decisions will not themselves be infected by impermissible racial considerations. Richard Wasserstrom observes that racism is implicit even in the case that is celebrated as one of the high points in the legal system's fight against racism. In the implementation decision in *Brown v. Board of Education* (*Brown* II), the Court held that school desegregation should proceed, not immediately, but "with all deliberate speed," in order to enable authorities to cope with "complexities arising from the tran-

113. The theoretical distinction between correcting government decisions and reforming the structure of society may, of course, break down in practice, because courts may find that a government that was truly impartial would undertake sweeping social reforms. The troubled history of school desegregation provides many illustrations. See J. Anthony Lukas, *Common Ground: A Turbulent Decade in the Lives of Three American Families* (New York: Vintage Books, 1986); J. Harvie Wilkinson, *From* Brown *to* Bakke: *The Supreme Court and School Integration, 1954–1978* (New York: Oxford University Press, 1979).

114. Ortiz, "The Myth of Intent in Equal Protection," p. 1113. David Strauss reaches the same conclusion in "Discriminatory Intent and the Taming of *Brown.*"

sition to a system of public education freed from racial discrimination."[115] This, Wasserstrom argues, was "a fantastic bit of nonsense." There was nothing so complicated about the dual school systems of the Southern states that they could not have been desegregated forthwith: it would have been easy enough to order that each student attend the nearest school. The Court, he concludes, may unconsciously have been influenced by the wretched state of black schools compared to white ones, so that it was simply unwilling to order white children to go to those schools. "The Supreme Court's solution assumed that the correct way to deal with this problem was to have black children go to their schools until the black schools were brought up to par or eliminated."[116] This example suggests that as long as racism is as pervasive as it is in the society from which decision makers (including judicial decision makers) are drawn, the requirements of process theory cannot be satisfied.

Beyond Virtual Representation

Ely's theory does not recognize the importance, for democracy, of certain kinds of citizen virtue. In a democracy, all citizens are, at least to some degree, government decision makers. If they are racist, then their racism will inevitably contaminate democratic decision making, and in ways that the judiciary cannot possibly remedy. One illustration can be drawn from Kimberle Crenshaw's analysis of popular discourse on the issue of poverty. The attitudes she describes obviously constrain the possibilities of political decision making in response to that problem.

> Believing both that Blacks are inferior and that the economy impartially rewards the superior over the inferior, whites see that most Blacks are indeed worse off than whites are, which reinforces their sense that the

115. 349 U.S. 294, 301, 299 (1955).

116. Richard A. Wasserstrom, "Racism, Sexism, and Preferential Treatment: An Approach to the Topics," 24 *U.C.L.A. L. Rev.* 581, 600 (1977). See also Lewis M. Steel, "Nine Men in Black Who Think White," in Leonard W. Levy, ed., *The Supreme Court Under Earl Warren* (New York: Quadrangle, 1972), pp. 82–92. A similar point has been made about *McCleskey v. Kemp.* "Perhaps it is only racial paranoia, but one wonders: If McCleskey were a white defendant convicted of killing a black during a felony in a state where whites were the victims of a justice system controlled by blacks, would the (white) Court's concern about the potential disruptive outcome of a reversal carry the same convincing weight?" Bell, *Race, Racism and American Law,* p. 857.

market is operating "fairly and impartially"; those who should logically be on the bottom are on the bottom. . . . The racial character of the rationalizations that legitimate poverty is exemplified by advocates who seek to educate the American public about the severity of the homelessness problem by revealing that many of the new homeless are white. This does not necessarily indicate that advocates prefer whites over Blacks; instead, it is an acknowledgement that such a problem can easily be disregarded as the result of personal failure if its victims are Black.[117]

The persistence of racism is a major cause of continuing black poverty even if, as many believe, the immediate causes of that poverty are unrelated to racism: the deindustrialization of cities, the exodus of the black middle class, and the increase in antisocial and self-destructive behavior in poor black neighborhoods. For racism cripples the political system's ability to respond to these conditions. It is unlikely that the nation would have been as willing as it has to casually discard its cities and urban public schools were the inhabitants of those places not disproportionately black. Opposition to programs that could ameliorate these conditions is heightened by the perception that those programs would primarily benefit blacks.[118] It is fashionable among conservatives to say that the welfare state has been a failure, but a broad range of possible measures has never been attempted, suggesting how shallow the political system's interest in these issues really is.[119] For example, the Reagan Administration proposed early on that tax incentives be used to attract job-creating capital investment to "enterprise zones" in the inner cities, but Reagan himself never used any of his considerable political capital to get this proposal enacted.[120] It is hard to believe that the appalling conditions of the inner cities would have been politically tolerable if they were being endured by white people.[121] If the conditions of the cities are the product of a patho-

117. Kimberle Williams Crenshaw, "Race, Reform, and Retrenchment: Transformation and Legitimation in Antidiscrimination Law," 101 *Harv. L. Rev.* 1331, 1380, 1384 n. 199 (1988).

118. See Boxill, *Blacks and Social Justice,* pp. 230–31.

119. The weakness of the political system's response to black poverty is made clear in Nicholas Lemann's brief history of federal welfare measures in *The Promised Land: The Great Black Migration and How It Changed America* (New York: Alfred A. Knopf, 1991), pp. 109–221; see esp. p. 219.

120. There is, of course, considerable disagreement about whether such incentives would have produced the desired result, but Reagan purported to believe in them.

121. It is also hard to prove this counterfactual, but Derrick Bell goes a long way in that direction with a striking thought experiment: Would the nation's reaction be the same if *white*

logical culture, some of the relevant pathology resides in the culture of the white majority.

One limitation of the theory of democracy implicit in the *Carolene Products* footnote is that it appears to rest on a pluralist model in which interest groups contend for whatever share of the pie they can get. The trouble with prejudice, according to this model, is that it prevents certain groups from striking bargains with potential coalition partners, and thus impedes them from getting their share of the goods. As Bruce Ackerman observes, even if the Constitution is read as endorsing the bargaining theory of democracy, "all that pluralist theory explains is why minority groups can expect to influence legislative outcomes some of the time; it is something very different to explain why minorities may dress up these expectations in the language of constitutional rights and demand judicial protection for them."[122] The thinnest sort of process-based theory would insist only on scrupulous enforcement of the Fifteenth Amendment. Ely, of course, wants to go beyond this, but he is able to do so only by relying on his theory of "virtual representation": the elected representatives have an obligation to represent *all* the people, not just those who voted for them. In, say, a direct democracy, as opposed to a representative one, it is not clear that Ely's theory could explain or justify an antidiscrimination norm.

Other theories of democracy, however, do provide such a norm. Strong conceptions of deliberative democracy require that there not be too great disparities of power among the citizens, because these distort the ability of the less powerful to participate freely in deliberation.[123] Concerns about factionalism are, moreover, familiar in democratic theory: divisions among voters must not become too deep or bitter, or the polity's deliberations will no longer concern the common good, but rather be taken over by the interests of the largest faction.[124] On this account, deep and permanent divisions among the

---

youth began exhibiting the low academic achievement, drug abuse, and crime that is endemic among black inner city youth? See Derrick Bell, *And We Are Not Saved: The Elusive Quest for Racial Justice* (New York: Basic Books, 1987), pp. 162–65.

122. Bruce A. Ackerman, "Beyond *Carolene Products*," 98 *Harv. L. Rev.* 713, 720 (1985).

123. See Cass R. Sunstein, "Beyond the Republican Revival," 97 *Yale L. J.* 1539, 1548–58, 1580–81 (1988).

124. The classic statements of this position are Jean-Jacques Rousseau, *On the Social Contract*, ed. Roger D. Masters, tr. Judith R. Masters (New York: St. Martin's Press, 1978), book II, ch. 3, p. 61; and Alexander Hamilton, James Madison, and John Jay, *The Federalist Papers*, ed. Clinton Rossiter (New York: New American Library, 1961), nos. 10, 51. For a recent restatement,

citizens will themselves prevent the machinery of democratic government from running as it should, even if voting rights are scrupulously maintained. And from this it readily follows that the elimination of racism is an appropriate end for the state to promote.

The most sustained application of strong democratic theory to antidiscrimination law is that developed by James Liebman. Like Ely, Liebman begins with the premise that all citizens must be accorded equal concern and respect in public decision making. Unlike Ely, however, he recognizes that in a liberal, pluralist democracy, this premise implies that a certain kind of civic virtue is required of the citizenry. Liberal pluralism, Liebman argues, is predicated on the ideas that all persons are equal in their capacity to define their own good, and that all goods so defined are equally worthy of the political process's concern and respect. "For pluralism to work, there must be a right to be plural—to be different—without for that reason being deemed inferior and made worse off in civil society." In their democratic deliberations, the people must "accept the principle that all persons are equal in their capacity to choose their own good lives and that all lives so chosen are equally deserving of the political process's respect and concern." From a liberal democratic perspective, legislative racism "entails as fundamental a 'structural' defect in a pluralistic political system as is imaginable because, by establishing a 'we are better than they' orthodoxy, it denies the validity of plurality and corrodes the [principle of equal concern and respect] that lies at the core of our pluralistic political system."[125]

Unlike Ely's theory of virtual representation, Liebman's "process defect" theory extends to citizen participation in the political process. "[O]nce mainstream equal protection theories acknowledge that 'I am better than she' logic has no place in the lawmaker's mind—whether or not the logic was that mind's own product or was implanted there by a constituent—those theories would seem equally to disavow the legitimacy of that logic whenever it appears in and incites the political process." Liebman's examination of equal protection theory arises in the context of a study of school desegregation law, and he argues that one of the strongest justifications of school desegregation is that it renders impossible the invidious decision making that the process the-

---

see Benjamin Barber, *Strong Democracy* (Berkeley: University of California Press, 1984), esp. pp. 206–7.

125. Liebman, "Desegregating Politics," pp. 1557, 1580, 1558, and 1582.

ory condemns. "Because desegregation inextricably intermingles, hence effectively brackets, the racial identities of children behind the schoolhouse walls, the white parental constituency cannot take advantaging aim at their own children or disadvantaging aim at African-American children without creating an unacceptably high risk that the effects of their actions will fall equally on children of the other race." Liebman also finds significance in studies that indicate that "racist attitudes fade in the years following desegregation." This encourages the hope that "desegregatively positioned children will matriculate to adulthood with more fully developed racial 'bonds of civic friendship' than did previous, racially estranged and unequal, generations."[126] Liebman is cautious about placing too much weight on the (encouraging) social science data, but it is clear to him that the process theory may require cultural transformation:

> Given the extent to which the social and political spheres are intertwined and the extent to which behavior in the former influences behavior in the latter, the legislature may well conclude that its duty to foster virtue among *citizens* in the political sphere . . . requires the extension of that duty to *persons* active in other "public" contexts. . . . Once we recognize that the "equal concern" duty applies to all individuals active in politics writ large, it requires only an empirical judgment that the class of citizens who inject their views into the political process roughly coincides with the class of persons involved in other walks of "public" life to support the educative extension of the "equal concern" duty to social activities conducted in a demonstrably "public" manner.[127]

This kind of strong democratic argument should not be unfamiliar, and is not the exclusive preserve of the political left. As we shall now see, something like it has been adopted by the most conservative members of the Supreme Court.

A Second Excursus on Reverse Discrimination

A second argument against reverse discrimination is that such discrimination is the product of a decision-making process corrupted by racial factionalism. This argument is the basis of the Supreme Court's decision in *City of Richmond*

126. Ibid., pp. 1564, 1616, 1643, and 1644.
127. Ibid., p. 1559 (emphases in original).

v. J. A. Croson Co., in which the Court invalidated a minority set-aside program in the awarding of municipal contracts and cast grave doubt on the constitutionality of any state program that includes racial preferences. Richmond, Virginia, with a black population of just over 50 percent, had responded to a study showing that only 0.67 percent of the city's recent prime construction contracts had been awarded to blacks by requiring 30 percent minority participation in subcontracting. The Court rejected the city's claim that the set-aside was a permissible response to past widespread discrimination in contracting. Racial classifications, whether they benefit whites or blacks, are suspect, Justice O'Connor explained in the majority opinion, because they may be "in fact motivated by illegitimate notions of racial inferiority or simple racial politics." They may thus "lead to a politics of racial hostility."[128] The danger that racial factionalism motivated the classifications was particularly apparent in this case, O'Connor wrote, because '[f]ive of the nine seats on the [Richmond] City Council are held by blacks."[129]

Racial factionalism is the implicit common denominator that permitted the *Croson* Court to deem the Richmond set-aside the constitutional equivalent of Jim Crow: in each case, the Court evidently thought, one faction had seized control of the government and made the law serve its private ends rather than the good of the whole. What is particularly worrisome about *racial* factionalism, Liebman and the Court evidently agree, is the historically demonstrated tendency (and not only in the United States) of racial factions to constitute large units, perpetuating themselves over generations, with loyalties that divide their members from other citizens. It is arguable that America owes its success in assimilating ethnic groups into a more or less harmonious polity to its refusal to give those groups any juridical recognition. The consequence of this nonrecognition of ethnic status was that ethnicity was not an inescapable aspect of identity, and individuals could look somewhere other than to their own ethnic leaders for political protection.[130] The big exception in this story is, of course, the case of people of color. That exception might nonetheless be taken to prove the rule: race was given juridical status for a long time. But the subordinate status of blacks is not attributable solely to juridical racism. Al-

128. 488 U.S. 469, 493 (1989); see also *Shaw v. Reno,* 113 S. Ct. 2816, 2832 (1993) (O'Connor, J.) (racial classification in electoral districting "may balkanize us into competing racial factions.").

129. *Croson,* p. 495.

130. See generally Nathan Glazer, *Affirmative Discrimination: Ethnic Inequality and Public Policy* (New York: Basic Books, 1975).

though there was little legally mandated segregation in the North after the Civil War, the inferior status of blacks persisted. Similarly, the salience of race in American society seems quite capable of perpetuating itself without the active assistance of the state.[131]

A democratic polity free from corruption would be one in which racial factionalism played no significant role in political decision making. The *Croson* Court thought that enforcing a rule of color blindness was the best way to police the decision-making process in order to purge it of such factionalism. The elimination of racial factionalism is clearly a job the judiciary must perform if anyone is to do it, since political decision makers (particularly, the Court seems to think, black ones) cannot be trusted to police themselves. But the soundness of this purportedly process-based approach depends on a prediction: that racism will have less influence, in the long run, in political decision making under a color-blindness rule than if benign racial preferences are permitted. The fear is that if government is permitted to give *any* juridical recognition to race, that recognition will teach each citizen the notion, corrosive of democracy, that her race is one of the most salient aspects of her public identity.

Unfortunately, citizens learn that lesson anyway, from the ordinary, common racism of civil society. It is far from clear that ignoring racism is the way to make it go away. If civil society is showing a robust capacity to perpetuate racism without the state's assistance, then government must, if it hopes to eradicate racism, intervene in the processes within civil society that reproduce it. There is reason to think that racial preferences are an important—perhaps indispensable—tool for doing that job. From this perspective, the rhetoric of color blindness is itself suspect, especially given its sources.

Consider a different scenario of racial factionalism. Suppose the government were taken over by a racial faction of whites who desired to concentrate wealth, power, and privilege in the hands of white people.[132] What would such a

131. A major weakness in the libertarian argument against antidiscrimination laws is the libertarians' failure to recognize that this is the case. The most sustained argument for the libertarian position is Epstein, *Forbidden Grounds*. This weakness is emphasized by Epstein's critics. See, e.g., J. Hoult Verkerke, "Free to Search," 105 *Harv. L. Rev.* 2080, 2089–94 (1992); Mark Tushnet, book review, 16 *Legal Stud. Forum* 251, 253 (1992); Samuel Issacharoff, "Contractual Liberties in Discriminatory Markets," 70 *Tex. L. Rev.* 1219, 1229–34 (1992). See generally symposium, 31 *San Diego L. Rev.* 1 (1994).

132. This is arguably an accurate description of the Reagan Administration and its key constituencies. See Edsall with Edsall, *Chain Reaction.*

faction have to get government to do now in order to bring about that result? Would it need to employ racial classifications? No. Because wealth, power, and privilege are *already* concentrated in the hands of whites, all it would need to do would be to *prevent re*distribution. A rule of color blindness would be, in this context, an effective instrument for that end.[133] The *Croson* Court's decision may thus give a judicial imprimatur to the precise evil that the Court says it seeks to eradicate.

The attractiveness of the color-blindness principle is that it stamps out one undoubtedly dangerous manifestation of racism, and does so by means of a rule that is easy to apply. However, the sole purpose of this rule is to minimize the influence of racism on government decision-making processes. There is reason to fear that racism will have *more* influence on decision making with a color-blindness rule than it would if racial preferences were permitted as a weapon against racism.

Let us concede that any alternative will require fine interpretative and predictive judgments that it is hard for the judiciary to make: in *Croson,* whether racial factionalism had infected the decision-making process in *this* case, and whether it was reasonable for the state to think that this set-aside would really help reduce racism rather than merely enriching some of the few local blacks who were already prosperous. Such a specific contextual inquiry, however, appears to be the only way to be certain that the Court is achieving, rather than thwarting, its desired end. The fatal weakness of *Croson* is the obtuse and ham-handed way the Court undertook this inquiry. Michel Rosenfeld observes that the majority opinion combines "an exceptionally stringent causal requirement with a completely abstract and acontextual grasp of the relevant facts," so that "Justice O'Connor appears to disconnect salient occurrences [the history of discrimination and the underrepresentation of blacks in the construction industry] from one another and from the broader context in which they emerge, and to accept the existence of causal links beween such occurrences only if every other plausible alternative must be ruled out."[134] The Court's holding, that the program must be invalidated because there was not sufficient

133. See generally Kennedy, "Persuasion and Distrust."

134. *Affirmative Action and Justice,* pp. 209, 212. The history ignored by the Court is detailed in Justice Marshall's dissent, and also in Peter Charles Hoffer, " 'Blind to History': The use of History in Affirmative Action Suits: Another Look at *City of Richmond v. J.A. Croson Co.,*" 23 *Rutgers L. J.* 271, 289–95 (1992); see also Thomas Ross, "The Richmand Narratives," 68 *Tex. L.*

evidence of past or ongoing racial discrimination in Richmond, Virginia is surreal. It suggests that, despite indications to the contrary, a colorblindness rule is what the Court has in fact adopted: if remedial classifications cannot be justified in Richmond, they probably cannot be justified anywhere. Any rule of law that is to substantially impede racial factionalism in all its manifestations must be less crude than this.

The larger lesson of this discussion is that the evil the *Croson* Court sought to eradicate may manifest itself in many ways other than racial classification. Racial factionalism is not simply a characteristic of certain statutes. It is a disease that plagues the polity as a whole. Justice O'Connor and James Liebman appear to agree on this much. From the perspective of strong democratic theory, racism is itself an obstacle to well-functioning government and should be eradicated.

The Limits of Process Theory

In sum, the process theorists agree that the defect with which they are concerned is the introduction of a contaminating element into the decision-making process: external preferences, malign preferences, desire to harm, or color-consciousness. In each case, however, that contaminating element is inadequately specified: Dworkin misdescribes its normative basis; Ely misdescribes the ways in which the process goes wrong; and the color-blindness theorists misdescribe both. We can conclude that a sound normative basis for process theory emerges from the debate between Ely and Dworkin: legislation (and perhaps other decisions as well) ought not to be based on malign preferences, that is, preferences that explicitly, implicitly, or even unconsciously deny equal concern and respect for some members of the polity.

None of these writers, however, offers an adequate account of where malign preferences originate, how they manifest themselves in the world, or how they perpetuate themselves. Such an account would have to look outside the decision-making process itself to the social context within which that process is situated. A process theory that does not say where the contamination is coming from is likely to overlook many of its points of entry into the decision-

---

Rev. 381 (1989); Charles R. Lawrence III, "The Word and the River: Pedagogy as Scholarship as Struggle," 65 *S. Calif. L. Rev.* 2231, 2282 (1992).

making system. It is with this gap in the process theory in mind that we turn to the next theory of equal protection, the stigma theory. As Charles R. Lawrence III has observed, unconscious racism originates in "widely shared, tacitly transmitted cultural values."[135] These values are reflected in stigma, the invidious cultural meaning of race. We shall find that the stigma theory takes us a long way toward filling the gaps in the process theory, and thus toward a more complete and satisfying account of the evil that antidiscrimination law seeks to eliminate.

135. Lawrence, "The Id, the Ego, and Equal Protection," p. 355.

2

Result-Based Theories

The Stigma Theory

Cultural meaning is the focus of a second group of antidiscrimination theorists. These writers identify the central concern of antidiscrimination law as the stigmatization of certain groups. Like the process theory, this view has roots in case law. In *Strauder v. West Virginia,* the first race discrimination case to reach the Supreme Court after the Civil War, the Court struck down a state law excluding blacks from juries. The Court declared that the Fourteenth Amendment protects blacks "from legal discriminations, implying inferiority in civil society."[1] *Plessy v. Ferguson* offered the tribute that vice pays to virtue when it declared that a segregation law *would* be unconstitutional if it were true that it "stamps the colored race with a badge of inferiority."[2] Similarly, in *Brown v. Board of Education,* Chief Justice Warren wrote that the segregation of black students is impermissible because it "generates a feeling of inferiority as to their status in the community that may affect their hearts and minds in a way unlikely ever to be undone."[3] In *Regents of Univ. of California v. Bakke,* four justices declared that the "cardinal principle" of the Fourteenth Amendment was "that racial classifications that stigmatize—because they are drawn on the presumption that one race is inferior to another

---

1. 100 U.S. 303, 308 (1880).
2. 163 U.S. 537, 551 (1896). "If this be so," the Court concluded, "it is not by reason of anything found in the act, but solely because the colored race chooses to put that construction upon it." Ibid. Charles Black observes that "the *Plessy* Court clearly conceived it to be its task to show that segregation did not really disadvantage the Negro, except through his own choice." The major premise laid down in *Strauder* was not questioned; "the fault of *Plessy* is in the psychology and sociology of its minor premise." Charles Black, "The Lawfulness of the Segregation Decisions," 69 *Yale L.J.* 421, 422 (1960).
3. 347 U.S. 483, 494 (1954).

or because they put the weight of government behind racial hatred and separatism—are invalid without more."[4]

The classic articulation of the stigma theory was given by Charles Black, one of the authors of the plaintiffs' brief in *Brown*, who argued that the correctness of *Brown* depended upon "what segregation means to the people who impose it and to the people who are subjected to it." Black argued that the Court could not properly ignore "a plain fact about the society of the United States—the fact that the social meaning of segregation is the putting of the Negro in a position of walled-off inferiority—or the other equally plain fact that such treatment is hurtful to human beings." Segregation, he concluded, was a clear violation of the Fourteenth Amendment, which "should be read as saying that the Negro race, as such, is not to be significantly disadvantaged by the laws of the states."[5] Paul Brest later elaborated upon the same theme, observing that "[d]ecisions based on assumptions of intrinsic worth and selective indifference inflict psychological injury by stigmatizing their victims as inferior. . . . Recognition of the stigmatic injury inflicted by discrimination explains applications of the antidiscrimination principle where the material harm seems slight or problematic."[6]

The strongest claims about stigma are those made by Kenneth Karst, who argues that the substantive core of the equal protection clause is "a principle of equal citizenship, which presumptively guarantees to each individual the right to be treated by the organized society as a respected, responsible, and participating member."[7]

> The principle of equal citizenship presumptively insists that the organized society treat each individual as a person, one who is worthy of respect, one who "belongs." Stated negatively, the principle presumptively forbids the organized society to treat an individual either as a member of an inferior or dependent caste or as a nonparticipant. Accordingly, the principle guards against degradation or the imposition of stigma. The inverse relationship between stigma and recognition as a person is evident. "By

4. 438 U.S. 265, 357–58 (1978) (opinion of Brennan, White, Marshall, and Blackmun, JJ., concurring in the judgment in part and dissenting in part).

5. Black, "The Lawfulness of the Segregation Decisions," pp. 426, 427, 421.

6. Paul Brest, "The Supreme Court, 1975 Term—Foreword: In Defense of the Antidiscrimination Principle," 90 *Harv. L. Rev.* 1, 8, 9 (1976).

7. Kenneth L. Karst, "The Supreme Court, 1976 Term—Foreword: Equal Citizenship Under the Fourteenth Amendment," 91 *Harv. L. Rev.* 1, 4 (1977).

definition, . . . we believe that the person with a stigma is not quite human." The relationship between stigma and inequality is also clear: while not all inequalities stigmatize, the essence of any stigma lies in the fact that the affected individual is regarded as an unequal in some respect. A society devoted to the idea of equal citizenship, then, will repudiate those inequalities that impose the stigma of caste and thus "belie the principle that people are of equal ultimate worth."[8]

In short, the equal citizenship principle "can be reduced to a claim to be free from stigma."[9]

Like the process theory, the stigma theory points beyond itself to a larger societal phenomenon. Indeed it does so more obviously, since the injury it specifies is the same whether it is inflicted by the state or by private actors.

> If a Negro child perceives his separation as discriminatory and invidious, he is not, in a society a hundred years removed from slavery, going to make fine distinctions about the source of a particular separation. The Court [in Brown] implied as much when it quoted with approval a statement by a lower-court judge to the effect that the detrimental consequences of school segregation were heightened—merely heightened—when segregation had the sanction of law.[10]

Our discussion of the stigma theory will focus on a different kind of issue from the one that preoccupied us with the process theory. The process theory rests on largely unexceptionable premises: that the state has a duty to be impartial, and that prejudice should not be allowed to cause people significant harm. The main question for us was whether these moral requirements demand a project of cultural transformation. For the stigma theory, the need for cultural transformation is not in question; the theory expressly requires that it be pursued. The problem is rather whether the stigma theory articulates a legitimate moral demand. I begin, then, with the arguments that support the view that there is a right to be free from racial stigma.

One argument against stigma draws on the process theory. The *Strauder*

8. Ibid., p. 6, quoting Erving Goffman, *Stigma: Notes on the Management of Spoiled Identity* (Englewood Cliffs, N.J.: Prentice-Hall, 1963), p. 5, and Robert E. Rodes Jr., *The Legal Enterprise* (Port Washington, N.Y.: Kennikat Press, 1976), p. 163.

9. Kenneth L. Karst, "Why Equality Matters," 17 *Ga. L. Rev.* 245, 249 (1983).

10. Alexander Bickel, *The Supreme Court and the Idea of Progress* (New Haven: Yale University Press, 1978), pp. 119–20.

Court argued that the exclusion of blacks from juries was "practically a brand upon them, affixed by the law, an assertion of their inferiority, and a stimulant to that race prejudice which is an impediment to securing to individuals of the race that equal justice which the law aims to secure to all others."[11] Stigma is the means by which process defect begets process defect: the exclusion of blacks was problematic not only because it was the product of a contaminated decision-making process, but also because it in turn reinforced racism and thereby increased the likelihood that blacks would not receive fair treatment in the courts. The prohibition of government actions that have stigmatizing effects may thus be necessary in order to ensure an unbiased political process.[12]

The main argument of the stigma theorists, however, is that stigma is itself an injury. Against this, some critics argue that the injury is only an intangible one, and that people ought to be thicker-skinned. The standard rejoinder is that in the case of race the stigmatizing meanings are so ubiquitous as to be inescapable. This theme is apparent in Martin Luther King Jr.'s classic description of the American system of racism:

> Perhaps it is easy for those who have never felt the stinging darts of segregation to say, "Wait." But when you have seen vicious mobs lynch your mothers and fathers at will and drown your sisters and brothers at whim; when you have seen hate-filled policemen curse, kick and even kill your black brothers and sisters; when you see the vast majority of your twenty million Negro brothers smothering in an airtight cage of poverty in the midst of an affluent society; when you suddenly find your tongue twisted and your speech stammering as you seek to explain to your six-year-old daughter why she can't go to the public amusement park that has just been advertised on television, and see tears welling up in her eyes when she is told that Funtown is closed to colored children, *and see ominous clouds of inferiority beginning to form in her little mental sky, and see her beginning to distort her personality by developing an unconscious*

11. 100 U.S. at 308.

12. For Ely, stigma is relevant if it affects the decision-making process, but not if it is only an outcome of that process. See John Hart Ely, *Democracy and Distrust* (Cambridge: Harvard University Press, 1980), p. 160, asterisk note. He does not consider the extent to which these two states of affairs tend to be intertwined, so that government actions reinforcing stigma, even if innocently motivated, may reinforce invidious cultural tendencies that will contaminate other government actions in the future.

bitterness toward white people; when you have to concoct an answer for a
five-year-old son who is asking, "Daddy, why do white people treat colored
people so mean?"; when you take a cross-country drive and find it necessary to sleep night after night in the uncomfortable corners of your
automobile because no motel will accept you; *when you are humiliated*
day in and day out by nagging signs reading "white" and "colored"; when
your first name becomes "nigger," your middle name becomes "boy" (how-
ever old you are) and your last name becomes "John," and your wife and
mother are never given the respected title "Mrs."; when you are harried by
day and haunted by night by the fact that you are a Negro, living constantly
at tiptoe stance, never quite knowing what to expect next, and are plagued
with inner fears and outer resentments; when you are fighting a degenerating
sense of "nobodiness"—then you will understand why we find it difficult
to wait.[13]

The italicized passages identify injuries that are less tangible than the others
on the list, but that are close to the core of what antidiscrimination law seeks
to combat, inasmuch as they enact the belief that blacks are intrinsically inferior to whites.

The most obvious harm caused by stigma is that of internalized self-hatred,
the "degenerating sense of 'nobodiness' " of which King writes. Kenneth Clark
writes that "[h]uman beings . . . whose daily experience tells them that almost
nowhere in society are they respected and granted the ordinary dignity and
courtesy accorded to others will, as a matter of course, begin to doubt their
own worth."[14] While it is evident that some blacks do suffer this kind of
damage, the most thorough aggregate studies of self-concept among blacks
have found that "personal self-esteem among black populations [is] either
equal to or greater than that among whites."[15] Black parents seem to do a very

13. Martin Luther King Jr., "Letter from Birmingham Jail," in *Why We Can't Wait* (New York:
Signet, 1964), pp. 81–82 (emphases added).

14. Kenneth Clark, *Dark Ghetto: Dilemmas of Social Power* (New York: Harper and Row, 1965),
pp. 63–64; see also Richard Delgado, "Words That Wound: A Tort Action for Racial Insults,
Epithets, and Name-Calling," 17 *Harv. Civ. Rts.–Civ. Liberties L. Rev.* 133, 136–49 (1982); Gordon
W. Allport, *The Nature of Prejudice* (Reading, Mass: Addison-Wesley, 1979), pp. 142–62. The
damage racism can inflict on one's self-respect is also a familiar theme in literature. See, e.g., Toni
Morrison, *The Bluest Eye* (New York: Pocket Books, 1972).

15. Judith R. Porter and Robert E. Washington, "Black Identity and Self-Esteem: A Review of

capable job of preparing their children to cope with racism, and blacks generally seem to give messages of inferiority no more credence than they deserve. Nonetheless, those who are constantly subjected to insults, even when they do not internalize the message, suffer a different kind of injury, that of resentment, tension, and anger. These can have a corrosive effect on one's psychological and even physical well-being despite one's knowledge that one holds the moral high ground. Dealing with racism is a distraction from other valued pursuits and a drain on one's time and energy. Whatever the precise proportion of blacks who suffer the various kinds of injuries attendant on racism, those injuries do occur, they are direct consequences of racism, and they are injustices.

A final consideration that supports making stigma central in antidiscrimination law is a historical one. Stigma was a central component of the system of slavery whose vestiges antidiscrimination seeks to eradicate. Orlando Patterson's comparative study of slavery finds that in many slave societies the slaves produced nothing of value for the master and were often economically dependent on him. The benefits that were always present were emotional rather than tangible, generating a sense of honor for the master and of dishonor for the slave: "The real sweetness of mastery for the slaveholder lay not immediately in profit, but in the lightening of the soul that comes with the realization that at one's feet is another human creature who lives and breathes only for one's self, as a surrogate for one's power, as a living embodiment of one's manhood and honor."[16] And this is a large part of the satisfaction of racism: the sense that one's identity as a white is confirmed and made valuable by the class of degraded persons to whom all whites are superior. It was the social distance between white and black, the stigmatization of the black as a nonperson, that made it seem normal and natural for blacks to be enslaved—or later subordinated—to whites. This is the existential basis of slavery as Hegel saw it: that because my sense of myself is largely derived from the image of myself I get from others, I will find it satisfying in a fundamental way to make another person into a slave, a living trophy of my superior value.[17] This

Studies of Black Self-Concept, 1968–1978," 5 *Ann. Rev. Sociology* 53, 62 (1979). See also Edgar G. Epps, "The Impact of School Desegregation on the Self-Evaluation and Achievement Orientation of Minority Children," 42 *Law and Contemporary Problems* 57 (Summer 1978). I am grateful to Jennifer Hochschild for directing me to these articles.

16. *Slavery and Social Death* (Cambridge and London: Harvard University Press, 1982), p. 78.

17. On Hegel's master-slave dialectic and its relevance to the antidiscrimination project, see

gratification was an important part of the value of slavery to (indeed, was largely constitutive of the personalities of) the Southern master class.[18] The Supreme Court appears to have had this analysis in mind when it held that the Thirteenth Amendment authorizes legislation against discrimination in housing, because Congress is empowered to legislate against "the badges and incidents of slavery" and "to eradicate the last vestiges and incidents of a society half slave and half free."[19] The stigmatization of blacks is not just a consequence of the fact that blacks were once slaves. That stigma was a *component* of the slave system, part of what made it function. To the extent that the stigma persists, slavery itself has not been wholly eradicated.

Stigma, then, is an essential part of racial injustice. However, the claim of the stigma theorists requires further clarification. Just as the color-blindness theorists did not explain why antidiscrimination law focuses solely on certain kinds of overgeneralization, so the stigma theorists do not say why the law concerns itself only with certain kinds of stigma. The theory's claim cannot be that stigma should never exist. Stigma is often, and appropriately, inflicted by the law itself—most pertinently, by a legal finding that a defendant has engaged in purposeful discrimination. As Brest has observed, "some insults to dignity are morally wrong while others are permissible or even desirable."[20] What, then, is especially bad about *racial* stigma?

An ambiguity in Ely's notion of malign preferences gives rise to a similar puzzle. It will be recalled that he defined these as preferences "involving the desire to deprive another person or group of an equal share of life's goods and opportunities." On that level of abstraction, any kind of stigma, such as that placed on criminals, might count as a malign preference. Since that does not appear to raise antidiscrimination concerns, it seems that Ely's conception, like Karst's, needs further specification. Later in the same article Ely does say that a malign preference is one "rooted in a belief that certain racial or other groups simply deserve less of life's good things than the rest of us,"[21] but the

---

my "Sex Equality and/or the Family: From Bloom vs. Okin to Rousseau vs. Hegel," 4 *Yale J. L. & Hum.* 399 (1992).

18. See Eugene Genovese, *The Political Economy of Slavery: Studies in the Economy and Society of the Slave South* (New York: Vintage, 1967), pp. 28–34.

19. *Jones v. Alfred H. Mayer Co.*, 392 U.S. 409, 440, 441 n. 78 (1968).

20. Paul Brest, "The Substance of Process," 42 *Ohio St. L. J.* 131, 141 (1981).

21. John Hart Ely, "Professor Dworkin's External/Personal Preference Distinction," 1983 *Duke L. J.* 959, 984, 985.

vague reference to "other groups" shows how much still needs to be said. We will not know which other groups to protect unless we know why we are especially concerned about the stigmatization of blacks.

In order to decide what kinds of stigma are impermissible, we must return to the logic of relevant reasons. The moral power of the stigma theory rests on the idea that certain reasons are *never* appropriate for imposing stigma. This is why the ascribed or immutable nature of such characteristics as race and sex are so ubiquitously cited in antidiscrimination discourse. One common way of stating the major premise of the stigma theory is that persons do not deserve to be, and should not be, stigmatized on the basis of ascribed or immutable characteristics.[22] This is not precisely right, though; the real claim is that persons should not be stigmatized unless there is some good reason for stigmatizing them. Ascription is simply strong evidence that no such reason can be offered. Even among instances of ascription, there are harder cases. It is not clear that the stigmatization of physical unattractiveness could be altogether eradicated without also ending admiration for beauty, and reasonable people disagree about whether that would be worth the cost. On the other hand, it is clear that this stigma produces gross injustice (physically unattractive people tend to receive severer sentences in criminal cases),[23] that there is no justification for making the lives of unattractive people as hard as they are, and that prevailing notions of beauty are themselves influenced by racism.[24] What is clear is that the impermissible kinds of stigma are not limited to those

22. See, e.g., *Frontiero v. Richardson*, 411 U.S. 677, 686 (1973) (plurality opinion): "[S]ince sex, like race and national origin, is an immutable characteristic determined solely by the accident of birth, the imposition of special disabilities upon the members of a particular sex because of their sex would seem to violate 'the basic concept of our system that legal burdens should bear some relationship to individual responsibility.'" Compare the United Nations definition of discrimination: "Discrimination includes any conduct based on a distinction made on grounds of natural or social categories, which have no relation either to individual capacities or merits, or to the concrete behavior of the individual person." *The main types and causes of discrimination*, U.N. publication, 1949, XIV, 3, 2, quoted in Allport, *The Nature of Prejudice*, p. 52. For a critique of the focus on immutability, see Janet E. Halley, "Sexual Orientation and the Politics of Biology: A Critique of the Argument from Immutability," 46 *Stan. L. Rev.* 503 (1994).

23. See Note, "Facial Discrimination: Extending Handicap Law to Employment Discrimination on the Basis of Physical Appearance," 100 *Harv. L. Rev.* 2035, 2039 (1987).

24. See generally Iris Marion Young, *Justice and the Politics of Difference* (Princeton: Princeton University Press, 1990), pp. 122–36. The phenomenon should be a familiar one. For instance, one hearing of a discrimination complaint revealed that an interview form contained the written comment that the black applicant had "unattractive, large lips." Note, "Facial Discrimination," p. 2042.

based on ascribed characteristics. (In Chapter 4, I shall discuss arguments for extending the stigma theory to protect religion and homosexual behavior.) The real issue is whether a relevant reason can be offered for the stigma.[25]

The argument that *racial* stigma is unjust typically focuses on the unchosen nature of race and relies on one or both of two premises, one having to do with the nature of moral reasoning, the other with the nature of persons. First, whatever the appropriate justifications are for stigma, a person should not be blamed for qualities he cannot do anything about. "Ought" implies "can"; moral blameworthiness intelligibly attaches only to a person who has behaved differently than she should have and could have.[26] Second, humanity is not naturally divided into superior and inferior races, with intrinsically different abilities and worth. It is not the case that, for example, white males are more

25. As Bernard Boxill observes, "a policy denying university admission to people who parted their hair on the right side would be unjust because the way in which people part their hair is irrelevant to a just policy of school admission. It does not matter in the least, in relation to the nature and object of education, that they choose how they part their hair. Similarly, even if black people could choose to become white, or could all easily pass as white, a law school or medical school that excluded blacks because they were black would still act unjustly." *Blacks and Social Justice* (Lanham, Maryland: Rowman & Littlefield, rev. ed. 1992), p. 16.

26. Ely attacks the relevance of ascription under a different name, "immutability," in the following well-known passage: "Surely one has to feel sorry for a person disabled by something that he or she can't do anything about, but I'm not aware of any reason to suppose that elected officials are unusually unlikely to share that feeling. Moreover, classifications based on physical disability and intelligence are typically accepted as legitimate, even by judges and commentators who assert that immutability is relevant. The explanation, when one is given, is that *those* characteristics (unlike the one the commentator is trying to render suspect) are often relevant to legitimate purposes. At that point there's not much left of the immutability theory, is there?" (*Democracy and Distrust*, p. 150, emphasis in original; quoted with evident approval in *City of Cleburne v. Cleburne Living Center*, 473 U.S. 432, 442 n. 10 [1985]).

This objection misses the point. There may be nothing wrong with *classifying* on the basis of immutable characteristics, as when congenitally blind people are forbidden to pilot airplanes. See *Democracy and Distrust*, pp. 154–55. But that kind of classification does not *stigmatize* the blind people. Their right to equal concern and respect is not at issue. Ely is likewise correct to say (pp. 150–51) that the amount of harm inflicted by a statute is generally irrelevant to judicial review, but what is at issue here is the *kind* of harm: not just stigma, but stigma on the basis of immutable characteristics. By treating stigma and immutability separately, Ely makes each seem less salient than it is. Even after *Cleburne*, the Court has continued to find immutability relevant. See *Bowen v. Gilliard*, 483 U.S. 587, 602 (1987), quoting *Lyng v. Castillo*, 477 U.S. 635, 638 (1986); *Lockhart v. McCree*, 476 U.S. 162, 175 (1986). Even Justice White, the author of *Cleburne*, acknowledged a year later (in an opinion for the Court) that the fact "[t]hat the characteristics of the complaining group are not immutable . . . may be relevant to the manner in which the case is adjudicated." *Davis v. Bandemer*, 478 U.S. 109, 125 (1986).

fully human and worthy of concern and respect than women or blacks. (Unless this second point is sufficiently emphasized, there is a danger that the first point will itself be implicitly racist. "She can't help it that she's black" implies that any reasonable person would avoid being black if she *could* help it.)

The most important objection to arguments that focus on ascription is that some of the most important human attachments depend upon discrimination among persons on the basis of ascribed characteristics. When Parsons and Shils introduced the concept of ascription, one example they provided was the commitment that parents feel for their children.[27] An infant does nothing to earn its parents' love. Objectively, there is no difference between it and any other infant, yet the parent cares for it more than for anyone else's child. We will hardly say that this discrimination is morally wrong. The point may be generalized to other local attachments: many communities are bound by constitutive ties that rest on ascribed characteristics. These ties not only create a salutary buffer between the individual and the state, but also are valuable in themselves. Such ties often entail hostility to outsiders—one's sense of oneself as a Protestant may be inseparable from a certain disdain toward Catholics— and they inevitably at least *devalue* outsiders. "The *McCleskey* statistics," Randall Kennedy observes, "do not represent something confined to race (because we all engage in differential valuations of human life according to clannish criteria—family, locality, nationality), nor even something that is wholly evil (that individuals feel greater identification with the victimization of members of a particular racial group bespeaks, after all, a certain sense of community)."[28]

27. Talcott Parsons and Edward A. Shils, *Toward a General Theory of Action* (Cambridge: Harvard University Press, 1951), p. 177. Parsons and Shils observed that when dealing with social objects, an actor must decide whether to act toward them in terms of what they are or in terms of what they do. With respect to cultural norms, which concern us here, "ascription" refers to "the normative pattern which prescribes that an actor in a given type of situation should, in his selections for differential treatment of social objects, give priority to certain attributes that they possess (including collectivity memberships and possessions) over any specific performances (past, present, or prospective) of the objects." "Achievement," on the other hand, refers to "the normative pattern which prescribes that an actor in a given type of situation should, in his selection and differential treatment of social objects, give priority to their specific performances (past, present, or prospective) over their given attributes (including memberships and possessions), insofar as the latter are not significant as direct conditions of the relevant performances." Ibid., pp. 82–83.

28. Randall Kennedy, "*McCleskey v. Kemp*: Race, Capital Punishment, and the Supreme Court," 101 *Harv. L. Rev.* 1388, 1442 (1988).

Can we, then, more precisely say how and when this ascription-based sense of community becomes an evil? We are after something less severe than Rousseau's universalistic view that "[a]ll the preferences of friendship are thefts committed against the human race and the fatherland. Men are all our brothers, they should all be our friends."[29] This seems mad or inhuman. Dworkin and Ely hold that the duty of equal concern and respect only applies in a bounded public sphere.[30] This produces the requirement of state neutrality— a requirement that does not restrict the state official or the voter in their ordinary relations as private citizens. I have already argued that, given the power of unconscious racism, even this limited kind of civic virtue is very hard to attain and cannot be achieved unless the power of racism in our culture is reduced. But the stigma theory is not only concerned about an uncorrupted government decision-making process.

The central concern of the stigma theory is to satisfy certain obligations that members of any community (not only a democratic one) owe to one another. For it is somewhat misleading to describe the stigma with which the antidiscrimination project concerns itself as something that insiders assign to outsiders. Stigma is itself an artifact of community. We have not yet defined stigma. Now let us try.

When we encounter another person, we tend to anticipate and to impute a certain identity and attributes to the person solely on the basis of the social setting of the encounter. Erving Goffman, in his study of stigma, calls this imputed identity "virtual social identity." Stigma arises when the individual fails to live up to these expectations; it "constitutes a special discrepancy between virtual and actual social identity."[31] This discrepancy produces a failure of acceptance and, if the individual himself internalizes the expectations, a damaged conception of self: "Those who have dealings with him fail to accord him the respect and regard which the uncontaminated aspects of his social identity have led them to anticipate extending, and have led him to anticipate receiving; he echoes this denial by finding that some of his own attributes warrant it." Put another way, a stigma is a mark, a perceived con-

---

29. See ibid., p. 1441 n. 239, quoting Jean-Jacques Rousseau, *Correspondence Générale de J.-J. Rousseau* (Paris: Librairie Armand Colin, 1925), v. 4, p. 82.

30. Rousseau adopts this distinction in other writings. See Jean-Jacques Rousseau, "Discourse on Political Economy," in Roger D. Masters, ed., *On the Social Contract,* tr. Judith R. Masters (New York: St. Martin's, 1978), p. 211.

31. Goffman, *Stigma,* pp. 3, 8–9.

dition of deviation from a prototype or norm, that defines the bearer as deviant, flawed, or otherwise undesirable. "To mark a person implies that the deviant condition has been noticed and recognized as a problem in the interaction or the relationship. To stigmatize a person generally carries a further implication that the mark has been linked by an attributional process to dispositions that discredit the bearer, i.e., that 'spoil' his identity."[32]

The deviant status of the stigmatized person is a consequence of the gap between what the individual is, on the one hand, and what it is thought that she should be, on the other. Consider the norm of professional comportment that is expected of those in positions of authority in contemporary society. As Iris Marion Young observes, this norm is rooted in nineteenth-century ideas of respectability that were associated with "'civilized' people, whose manners and morals are more 'advanced' than those of 'savage' or backward peoples. In this schema people of color are naturally embodied, amoral, expressive, undisciplined, unclean, lacking in self-control." The racist connotations of the norm continue to obstruct the aspirations of blacks and women, for example, to professional status: "Even if they successfully exhibit the norms of respectability, their physical presence continues to be marked, something others take note of. . . . Upon first meeting someone they must 'prove' through their professional comportment that they are respectable, and their lives are constantly dogged by such trials, which though surely not absent from the lives of white men, are less regular."[33]

The exclusionary result, in other words, is as much a product of the norm as of the person who is thought to deviate from it. "Difference can be understood not as intrinsic but as a function of relationships, as a comparison drawn between an individual and a norm that can be stated and evaluated," Martha Minow writes. "Existing arrangements that make some traits stand out as different are neither natural nor necessary; the relationship between the status quo and the assignment of difference can be renovated."[34] Moreover, particular identities are dependent upon the rejection of difference. "An identity is

32. Edward E. Jones, Amerigo Farina, Albert H. Hastorf, Hazel Markus, Dale T. Miller, Robert A. Scott, and Rita de S. French, *Social Stigma: The Psychology of Marked Relationships* (New York: W. H. Freeman, 1984), p. 8.

33. *Justice and the Politics of Difference*, pp. 138, 141.

34. Martha Minow, *Making All the Difference: Inclusion, Exclusion, and American Law* (Ithaca and London: Cornell University Press, 1990), p. 80.

established in relation to a series of differences," observes William Connolly. "These differences are essential to its being. If they did not coexist as differences it would not exist in its clarity and solidity."[35] Identity need not entail the creation of a caste of stigmatized others, but too often it does. American identity, for example, has persistently been a *white* identity, defined against a degraded racial other.[36]

Stigma inflicts its greatest harm when the individual is part of the same community of shared meanings as those who stigmatize him. "[T]he very notion of *shameful* differences assumes a similarity in regard to crucial beliefs, those regarding identity."[37] If the individual did not internalize the stigma, then it would be considerably less harmful to him.

> [I]t seems possible for an individual to fail to live up to what we effectively demand of him, and yet be relatively untouched by this failure; insulated by his alienation, protected by identity beliefs of his own, he feels that he is a full-fledged normal human being, and that we are the ones who are not quite human. He bears a stigma but does not seem to be impressed or repentant about doing so. This possibility is celebrated in exemplary tales about Mennonites, Gypsies, shameless scoundrels, and very orthodox Jews.[38]

Part of the case against stigma, it will be recalled, is that it weighs on the individual in a way he cannot escape. The separation of a community into mutually disdainful ethnic enclaves need not imply the stigmatization of any one of them, so long as each has the resources to maintain its own self-understandings as against those assigned to it by the others. The problem in contemporary America is, of course, that certain communities have been unable to do this. The life of the Southern community under Jim Crow, for

35. William E. Connolly, "Identity and Difference in Liberalism," in R. Bruce Douglass, Gerald M. Mara, and Henry S. Richardson, eds., *Liberalism and the Good* (New York and London: Routledge, 1990), p. 59.

36. See Rogers M. Smith, "Beyond Tocqueville, Myrdal, and Hartz: The Multiple Traditions in America," 87 *Am. Pol. Sci. Rev.* 549 (Sept. 1993); Kimberle Williams Crenshaw, "Race, Reform, and Retrenchment: Transformation and Legitimation in Antidiscrimination Law," 101 *Harv. L. Rev.* 1331, 1370–76 (1988); Toni Morrison, *Playing in the Dark: Whiteness and the Literary Imagination* (Cambridge and London: Harvard University Press, 1992).

37. Goffman, *Stigma*, p. 131, emphasis in original.

38. Ibid., p. 6.

example, was one "not of mutual separation of whites and Negroes, but of one in-group enjoying full normal communal life and one out-group that is barred from this life and forced into an inferior life of its own."[39]

Where stigma exists, there is already community—and therefore communal obligations. Dworkin observes that discrimination in favor of members of one's own group may

> conflict, not just with duties of abstract justice the group's members owe everyone else, but also with associative obligations they have because they belong to larger or different associative communities. For if those who do not belong to my race or religion are my neighbors or colleagues or . . . my fellow citizens, the question arises whether I do not have responsibilities to them, flowing from those associations, that I ignore in deferring to the responsibilities claimed by my racial or religious group.[40]

If two groups of unequal power live in the same community, then the dominant group has a prima facie obligation to recognize those in the less powerful group as full members of that community. Consider an illustration from Goffman:

> Dear Ann Landers:
>
> I'm a girl 12 years old who is left out of all social activities because my father is an ex-convict. I try to be nice and friendly to everyone but it's no use. The girls at school have told me that their mothers don't want them to associate with me because it will be bad for their reputations. My father had some bad publicity in the papers and even though he has served his time nobody will forget it.
>
> Is there anything I can do? I am very lonesome because it's no fun to be alone all the time. My mother tries to take me places with her but I want to be with people my own age. Please give me some advice—An OUTCAST.[41]

---

39. Black, "The Lawfulness of the Segregation Decisions," p. 425.

40. Ronald Dworkin, *Law's Empire* (Cambridge: Belknap Press of Harvard University Press, 1986), pp. 202–3.

41. *Berkeley Daily Gazette*, April 12, 1961, quoted in Goffman, *Stigma*, p. 30. An equally impressive illustration appears in Patricia J. Williams, *The Alchemy of Race and Rights* (Cambridge and London: Harvard University Press, 1991), p. 89.

This girl is suffering because recognition as a valued, respected member of society is a basic human need, which she is arbitrarily being denied. As Steven Smith observes, "[t]he desire to be recognized is not just another desire that we happen to have; it is the core human desire, central to our sense of well-being, our sense of who and what we are."[42] Much of the value of sociality per se, as contemporary communitarians such as Michael Sandel insist, is that it endows us with a determinate identity in which our activities have meaning.[43] But if that is what community is for, then there are grounds for complaint when this benefit is withheld from some members on arbitrary grounds. Simply because this girl is part of a community, its other members have an obligation to recognize and accept her as one of them. This obligation binds only the members of *her* community, but it does not derive from the particular customs of that community; rather, it is a basis for judging those customs. When certain communities endow some of their members with spoiled identities, identities that are constituted by exclusion and insult, exercise of power requires justification. The fact that the needed recognition can only be provided by the community creates a prima facie obligation on the part of the community to provide it. As William Frankena defines it, "Something is a prima facie duty if it is a duty other things being equal, that is, if it would be an actual duty if other moral considerations did not intervene."[44] In some cases, the justification will be forthcoming: most criminals, for example, deserve to be held in contempt for what they have done. But the idea of desert cannot justify stigma in some cases, notably when stigma is based on ascribed characteristics.

The fact that antidiscrimination law focuses its moral concern on stigma based on race and other ascribed characteristics, while ignoring social class, opens it to the charge that it implicitly embraces the capitalist myth of equal opportunity and thus legitimates the massive inequalities of wealth in our society. By focusing on a single defect in distributive justice, it implies that

---

42. Steven B. Smith, *Hegel's Critique of Liberalism: Rights in Context* (Chicago: University of Chicago Press, 1989), p. 117. See also Isaiah Berlin's useful discussion of the importance of recognition in "Two Concepts of Liberty," in *Four Essays on Liberty* (Oxford: Oxford University Press, 1969), pp. 154–62.

43. See Michael J. Sandel, *Liberalism and the Limits of Justice* (Cambridge: Cambridge University Press, 1982).

44. William K. Frankena, *Ethics* (Englewood Cliffs, N.J.: Prentice-Hall, 1963), p. 24.

others are unimportant or perhaps even justified. Even if there is some truth to this charge, it is also true that our society's tendency to judge individuals on the basis of characteristics that are within their power provides incentives for desired behavior.[45] Whether free will is an illusion and *all* characteristics are beyond the control of the individual, so that no one can be said to deserve anything, is an exceedingly difficult question.[46] Its difficulty, however, may itself be sufficient reason for drawing this limit on antidiscrimination law, that it concerns itself only with those kinds of stigma that are plainly unjustified. Thus the project does not extend to stigma based on characteristics such as intelligence, that is, characteristics neither wholly dependent nor wholly independent of the will. There is no question that one's intellectual performance is to some extent the result of one's genetic endowment and environment, but effort also seems to have something to do with it, leaving us in doubt to what extent the opprobrium that attaches to the failing student is justified. It simply is not clear that the demand for relevant reasons cannot be satisfied here. Put another way, the justification for these stigmas is that we have good reason to doubt whether our society, or any advanced industrial society, could function without them.

The difficult cases set a reasonable boundary upon the scope of the principle. Within the area bounded by these difficult cases, however, there is no ambiguity at all: the illegitimate status of racism is clear to meritocrats and levelers alike. We are, once again, in the region of overlapping consensus. To

45. Owen Fiss finds both factors to be at work in the moral basis of antidiscrimination law: "Individual control is a value because it provides the prospect for upward mobility, an important incentive to self-improvement and efficient performance. Further, it is valuable because it rationalizes, and thus makes more tolerable, the unequal distribution of status and wealth among people in the society: failure is the individual's own fault. The principle that the individual should control his own fate also assumes that the allocation of scarce employment opportunities represents, to some extent, a reward. The reward may serve an instrumental purpose; it may be an incentive to develop the necessary qualities or skills or to perform well. Or the reward or allocation may be, for the individual, an end in itself. In either event, responsibility is a necessary condition for being rewarded, and individual control is a necessary condition for responsibility." (Owen Fiss, "A Theory of Fair Employment Laws," 38 *U. Chi. L. Rev.* 235, 241–42 [1971]). See also Cass R. Sunstein, *The Partial Constitution* (Cambridge and London: Harvard University Press, 1993), pp. 341–42. The concern with choice may also, however, be rooted in religious notions of free will and the equality of souls before God, or the Kantian-Rawlsian view of persons as essentially "free and equal rational beings." John Rawls, *A Theory of Justice* (Cambridge: Harvard University Press, 1971), p. 252. For our purposes, it suffices to say that this concern seems philosophically justified and that its widespread acceptance is causally overdetermined.

46. See Sandel, *Liberalism and the Limits of Justice*, pp. 66–103.

say it once more, whatever aspects of distributive justice may be unclear or controversial, we are confident that racism is wrong. It is not just another preference; it has destructive effects on the individual and the community alike. The communitarian basis of the stigma theory shows how the notion of malign preference can be extended from governmental to private decision making. From the standpoint of communal obligation, a preference that stigmatizes on the basis of race is malign, whether it is manifested in the actions of government or of private citizens. The obligation of members of a community to recognize one another's worth is not satisfied by (although it may demand) the law's recognition of their formal equality; that obligation governs their interactions with one another. They are not obligated to love one another as much as they love their own children, but they are obligated to cultivate a certain level of concern for one another, and this obligation is inconsistent with racially selective sympathy and indifference.

The defender of communal identity may reply that stigma based on ascribed characteristics is sometimes deeply rooted in traditions that give coherence to the daily life of existing communities. Any assault on those traditions risks being an assault on those communities. But this proves no more than that such assaults are best launched from *within* communities, by members who seek to reinterpret tradition to include those who have, in the past, been wrongly excluded. The antidiscrimination project derives its moral force from an understanding of the importance of community. Its goal is not to burn down the ancient halls, but to bring more people inside.[47] Thus, it is better if a community voluntarily desegregates its schools because it decides that is what its own ideals require than if a federal judge orders it to do so. Sometimes, however, communities cannot be reformed from within. When they cannot, coercive intervention from outside may be justified. Eisenhower was right to send the troops to Little Rock.

If the major premise of the stigma theory is that persons do not deserve to be, and should not be, stigmatized without sufficient reason, the minor premise is that there is a broad range of deeply entrenched meanings, practices, and institutions in American society that reproduce and maintain the perva-

---

47. To the extent that racism is itself part of the architecture, this will require some reconstruction, but the basic model is renovation, not arson. Cf. Michael Walzer, *Interpretation and Social Criticism* (Cambridge and London: Harvard University Press, 1987), p. 27: "Insofar as we can recognize moral progress, it has less to do with the discovery or invention of new principles than with the inclusion under the old principles of previously excluded men and women."

siveness of the unjustifiable belief that some classes of human beings—paradigmatically, blacks—are intrinsically less worthy or deserving than others. Because of the pervasiveness of that belief, the attempt to erase it from all the places it has been inscribed will necessarily touch each of us intimately. As we saw in Chapter 1, although racism is now generally stigmatized, it continues to exert a powerful, often unconscious, influence on the distribution of rewards and punishments in our society. It also can affect our sense of who we are. As Martin Luther King Jr. wrote, "All segregation statutes are unjust because segregation distorts the soul and damages the personality. It gives the segregator a false sense of superiority and the segregated a false sense of inferiority."[48] If the major premise offered above is accepted, then King's use of the word "false" in the sentence just quoted is analytically precise. The segregator's sense of superiority and the segregated's sense of inferiority are both predicated on the false belief that differing pigmentations are an appropriate basis for differing degrees of prestige and stigma. Each has a false sense of self: he does not know himself. King suggests that segregation is an obstacle to self-knowledge. The point is more than metaphorical. If people should not be stigmatized on the basis of ascribed characteristics, and if my sense of my own identity rests in significant part on my understanding of your status as degraded, and if that degraded status is one that you do not really deserve, then my self-understanding is literally false.[49]

It would be imprecise, but not very imprecise, to say that the stigma theory seeks to eradicate racism. Other things being equal, people should be free to think what they want, and some racism in the hearts and minds of whites is tolerable so long as it does not affect the social identities of blacks. Nonetheless, to end the damage to identity of which King speaks, there would have to be a lot less racism in the hearts and minds of members of both races than there is now. The institutions and practices that reproduce racial stigma (and we

48. Martin Luther King Jr., "Letter from Birmingham Jail," p. 82.

49. King's notion of distorted self-knowledge invites comparison with Hegel's remarkably similar critique of hierarchy. See my "Sex Equality and/or the Family." As a graduate student, King had studied Hegel's work closely. See David J. Garrow, *Bearing the Cross: Martin Luther King, Jr., and the Southern Christian Leadership Conference* (New York: William Morrow, 1986), pp. 46–47. Hegel and King converge on the thought that hierarchy engenders a false sense of self. Both attack certain hierarchies because they assign to those at the top and bottom undeserved rewards and penalties, and thereby pervert everyone's self-knowledge.

shall shortly discuss what these are) should be, if not eradicated, at least greatly reduced in size and scope. Their marginalization should be sufficient to "protect people who are [now] the objects of systematic prejudice from suffering [in the world we seek to bring into existence] any serious or pervasive disadvantage from that prejudice."[50] The stigma should no longer be an inescapable identity. Our attitude toward the institutions that reproduce such stigma should be that of a gardener toward weeds, which can be tolerated so long as their size and number are small enough for them to be harmless to the plants that are the objects of the gardener's concern.[51]

Finally, like the process theory, the stigma theory is incomplete. Stigma, strictly speaking, is a meaning, but Karst also wants to discuss the effects that are brought about by this meaning. Thus he writes that "the harms from stigma are not merely psychological," because "society also acts toward the stigmatized person on the basis of the stigma." "Jim Crow demeaned its black victims, but it also deprived them of a wide range of goods, from lunch counter service to legislative representation."[52] What Karst is concerned about is not limited to the stigma itself, but includes the whole complex of practices and institutions that are predicated on it. Elsewhere he writes:

For all its importance, status equality cannot stand by itself. Just as Jim Crow employed a mixture of formal legal disabilities and informal social and economic sanctions, it will take more than the elimination of formal legal inequalities to end the status harm that is the main evil of a system of caste. To speak of equal citizenship as a status goal, then, is to identify an objective that includes a measure of substantive equality along with formal equality before the law. The best evidence of an end to the harms

50. Ronald Dworkin, "What Is Equality? Part 3: The Place of Liberty," 73 *Iowa L. Rev.* 1, 37 (1987). My insertions in square brackets are, I think, necessary in order to save the project described in the quotation from becoming definitionally impossible. It is not clear how Dworkin imagines that people could continue in the future to be the objects of systematic prejudice without suffering any serious or pervasive disadvantage from that prejudice. The only fully effective remedy for their plight is to eliminate or at least marginalize the prejudice.

51. Nancy Rosenblum has argued persuasively that illiberal beliefs and associations are not invariably corrosive of liberal society, and can sometimes even strengthen it, for example by promoting the experience of pluralism. See her "Civil Societies: Liberalism and the Moral Uses of Pluralism," 61 *Soc. Research* 539 (1994); and "Democratic Character and Community: The Logic of Congruence?," 2 *J. Pol. Phil.* 67 (1994).

52. Karst, "Equal Citizenship," pp. 7–8.

that are black people's legacy from the racial caste system would be for blacks and whites to be ranged along the socioeconomic scale in approximately the same distribution.[53]

The concept of stigma suggests, but does not fully comprehend, the harm inflicted by racism. "Stigma" thus appears to be an unduly limited and potentially misleading term for the evil it seeks to describe. The danger created by an excessive emphasis on stigma is that it will encourage an empty, symbolic politics, more concerned with gestures of respect for blacks than with concrete measures to improve their lot.[54] Like the process theory, the stigma theory properly understood points away from itself toward a larger and subtler dynamic. To understand that dynamic, we must understand the tangible world that is called into being by the stigmatization of blacks. That tangible world is emphasized by the third theory we shall examine.

The Group-Disadvantage Theory

The group-disadvantage theory looks beyond process and signification to the substantive social position of blacks and other disadvantaged groups. Both the process and the stigma theories focus on the ideas in people's heads: either the heads of the people doing the discriminating or those of the people suffering the stigma, or perhaps both. Against all this, some writers object that antidiscrimination law should really be concerned with concrete things that happen in the world. The principal complaint about segregation, after all, was that it massively limited blacks' life chances in a material way. The group-disadvantage theorists claim that as soon as antidiscrimination law looks away from material results, it begins to lose its way. Their critiques of the process and stigma theories reveal the incompleteness of those theories, yet their own theories are equally incomplete: they do not explain why the material disadvantaging of *groups* raises any greater normative concern than inequality between individuals does. Such an explanation must look to what the group-disadvantage theorists deem irrelevant: process and stigma.

53. Kenneth L. Karst, *Belonging to America: Equal Citizenship and the Constitution* (New Haven and London: Yale University Press, 1989), p. 135.

54. Adolph L. Reed Jr. argues that this excessive concern with symbolic gains has hurt the prospects for a viable black political movement. See *The Jesse Jackson Phenomenon* (New Haven and London: Yale University Press, 1986).

From the standpoint of concrete results, both theories considered so far arguably have too-limited ambitions. The stigma theory promises only symbolic gains, an end to racial insult. The process theory does not even promise this, only that decision makers will act with pure hearts. A cynic could say that according to process theory, the only harm the Constitution recognizes is the harm caused to the souls of white people when they commit the sin of racism.[55]

This argument is made most pointedly by Alan Freeman. In the most important critique of antidiscrimination law to emerge from the Critical Legal Studies movement, he castigates the Court for devising a doctrine of antidiscrimination law on the basis of the "perpetrator perspective," from which racial discrimination appears to be merely "the misguided conduct of particular actors" in "a world where, but for the conduct of these misguided ones, the system of equality of opportunity would work to provide a distribution of the good things in life without racial disparities and where deprivations that did correlate with race would be 'deserved' by those deprived on grounds of insufficient 'merit.' " By requiring that any civil rights claimant show that she is the individual victim of intentional discrimination, the perpetrator perspective allows the Court to say "that Black Americans can be without jobs, have their children in all-black, poorly funded schools, have no opportunities for decent housing, and have very little political power, without any violation of antidiscrimination law." Freeman thinks antidiscrimination law should instead be based upon the "victim perspective," which "would ask in each case whether the particular conditions complained of, viewed in their social and historical context, are a manifestation of racial oppression." Rather than

55. It must be acknowledged that even the theorists of process and stigma sometimes acknowledge that the disadvantaging of groups is relevant to questions of social justice. Dworkin thinks that an idealist argument can reasonably be offered in support of preferential treatment for blacks, that "whatever effect minority preference will have on average welfare, it will make the community more equal and therefore more just." "Reverse Discrimination," in *Taking Rights Seriously* (Cambridge: Harvard University Press, 1978), p. 232. Black focuses on social meaning, but his aim is clearly to accomplish tangible results. "If at the end of the century, it is still a thing to be told in every traveler's tale that American Negroes are in poverty and misery, if they are still in fact discernibly disadvantaged because of their race, and if during that century the states have maintained legal regimes which did not put forth all reasonably possible affirmative effort to relieve this suffering and practical subordination, are our descendants going to be able to say that the century has been marked by 'equal protection of the laws' for Negroes?" Charles L. Black Jr., "Foreword: 'State Action,' Equal Protection, and California's Proposition 14," 81 *Harv. L. Rev.* 69, 98 (1967).

searching for a guilty perpetrator, such a perspective would entail "a demand for results." From the victim perspective, "the problem will not be solved until the conditions associated with it have been eliminated. To remedy the condition of racial discrimination would demand affirmative efforts to change the condition."[56]

Freeman's critique of existing doctrine as an ideological rationalization of the status quo is a powerful one, but he is on less certain ground when he tries to devise an alternative. The difficulty begins when he tries to define the victims:

> In the context of race, "victim" means a current member of the group that was historically victimized by actual perpetrators or a class of perpetrators. Victims are people who continue to experience life as a member of that group and continue to experience conditions that are actually or ostensibly tied to the historical experience of actual oppression or victimization, whether or not individual perpetrators, or their specific successors in interest, can be identified now. The victim perspective is intended to describe the expectations of an actual human being who is a current member of the historical victim class—expectations created by an official change of moral stance toward members of the victim group. Those expectations, I suggest, include changes in conditions.[57]

In order to make any persuasive claim, however, it is not enough to cite the expectations of certain persons: one must say why those persons' expectations should defeat rival claims. The feeling of injury is not enough. As Nathan Glazer has argued, "If we feel that a perception is wrong, one of our duties is to try to correct it, rather than assume that the perception of being a victim must alone dictate the action to be taken. False perceptions are to be responded to sympathetically, but not as if they were true."[58]

56. Freeman, "Legitimizing Racial Discrimination Through Antidiscrimination Law," pp. 1054, 1050, 1070, 1098, 1053.

57. Ibid., p. 1053 n. 16. Mari J. Matsuda similarly claims that the perspective of the suffering provides norms. "When notions of right and wrong, justice and injustice, are examined not from an abstract position but from the position of groups who have suffered through history, moral relativism recedes and identifiable normative priorities emerge." "Looking to the Bottom: Critical Legal Studies and Reparations," 22 *Harv. Civ. Rts.–Civ. Liberties L. Rev.* 323, 325 (1987).

58. Nathan Glazer, *Affirmative Discrimination: Ethnic Inequality and Public Policy* (New York: Basic Books, 1975), pp. 97–98. Judith Shklar makes the same point in *The Faces of Injustice* (New Haven and London: Yale University Press, 1990), pp. 3–4.

What is missing from Freeman's account is a criterion for distinguishing meritorious claims of injury from unjustified ones. Such a criterion is implicit in his value-laden descriptive terms: blacks are "victimized" and "oppressed," but presumably Confederate slaveholders who were deprived of their property without compensation were not. Freeman does not explain the concept of oppression on which he is relying.[59] Evidently it is not limited to material "conditions." It may be true that "since racial minorities bear so disproportionately the burdens of economic class in the United States, any claim for substantive distributive justice is in essence a claim on behalf of those minorities."[60] But the reverse is not the case. The claim for racial justice is not only a claim for distributive justice: the fact that disproportionate numbers of the poor are black adds something to their claim. Poverty is bad if it is simply a misfortune, but it is worse if it is the objective expression of social stigma. That additional grievance seems to be what antidiscrimination law in particular is concerned about, but its place in Freeman's account is obscure. Social reality is indeed distorted by a legal doctrine that "presupposes a world composed of atomistic individuals whose actions are outside of and apart from the social fabric and without historical continuity."[61] That said, however, a positive program for antidiscrimination law must explain what historical events count as "oppression," why history imposes obligations on the present generation, what those obligations are, and what kinds of "results," material and symbolic, the present generation ought to strive to bring about.

A similar gap is visible in the writing of Catharine MacKinnon, who, like Freeman, seeks to theorize "on the basis of the experience of the subordinated, the disadvantaged, the dispossessed, the silenced."[62] MacKinnon persistently attacks Herbert Wechsler's claim that "the main constituent of the judicial process is precisely that it must be genuinely principled, resting with respect

59. Freeman does say that, unlike the perpetrator perspective, the victim perspective is "rooted in social reality," and that reality is "revolting." Alan Freeman, "Antidiscrimination Law: The View From 1989," in David Kairys, ed., *The Politics of Law* (New York: Pantheon, rev. ed. 1990), pp. 124, 128. Revulsion, however, is not much of a principle with which to adjudicate claims.

60. Freeman, "Legitimizing Racial Discrimination Through Antidiscrimination Law," p. 1061. Freeman has developed this point in other writings. See his "Racism, Rights, and the Quest for Equality of Opportunity: A Critical Legal Essay," 23 *Harv. Civ. Rts.–Civ. Liberties L. Rev.* 295, 362–85 (1988); and "Race and Class: The Dilemma of Liberal Reform," 90 *Yale L. J.* 1880 (1981).

61. Freeman, "Legitimizing Racial Discrimination Through Antidiscrimination Law," p. 1054.

62. Catharine MacKinnon, *Toward a Feminist Theory of the State* (Cambridge and London: Harvard University Press, 1989), p. xiv.

to every step that is involved in reaching judgment on analysis and reasons quite transcending the immediate result that is achieved."[63] Although, in demonstrating the bias inherent in putatively "neutral" legal standards, MacKinnon purports to repudiate Wechslerian neutrality as such,[64] her most enduring contribution to antidiscrimination theory has been her unmasking of the bias that hides behind purportedly "neutral" norms. A recurrent theme in her writing, which primarily addresses issues of sex equality, is the use of male practices as the norm against which women's claims are measured. Thus, for example, MacKinnon notes that when efforts to provide pregnancy leave for workers are condemned as special treatment for women, the notion of neutrality invoked is bogus. The perspective MacKinnon criticizes "says it is sex discrimination to give women what we need, because only women need it. It is not sex discrimination not to give women what we need because then only women will not get what we need."[65] The fundamental problem of sex inequality, MacKinnon argues, is not that women who are situated similarly to men are treated differently; it is that there is a system of sexual subordination that ensures that hardly any women *will* be situated similarly to men.[66] The standard itself is thus unmasked as discriminatory. "Why should you have to be the same as a man to get what a man gets simply because he is one?"[67] A norm is already implicit in this unmasking:

Many readers (in the Kantian tradition) say that if a discourse is not generalized, universal, and agreed-upon, it is exclusionary. The problem, however, is that the generalized, universal, and agreed-upon never did solve the disagreements, resolve the differences, cohere the specifics, and generalize the particularities. Rather, it assimilated them to a false universal that imposed agreement, submerged specificity, and silenced particularity. The anxiety about engaged theory is particularly marked among those whose particularities formed the prior universal. What they

63. Herbert Wechsler, "Toward Neutral Principles of Constitutional Law," 73 *Harv. L. Rev.* 1, 15 (1959).

64. See Catharine MacKinnon, *Sexual Harassment of Working Women: A Case of Sex Discrimination* (New Haven and London: Yale University Press, 1979), pp. 126–27; idem, *Feminism Unmodified: Discourses on Life and Law* (Cambridge and London: Harvard University Press, 1987), p. 165; idem, *Toward a Feminist Theory of the State*, pp. 162, 292 n. 27.

65. MacKinnon, *Feminism Unmodified*, p. 36.

66. See MacKinnon, *Toward a Feminist Theory of the State*, p. 224.

67. MacKinnon, *Feminism Unmodified*, p. 37.

face from this critique is not losing a dialogue but beginning one, a more equal and larger and inclusionary one.[68]

The aspiration in the final sentence appears to be one of genuine unforced agreement. But what does this mean except to "solve the disagreements, resolve the differences, cohere the specifics, and generalize the particularities"? As we saw in our critique of Freeman, in order to make a case for reform it is not enough to show what the world looks like from the victim's perspective; one must also say why that person's expectations should defeat rival claims. "Although human voices can be heard on both sides of any legal dispute," writes Judge Patricia Wald, "we ultimately are forced back to some abstract principle or value to compare, weigh and choose between these human voices."[69]

The most important attempt to fill this normative gap is that of the pioneering theorist of group disadvantage, Owen Fiss. Fiss argues that the equal protection clause should be read as presumptively prohibiting any state law or practice which "aggravates (or perpetuates?) the subordinate position of a specially disadvantaged group." It is appropriate to protect such a group when that group has been (or will be) in a position of subordination for a long time. In order to be recognizable, such a social group must, first, have "a distinct existence apart from its members," so that "[y]ou can talk about the group without reference to the particular individuals who happen to be its members at any one moment"; second, the group must be interdependent, so that "[m]embers of the group identify themselves—explain who they are—by reference to their membership in the group; and their well-being or status is in part determined by the well-being or status of the group." Thus, to take the paradigmatic example, "[b]lacks are viewed as a group; they view themselves as a group; their identity is in large part determined by membership in the group; their social status is linked to the status of the group; and much of our action, institutional and personal, is based on these perspectives." A social group should be eligible for protection under the equal protection clause if "the group has been in a position of perpetual subordination; and . . . the political power of the group is severely circumscribed."[70] Once again, it is

68. MacKinnon, *Toward a Feminist Theory of the State*, pp. xv–xvi.

69. Patricia M. Wald, "Disembodied Voices—An Appellate Judge's Response," 66 *Tex. L. Rev.* 623, 625 (1988).

70. Owen Fiss, "Groups and the Equal Protection Clause," in Marshall Cohen, Thomas Nagel,

blacks, whose subordination the Fourteenth Amendment was primarily intended to end, that Fiss primarily has in mind.

Such an approach "may be rooted in a theory of compensation—blacks as a group were *put* in that position by others and the redistributive measures are *owed* to the group as a form of compensation."[71] We shall consider this argument presently, but Fiss does not rely on it. "The redistributive strategy could give expression to an ethical view against caste, one that would make it undesirable for any group to occupy a position of subordination for any extended period of time."[72] History is of interest only because it is evidence that the subordination of blacks will continue unless remedial steps are taken. "Similarly, if we are told that today a period of perpetual subordination is about to begin for another group, we should be as concerned with the status of that group as we are with the blacks."[73]

Fiss's theory has been attacked for its indifference to history. Brest argues that while "a group theory is essentially indifferent to the history that led to the unequal distribution," blacks need to stress the link between their disadvantage and past injustices, because "as the claims to compensation based on the past injustices of human institutions become attenuated, they begin to compete with claims based on the vagaries of fate, and thus become indistinguishable from demands for greater distributive justice among all individuals."[74] Similarly Paul Gewirtz: "Inevitably, a general distributive theory

---

and Thomas Scanlon, eds., *Equality and Preferential Treatment* (Princeton: Princeton University Press, 1977), pp. 134, 127–28, 125, 131–32.

71. Ibid., p. 127, emphases in original.

72. Ibid., p. 128. "Changes in the hierarchical structure of society—the elimination of caste—might be justified as a means of (a) preserving social peace; (b) maintaining the community as a community, that is, as one cohesive whole; or (c) permitting the fullest development of individual members of the subordinated group who otherwise might look upon the low status of the group as placing a ceiling on their aspirations and achievements." Ibid. This plainly cannot exhaust all the available arguments. Since social peace can also be preserved by systematic repression, (a) seems the weakest of the three, and (b) has a similar difficulty inasmuch as social cohesion can be quite strong in caste societies, and is arguably stronger there than in competitive, individualistic liberal societies. There is a great deal of power in (c), but it seems an incomplete account of the evil of caste: did a member of the black upper class in 1915, who might have been wealthier than the majority of whites, or W. E. B. DuBois, one of the most accomplished literary figures of his time, have nothing to complain of from racism?

73. Ibid., p. 128 n. 67.

74. Brest, "In Defense of the Antidiscrimination Principle," pp. 49, 42. The trouble with this

sacrifices the *distinctive moral power of a plea for racial justice,* holding it hostage until broader distributive ideas gain acceptance."[75] Once more, if the problem is persistent material deprivation, then the answer is simply redistribution. Race plays no part in the description of either the problem or the solution. This would be a strange account of an ideal of racial justice.

Poverty is one thing that constrains people's freedom. The reason the group-disadvantage theory does not collapse into a general redistributive theory, as Brest and Gewirtz claim, is that racism is another, distinct obstacle to human freedom. One way of describing the injustice of a system of social class is to note that if one enters a hospital ward of healthy newborn babies, one can predict with a high degree of accuracy the eventual positions of those children in society on the basis of their social class.[76] One cannot do that with race— a black child may well end up in the upper income stratum, particularly if her parents are already there. But a similar type of injustice is present: one knows that the black child in the ward will be subject to certain disadvantages and humiliations that no white child will have to endure. Moreover, while the injury of poverty can be understood in terms of the deprivation of individuals, the injury of racism cannot be described without reference to groups and group behavior.

This kind of argument *may* be deployed to justify the recognition of group disadvantage as a cognizable injury, without reference to process defect or stigma. Cass Sunstein argues that the principle that underlies antidiscrimination law is an "anticaste principle," which holds that

> differences that are irrelevant from the moral point of view ought not without good reason to be turned, by social and legal structures, into social disadvantages. They certainly should not be permitted to do so if the disadvantage is systemic. A systemic disadvantage is one that operates along standard and predictable lines in multiple important spheres of life, and applies in realms that relate to basic participation as a citizen in a democracy.... The anticaste principle might suggest that with respect to

---

formulation is that it suggests that the only injustice blacks suffer is their socioeconomic disadvantage.

75. Paul Gewirtz, "Choice in the Transition: School Desegregation and the Corrective Ideal," 86 *Columb. L. Rev.* 728, 737 (1986), emphasis in original.

76. See James S. Fishkin, *Justice, Equal Opportunity, and the Family* (New Haven: Yale University Press, 1983), p. 4.

basic human capabilities and functionings, one group ought not to be systematically below another.[77]

Not all morally irrelevant differences can be prevented from becoming the basis of advantages and disadvantages. Markets inevitably reward some such differences, such as valuable native capabilities, but markets cannot be reasonably dispensed with. For this reason, Sunstein concludes that the anticaste principle is limited in scope. Its appeal is greatest "in discrete contexts in which gains from current practice to the least well-off are hard to imagine; in which second-class citizenship is systemic and occurs in multiple spheres and along easily identifiable and sharply defined lines; in which there will be no major threat to a market economy; and in which the costs of implementation are most unlikely to be terribly high."[78]

Sunstein's formulation makes clear, as Fiss's does not, how a group-disadvantage principle can be developed without reference to process defect or stigma. There may be a practice that has the effect of systemically disadvantaging a group, even though that group is not stigmatized and its interests are fairly taken into account in the political process. Thus Sunstein's anti-caste principle vindicates the claims of disabled people, who are not particularly despised or devalued, and whose disadvantages are often the result of practices that merely neglect to take their needs into account. For just this reason, however, Sunstein's principle does not fully capture the wrongs associated with racial injustice. The word "caste" has connotations of devaluation and knowing oppression, connotations that are not part of the principle as Sunstein defines it.[79] To understand *racial* injustice, one must look to the reasons that have been invoked to justify blacks' subordination.

It is because the stigmatization of blacks affects the process by which decisions affecting them are made that Fiss is right to say that "their well-being or status is in part determined by the well-being or status of the group."[80] Fiss, however, never makes clear how culture fits into his account of group disadvantage. At one point, he suggests that group disadvantage consists in a

77. Sunstein, *The Partial Constitution*, p. 339.

78. Ibid., p. 342.

79. Sunstein does, however, rely on such considerations when he defends his principle against objections. See Cass Sunstein, "The Anticaste Principle," 92 *Mich. L. Rev.* 2410, 2431–33 (1994). He thus appears to conceive stigma to be at least partly constitutive of the evil that the Fourteenth Amendment seeks to remedy, even though he makes it no part of his definition of that evil.

80. Fiss, "Groups and the Equal Protection Clause," p. 125.

combination of "socioeconomic status" and "political status,"[81] neither of which directly implicates structures of signification, but elsewhere he says that stigma is a cognizable harm.[82] Without reference to culture, a group's socioeconomic and political powerlessness is merely an aggregate of disadvantages suffered by individuals. In other words, Fiss's group-disadvantage theory is incomplete without reference to process defect and stigma. I therefore turn to Iris Marion Young, who is more attentive to the multifaceted nature of group oppression.

Like the other group-disadvantage theorists, Young builds her theory upon the experiences of those who have been excluded from power in the United States—women, blacks, Native Americans, gays, lesbians, and the poor.[83] Unlike Fiss and Freeman, she is clearly concerned as much with intangible as with material harms, and she pays close attention to the ways in which these reinforce one another. The theory of justice she develops has groups as its focus, because the injustices it identifies—oppression and domination—are group-based and can only be described by reference to groups.[84] "Oppression consists in systematic institutional processes which prevent some people from learning and using satisfying and expansive skills in socially recognized settings, or institutionalized social processes which inhibit people's ability to play and communicate with others or to express their feelings and perspective on social life in contexts where others can listen." "Domination consists in institutional conditions which inhibit or prevent people from participating in determining their actions or the conditions of their actions."[85] Oppression is the form of disadvantage suffered specifically by those groups on whose behalf Young writes.

81. Ibid., p. 128. Fiss includes "prejudice" in his picture only as one of the causes of blacks' political powerlessness: the "fear, hatred, and distaste that make it particularly difficult for them to form coalitions with others (such as the white poor) and that make it advantageous for the dominant political parties to hurt them—to use them as a scapegoat." Ibid., p. 129. As we saw in our discussion of Ely in Chapter 1, however, prejudice is often subtler than "fear, hatred, and distaste."

82. Ibid., p. 94. It is the ambiguity of Fiss's notion of "status-harm" that enables Karst to say that his principle of equal citizenship, which is primarily concerned with stigma, is "consistent" with Fiss's argument. Karst, "Equal Citizenship," p. 8 n. 37.

83. Young, *Justice and the Politics of Difference*, pp. 4–7.

84. "The achievement of formal equality does not eliminate social differences, and rhetorical commitment to the sameness of persons makes it impossible even to name how those differences presently structure privilege and oppression." Ibid., p. 164.

85. Ibid., p. 38.

Briefly, a group is oppressed when one or more of the following conditions occurs to all or a large portion of its members: (1) The benefits of their work or energy go to others without those others reciprocally benefiting them (exploitation); (2) they are excluded from participation in major social activities, which in our society means primarily a workplace (marginalization); (3) they live and work under the authority of others and have little work autonomy and authority over others themselves (powerlessness); (4) as a group they are stereotyped at the same time that their experience and situation is invisible in the society in general, and they have little opportunity and little audience for the expression of their experience and perspective on social events (cultural imperialism); (5) group members suffer random violence and harassment motivated by group hatred or fear.[86]

What all of these have in common is that they systematically immobilize or diminish specific groups. "[S]ocial justice means the elimination of institutionalized domination and oppression."[87]

Young's description of oppression is the most comprehensive devised by any of the group-disadvantage theorists. The process and stigma theories may be understood as identifying particular aspects of oppression: process defect is a form of powerlessness, and stigma is a form of cultural imperialism. For our purposes, it helps to emphasize what Young does not: the centrality of cultural imperialism among the faces of oppression. Group status is an artifact of culture if it is anything at all. It is the distribution of honor and stigma that determines *who* is going to be exploited, marginalized, powerless, identified as culturally deviant, or violently harmed.[88] "The symbolic meanings that people attach to other kinds of people and to actions, gestures, or institutions often significantly affect the social standing of persons and their opportunities." Put another way, cultural imperialism is the hub from which the other injuries radiate whenever the distribution of other forms of oppression is not random, but falls on particular groups. "Nearly all, if not all, groups said by contemporary social movements to be oppressed suffer cultural imperial-

86. Iris Marion Young, "Polity and Group Difference," in *Throwing Like a Girl and Other Essays in Feminist Philosophy and Social Theory* (Bloomington and Indianapolis: Indiana University Press, 1990), p. 123; see idem, *Justice and the Politics of Difference*, pp. 48–63.

87. Young, *Justice and the Politics of Difference*, p. 15.

88. Young acknowledges that these connections are sometimes present, but places causal or explanatory questions outside the scope of her discussion. See ibid., p. 65.

ism."[89] More than the other group-disadvantage theorists, Young recognizes the importance of stigma in biasing societal decision making and perpetuating the inferior status of certain groups. Culture is the means by which groups are selected for disadvantage.

> The behavior, comportments, images, and stereotypes that contribute to the oppression of bodily marked groups are pervasive, systemic, mutually generating, and mutually reinforcing. They are elements of dominant cultural practices that lie as the normal background of our liberal democratic society. Only changing the cultural habits themselves will change the oppressions they produce and reinforce, but change in cultural habits can occur only if individuals become aware of and change their individual habits.[90]

Young is also more explicit than Fiss about the normative basis of group-disadvantage theory. The injuries that constitute oppression are injustices because they systematically frustrate the realization of two aspects of the good life: "(1) developing and exercising one's capacities and expressing one's experience . . . and (2) participating in determining one's action and the conditions of one's action."[91] These values "are universalist values, in the sense that they assume the equal moral worth of all persons."[92] They are, in fact, the values of mainstream liberalism, which holds that we should promote human freedom, and so should give people a reasonable range of valuable choices about the course of their lives. Liberalism cannot be indifferent to distributive outcomes.[93]

The greatest weakness of the group-disadvantage theorists is their failure adequately to attend to the reasons for the disadvantages. Even Young does not fully specify the normative basis of her commitment to group-based justice.[94] She claims that her conception of justice does not "devalue or exclude

---

89. Ibid., pp. 23, 64.
90. Ibid., p. 152.
91. Ibid., p. 37.
92. Ibid.
93. See Steven Lukes, "Equality and Liberty: Must they Conflict?," in David Held, ed., *Political Theory Today* (Cambridge, Eng.: Polity Press, 1991), pp. 48–66; see generally Amy Gutmann, *Liberal Equality* (Cambridge: Cambridge University Press, 1980).
94. This weakens some of Young's descriptive apparatus. Her concept of exploitation, for example, appears to depend on some idea of unfair exchange, but any such idea is necessarily

any particular culture or way of life,"[95] but if this were true, she would be incapable of distinguishing the claims of worthy groups from those of unworthy ones, such as Nazis, that also are powerless, stigmatized, and marginalized.[96] Sometimes these disadvantages can be justified. Sometimes, by contrast, the reason for the disadvantages makes them worse. A formulation of the relevant reasons for disadvantage can no more be dispensed with in the context of group-disadvantage theory than it can with respect to other theories.

As with the other theories, a relevant-reasons argument completes and reinforces the group-disadvantage theory. The reason the material disadvantages of blacks are of greater concern to liberals than other distributive injustices is that *these* disadvantages result from and reinforce an ideology that is contrary to any legitimate distributive theory—one that, to borrow Dworkin's metaphor, takes up the same conceptual space as any such theory. The disproportionate poverty of blacks is embedded in a racial narrative in which those disadvantages seem legitimate. Unlike material disadvantage per se, the disproportionate poverty of blacks operates as a racist signifier, a badge of the inferior status of all blacks. The self-legitimating character of group oppression is rooted in part in the tendency of all human beings—seeking to reduce cognitive dissonance by bringing their beliefs into line with existing practice—to believe in a just world, in which inequalities are deserved or desired.[97] The ideological upshot is well summarized by Charles Lawrence: "The law requires that we treat blacks and whites equally. We are a law-abiding country, and the courts tell us that in the vast majority of instances the law is obeyed. Thus, if we are treating blacks and whites equally, and blacks continue to be represented at the bottom of the socioeconomic ladder, it must be either because they are failing to avail themselves of the opportunities available to them or

---

dependent on a conception of fairness that remains to be specified. I am grateful to James W. Bailey for this point.

95. Young, *Justice and the Politics of Difference*, p. 37.

96. See Stephen Macedo, "Liberal Civic Education and Religious Fundamentalism: The Case of God v. John Rawls?," 105 *Ethics* 468, 468–69 (1995). Elsewhere Young offers a more nuanced view, criticizing definitions of human nature because they threaten "to devalue or exclude some *acceptable* individual desires, cultural characteristics, or ways of life." See her *Justice and the Politics of Difference*, p. 36 (emphasis added).

97. See Cass R. Sunstein, "Three Civil Rights Fallacies," 79 *Calif. L. Rev.* 751, 759–60 (1991), and sources cited therein.

because they are not capable of availing themselves of those opportunities."[98] The material disadvantages thus themselves reinforce the narrative that legitimates them. This should not be news. The point was developed at considerable length in Gunnar Myrdal's classic study of American race relations, *An American Dilemma*, in 1944. Myrdal claimed that there existed "a general interdependence between all the factors in the Negro problem. White prejudice and discrimination keep the Negro low in standards of living, health, education, manners, and morals. This, in its turn, gives support to white prejudice. White prejudice and Negro standards thus mutually 'cause' each other."[99]

If the material disadvantages of blacks are legitimated by a narrative in which those disadvantages are deserved, the product of blacks' own inferiority, then a probable prerequisite for the amelioration of those disadvantages is the promulgation of a different narrative, a counternarrative. The most promising such narrative is one that attributes those disadvantages to past wrongs. Discussions of racial justice that stress past wrongs often invoke the idea of reparations.[100] Any claim that whites ought to compensate blacks for their historical injuries produces deep difficulties, as Richard Epstein explains:

> [T]ime and circumstance ravage any simple conception of legal relief between two immediate parties. Many of those who did prosper spent or dissipated their ill-gotten wealth and died; others in the next generation, black and white alike, have been burdened by past segregationist practices that reduce their overall productivity and freedom *and* the present, expensive efforts to ameliorate such practices. It is not as though the population at large (old settler and new immigrant, black civil rights supporter and white Klan member) has received huge gains from past segregation that can now be disgorged to its original owners or their descendants. There is no fund of specific assets descended from one generation to the next from which restitution or compensation can be made.

98. Charles R. Lawrence III, " 'Justice' or 'Just Us': Racism and the Role of Ideology," 35 *Stan. L. Rev.* 831, 844 (1983).

99. Gunnar Myrdal, *An American Dilemma: The Negro Problem and Modern Democracy* (New York and London: Harper & Brothers, 1944), p. 75.

100. The case for reparations is succinctly presented in Derrick Bell, *Race, Racism and American Law* (3rd ed.; Boston: Little, Brown, 1992), § 1.15, pp. 50–55.

Many people today are not descendants of past wrongdoers, who in any event had little if anything to leave at their death.[101]

The trouble with this facile dismissal of the reparations claim is that in the case of blacks, the causal connection between past wrongs and present disadvantage remains clear. Blacks were deliberately placed into their present situation of disproportionate disadvantage, and this was done by men who intended that power, wealth, and prestige in America remain in white hands. Disproportionate black poverty and powerlessness are precisely what they intended to bring about. And unless something is done to remedy the situation, the wrong is likely to perpetuate itself into future generations.[102]

The reparations claim is necessarily forward-looking as much as backward-looking.[103] Unless the connection between past wrongs and continuing disadvantage is emphasized, the reparations claim not only loses its moral force

---

101. Richard Epstein, "The Paradox of Civil Rights," 8 *Yale L. & Pol'y Rev.* 299, 308 (1990).

102. The reasons the market is unlikely to dispel these patterns have been thoroughly explored. See Glenn C. Loury, "Why Should We Care About Group Inequality?," 5 *Soc. Phil. & Pol'y* 249, 253–59 (Aut. 1987); David Strauss, "The Law and Economics of Racial Discrimination in Employment: The Case for Numerical Standards," 79 *Georgetown L. J.* 1619 (1991); and Cass R. Sunstein, "Why Markets Don't Stop Discrimination," 8 *Soc. Phil. & Pol'y* 22 (Spr. 1991).

103. On the mutually reinforcing nature of backward-looking and forward-looking claims, see Boxill, *Blacks and Social Justice*, pp. 147–72. The most fully developed argument for compensation, Boris I. Bittker's *The Case for Black Reparations* (New York: Vintage, 1973), responds to concerns such as Epstein's by "focus[ing] on the wrongs of the recent past, the consequences of which are everywhere to be seen" (p. 28). "As one surveys American life *today* . . . the day seems unfortunately far off when one will be able to say that the consequences of segregation and other forms of official discrimination have so totally evaporated that remedial action has become an anachronism." Ibid., p. 126, emphasis added. At crucial points in his argument, Bittker finds it necessary to shift his focus from historical wrongs to the fact that blacks continue to be second-class citizens in American society. This suggests that the need for social change arises out of their present status rather than past wrongs. At one point he acknowledges that if the present status of blacks were equal to that of other groups, then the fact that blacks were injured in the past would not state a valid claim. See ibid., pp. 11–12. The past wrongs are important because they point to what the present material inequalities signify: not just a failure of distributive justice, but the continuing inferior status of blacks.

Mari Matsuda's recent restatement of the reparations claim similarly acknowledges that "[r]eparations claims are based on continuing stigma and economic harm." "Looking to the Bottom," p. 381. "Members of the dominant class continue to benefit from the wrongs of the past and the presumptions of inferiority imposed upon victims." Ibid., p. 379. She also notes that this is an indispensable part of a valid reparations claim: "The outer limit should be the ability to identify a victim class that continues to suffer a stigmatized position enhanced or promoted by the wrongful act in question." Ibid., p. 385.

but threatens to have a poisonous effect on democratic politics. Probably every ethnic group in the United States has, at some time in its history, suffered some terrible injustice. It is therefore not possible to confer public status on the injustices faced by some groups without thereby implicitly devaluing the injustices endured by others. And there is no way to decide which injustices deserve such recognition—whether, for example, the Holocaust was a more profound evil than slavery. "We cannot expect that the normal means of argument and persuasion will reconcile divergent perceptions among ethnic groups about the relative moral affront which history has forced upon them," Glenn Loury observes. "We must not, therefore, permit such disputes to arise, if we are to maintain an environment of comity among groups in this ethnically diverse society."[104] The purpose of reparations, properly conceived, is not to rank the historical wrongs that different groups have suffered, but to end the continuing subordinate status of blacks. As Thomas Hill observes,

> the question to ask is not merely, "What will promote respectful and trusting racial and gender relations in future generations?," but rather, "Given our checkered past, how can we appropriately express the social value of mutual respect and trust that we want, so far as possible, to characterize our history?" We cannot change our racist and sexist past, but we also cannot express full respect for those present individuals who live in its aftermath if we ignore it.[105]

The reparations-based argument for ameliorating group disadvantage is an important part of a counternarrative.

The narrative dimension is also crucial to the evaluation of the approach that now prevails in the Supreme Court, in which race-based remedies are only available for precisely identifiable past wrongdoing.[106] The message sent by that doctrine, as Hill observes, is that "We would rather let the majority of white males enjoy the advantages of their unfair head start than risk compensating one of you who does not deserve it."[107] The Supreme Court's affirmative action jurisprudence, consciously or unconsciously, reflects and

104. Loury, "Why Should We Care About Group Inequality?," p. 261.

105. Thomas E. Hill Jr., "The Message of Affirmative Action," 8 *Soc. Phil. & Pol'y* 108, 124 (Spr. 1991).

106. See, e.g., *City of Richmond v. J. A. Croson Co.*, 488 U.S. 469 (1989); *Wygant v. Jackson Board of Education*, 476 U.S. 267 (1986).

107. Hill, "The Message of Affirmative Action," p. 126.

reinforces the hoary notion that there is something particularly outrageous about giving undeserved benefits to blacks, because this rewards them for their laziness and incompetence.[108] It is impossible to create the status quo ante that would exist in the absence of the wrongs of racism, because it is impossible for us to know what that world would look like.[109] What we can seek to produce instead is a world in which those past wrongs do not obviously produce present disadvantage for anyone.

In short, to capture what is missing from the group-disadvantage theories of antidiscrimination law, it is necessary to talk about how the group disadvantages came about, how they perpetuate themselves, and what they mean to society today. These are, however, precisely what the process and stigma theories focused upon. Just as their inadequacies pointed us toward a group-disadvantage theory, so the inadequacies of the group-disadvantage approach point us back toward defective process and stigma. It is these meanings that perpetuate the disadvantaged status of groups. We are moving in a circle.

None of these writers is wrong, strictly speaking. But in each case, we have found that the problem upon which each of them focuses points beyond itself to a larger system of injury. Like the blind men who surrounded the elephant in the fable, each writer has seized on a part of the thing he is trying to identify and calls it the whole. It is time to say how the pieces fit together.

A Synthesis: The Social Construction of Stigmatized Classes

Antidiscrimination law is best understood as part of a project of social reconstruction. The social reality this project seeks to reconstruct operates on several levels: the beliefs and values shared by the members of society; the practices that are constructed by (and, in turn, construct) those beliefs; and the distribution of wealth and power that emerges out of those practices. The central evil this social reconstruction project seeks to eliminate—central in the sense that is the source of all the others, and the others fall within the ambit of

---

108. This is particularly striking in Justice O'Connor's suggestion in *Croson* that the miniscule percentage of minority contractors in Richmond may be the product not only of discrimination but also of "both black and white career choices." *Croson*, at 503. The implication is that blacks are not interested in lucrative construction jobs, but prefer being janitors, maids, and cooks.

109. See Sunstein, "Three Civil Rights Fallacies," pp. 761–65; David Strauss, "Discriminatory Intent and the Taming of *Brown*," 56 *U. Chi. L. Rev.* 935, 971–75 (1989); Boxill, *Blacks and Social Justice*, p. 154.

antidiscrimination law only by virtue of their connection with it—is the embedding, in habitual social practice, of the idea that certain classes of people are intrinsically inferior and unworthy because of their race. The consequences of that idea are part of the evil to be eliminated, not only because of their intrinsic perniciousness, but also because they reproduce the idea itself. As I have said, the existence in so many cities of zones of poverty, ignorance, crime, and hopelessness would be a great evil regardless of who lived there, but it is made both more politically intractable and worse in itself by the fact that disproportionate numbers of those who do live there are black. The injury of poverty is compounded by the insult of racism. It is this last increment of evil that antidiscrimination law is specifically concerned about. Thus, the law of racial equality seeks to eliminate racial meanings, such as the belief that blacks are intrinsically inferior to whites; racially significant practices, such as school segregation and job discrimination; and racially tainted distribution, such as the existence of a large black underclass.

This is a complex task. Systems of stigmatizing meaning reproduce themselves systemically. If our aim is to disrupt the processes by which this happens, then we must understand those processes in order to understand how the undertaking should proceed. What we need is an account of the etiology of the disease, a theory of how social meanings—and racism is a social meaning—become institutionalized. A theory of antidiscrimination law, in other words, must presuppose a theory of the sociology of knowledge.

Berger and Luckmann observe that "social order is a human product, or, more precisely, an ongoing human production." It exists only insofar as it is recognized by human minds. While social order, because it is a human product, appears in enormously varied forms, some kind of social order is constructed in every human society. Social order is a human product, but humanity is reciprocally a social product. In every society, patterns of behavior and interaction become habitualized and institutionalized.[110] With this institutionalization comes legitimation, the development of a commonly held set of meanings that explain what the members of society are doing and why they are doing it. Over a period of generations, behaviors and meanings tend to

110. Peter L. Berger and Thomas Luckmann, *The Social Construction of Reality: A Treatise in the Sociology of Knowledge* (Garden City, N.Y.: Anchor, 1967), p. 52. "Institution" does not necessarily refer to a locus of official power. "Institutionalization occurs whenever there is a reciprocal typification of habitualized actions by types of actors. Put differently, any such typification is an institution." Ibid., p. 54.

crystallize into reified, objective-seeming patterns that take on the appearance of "a comprehensive and given reality confronting the individual in a manner analogous to the reality of the natural world." In spite of this apparent concreteness, no system of meanings can endure unless human beings actively maintain it. "*All* social reality is precarious. *All* societies are constructions in the face of chaos."[111] A system of meanings must be maintained among a society's members and transmitted to the next generation, and this implies some degree of control over the minds and bodies of the members.

While a symbolic universe is a human construct, its inhabitants typically live naively within it, taking its meanings for granted as a quasi-natural reality. To the extent that this is the case, "the symbolic universe is self-maintaining, that is, self-legitimating by the sheer facticity of its objective existence in the society in question." But in no society is this completely the case. Every social world is, to some extent, problematic for its inhabitants, and the more this is so, the more a society's practices require increasingly elaborate activities and institutions of legitimation, which may be described as "machineries of universe-maintenance."[112]

As a number of commentators have pointed out, Berger and Luckmann do not consider the extent to which socially constructed meanings may reflect and reinforce the disparate power of ruling elites.[113] The social meanings that societies reproduce sometimes include meanings which divide members of society into classes on the basis of ascribed characteristics and assign some of these classes lower status, in terms of power and prestige, than others.[114] These meanings stigmatize the people at the bottom of the hierarchy, branding them as intrinsically less worthy of concern and respect than others. Thus, as Iris Marion Young has put it, "the difference of women from men, American

111. Ibid., pp. 61–62, 59, 103, emphases in original.

112. Ibid., p. 105.

113. See, for example, John Gaventa, *Power and Powerlessness: Quiescence and Rebellion in an Appalachian Valley* (Urbana: Univ. of Ill., 1980), p. 15 n. 47; Richard Lichtmann, "Symbolic Interaction and Social Reality: Some Marxist Queries," 15 *Berkeley J. Sociology* 75, 89 (1970); and MacKinnon, *Toward a Feminist Theory of the State,* p. 270 n. 18.

114. Compare A. L. Kroeber's classic definition of caste as "an endogamous and hereditary subdivision of an ethnic unit occupying a position of superior or inferior rank or social esteem in comparison with other such subdivisions." "Caste," in *Encyclopedia of the Social Sciences* (New York: Macmillan, 1930), v. 3, p. 254. The phenomenon I am describing here is broader than that of caste thus defined, since it can embrace characteristics such as gender that are not endogamous or hereditary.

Indians or Africans from Europeans, Jews from Christians, homosexuals from heterosexuals, workers from professionals, becomes reconstructed largely as deviance and inferiority." As with social reality generally, this reality legitimates itself by its very existence. "Since only the dominant group's cultural expressions receive wide dissemination, their cultural expressions become the normal, or the universal, and therefore the unremarkable."[115] Members of the privileged groups will find that their taken-for-granted norms include using their greater power in ways that maintain the stigmatized groups' subordinate status symbolically, politically, and materially. Those in the stigmatized groups may themselves internalize the reigning values, and so may develop such a low opinion of themselves that they do not, either overtly or covertly, challenge their position in society. The process need not signify a conspiracy by the ruling classes to promote oppression. The social construction of reality takes place in every society, and it has consequences for the distribution of wealth, power, and prestige. The degree of monolithic facticity that attaches to stigmatizing meanings will, however, vary across societies and across time within societies.[116] In at least some societies, these meanings will be objects of vigorous contestation. America is such a society, and with the enactment of the Civil War amendments, the Constitution switched sides in the contest.

Antidiscrimination law is part of a project of social reconstruction. It seeks to disrupt the machineries of universe-maintenance that reproduce unjustifiably stigmatizing meanings, and thereby to reshape the socially constructed reality of American society. The various interpretations of the Fourteenth Amendment I have surveyed all converge on the idea that the state is forbidden from placing its authority behind such constructs and coercively maintaining them. This is why the stigma theory is as persuasive as it is. As Charles Lawrence observes, "*Brown* held that segregated schools were unconstitutional primarily because of the *message* segregation conveys—the message that black children are an untouchable caste, unfit to be educated with white children."[117] Similarly, in *Shelley v. Kraemer,* the Court held that judicial enforcement of racially restrictive covenants violated the Fourteenth Amendment. While such

115. Young, *Justice and the Politics of Difference*, p. 59.

116. It is thus important to avoid the temptation to present oppression as so pervasive that it becomes hard to imagine where a sense of alternatives or resistance could possibly come from. See, e.g., MacKinnon, *Toward a Feminist Theory of the State*, pp. 102–5.

117. Charles Lawrence III, "If He Hollers Let Him Go: Regulating Racist Speech on Campus," 1990 *Duke L.J.* 431, 439.

covenants were originally the product of private agreements, the Court observed, judicial action enforcing them "bears the clear and unmistakable imprimatur of the State."[118] The civil rights statutes go further, but their purpose and strategy are similar: they forbid individuals from using private power in ways that maintain the stigmatized status of blacks and certain other groups. Both point to a larger and more ambitious project.

Let us review where we have come. Process theory, we saw, pointed beyond itself toward a larger problem that infected government decisionmaking. In search of that larger problem, we turned toward stigma theory. But stigma theory failed to specify which sorts of stigma are impermissible and why, and it too pointed beyond itself to a larger social reality in which stigma is inscribed and reproduced. Finally, we examined the group-disadvantage theorists, who sought to focus directly on social reality. But we found that by paying too little attention to symbolic considerations, these writers lost sight of what was distinctive about the antidiscrimination project. Each theory pointed toward one of the others, and we found ourselves moving in a circle. We then made a fresh start by building upon the sociology of knowledge, and examined the ways in which stigmatizing beliefs could both shape and be shaped by social reality. With this framework, it is now possible to place all three theories in perspective.

The stages through which social reality is constructed are usefully summarized by Berger:

> The fundamental dialectic process of society consists of three moments, or steps. These are externalization, objectivation, and internalization. Only if these three moments are understood together can an empirically adequate view of society be maintained. Externalization is the ongoing outpouring of human being into the world, both in the physical and the mental activity of men. Objectivation is the attainment by the products of this activity (again both physical and mental) of a reality that confronts its original producers as a facticity external to and other than themselves. Internalization is the reappropriation by men of this same reality, transforming it once again from structures of the objective world into structures of the subjective consciousness. It is through externalization that society is a human product. It is through objectivation that society be-

118. 334 U.S. 1, 20 (1948).

comes a reality *sui generis*. It is through internalization that man is a product of society.[119]

We can discern all three of these moments in the social construction of ascribed stigma. In the decision-making process, the stigmatic meanings (Ely's "malign external preferences") are externalized into the world; there they become objective in a distribution of prestige, power, and tangible goods; through the experience of this objective reality, the meanings are then internalized anew by the members of society. Each of the theories we have examined has focused on one of the moments through which a stigmatizing reality reproduces itself. The process theorists focus on the moment of externalization, when stigmatizing meanings manifest themselves in decision making. The group-disadvantage theorists focus on the moment of objectivation, the concrete reality that these meanings create. The stigma theorists focus on the moment of internalization, when the meanings are absorbed by the participants in the culture.

Each of these moments is necessary to the meaning-producing process, and the disruption of any one of them would help to derange the process.[120] It does not follow, however—and this is the weakness of each theory standing alone—that attacking any one of the parts is sufficient to destroy the whole. For example, Freeman notes that Myrdal was too optimistic in thinking that the pattern of cumulative causation by which racism perpetuated itself could be remedied simply by changing the racial beliefs of whites: not only has racism deeper psychological roots than Myrdal imagined, but the American class structure impedes the upward mobility of blacks independently of racism.[121] As we have noted, disproportionate black poverty itself reinforces racism. In short, one can better fight the beast if one can see it whole.

As Lawrence observes, "ultimately the proponents of the process defect theory and the stigma theory have identified different manifestations of the same cultural phenomenon." A correct understanding of that phenomenon

---

119. Peter L. Berger, *The Sacred Canopy: Elements of a Sociological Theory of Religion* (Garden City, N.Y.: Anchor, 1969), p. 4. Berger and Luckmann note that each of these moments "corresponds to an essential characterization of the social world. *Society is a human product. Society is an objective reality. Man is a social product.*" Berger and Luckmann, *The Social Construction of Reality*, p. 61, emphases in original.

120. Cf. Allport, *The Nature of Prejudice*, p. 506; Myrdal, *An American Dilemma*, pp. 75–78.

121. See Freeman, "Antidiscrimination Law: The View from 1989," p. 142; Freeman, "Racism, Rights, and the Quest for Equality of Opportunity," pp. 354–85.

"locates the origin of racial stigma in the accumulation of the individual un-conscious and finds the origin of unconscious racism in the presence of widely shared, tacitly transmitted cultural values."[122] It is true that, as Ely claims, "unconstitutionality in the distribution of benefits that are not themselves constitutionally required can intelligibly inhere only in the way the distribu-tion was arrived at,"[123] but what one is looking for in the process is imper-missible substance[124]—the stigma that unjustifiably signifies the lesser worth of some citizens. This and only this type of stigma is the kind of malign preference that raises antidiscrimination concerns. Each wrong generates the other: unjustifiable stigma contaminates the process, and is in turn a result that only a contaminated process can produce. In this context, the distinction (insisted upon by Ely) between process and substance, or the question whether the process theory or the stigma theory better captures the aims of antidis-crimination law, makes little sense. The wrong of racial oppression is reducible neither to a tainted decision-making procedure, nor to a set of stigmatic mean-ings, nor to a maldistribution of material goods. Rather, it is all of these.

All three theories of antidiscrimination law ultimately rest on the same ethical claim: the denial of the belief that some persons deserve less concern and respect because of their race. The distortions identified by Dworkin and Ely produce a decision-making process that is defective because it is tainted by this false belief. The stigma identified by Black and Karst is intolerable because it rests on this false belief. The group disadvantages cited by Freeman, MacKinnon, Fiss, and Young are worse than the general run of material ine-quality because they are the product of the false belief and help to perpetuate it. The foundational commitment of antidiscrimination law is the commit-ment to this ethical claim.

Each of the three diagnoses of the problem points to an aspiration that cannot be realized if only that particular symptom is addressed. The decision-making process cannot be repaired without sealing off the source of the con-tamination, which turns out to be the racism entrenched within the larger

122. Charles R. Lawrence III, "The Ego, the Id, and Equal Protection: Reckoning With Un-conscious Racism," 39 *Stan. L. Rev.* 317, 355 (1987).

123. Ely, *Democracy and Distrust*, p. 145.

124. This has been stressed by Ely's critics. See Brest, "The Substance of Process," pp. 134–37; Laurence Tribe, "The Puzzling Persistence of Process-Based Constitutional Theories," 89 *Yale L. J.* 1063, 1072–77 (1980); Bruce Ackerman, "Beyond *Carolene Products*," 98 *Harv. L. Rev.* 713, 739–40 (1982).

culture. Racial stigma cannot be ended without changing the social facts in which that stigma is inscribed and which in turn daily reinscribe it. Material inequalities cannot be addressed without changing the process by which they are generated and legitimated. All three theories point toward a larger problem.

If the problem's strength lies largely in its invisibility, then the preeminent strategy for fighting it must be education. Americans must be made more aware of the subtle and pernicious influence of racism on ordinary, taken-for-granted processes of reasoning, so that they are able to fight these tendencies within themselves and avoid passing them on to their children. At the same time, the material reality that works to reinforce racism must also be transformed, most particularly in the inner cities that now operate so efficiently to produce a disproportionately black population of criminals. And, of course, the judiciary must do what it can to police the decision-making process for the subtle influence of racism, conscious and unconscious. The antidiscrimination project, in short, must adopt a multifaceted strategy to address a problem that is itself multifaceted.

The problem is, indeed, so pervasive that Derrick Bell can make a powerful case that "racism is an integral, permanent, and indestructible component of this society." Perhaps this is true. Perhaps "an honest assessment of our current status is cause for despair so profound it tempts surrender." Bell's answer to this temptation is that resistance is worth undertaking even if it is bound to fail, because it makes one's suffering meaningful.[125] Another is that it is foolishly arrogant to be confident of one's ability to predict the future. The earliest abolitionists had little reason to believe that slavery, which had existed since antiquity, could ever be abolished. Similarly, racism is as old as this country, but it, too, may not be immortal. The only way to find out is to do all one can to kill it.

A Final Excursus on Reverse Discrimination

The history of caste domination has made us the inheritors of a society that is pervasively racist. Race continues to exert a subtle yet powerful influence on Americans' beliefs and even perceptions. As T. Alexander Aleinkoff has

---

125. Derrick Bell, *Faces at the Bottom of the Well: The Permanence of Racism* (New York: Basic Books, 1992), quotes on pp. xiii, xi; see generally pp. ix–xvi, 195–200.

observed, "Most blacks have to overcome, when meeting whites, a set of assumptions older than this nation about one's abilities, one's marriageability, one's sexual desires, and one's morality." Racial considerations influence "the people we choose to spend our time with or marry, the neighborhoods in which we choose to live, the houses of worship we join, our choice of schools for our children, the people for whom we vote, and the people we allow the state to execute."[126] The goal of the antidiscrimination project is to change this pattern. Racial preferences *may* be a crucial means to this end.

Cognitive psychologists have found that racial categories are inherent in the way that contemporary Americans organize and process our experience. The human mind has a tendency to heighten the salient differences between members of the categories it employs, to deemphasize or overlook differences between members of the same category, and to resist information that contradicts established categories. All this readily applies to racial categories. People are more likely to notice and remember information when it confirms previously held stereotypes, and to interpret behavior as reconfirming and validating those stereotypes.[127] These tendencies, which operate unconsciously, can have a direct effect on the shaping of public policy, even when those policies are formally color blind.

A large part of the reason why whiteness appears to be a signifier for full humanity is that the positions in our society that are most admired and valued, that represent our human ideals, are prototypically occupied by whites.[128] Linguists investigate the cognitive tagging of social categories by manipulating phrases. When a native speaker senses that something is not quite right about a phrase, this suggests that the nonarticulated but underlying semantic structure is such that the information contained in that phrase is inappropriate. Thus, for example, "female nurse" sounds strange to the native speaker of English, but "male nurse" does not, because nurses are thought of as prototypically female, so that the first adjective is redundant. Given this phenom-

126. T. Alexander Aleinikoff, "A Case for Race-Consciousness," 91 *Columb. L. Rev.* 1060, 1066–67 (1991).

127. See Mark Snyder, "On the Self-Perpetuating Nature of Social Stereotypes," in David L. Hamilton, ed., *Cognitive Processes in Stereotyping and Intergroup Behavior* (Hillsdale, N.J.: Lawrence Erlbaum, 1981), pp. 183–212; David L. Hamilton and Tina K. Trolier, "Stereotypes and Stereotyping: An Overview of the Cognitive Approach," in John F. Dovidio and Samuel L. Gaertner, eds., *Prejudice, Discrimination, and Racism* (Orlando: Academic Press, 1986), pp. 127–63.

128. In this paragraph I am indebted to conversations with Prof. Steven Winter of the University of Miami Law School.

enon, the lack of symmetry between "white doctor"/"black doctor," "white lawyer/black lawyer," "white company president"/"black company president" has disturbing implications. (The same phenomenon occurs with gender: "male doctor"/"female doctor," "male lawyer/female lawyer," "male company president"/"female company president.") The fact that the first phrase of each pair, if used in ordinary conversation, would sound strangely redundant in a way the second would not suggests that speakers of English still regard it as strange and abnormal for blacks (or women) to occupy such positions. To change these cognitive processes, it is necessary to rearrange the distribution of positions, so that people experience blacks and women differently.[129] Banning racial preferences in hiring and professional school admissions would make that harder.[130] Such preferences cannot, of course, do the whole job; the existence of a large black underclass also reinforces racism, and there is no evidence that racial preferences have done anything to ameliorate the situation of that underclass.[131] The project's *reasons* for being concerned about that underclass, however, are also reasons for preferential treatment of blacks. Private institutions and businesses that use such preferences are furthering the project in ways in which the state cannot.

This is, of course, a predictive argument, and it may be countered by other predictive arguments. Glenn Loury has argued that the use of racial preferences reinforces, rather than undermines, racial stereotypes. "If, in an employment situation say, it is known that differential selection criteria are used

---

129. Justice Stevens has made a similar argument in *Wygant v. Jackson Board of Education*, 476 U.S. 267, 315 (1986). The argument is most often made by emphasizing the importance of "role models," but because this way of putting it neglects the cognitive dimensions of the problem, it is too easily trivialized and rejected. See, e.g., Richard A. Posner, "The DeFunis Case and the Constitutionality of Preferential Treatment of Racial Minorities," 1974 *Sup. Ct. Rev.* 1, 17–18; Richard Delgado, "Affirmative Action as a Majoritarian Device: Or, Do You Really Want To Be a Role Model?," 89 *Mich. L. Rev.* 1222 (1991).

130. William Van Alstyne has argued that "one gets beyond racism by getting beyond it now: by a complete, resolute, and credible commitment *never* to tolerate in one's own life—or in the life or practices of one's government—the differential treatment of other human beings by race." "Rites of Passage: Race, the Supreme Court, and the Constitution," 46 *U. Chi. L. Rev.* 775, 809 (1979). The problem with this formulation is that it is not possible, except superficially, to get beyond it now. Given how deeply entrenched racism is in our cognitive processes, the kind of commitment Van Alstyne advocates may be resolute indeed, but it will not be very credible.

131. See William Julius Wilson, *The Truly Disadvantaged: The Inner City, the Underclass, and Public Policy* (Chicago: University of Chicago Press, 1987), pp. 109–24. Wilson observes that this is equally true of laws that prohibit first-order discrimination.

for different races, and if it is further known that the quality of performance on the job depends on how one did on the criteria of selection, then in the absence of other information it is a rational statistical inference to impute a lower perceived quality of performance to persons of the race that was preferentially favored in selection."[132] In positions that are filled by competition, Charles Murray has argued, racial preference produces a systematic mismatch between the abilities of blacks and the abilities of whites, and thus "segments whites and blacks who come into contact with each other so as to maximize the likelihood that whites have the advantage in experience and ability."[133] The consequence, Murray claims, is that not only do blacks who receive preferential treatment get little respect from whites; they also come to doubt their own capacities.[134]

This is not an implausible story. It is equally plausible, however, that the absence or near-absence of blacks from valued positions would also reinforce racism; that in many contexts racial preferences do not produce any great variation in competence; that racial preferences compensate for the subtle influence of racism in the selection process and thus make that process more meritocratic than it would otherwise be; and that blacks dismiss whatever stigma attaches to them as due to prejudice.[135] Both of these stories are probably true some of the time, and which is closer to the truth in any particular case, or in the general run of cases, is an empirical question that ought to be investigated as such.[136] The consequentialist critique of reverse discrimination

132. Glenn C. Loury, "Beyond Civil Rights," in Russell Nieli, ed., *Racial Preference and Racial Justice: The New Affirmative Action Controversy* (Washington, D.C.: Ethics and Public Policy Center, 1991), p. 447.

133. Charles Murray, "Affirmative Racism," in Nieli, ed., *Racial Preference and Racial Justice*, p. 408. See also Thomas Sowell, "Are Quotas Good for Blacks?," in Nieli, ed., *Racial Preference and Racial Justice*, p. 422–23.

134. See Murray, "Affirmative Racism," p. 406.

135. Christopher Jencks argues powerfully that "when reverse discrimination leads to visible racial differences in job performance, its political costs outweigh its economic benefits." *Rethinking Social Policy: Race, Poverty, and the Underclass* (Cambridge: Harvard University Press, 1992), p. 63. Jencks acknowledges, however, that there is considerable uncertainty about the validity of traditional selection standards, that racism commonly infects evaluations of merit, and that an intelligent weighing of which preferential treatment programs should be retained must await the resolution of this uncertainty. Ibid., pp. 64–69.

136. So is the question whether, as Stephen Carter suggests, there is at last a critical mass of blacks in the professions and the skilled trades, so that racial preferences have now completed their most important work and have outlived their usefulness. See *Reflections of an Affirmative Action Baby* (New York: Basic Books, 1991).

simply cannot be developed persuasively or answered by political philosophy alone. Racial preferences have now been in place for enough years to provide a rich lode of data on which kinds of programs (if any) produce the positive results that proponents of racial preference hope for, and which (if any) produce the negative consequences that critics fear. It would probably even be possible to disaggregate these effects in cases where both are present—to determine, say, the point past which a college is digging so deep into the applicant pool to find blacks that those thereby admitted are unlikely to be able to perform to the school's standards. One of the most disheartening features of the endless debate over reverse discrimination is that most of the scholarship that has been undertaken on the issue has been the work of philosophers puzzling out whether it violates the rights of whites, rather than empirical social scientists investigating whether it ameliorates the condition of blacks.[137] None of these claims can be assessed without an examination of the evidence, but for the most part the evidence has not even been gathered.

Judicial Implications

What is the upshot of the antidiscrimination project for judicial practice? Assume for a moment (what it has not been possible to argue here) that at least one of the three theories we have been considering is a sound reading of the equal protection clause of the Fourteenth Amendment. We have seen that, inasmuch as each theory's aspirations cannot be realized without also realizing those of the others, each theory entails the others, and thus entails the broader antidiscrimination project as it has been described here. It follows that the equal protection clause obligates the state to act in furtherance of the project, to the extent that it reasonably can.

Such action, like policymaking in general, necessarily involves a multitude of prudential and predictive judgments, of a kind for which courts are not particularly well suited. For example, it is hard to imagine what a judicial remedy for the miserable condition of the urban underclass would even look like. This hardly implies, however, that the Fourteenth Amendment is judicially unenforceable. The amendment's language is prohibitive rather than

---

137. This is noted by Jennifer Hochschild in *Facing Up to the American Dream: Race, Class, and the Soul of the Nation* (Princeton: Princeton University Press, 1995), p. 100.

directive, and each of the three theories we have been considering here entails (though it is not exhausted by) an interpretation of this prohibition. If all three are correct as far as they go, then the prohibition is broad and multifaceted, and the courts have plenty of work to do.

The stigma theory, which we have argued points to the central evil the project seeks to eliminate, holds that government ought not to give its imprimatur to the social construction of unjustifiably stigmatized classes. This implies that one appropriate test for determining what should trigger heightened scrutiny is the "cultural meaning" test devised by Charles Lawrence.

> This test would evaluate governmental conduct to see if it conveys a symbolic message to which the culture attaches racial significance. The court would analyze governmental behavior much like a cultural anthropologist might: by considering evidence regarding the historical and social context in which the decision was made and effectuated. If the court determined that a significant portion of the population thinks of the governmental action in racial terms, then it would presume that socially shared, unconscious racial attitudes made evident by the action's meaning has influenced the decisionmakers. As a result, it would apply heightened scrutiny.[138]

Thus, for example, the social meaning of the segregation that was at issue in *Brown v. Board of Education* was obvious. "Given this common knowledge, it is difficult, if not impossible, to envision how a governmental decision maker might issue an order to segregate without intending, consciously or unconsciously, to injure blacks."[139] Lawrence's test produces a similar result in *Village of Arlington Heights v. Metropolitan Housing Development Corp.*,[140] one of the cases in which the Supreme Court announced that the Constitution prohibited only intentional discrimination. The case involved a nearly all-white suburban village's refusal to permit the construction of an integrated low-income housing project. Lawrence notes that segregated housing itself carries a message of inferiority, and that race was a prominent theme on both sides of the debate over whether to permit the project. Moreover, the maintenance of an all-white suburb itself is interpreted in our culture "as evidence of blacks'

---

138. Lawrence, "The Id, the Ego, and Equal Protection," p. 356.
139. Ibid., p. 363.
140. 429 U.S. 252 (1977).

continued untouchability."[141] This test is the one most appropriate to the understanding of antidiscrimination law advanced here, because it targets the evil we have called foundational: the institutionalization of the unjustified idea that some groups of persons have lesser worth.

There is even reason to believe that Lawrence's test does not go far enough in combatting unconscious racism. The cultural meaning test looks to the effects of racism, but the antidiscrimination project is equally concerned about identifying racism's causes. Even without the pervasive pattern of significations that devalue some persons on the basis of ascribed characteristics, persons tend to categorize themselves by groups and to devalue other groups. Even in laboratory experiments where the experimenter told the subjects that he was arbitrarily creating group assignments, subjects still showed bias in favor of their own groups.[142] There is considerable evidence that continuing, day-to-day contact between groups is necessary (though not sufficient) for the re-duction of prejudice.[143] "If equal opportunities are to be given to all groups, ethnic contact, intergroup communications, and relationships have to become a way of life."[144] De facto segregation may teach racism even if that is not its cultural meaning.

Among the justifications that have been offered for school desegregation—equal educational opportunity, integration as a good in itself, compensation for past wrongs, prohibition of future wrongs, preventing biased decision making—one rarely finds the argument that school desegregation helps to eliminate racism.[145] Certainly this argument has not been given much weight by the courts. Yet there is reason to think that school integration is the most effective way the state can directly address racism itself:

> Black and white adults who previously attended desegregated elementary
> and secondary schools (after proper controls) seem to be less likely to

141. Lawrence, "The Id, the Ego, and Equal Protection," p. 369.

142. David A. Wilder, "Social Categorization: Implications for Creation and Reduction of Intergroup Bias," 19 *Adv. in Experimental Soc. Psych.* 291, 311–12 (1986).

143. See Yehuda Amir, "The Role of Intergroup Contact in Change of Prejudice and Ethnic Relations," in Phyllis A. Katz, ed., *Towards the Elimination of Racism* (New York: Pergamon Press, 1975), pp. 245–308.

144. Ibid., p. 294.

145. The most prominent theories of desegregation are usefully catalogued and critiqued in James S. Liebman, "Desegregating Politics: 'All-Out' School Desegregation Explained," 90 *Colum. L. Rev.* 1463, 1484–1539 (1990).

express negative views about members of the other race and are significantly more comfortable in integrated work and social settings than are black and white graduates of segregated schools. Likewise, black graduates of desegregated schools are less likely than graduates of segregated schools to believe that antiblack discrimination is widespread. Most heartening is evidence that, upon graduating from desegregated schools, both blacks (as to whom the evidence is stronger) and whites vote with their feet in ways that suggest that they carry 'equal concern' virtue with them outside the public educational sphere—indeed outside the public sphere—and into their private lives: Members of both races who attended integrated schools (again, after proper controls) live in integrated neighborhoods and report having personal relationships with persons of the other race in significantly higher proportions than do blacks and whites who went to segregated schools.[146]

Given the evidence that this is the case, and that integration does white children no harm whatsoever,[147] it is revealing that deliberate integration almost never happens unless it is imposed by courts or federal agencies. Once again, it appears that racially selective sympathy and indifference is playing a large role in government decision making. This is a defect in the decision-making process that the cultural meaning test is unlikely to discern.

There is also a more immediate difficulty with Lawrence's theory—one that presses in the other direction, toward restraint. His cultural meaning test, he says, should be used "in order to determine whether to subject an allegedly discriminatory act to strict scrutiny."[148] Here we begin to confront the limits of the antidiscrimination project. If every racially significant government action is to be subjected to strict scrutiny—scrutiny that, as Gerald Gunther has observed, is " 'strict' in theory and fatal in fact"[149]—then will not the commitment to eradicating racism effectively override every other commitment that our society has? And in a complex and pluralistic society, can any commitment be given that overwhelming degree of priority?

146. Ibid., pp. 1626–27 (footnotes omitted).

147. See ibid., p. 1621.

148. Lawrence, "The Id, the Ego, and Equal Protection," p. 355.

149. Gerald Gunther, "The Supreme Court, 1971 Term—Foreword: In Search of Evolving Doctrine on a Changing Court: A Model for a Newer Equal Protection," 86 *Harv. L. Rev.* 1, 8 (1972).

Thus, for example, when Lawrence reviews *Washington v. Davis*[150] under his test, he finds an invidious racial meaning in the city police department's use of a civil service exam which blacks failed at a rate roughly four times that of whites. That racial meaning is conveyed through the maintenance of a disproportionately white police force. "To the extent that our culture attaches specific meaning to the assignment of racial groups to certain occupational and hierarchical roles, behavior that maintains those role assignments will have racial meaning."[151] Moreover, racism is promoted by the test results themselves. "If larger numbers of blacks than whites fail the test, this will be seen as proof that blacks are not smart enough for the job."[152]

Lawrence assures us that "evidence of cultural meaning must include more than racially disparate impact,"[153] because the plaintiffs will have to produce evidence that this disparate impact will be interpreted by the general population as signifying the inferior ability of blacks. In the case of any screening device that purports to measure intelligence, however, this burden will always be easy to meet. The point reaches beyond civil service examinations. What about medical school admissions? Disproportionate numbers of white doctors would seem to convey the same kind of invidious message as disproportionate numbers of white police. And then, what about college admissions? College grades? High school grades? Should strict (therefore fatal) scrutiny be applied to any governmentally administered measure of ability at which whites do substantially better than blacks?

Part of the difficulty here is that Lawrence's test is really two tests: one that monitors decision-making inputs for process defect, as in *Arlington Heights,* and one that monitors decision-making outputs for stigma, as in *Washington v. Davis.* It seems to work better as a stigma test than as a process test, because the only process defects it will capture are those where the stigmatizing effect is known, consciously or unconsciously, to the decision maker ex ante. (On the other hand, the stigma theory, more than the others, is centrally concerned with cultural meaning.)[154] One of the starkest cases of unconscious racism is *McCleskey v. Kemp,* discussed in Chapter 1, but in many states with similar disparities, it is not clear that the death penalty is understood by legislators,

150. 426 U.S. 229 (1976).
151. Lawrence, "The Id, the Ego, and Equal Protection," p. 372.
152. Ibid., p. 373.
153. Ibid.
154. Lawrence recognizes this. See ibid., pp. 355, 357 n. 182.

prosecutors, or juries to have *any* racial connotations. Moreover, even conscious discrimination will often be hidden; racial redlining by bankers conveys no invidious cultural meaning until it is uncovered.[155] It thus appears that the cultural meaning test must be one of a number of tests for a constitutional violation. Like the other theories considered above, it identifies only one part of a very large problem. Once again, racism is so pervasive and multifaceted that no single theory will capture all the harm it does.

The antidiscrimination project's ambitions are so great—or, to put it another way, the evil it seeks to combat is so deeply woven into our culture—that the attempt to realize the project will inevitably have costs. Sometimes the costs are too high. Other values can sometimes trump those of the antidiscrimination project.

The trouble with contemporary antidiscrimination law is that the other values win too easily and too often. Daniel Ortiz has shown that the Court's approach to government decisions that have a disparate impact on minorities, at least with respect to housing and public employment, amounts in practice to minimal scrutiny. "Instead of asking whether the decision maker *would* have made the same decision without the discriminatory motivation, the Court asks something a bit closer to whether it *could* have done so."[156] This approach fails to satisfy the requirements of process theory, because "the presence of permissible goals—even very substantial ones—does not reveal how important the impermissible goals were." With this approach, "impermissible motivation might have changed the ultimate result of the decision-making process and still be excused."[157] The bottom line, as Freeman has observed, is that antidiscrimination law tends to lose all its bite as soon as it comes into

155. Henry Louis Gates Jr. marshals this example against Lawrence in "War of Words: Critical Race Theory and the First Amendment," in Henry Louis Gates Jr. et al., *Speaking of Race, Speaking of Sex: Hate Speech, Civil Rights, and Civil Liberties* (New York and London: New York University Press, 1994), p. 54.

156. Daniel R. Ortiz, "The Myth of Intent in Equal Protection," 41 *Stan. L. Rev.* 1105, 1115 (1989), emphases in original. Thus in *Washington v. Davis*, 426 U.S. 229, 246 (1976), the Court found the employment test was "neutral on its face and *rationally* may be said to serve a purpose the government is *constitutionally empowered* to pursue." In *Village of Arlington Heights v. Metropolitan Housing Development Corp.*, 429 U.S. 252, 279 n. 25 (1977), the exclusion of blacks by the village's refusal to rezone for low-income housing was described as "essentially an unavoidable consequence of a legislative policy that has in itself always been deemed to be *legitimate.*" (The emphases are added in both these quotations.) The emphasized words, Ortiz observes (p. 1115), "resonate with the language of reduced scrutiny.".

157. Ortiz, "The Myth of Intent," p. 1116.

conflict with other values, such as "local autonomy of the suburbs, or previously distributed vested rights, or selection on the basis of merit."[158]

It is neither the case (as Lawrence seems inclined to think) that antidiscrimination should always trump other values or (as the Court seems inclined to think) that such values should always trump antidiscrimination. The world is simply more complicated than that. These are hard cases. Once we acknowledge that the antidiscrimination project must compete with other considerations, Edmund Burke's warning presses on us with some urgency:

> The nature of man is intricate; the objects of society are of the greatest possible complexity; and therefore no simple disposition or direction of power can be suitable either to man's nature, or to the quality of his affairs. . . . If you were to contemplate society in but one point of view, all these simple modes of polity are infinitely captivating. In effect each would answer its single end much more perfectly than the more complex is able to attain all its complex purposes. But it is better that the whole should be imperfectly and anomalously answered, than that, while some parts are provided for with great exactness, others might be totally neglected, or perhaps materially injured, by the over-care of a favourite member.[159]

The point is that in each case, the competing value needs to be specified and an argument made why this value should or should not trump the antidiscrimination value. When a law or a private activity raises antidiscrimination concerns, it should be subjected to neither strict (therefore automatically fatal) nor minimal (therefore automatically deferential) scrutiny, but to something in between.

All three of the theories we have considered require, in the end, judicial balancing of the antidiscrimination goal against other societal goals. The best understanding of the process theory, David Strauss has argued, would require a court to ask, "suppose the adverse effects of the challenged government decision fell on whites instead of blacks, or on men instead of women. Would the decision have been different?"[160] Strauss observes that this standard is

---

158. Freeman, "Legitimizing Racial Discrimination Through Antidiscrimination Law," p. 1050.

159. Edmund Burke, *Reflections on the Revolution in France,* ed. Conor Cruise O'Brien (1790; London: Penguin, 1968), pp. 152–53. Berlin's "Two Concepts of Liberty" makes essentially the same point.

160. Strauss, "Discriminatory Intent and the Taming of *Brown,*" p. 957.

inadequate, because in hard cases it dissolves into speculative or meaningless questions, such as "Would abortion be outlawed if men could get pregnant?" But there are cases in which a clear answer is available. As noted above, Warren McCleskey succeeded in showing that if his victim had been black, he would probably not have been sentenced to death. The harms that the stigma and group-disadvantaging theories identify are not sufficient without balancing to make out a Fourteenth Amendment claim, because the prevention of these harms is not an absolute goal. The question arises again whether the law would find these injuries a price worth paying if they fell on whites.[161]

A useful model is the rule of *Griggs v. Duke Power Co.*, which asks whether the competing value has any substance at all. *Griggs* interpreted the Civil Rights Act of 1964 to mean that "[i]f an employment practice which operates to exclude Negroes cannot be shown to be related to job performance, the practice is prohibited." When a practice that appears neutral on its face has a disproportionate impact on blacks, the *Griggs* Court held, that practice must be justified.[162] In *Washington v. Davis*,[163] however, the Court refused to impose

161. For a defense of judicial balancing, see Theodore Eisenberg, "Disproportionate Impact and Illicit Motive: Theories of Constitutional Adjudication," 52 *N.Y.U. L. Rev.*, 36, 68–73 (1977). Strauss has observed that while such balancing involves value judgments of the sort ordinarily left to legislatures, legislatures cannot be the final arbiters of whether their decisions have complied with the Constitution. "The Equal Protection Clause reflects an unmistakable determination that state legislatures are not to be trusted to refrain from engaging in racial discrimination. The drafters of that provision were clear in their intention to establish some means to police state action to ensure that it is not discriminatory. State political processes were not to have the last word on the question whether they were discriminating on the basis of race." "Discriminatory Intent and the Taming of *Brown*," p. 985. Given courts' tendency to give too little weight to the antidiscrimination project, it may make sense to require that any countervailing state interest be especially compelling, as Fiss proposes. See "Groups and the Equal Protection Clause," pp. 143–45.

162. 401 U.S. 424, 431 (1971). I take no position here on whether, as some have claimed, lower courts have interpreted *Griggs* in a way that makes it unreasonably difficult for businesses to show that criteria are related to job performance. See, e.g., Christopher Jencks, *Rethinking Social Policy: Race, Poverty, and the Underclass* (Cambridge: Harvard University Press, 1992), pp. 66–69; Epstein, *Forbidden Grounds*, pp. 205–41. *Griggs* was essentially overruled in *Wards Cove Packing Co. v. Atonio*, 490 U.S. 642 (1989), which required the employee to show that the employment practices resulting in disparate impact do not have an adequate business justification, rather than requiring the employer to show that they do. This essentially made disparate impact suits impossible to win by requiring the plaintiff to prove a negative. *Wards Cove* in turn was nullified, and the *Griggs* rule restored, by the Civil Rights Act of 1991, Pub. L. 102-166.

163. 426 U.S. 229 (1976).

the same requirement on state actors via the Fourteenth Amendment: the state does not even bear the burden of justifying a practice with a disproportionate impact on blacks unless the plaintiff can first do what is nearly impossible by proving discriminatory intent. *Griggs* makes more sense than *Davis* because it requires a weighing of the equities on each side, instead of placing an effectively irrebuttable presumption on either.

Ethical Implications

The prudent weighing of considerations counseled by Burke is inevitably an imprecise business. It is no less so when individuals decide how much of a burden they should undertake in daily life to combat racism. For cultural transformation cannot be accomplished by the state alone. Setting aside the limits to the state's legitimate involvement with the ideas in people's heads— limits that will be taken up in Chapters 5 and 6—there are limits to what the state *can* do. As this is written in the mid-1990s, more than forty years of Communist domination of Eastern Europe has come to an end—forty years of rule by governments determined to stamp out ethnic rivalries and unhampered by liberal scruples. It has all been a failure. The liberation of these areas has inaugurated a new era of persecutions and civil wars. The project of eradicating racism and its practices and institutions is so large that, perhaps paradoxically, it entails a limited role for the law. The problem is so pervasive that it cannot be remedied by the state alone without totalitarian control of civil society, and probably not even then.[164] The law's proper role is therefore one of abetting, rather than leading, an egalitarian social movement.

Each of us, in our daily activities, constitutes the culture in which we live, and each of us at least to that extent has the ability, and therefore the obligation, to reshape that culture. As Patricia Williams observes, "a part of ourselves is beyond the control of pure physical will and resides in the sanctuary of those around us; a fundamental part of ourselves and of our dignity depends on the uncontrollable, powerful, external observers who make up a society. Surely a part of socialization ought to include a sense of caring responsibility

164. It should go without saying that the project is beyond the capacity of courts, which, except in unusual circumstances, appear to be unable to bring about significant social change without the help of other branches of government. See generally Gerald N. Rosenberg, *The Hollow Hope: Can Courts Bring About Social Change?* (Chicago and London: University of Chicago Press, 1991).

for the images of others that are reposited within us."[165] Racism is an automatic component of the thought processes even of whites who consciously and sincerely reject it. Unless they actively strive to inhibit it, it will infect their deliberations.[166] If we have an obligation not to stigmatize others, then we have a corresponding obligation to learn how racism works and what we tend to do, in our daily routines, that reinforces racism. This implies, at least, that education ought (among its other aims) to make students aware of the racial impact of taken-for-granted practices and symbols. If there is resistance to the teaching of "sensitivity," this is due, I suspect, to the ambiguity of this word: it describes a certain moral virtue, which, critics reasonably object, cannot be taught in the classroom. What these critics miss, however, is that it also describes an intellectual virtue, the virtue of being aware of what one is in fact doing, in this case "what practices, habits, attitudes, comportments, images, symbols, and so on contribute to social domination and group oppression."[167]

Since it is ordinary day-to-day activities that reproduce the taken-for-granted meanings of race in our society, it is those activities that must be changed, and it ultimately is up to us ordinary citizens, rather than the state, to change them. A key step in this process of change is the public identification and condemnation of routine but stigmatizing behaviors. (This kind of activity has had notable successes, such as ending the exclusion of black models from advertising.) It should not be surprising if this activity makes many people feel self-conscious and uncomfortable. This discomfort is reflected in the recent and ongoing reaction throughout the popular press against the pressure toward "political correctness"—the tendency of some "thought police," as they are sneeringly called, to monitor the production of symbolic representations for signs of racism, sexism, or homophobia. Doubtless many who engage in this activity are humorless, heavy-handed, dogmatic, and intolerant. Some such activists have embraced foolish ideologies of racial determinism and education-as-therapy that are as dangerous as the tendencies they seek to combat. The monitoring of culture is, however, absolutely indispensable if the

165. Williams, *The Alchemy of Race and Rights*, p. 73; see also Young, *Justice and the Politics of Difference*, pp. 148–51.

166. See Patricia G. Devine, "Stereotypes and Prejudice: Their Automatic and Controlled Components," 56 *J. Personality & Soc. Psych.* 5 (1989); Patricia G. Devine, Margo J. Monteith, Julia R. Zuwerink, and Andrew J. Elliot, "Prejudice With and Without Compunction," 60 *J. Personality & Soc. Psych.* 817 (1991). I am grateful to Steven Winter for directing me to these articles.

167. Young, *Justice and the Politics of Difference*, p. 86.

goals of the antidiscrimination project are ever to be attained.[168] Opponents of such monitoring charge that its purpose, even when it does not attempt to invoke the coercive power of the state, is to create a new orthodoxy. But orthodoxy is what the antidiscrimination project must create—not in the sense that some central scrutinizer should be empowered to punish deviations from it, but in the sense that on certain issues there ought to be a high degree of uniformity of opinion among the citizens. The popular press no longer debates whether blacks are genetically closer to apes than to whites, or whether there is an international Jewish conspiracy to dominate the world. The absence of diversity of opinion on these matters is a great social good.

The question of the desirable limits of such orthodoxy is a complex one, not usefully addressed by slogans. Any social convention that imposes intellectual conformity (and the taboo against expression that could be construed as racist is only one of many such conventions) will induce some persons whose beliefs are sound, but whose views challenge some aspect of the conventional wisdom, to avoid candid expression of their opinions. As a consequence, honest examination of pressing public problems may be precluded in favor of a sanitized, impoverished public discourse.[169] This may have harmful effects even upon the realization of the project. The consequentialist critique of reverse discrimination, to the extent that it is correct, is a powerful argument that such programs do not promote the aims of the project. It is arguable that one reason these consequences have not been investigated is that researchers fear that, if they conclude that reverse discrimination *does* have counterproductive effects, they will be labeled as racists. So the research is not done, and the bad consequences (if they exist) continue, promoted by people who believe themselves thereby to be fighting racism. One of the paradoxes of the project is that it requires both intellectual conformity and intellectual courage, and these requirements work at cross-purposes.

The practical judgment that the project requires of us is judgment of a uniquely complex kind. For individuals, no less than for the state, the campaign against racism cannot be all-consuming. These obligations must be balanced against others, to those we care most about and to ourselves. To

168. For a balanced assessment of this movement, see Louis Menand, "The Culture Wars," *N.Y. Rev. of Books,* Oct. 6, 1994, pp. 16–21.

169. See Glenn C. Loury, "Self-Censorship in Public Discourse: A Theory of Political Correctness and Related Phenomena," in *One by One from the Inside Out: Essays and Reviews on Race and Responsibility in America* (New York: Free Press, 1995), pp. 145–82.

complicate matters further, unlike Burke, we cannot rely on our untutored prejudices and the ordinary decent person's opinions to see us through to the right balance, because these are among the things that the antidiscrimination project calls into question. Our biases are likely even to impair our ability to tell when racism has affected, or is reinforced by, our actions. The disposition of character that the project seeks to foster is an unstable mix of courage and self-doubt: a willingness to say fearlessly what one believes, while remaining acutely aware that one's convictions are always in danger of being tainted by unconscious racism. The project requires us to make fine-grained practical judgments at the same time that we cultivate suspicion of our own powers of judgment. The antidiscrimination project thus tends to foster, among whites who subscribe to it, a nervous, guilty disposition, apologetic and distrustful of itself. One must perpetually navigate a way between the Scylla of suburban obliviousness and the Charybdis of intellectual ossification. The guilty white liberal is not a particularly heroic human type, but seems in many ways abject and comical. Under the circumstances American whites live in, though, the alternatives are worse.[170] The solution is to change the circumstances. Racism exacts a moral price from whites as well as blacks. The promise that the antidiscrimination project holds forth for whites is of a world in which these intractable dilemmas are no longer the common currency of everyday life.

170. See Randall Kennedy, "On Cussing Out White Liberals," 235 *The Nation* 169, 172 (1982).

3

Women

With which groups should the antidiscrimination project be concerned? The Court, we noted in Chapter 1, has not made it clear how it decides which classifications are "suspect" and therefore subject to heightened judicial scrutiny under the Fourteenth Amendment. (Nor has clarification come from Congress or state legislatures, bodies that need not enunciate any principled basis for deciding which categories of discrimination to prohibit.) Paul Brest has suggested that the criteria for extending the antidiscrimination principle to nonracial classifying traits have simply been whether they "tend to be especially harmful" (presumably because they "are pervasive and have traditionally operated in the same direction—to the disadvantage of members of the minority group") "and have little social utility."[1] This may account for statutory inclusion of statuses that are not particularly stigmatized.[2] But for our purposes, this rationale sweeps too broadly. Not all forms of discrimination that satisfy Brest's criteria justify the kind of ambitious project of cultural reconstruction described in the last chapter—or at least, the two criteria have to be satisfied with special force, as they are in the case of race. Racism is pervasive in American culture, and from a liberal perspective its social utility is negative in a special way: it incorporates beliefs that imply the denial of liberalism's fundamental tenets. If the project of cultural reconstruction is directed against more than racism, it is because racism is not the only ideology that fits that description.

"Racial classifications that disadvantage minorities are 'suspect,' " writes

---

1. Paul Brest, "The Supreme Court, 1975 Term—Foreword: In Defense of the Antidiscrimination Principle," 90 *Harv. L. Rev.* 1, 10–11 (1976).

2. See, e.g., *N.Y. Executive Law* §296 (McKinney 1982) (outlawing employment discrimination on the basis of, inter alia, marital status).

Ely, "because we suspect that they are the product of racially prejudiced thinking of a sort we understand the Fourteenth Amendment to have been centrally concerned with eradicating."[3] This statement remains correct, if at a somewhat higher level of abstraction, if the words "racial" and "racially" are deleted. The premise of the antidiscrimination project is that there is a broad range of deeply entrenched meanings, practices, and institutions in American society that reproduce and maintain the pervasive, unjustifiable belief that certain classes of human beings are less worthy or deserving than others. These meanings, practices, and institutions impede the political participation, economic well-being, self-respect, and autonomy of members of those classes. Discrimination against a group should be prohibited, and the culture that fosters such discrimination should be changed, if that discrimination is likely to be predicated on, reflect, or reproduce this kind of belief, or if it tends to produce these kinds of harm.[4] The question whether any group should be protected by antidiscrimination law turns on the following inquiry: does the prevailing understanding of that group unjustifiably stigmatize or socially construct its members in a way that reduces the group's political power, material wealth, and autonomy? In this chapter, I shall take up this inquiry with respect to the case of women.

The case for cultural reconstruction, we have seen, can rest on any of the three kinds of harm described by the theories of antidiscrimination we have considered. It is strongest when all three are present. In this chapter, I shall argue that all three are indeed present in the case of women, and that, as with racism, they are mutually reinforcing. The antidiscrimination project is therefore appropriately extended to women as well as blacks.

Of the three theories of discrimination, the applicability of the group-

3. John Hart Ely, *Democracy and Distrust* (Cambridge: Harvard University Press, 1980), p. 243 n. 11.

4. Some judges have read the equal protection case law in a way that is consistent with this analysis. See, e.g., *Watkins v. United States Army*, 847 F.2d 1329, vacated, 847 F.2d 1362 (9th Cir. 1988), aff'd on other grounds, 875 F.2d 699 (9th Cir. 1989) (en banc), cert. denied, 498 U.S. 957 (1990), which holds that three factors guide the determination of whether a characteristic warrants judicial protection: the unfairness of using that characteristic as a basis for decision making, a history of purposeful discrimination against the group possessing that characteristic, and that group's traditional lack of political power. The appearance of these factors in combination strongly suggests that a system of subordination, of the kind described in the text above, is at work. Cf. *City of Cleburne v. Cleburne Living Center*, 473 U.S. 432, 472–73 n. 24 (1985) (Marshall, J., concurring in the judgment in part and dissenting in part).

disadvantaging theory is the easiest to show in this case. Although discrimination against women has diminished in recent years, their economic status remains inferior to that of men, and prosperous women tend to owe their status to their economic dependence on men.

Is the prevailing cultural meaning of gender responsible for this state of affairs? Surprisingly, feminists and antifeminists agree that the answer is yes, although they disagree about *which* aspects of the culture are to blame. Feminists point to the traditions of assigning women primary responsibility for child care and of structuring most jobs with a male worker in mind, so that it is assumed the worker does not have child care responsibilities. This handicaps women in the job market even if no employer discriminates against them: well-paying jobs are structured in such a way that most women, who *do* have child care responsibilities, really are less qualified for those jobs.[5] Antifeminists also blame the culture, but their ire is focused on the new rather than the old: the devaluation of women's traditional roles and the destigmatization of divorce, which has greatly lowered the social costs imposed on men who leave their wives.[6] (A complete explanation would also, of course, have to take account of the simultaneous decline in middle-class wages and boom in service-sector jobs, which have compelled many women to enter the paid workforce whether they wished to or not.)[7] Both explanations have some power, although the antifeminists considerably exaggerate the economic security that women were able to rely on in former times, and neither in principle excludes the other, although each obviously points toward a different prescription. Neither relates in an unmediated way to the social meaning of gender per se. To make the case for the deliberate transformation of that social meaning, it is necessary to show that women are stigmatized and that their stigmatization contaminates public and private decision-making processes in ways that materially disadvantage them.

5. See Susan Moller Okin, *Justice, Gender, and the Family* (New York: Basic Books, 1989), pp. 134–69.

6. See., e.g., Phyllis Schlafly, *The Power of the Positive Woman* (New Rochelle, N.Y.: Arlington House, 1977). Feminists have also called attention to this development, however. See, e.g., Barbara Ehrenreich, *The Hearts of Men: American Dreams and the Flight from Commitment* (Garden City, N.Y.: Anchor, 1983).

7. "Two-thirds of all women in the labor force either are supporting themselves and their families or are married to men earning less than $15,000 a year." Mary Ann Mason, *The Equality Trap: Why Working Women Shouldn't Be Treated Like Men* (New York: Touchstone, 1988), p. 112.

The question whether any given set of practices is stigmatizing is necessarily answered by interpreting the meanings that are shared at a particular time and place.[8] The Court confused this issue when it declared in *Brown* that "[s]eparate educational facilities are inherently unequal"[9] and thereby inadvertently created huge and unnecessary difficulties for black (and, later, women's) colleges.[10] The statement was correct insofar as it recognized the implausibility of the "separate but equal" claim in the context of Jim Crow, but incredible insofar as it was phrased in terms of what Charles Black called "the metaphysics of sociology: 'Must Segregation Amount to Discrimination?' "[11] Black's comment remains instructive:

> That is an interesting question; someday the methods of sociology may be adequate to answering it. But it is not our question. Our question is whether discrimination inheres in that segregation which is imposed by law in the twentieth century in certain specific states in the American Union. And that question has meaning and can find an answer only on the ground of history and of common knowledge about the facts of life in the times and places aforesaid.[12]

It is therefore necessary to explore the social meaning of any particular effort to push individuals into specific social roles.[13]

The most obvious difficulty with such an exploration is that it requires the courts to inquire into highly contestable social meanings. Even if the stigmatizing meaning of segregation was, as Black argued, a plain fact, the meaning of many other government actions are not. Such considerations led Justice Powell in the *Bakke* case to reject Brennan's proposed stigma test: "There is no principled basis for deciding which groups would merit 'heightened

---

8. Such interpretation of cultural meaning is a familiar part of the job courts do. See Charles Lawrence III, "The Ego, the Id, and Equal Protection: Reckoning With Unconscious Racism," 39 *Stan. L. Rev.* 317, 358–62 (1987).

9. *Brown v. Board of Education*, 347 U.S. 483, 495 (1954).

10. See Derrick Bell, *Race, Racism, and American Law* (3d ed.; Boston: Little, Brown, 1992), pp. 661–82; Ruth Colker, "Anti-Subordination Above All: Sex, Race, and Equal Protection," 61 *N.Y.U. L. Rev.* 1003, 1049–58 (1986); *United States v. Fordice*, 112 S.Ct. 2727, 2744–46 (1992) (Thomas, J., concurring).

11. Charles Black, "The Lawfulness of the Segregation Decisions," 69 *Yale L. J.* 421, 427 (1960).

12. Ibid.

13. This is why Lawrence's cultural meaning test, which we examined in Chapter 2, is an appropriate standard for heightened scrutiny.

judicial solicitude' and which would not. Courts would be asked to evaluate the extent of the prejudice and consequent harm suffered by various minority groups. . . . The kind of variable sociological and political analysis necessary to produce such rankings simply does not lie within the judicial competence— even if they otherwise were politically feasible and socially desirable."[14] Richard Epstein concludes that "the best way to take into account the full range of symbols, good and bad, noble and vain, is for the legal system to *ignore* them all—mine and yours alike."[15] The trouble with this solution is that the central evil antidiscrimination law seeks to remedy is among the things ignored. These arguments are reminiscent of the old joke about the drunken man who was found looking for his keys under a streetlamp far from the place where he had dropped them, because, as he explained, the light was better there.

Sex discrimination presents a difficult case because its significance is contested. Unlike race, traditional sex roles are not generally agreed to entail the degradation of a group: the Equal Rights Amendment was defeated in large part by a grassroots movement of women. Bernard Williams argues (in another context) that equal concern is not in principle inconsistent with "some kind of hierarchical society, so long as the hierarchy maintained itself without compulsion, and there was human understanding between the orders. In such a society, each man would indeed have a very conspicuous title which related him to the social structure; but it might be that most people were aware of the human beings behind the titles, and found each other for the most part content, or even proud, to have the titles that they had."[16] Williams thinks that "what keeps stable hierarchies together is the

14. *Univ. of Calif. Regents v. Bakke*, 438 U.S. 265, 296–97 (1978) (opinion of Powell, J.). See also, for a similar argument, Richard A. Posner, "The Defunis Case and the Constitutionality of Preferential Treatment of Minorities," 1974 *Sup. Ct. Rev.* 1, 21–26. During the *Brown* litigation, Justice Jackson had similar reservations, as evidenced by a memorandum he wrote in February 1954: "I do not think we should import into the concept of equal protection of the law these elusive psychological and subjective factors. They are not determinable with satisfactory objectivity or measurable with reasonable certainty. If we adhere to objective criteria the judicial process will still be capricious enough." Quoted in Richard Kluger, *Simple Justice: The History of 'Brown v. Board of Education' and Black America's Struggle for Equality* (New York: Random House, 1976), p. 689. In the event, however, Jackson joined the opinion of the Court.

15. Richard Epstein, *Forbidden Grounds: The Case Against Employment Discrimination Laws* (Cambridge and London: Harvard University Press, 1992), pp. 498–99 (emphasis in original).

16. Bernard Williams, "The Idea of Equality," in *Philosophy, Politics, and Society, Second Series,* ed. Peter Laslett and W. G. Runciman (Oxford: Basil Blackwell, 1962), p. 119. Cf. Alexis de

idea of necessity, that it is somehow foreordained or inevitable that there should be these orders; and this idea of necessity must be eventually undermined by the growth of people's reflective consciousness about their role, still more when it is combined with the thought that what they and the others have always thought about their roles in the social system was the product of the social system itself."[17] But at least some contemporary women, on reflection, value their traditional roles and feel threatened by a conception of equality that condemns those roles.[18] This fact must somehow be reconciled with the idea that sexism is an evil that must be eradicated. Moreover, why is Williams so confident that equal respect is violated when hierarchy is maintained through "compulsion"? It is at least in principle possible for the power holder to say, "no disrespect intended, but this is your social role, and everyone has an equal duty to carry out the responsibilities of his or her social role. The king has no right to abdicate his role, just as the peasant's

---

Tocqueville, *Democracy in America*, tr. George Lawrence (orig. ed. 1835–40; Garden City, N.Y.: Doubleday Anchor, 1969), pp. 13–14.

17. Williams, "The Idea of Equality," pp. 119–20. Similarly John Rawls, *A Theory of Justice* (Cambridge: Harvard University Press, 1971), p. 547: "[I]n a feudal or in a caste system each person is believed to have his allotted station in the natural order of things. His comparisons are presumably confined to within his own estate or caste, these ranks becoming in effect so many noncomparing groups established independently of human control and sanctioned by religion and theology. Men resign themselves to their position should it ever occur to them to question it; and since all may view themselves as assigned their vocation, everyone is held to be equally fated and equally noble in the eyes of providence." Rawls rejects this vision of society by saying that a well-ordered society must not be founded on "false or unfounded beliefs" (ibid.), and that "when the belief in a fixed natural order sanctioning a hierarchical society is abandoned, assuming here that this belief is not true, a tendency is set up that points in the direction of [liberal] principles of justice"(ibid., p. 548). The problem is that in the case of sexism, it is not generally accepted that this belief is not true.

Michael Walzer, too, accepts that a caste system may be just if the members of the lower orders "really do accept the doctrines that support the caste system." *Spheres of Justice: A Defense of Pluralism and Equality* (New York: Basic, 1983), p. 314. "In a society where social meanings are integrated and hierarchical, justice will come to the aid of inequality" (ibid., p. 313). The point should not be too readily accepted with reference to any existing society, however. "For an inquiry into the preferences of the oppressed to mean anything at all, one would have to conduct it under conditions that make it possible for the most deprived members of society to speak without fear and with adequate information. How else can one know whether they really share the values of the masters?" Judith N. Shklar, *The Faces of Injustice* (New Haven and London: Yale University Press, 1990), p. 115.

18. See, e.g., Schlafly, *The Power of the Positive Woman*.

wife has no right to abdicate hers; the social order is a common good, which all have a responsibility (each in his or her own ascribed way) to maintain."[19] Such a rationale was used not very long ago to explain why women should be held to the duties traditionally deemed appropriate for their sex.[20]

One may understand the project of sex equality as one of ending well-intentioned customs that happen to have disadvantaged women. Women would then be protected by Sunstein's anti-caste principle, which holds that "differences that are irrelevant from the moral point of view ought not without good reason to be turned, by social and legal structures, into social disadvantages."[21] Some women do value their traditional roles, but many others do not, and the latter confront a far narrower range of options than men have. As with race, however, this principle understates both the wrong that is done by sex inequality and the deep cultural roots of that wrong. The problem is not simply that "women were victimized by policies designed to protect them";[22] it is that women have been devalued by the prevailing culture.

Sherry Ortner argues that three types of data constitute evidence that a culture regards women as inferior:

(1) elements of cultural ideology and informants' statements that *explicitly* devalue women, according them, their roles, their products, and their social milieux less prestige than that accorded men and the male correlates; (2) symbolic devices, such as the attribution of defilement, which may be interpreted as *implicitly* making a statement of inferior valuation; and (3) social-structural arrangements that exclude women from participation in or contact with some realm in which the highest powers of the society are felt to reside.[23]

19. Several Shakespearean characters eloquently articulate such a view. See Ulysses' speech on degree in *Troilus and Cressida*, I, iii, 75–137, or Menenius' organic vision of the body politic in *Coriolanus*, I, i, 99–158, which Allan Bloom nostalgically quotes in *The Closing of the American Mind* (New York: Simon & Schuster, 1987), pp. 110–11.

20. See, e.g., *Bradwell v. Illinois*, 83 U.S. (16 Wall.) 130, 141 (1872) (Bradley, J., concurring).

21. Cass Sunstein, *The Partial Constitution* (Cambridge: Harvard University Press, 1993), p. 339.

22. David L. Kirp, Mark G. Yudof, and Marlene Strong Franks, *Gender Justice* (Chicago: University of Chicago Press, 1986), p. 29.

23. Sherry Ortner, "Is Male to Female as Nature Is to Culture?," in Michelle Zimbalist Rosaldo and Louise Lamphere, eds., *Woman, Culture, and Society* (Stanford: Stanford University Press,

Our problem arises because in the contemporary United States it is contested whether the first type of cultural data even exist: although some Americans find express misogyny banally common in our culture, others claim that it is rare and is itself stigmatized. The only one of Ortner's categories whose applicability is uncontroversially obvious is the third: no one can dispute women's almost complete exclusion from the top echelons of business, government, and organized religion. Nonetheless, some evidence of overt stigma must be noted. Whether or not women are devalued per se, our culture devalues many things *about* them, attaching low prestige to the traditionally female roles of wife, mother, nurse, and secretary and also regarding women's concerns as silly and trivial.[24] (When two men talk together, they have a discussion; when two women do, they gossip.)

The evidence of implicit devaluation, by contrast, is overwhelming. The stereotypes of women and of blacks of both sexes are similar: as Sandra Lee Bartky notes, both "have been regarded as childlike, happiest when they are occupying their 'place'; more intuitive than rational, more spontaneous than deliberate, closer to nature, and less capable of substantial cultural accomplishment."[25] Our language and institutions alike regard women as deviations from the prototypical norm of humanity. The common term that designates human beings in general is "man."[26] Catharine MacKinnon observes, "Men's physiology defines most sports, their needs define auto and health insurance coverage, their socially designed biographies define workplace expectations and successful career patterns, their perspectives and concerns define quality in scholarship, their experiences and obsessions define merit, their objectification of life defines art, their military service defines citizenship, their pres-

---

1974), p. 69. A more differentiated index may be necessary to compare with precision the status of women in different societies—see Naomi Quinn, "Anthropological Studies of Women's Status," 6 *Ann. Rev. Anthropol.* 181 (1977)—but Ortner's will do for present purposes.

24. Corresponding to this are the valorization of the incidents, such as power, of traditional male roles. See Richard D. Ashmore, "Sex Stereotypes and Implicit Personality Theory," in David L. Hamilton, ed., *Cognitive Processes in Stereotyping and Intergroup Behavior* (Hillsdale, N.J.: Lawrence Erlbaum, 1981), pp. 77–78.

25. Sandra Lee Bartky, *Femininity and Domination* (New York and London: Routledge, 1990), p. 23; see also William H. Chafe, *Women and Equality: Changing Patterns in American Culture* (Oxford: Oxford University Press, 1977), pp. 47–49.

26. Simone de Beauvoir, *The Second Sex*, H. M. Parshley trans. (New York: Vintage, 1974), p. xviii. This is, of course, only the tip of a very large iceberg. The English language reflects the assumption of female subordination and subservience in a multitude of ways. See generally Robin Lakoff, *Language and Woman's Place* (New York: Harper Torchbooks, 1975).

ence defines family, their inability to get along with each other—their wars and rulerships—defines history, their image defines god, and their genitals define sex."[27] Another indicator of implicit devaluation, not mentioned by Ortner, is the most insidious consequence of stigma: a tendency for the members of the stigmatized class to devalue themselves. "Both clinical and empirical evidence suggests that women tend to devalue their own performance, undervalue their labor, and to ascribe their failures to internal rather than external causes."[28] As for the symbolic device Ortner does mention, the attribution of defilement, I submit for your inspection one of the commonest of obscenities, the verb *fuck*. The term refers in a vulgar way to sexual intercourse, but as Robert Baker has observed, it also is ordinarily used to indicate harm, and the fact that this metaphor makes sense to us suggests that "we conceive of the female role in intercourse as that of a person being harmed (or being taken advantage of)."[29] The word implies "that intercourse is both the normal use of a woman, her human potentiality affirmed by it, and a violative abuse, her privacy irredeemably compromised, her selfhood changed in a way that is irrevocable, unrecoverable."[30]

Even certain ostensibly valorizing aspects of the culture carry insulting connotations. When women have been praised for their superior competence at performing traditionally female roles, for example, this valorization has been in terms of their usefulness to (male) society. An unmistakable element of contempt is implicit in "[t]he tendency to regard men as complete persons with potentials and rights, but to define women by the functions they serve in relation to men."[31] The idealized aspects of femininity also become the basis for what may be called *compound stigmatization*: the positing of a norm for a group that both carries degrading connotations and includes require-

27. Catharine MacKinnon, *Feminism Unmodified: Discourses on Life and Law* (Cambridge: Harvard University Press, 1987), p. 36.

28. Deborah L. Rhode, *Justice and Gender* (Cambridge: Harvard University Press, 1989), p. 182, and citations therein.

29. Robert Baker, " 'Pricks' and 'Chicks': A Plea for 'Persons,' " in Robert Baker and Frederick Elliston, eds., *Philosophy and Sex* (Buffalo: Prometheus, 1975), p. 60. See also Laurie Shrage, "Should Feminists Oppose Prostitution?," 99 *Ethics* 347 (1989).

30. Andrea Dworkin, *Intercourse* (New York: Free Press, 1987),p. 122. One can recognize the pervasiveness of this view in our culture without leaping to the conclusion that "intercourse itself is immune to reform" (ibid., p. 137), or that "intercourse itself determines women's lower status" (ibid., p. 138).

31. Susan Moller Okin, *Women in Western Political Thought* (Princeton: Princeton University Press, 1979), p. 304.

ments that some and perhaps most members of the already stigmatized group cannot satisfy. The valorization of female beauty, for example, not only reduces women to their bodies; it also devalues the bodies that most women have. As Bartky observes,

> The imperative not to neglect our appearance suggests that we can neglect it, that it is within our power to make ourselves look better—not just neater and cleaner, but prettier, and more attractive. What is presupposed by this is that we don't look good enough already, that attention to the ordinary standards of hygiene would be insufficient, that there is something wrong with us as we are. . . . Even within an already inferiorized identity (i.e., the identity of one who is principally and most importantly a body), I turn out once more to be inferior, for the body I am to be, never sufficient unto itself, stands forever in need of plucking or painting, of slimming down or fattening up, of firming or flattening.[32]

Compound stigmatization takes a variety of forms. The oppression that black women suffer, for example, is distinct in many ways from that experienced by white women. Nonetheless, there is a common denominator in the stigmatization of womanhood as such: whatever else one is, the status of being a woman means that one is a defective and inferior version of that.[33]

All this may be conceded, and yet it may be argued that traditional sex roles, such as the assignment of primary responsibility for child care to women, are no necessary part of this stigmatization. The argument over whether traditional notions of femininity stigmatize women arises out of the historical circumstance that an ideology of "separate spheres," now in decline, did valorize women's domestic role and did manage, for a good part of the nineteenth century, to improve considerably the social status of middle-class white women. (It appears to have compounded the stigmatization of working-class white women and of most women who were not white, since these women were unable to conform to the domestic ideal.)[34] In the eighteenth century, nothing about women or their social role was particularly admired, and their husbands' authority over them in all things was taken for granted. By 1850,

32. *Femininity and Domination*, p. 29; see also pp. 63–82.

33. See Catharine A. MacKinnon, "From Practice to Theory, or What is a White Woman Anyway?," 4 *Yale J. L. & Feminism* 13 (1991).

34. See Kimberle Crenshaw, "A Black Feminist Critique of Antidiscrimination Law and Politics," in David Kairys, ed., *The Politics of Law* (New York: Pantheon, rev. ed. 1990), pp. 195–218.

as Glenna Matthews observes, "all of this had changed. The home was so much at the center of the culture that historians speak of a 'cult' of domesticity in the early to mid-nineteenth century. Women in their homes were the locus of moral authority in society."[35] Greater material prosperity and a widespread concern for how to socialize the citizens of the new American republic created the possibility and inclination for a sentimental valorizing of both domestic life and the woman who presided over it. Middle-class white women continued to be confined to the home, but their role there came to be understood to be, and to make them, uniquely valuable. Domesticity, Carl Degler writes, "was an alternative to patriarchy, both in intention and in fact. By asserting a companionate role for women, it implicitly denied patriarchy."[36] The ideology of separate spheres eventually became a basis for women's claim to political influence as female reformers began to attack aspects of male culture, such as slavery, prostitution, and the consumption of alcohol, in the name of their own higher virtue.[37]

The domesticity movement was based on an important truth. The work traditionally assigned to women is, in fact, intrinsically valuable. Child care, in particular, is both more important and more personally rewarding than quite a lot of the work people get paid to do. Yet as the title of Matthews' study indicates, the domesticity movement ultimately failed, and the women who today identify themselves as "just housewives" tend not to be highly esteemed for that work by others or themselves. The significant functions that the home gained in the nineteenth century, Matthews argues, had disappeared by the early twentieth. The rise of Darwinism, which viewed the home as irrelevant to or a burden on human progress, had deprived it of its claim to political significance. Its capacity to be an arena for the display of peculiarly female skills had been eroded by the advent of ready-made foods (typically far inferior to the dishes they replaced) and the new home economics profession's denigration of traditional female skills. The religious significance of the home lost its salience together with religion itself. What remained was the

35. Glenna Matthews, "Just a Housewife": The Rise and Fall of Domesticity in America (New York and Oxford: Oxford University Press, 1987), p. 6.

36. Carl N. Degler, At Odds: Women and the Family in America from the Revolution to the Present (Oxford: Oxford University Press, 1980), p. 28. See also Nancy F. Cott, The Bonds of Womanhood: "Woman's Sphere" in New England, 1780–1835 (New Haven: Yale University Press, 1977).

37. See Matthews, "Just a Housewife," pp. 66–91; Degler, At Odds, pp. 279–327.

home's heightened emotional role. Here too, however, the growth of professional expertise—in this case, the science of psychology—undermined confidence in women's ability to perform their roles well.[38]

Matthews observes that domesticity was more valuable as a tactic than as a long-term strategy for valorizing women, because it deprived women of the natural rights case for their equal participation in society. The emphasis on women's special qualities created an opening for the claim that those qualities might be negative ones, such as lesser intellectual ability. No amount of ingenuity could portray some public issues, such as those involving foreign policy and warfare, as appropriate objects of domestic influence; in these areas, the ideology of domesticity always continued to legitimate women's exclusion from politics. And finally, "as the home changed, as domesticity declined in cultural value, woman's moral nature, identified as different by women themselves, could once again be trivialized as it had been in earlier periods of American history."[39]

Moreover, women's confinement to the home, however sentimentalized it might have been, entailed their exclusion from the activities that constituted first-class citizenship.[40] The consequence was precisely the rupture between expected and actual social identity that Goffman defines as the essence of stigma: the individual possesses "an attribute that makes [her] different from others in the category of persons available for [her] to be, and of a less desirable kind."[41] Bartky's description of modern women's oppression is applicable only in lesser degree to the golden age of domesticity: women were "caught in the double bind of society which both affirms my human status and at the same time bars me from the exercise of many of those typically human functions that bestow this status. To be denied an autonomous choice of self, forbidden cultural expression, and condemned to the immanence of mere bodily being is to be cut off from the sorts of activities that define what it is to be human."[42]

What remains today of the ideology of domesticity is the idea that women have greater responsibility than men for taking care of the home. That respon-

38. Matthews, *"Just a Housewife,"* p. 181.

39. Ibid., p. 90.

40. See generally Rogers M. Smith, " 'One United People': Second-Class Female Citizenship and the American Quest for Community," 1 *Yale J. L. & Hum.* 229 (1989).

41. Erving Goffman, *Stigma: Notes on the Management of Spoiled Identity* (Englewood Cliffs, N.J.: Prentice-Hall, 1963), p. 3.

42. Bartky, *Femininity and Domination*, p. 31.

sibility, however, is not valorizing, but stigmatizing: housework is now thought of as mindless and degrading, and child care is not accorded much prestige. Moreover, women's increasing presence in the workforce has exacerbated this devaluation. What was often an attempt to share in the higher esteem that attached to paid workers has not worked out that way for most women. As noted earlier, the fact that women, but not men, must combine paid work with housekeeping and child care responsibilities has tended to segregate women into part-time jobs without benefits or low-paid professions such as clerical work and elementary school teaching.[43] While they are thus handicapped in the workplace, where employers understand that women with children are less able than men to devote their full attention to their jobs, they are also often accused of neglecting their children when they work. (Of course, a special stigma is reserved for the woman who has no children.) In short, women tend to be stigmatized whether they are mothers or workers or both. Domesticity has become the basis for new forms of compound stigmatization. Often, to the extent that a woman mothers, she is regarded as a bad worker, and to the extent that she works, she is regarded as a bad mother. Whatever women do in either sphere stamps them with a badge of inferiority in the other. And women often internalize this sense of inferiority: they come to feel that it is their fault they cannot measure up to the demands of work and home, that a better woman, a "superwoman," would be able to "have it all." Whatever the value of the nineteenth-century ideal, however, for most women it is not possible to return to those days; the single-paycheck family in America is largely a thing of the past. The attraction of antifeminism to women today is rooted in nostalgia for the nineteenth century, when white, middle-class housewives had considerably better social status and security than they do now. Any claim that women are not in fact stigmatized is a comforting delusion.

Process Theory and Gender

This stigmatization of women infects and thereby deforms the process of political decision making. Ely places great weight on the facts that women now have the vote and that traditional gender stereotypes are now commonly questioned. Because any recently enacted statute that classifies on the basis of sex is

43. See Mason, *The Equality Trap*, pp. 123–44; Okin, *Justice, Gender, and the Family*, pp. 153–56.

the product of a democratic process in which women, who represent more than half the electorate, have had a fair chance to participate, Ely thinks such statutes should be upheld by the courts.[44] Here, as with race, however, Ely fails to notice all the places in which malign considerations contaminate the political process, and thus he is too easily satisfied that the taint has been eliminated from the process.

Diffuse majorities often have a harder time than insular minorities in organizing to influence legislative decisions.[45] Consciousness of one's group has been more difficult for women to achieve than for blacks, because women live closer to the group holding power over their lives than they do to each other. As a consequence, women have been less able than blacks to construct a counterculture to resist their ascribed, inferior status.[46] Living in a world that has been predominantly constructed by men, women have, far more than blacks, internalized the prevailing stereotypes, at least to the extent that they have believed that whatever problems they faced were the consequence of their individual situation rather than their social status as women.[47] Moreover, the critique of male dominance is not yet fully developed. Feminists continue to probe into areas of the law, such as abortion, pornography, and prostitution, whose relevance to sex equality was only beginning to be seen in the 1970s, when Ely formulated his process theory. It is therefore likely that sexism continues to infect government decision making in ways that have as yet not even been identified.

Ely has recognized women's traditional powerlessness and the obstacles it presented to their formation of political consciousness; this is why he would invalidate all but the most recent laws that disadvantage women. "To put on the group affected the burden of using its recently unblocked access to get the offending laws repealed would be to place in their path an additional hurdle that the rest of us do not have to contend with in order to protect

44. Ely, *Democracy and Distrust,* pp. 164–70.

45. See Bruce Ackerman, "Beyond *Carolene Products,*" 98 *Harv. L. Rev.* 713 (1985).

46. " 'Some of my best friends are Negro' got to be a parody of white hypocrisy, but *the* best friend of most men really is a woman, which eliminates the real hostility and fear that persists among the races." Ely, *Democracy and Distrust,* p. 257 n. 94. Ely does not recognize that this fact cuts both ways: the close association of men and women has produced a reluctance among women to criticize male privileges and female disadvantages. Often a woman knows that such views are likely to receive an unsympathetic hearing from the person whose sympathy she most desires.

47. See Chafe, *Women and Equality,* pp. 55–57.

ourselves—hardly an appropriate response to the realization that they have been unfairly blocked in the past."[48] But if sexism is indeed pervasive in our culture, then women face this additional hurdle at many sites other than statutes that expressly classify on the basis of sex. As noted earlier, for example, the structures of family life and work operate together, in ways so familiar that they seem neutral and unbiased, to disadvantage women in both spheres. There is a good deal that law could do to change the workplace, at least, in order to make it more accommodating of women; there is nothing neutral about "setting the norm by reference to the center of the male bell curve."[49] However, these same structures operate to exclude women from the political sphere by confining them to the sorts of lives that do not lead to the holding of elective office, and most (male) elected officials are not likely to have sex equality issues at the top of their priority list. "Voters, male and female alike, are typically confronted not with single-issue referenda but rather with packages of attitudes, packages we call candidates."[50] That such candidates have until recently almost always been male has usually attracted little remark.

The same kinds of unconscious prejudices that can inject racism into an ostensibly neutral decision-making process, as we saw in Chapter 1, are equally likely to bring sexism into the process. Compound stigmatization is rampant. A woman who fails to conform to the self-effacing maternal ideal can arouse irrational fear and anger in persons of both sexes that date back to their own early frustrations with their mothers.[51] Also, once again, rational as well as irrational forces contribute to prejudiced decision making: people naturally think in categories, and the categories associated with sex are learned at an early age and are not easily revised. It is taken for granted that "working mothers," for example, are a deviant case of the prototypical "mother," and from this it is inferred that they cannot "mother" as well as those who do not work.[52]

48. Ely, *Democracy and Distrust*, p. 169, asterisk note.

49. Christine A. Littleton, "Reconstructing Sexual Equality," 75 *Calif. L. Rev.* 1279, 1325 (1987).

50. Ely, *Democracy and Distrust*, p. 164.

51. See generally Dorothy Dinnerstein, *The Mermaid and the Minotaur: Sexual Arrangements and Human Malaise* (New York: Harper Colophon, 1977). For a striking illustration, see *Price Waterhouse v. Hopkins*, 490 U.S. 228 (1989).

52. See George Lakoff, *Women, Fire, and Dangerous Things: What Categories Reveal about the Mind* (Chicago: University of Chicago Press, 1987), pp. 79–84.

Similar assumptions can, of course, be found throughout the judicial system. The hidden psychic roots of lawmaking are particularly apparent in rape law, which for many years treated complainants with a suspicion unparalleled in the treatment of victims of any other crime. The presumption "that women often desire, and hence invent or invite, forced sex" appears to be "grounded in male rather than female fantasies,"[53] but it continues to play a large role in this area of the law.[54] As we shall see, the tendency of male judges to regard the work women do as trivial and valueless has had catastrophic consequences for women in divorce litigation. Illustrations could be multiplied.[55]

The ubiquity of unconscious sexism has sobering implications for process theory. These implications parallel those we noted in Chapter 1 in the case of racism. Not only does sexism continue to infect the decision-making process, but it infects it so pervasively that judicial review is incapable of remedying the problem. Indeed, it can often be found in the opinions of those judges who are most concerned about sex equality.[56] Whether we like it or not, the courts cannot police the democratic process in a way that relieves women of the burden of protecting themselves from the present effects of past sexism. All the courts can do is to try to abet the larger social movement to eradicate the cultural tendencies that distort decision-making processes to women's detriment. The requirements of process theory cannot be satisfied without a massive transformation of the cultural meaning of gender.

53. Rhode, *Justice and Gender*, p. 247.

54. See generally Susan Estrich, *Real Rape* (Cambridge: Harvard University Press, 1987).

55. See generally Rhode, *Justice and Gender*; for a briefer overview, see Nadine Taub and Elizabeth M. Schneider, "Women's Subordination and the Role of Law," in David Kairys, ed., *The Politics of Law* (New York: Pantheon, rev. ed. 1990), pp. 151–76.

56. See, for example, Justice Blackmun's remarkable concurrence in the result in *Michael M. v. Superior Court*, 450 U.S. 464, 481–87 (1981), in which he expressed discomfort with upholding a statutory rape conviction, given that the defendant's partner "appears not to have been an unwilling participant in at least the initial stages of the intimacies that took place" the night they had intercourse. Ibid., p. 483. Blackmun's footnote, which quotes the trial transcript, reveals that the woman had been kissing the defendant, but that she "let him do what he wanted to do" only after he punched her in the face two or three times. Her acquiescence, even under these circumstances, came close enough to consent to make Blackmun feel that the case was "an unattractive one to prosecute at all." Ibid., p. 485. Blackmun was one of the Supreme Court's leading defenders of sex equality, but he seems to have internalized the prevailing notion that any man who has been deliberately aroused by a woman cannot be guilty of rape.

The Supreme Court and Role Theory

Before taking up the question of what remedies this argument implies, something must be said about the Supreme Court's understanding of the problem of sex discrimination. The Court's views are of interest here not only because they shape the law but also because they are typical of more widespread beliefs. The Court evidently imagines that the central evil to be eradicated is the crudest of process defects: error. The vague verbal formula of *Craig v. Boren*, which held that to withstand challenge under the equal protection clause, sex-based classifications "must serve important governmental objectives and must be substantially related to the achievement of those objectives,"[57] has in practice been taken to mean that the central evil that sex discrimination law seeks to eradicate is "stereotyping." Stereotyping is surely part of the problem, but to make it the center of one's concerns implies that sex inequality is merely a mistake—either one of overgeneralizing on the basis of gender or one of forcing people into roles to which they are unsuited. As a result, the focus on stereotyping is ineffective in ameliorating gender inequality, and in some cases it has even exacerbated it.

"Legislative classifications which distribute benefits and burdens on the basis of gender carry the inherent risk of reinforcing stereotypes about the 'proper place' of women and their need for special protection," declares Justice Brennan's opinion for the Court in *Orr v. Orr*, which is typical of the Court's statements on sex discrimination.[58] Stereotypes, it appears, consist of two ideas: "the 'proper place' of women and their need for special protection." If the stereotype is normative, as where the state has a "preference for an allocation of family responsibilities under which the wife plays a dependent role," and "seek[s] . . . the reinforcement of that model among the State's citizens,"[59] then what is wrong with it is that this norm unnecessarily confines human potential. "No longer is the female destined solely for the home and the rearing of the family, and only the male for the marketplace and the world of ideas."[60] If the stereotype is empirical, then it is even clearer that what is wrong with it is the likelihood of error.[61] When the Court has focused its concerns spe-

57. 429 U.S. 190, 197 (1976).
58. 440 U.S. 268, 283 (1979).
59. Ibid., p. 279.
60. *Stanton v. Stanton*, 421 U.S. 7, 14–15 (1975).
61. This is consistent with the meaning of "stereotyping" one finds in Ely. According to Ely, the courts should be concerned when the legislature, because of its propensity to divide the world

cifically on empirical claims based on sex, it has placed great weight on the fact that those claims were false, or at least were true less often than the decision maker might have believed.[62]

According to the "stereotyping" theory, the rights that are violated by discrimination are wholly individualistic. Stereotyping is wrong because it forces unique human beings into roles they may find confining. If the stereotype is normative, it is not appropriate for the individual and her needs; if empirical, it is not true, or is true less often than the decision maker thought. The trouble with this theory is that this kind of injury is not inflicted only by cultural systems of ascriptive stigma, or even only by patterns of discrimination that fit Brest's criteria, noted earlier, of being "especially harmful" and having "little social utility." The complaint about empirical stereotyping could be made by a person who would do a civil service job very capably, but who cannot pass the exam.[63] The complaint about normative stereotyping could be made against any culture, because any social world limits human potential. "[T]here is no social world without loss—that is, no social world that does not exclude some ways of life that realize in special ways certain fundamental values. By virtue of its culture and institutions, any society will prove uncon-

---

into "we-they" categories, has enacted a law "involving a generalization whose incidence of counterexample is significantly higher than the legislative authority appears to have thought it was." *Democracy and Distrust*, p. 157. This misapprehension "will have distorted the entire decision. Just as we would want reconsidered any important decision that was made under the influence of an erroneous assumption about the relevant facts, so should we here." Ibid. He finds stereotyping to be the central concern of sex discrimination law: "[E]xaggerated stereotyping—typically to the effect that women are *unsuited* to the work of the world and therefore *belong* at home— has long been rampant throughout the male population and consequently in our almost exclusively male legislatures in particular." Ibid., p. 164, emphases added. The italicized words should reveal what is wrong with Ely's notion that "[s]tereotypes are not true or false (save only, I suppose, in the unlikely event that *no* member of the class in question possesses the attributed characteristic), but rather are distinguished by their relative incidence of counterexample." Ibid., p. 252 n. 70, emphasis in original. What would be a counterexample to the notion that women belong at home? This simply is not an empirical claim. To speak of counterexamples makes no sense. The Court at least addresses both normative and empirical stereotypes. Ely, characteristically, seizes one of the elephant's limbs and calls it the whole.

62. See, e.g., *City of Cleburne v. Cleburne Living Center, Inc.*, 473 U.S. 432, 441 (1985); *Mississippi University for Women v. Hogan*, 458 U.S. 718, 725–26 (1982); *Roberts v. United States Jaycees*, 468 U.S. 609, 625 (1984); *Frontiero v. Richardson*, 411 U.S. 677, 686 (1973) (plurality opinion). The problems that this exclusive focus on error has produced in the sex discrimination jurisprudence of both the left and right wings of the Court are explored more fully in Ann E. Freedman, "Sex Equality, Sex Differences, and the Supreme Court," 92 *Yale L.J.* 913 (1983).

63. Cf. Ely, *Democracy and Distrust*, pp. 155–56.

genial to some ways of life. But these social necessities are not to be mistaken for arbitrary bias or for injustice."[64] The injuries of stereotyping are of a kind that no society can avoid inflicting on its members. It therefore is unclear why they should arouse special concern in any particular case. More must be said about the patterning of errors, and the cultural sources of the pattern. We already encountered this problem in our examination in Chapter 1 of the color-blindness theory, to which the stereotyping theory bears some resemblance. Predictive pigeonholing is only part of the harm that stigmatizing cultural systems inflict, and not the most important part. (Also like the color-blindness theory, the stereotyping theory is unable to distinguish the victims of discrimination from the beneficiaries.[65] It has become notorious that in almost all the major sex discrimination cases decided by the Supreme Court, the prevailing plaintiff was a man.)[66]

The stereotyping approach is rooted in the role theory of gender, which holds that persons are forced into gendered patterns of behavior by cultural expectations that limit their human possibilities. The subordination of women is the result of role expectations that define them as helpmates with passive and expressive characters. The obvious solution that follows from this theory is to change the expectations. The trouble with role theory, R. W. Connell observes, is that the theory "focuses on attitudes and misses the realities that the attitudes are about. The political effect is to highlight the pressures that create an artificially rigid distinction between men and women, and to play down the economic, domestic and political power that men exercise over women."[67] This kind of mystification does not occur when other inequalities are considered: "we do not speak of 'race roles' or 'class roles' because the exercise of power in these areas of social life is more obvious to sociologists."[68]

64. John Rawls, "The Priority of Right and Ideas of the Good," 17 *Phil. & Pub. Aff.* 251, 265–66 (1988).

65. "Brennan's argument in *Frontiero* [*v. Richardson*, 411 U.S. 677 (1973), in which a plurality of the Court first endorsed heightened scrutiny of sex-based classifications] implies that, since *women* have been subject to disabilities, *sex* must be a suspect classification—whether a particular law injures women or benefits them. And that conclusion does not follow from that premise." Judith A. Baer, *Equality Under the Constitution: Reclaiming the Fourteenth Amendment* (Ithaca and London: Cornell University Press, 1983), p. 124.

66. See David Cole, "Strategies of Difference: Litigating for Women's Rights in a Man's World," 2 *L. & Inequality* 33, 34 n. 4 (1984) (collecting cases).

67. R. W. Connell, *Gender and Power* (Stanford: Stanford University Press, 1987), p. 50.

68. Ibid.

The Court's sex discrimination doctrine implies that the problem is all in people's minds. There is some truth to this—stigma is an idea—but it loses sight of the fact that this idea is externalized in the world and becomes objective. "Ultimately, then, role theory is not a social theory at all. It comes right up to the problem where social theory logically begins, the relationship between personal agency and social structure; but evades it by dissolving structure into agency."[69] The goal of the antidiscrimination project is a liberal one of freeing people from the subordinate roles traditionally prescribed for them,[70] but it is a remarkably deluded liberalism that imagines that all obstacles to liberty can simply be willed away. Like the other process theories we have examined, the Court's approach seizes on one part of the problem and calls it the whole.

The part that gets left out—the cultural apparatus that, without anyone deliberately making it happen, makes women an inferior class—is the part doing most of the harm to women today. As we noted in Chapter 2, it is poor strategy to attack a single part of a multifaceted problem as if it were the whole. To continue the metaphor of the blind men and the elephant, to attack only sex-based classification as if it were the whole of sexist oppression is taking the tail to be the whole elephant and trying to kill the elephant by whacking its tail with a hammer: one may do some damage to the tail, but one will soon find out about the rest of the elephant in a most unpleasant way.

The counterproductive tendencies of the present approach have been most notably revealed in the recent changes in divorce law. The most pressing sex equality issue the nation faces today is the massive impoverishment of single (usually divorced) women with children. The project of eliminating "stereotypes" from the law has not only prevented the law from addressing this state of affairs but threatens to make it worse if pushed to its logical conclusions.

By eschewing old notions of female dependency (thus eliminating normative stereotypes) and presuming that men and women are equally capable of supporting themselves after divorce (thus eliminating empirical stereotypes), courts have ignored the ways marriage itself economically disables women,

69. Ibid.
70. See Chafe, *Women and Equality*, p. 73; Linda Nicholson, *Gender and History: The Limits of Social Theory in the Age of the Family* (New York: Columbia University Press, 1986), pp. 55–56.

since wives rather than husbands tend to forgo educational and career opportunities for the sake of child-rearing.[71]

If the divorce rules do not give her a share of his enhanced earning capacity (through alimony and child support awards), and if divorce rules expect her to enter the labor market as she is, with few skills, outdated experience, no seniority, and no time for retraining, and if she continues to have the major burden of caring for young children after divorce, it is easy to understand why the divorced woman is likely to be much worse off than her former husband. Faced with expectations that she will be "equally" responsible for the financial support of their children and herself, she has been unequally disadvantaged by marriage and has fewer resources to meet those expectations.[72]

There is considerable controversy among scholars over whether the economic changes of the past several decades have benefited or harmed women.[73] What is less controversial is that the divorce rate has risen, that women's economic status tends to decline after divorce,[74] and that the formal equality analysis employed by the Court has proved incapable of recognizing—much less addressing—this problem. Under the present regime, if a marriage fails, the consequences will be catastrophic for the woman but not for the man. Because wives are aware of this fact, it is likely that they "take it into consid-

71. Susan Okin argues that the reason this happens is not that people prefer traditional patterns or find them efficient in terms of the family's total welfare. Rather, "the major reason that husbands and other heterosexual men living with wage-working women are not doing more housework is that *they do not want to, and are able, to a very large extent, to enforce their wills.*" *Justice, Gender, and the Family*, p. 153, emphasis in original; see pp. 153–55 and sources cited therein. See also Arlie Hochschild, *The Second Shift: Working Parents and the Revolution at Home* (New York: Viking, 1989).

72. Lenore Weitzman, *The Divorce Revolution* (New York: Free Press, 1985), p. xii. Richard Posner endorses a similar analysis of the opportunity costs marriage often imposes on women in *Economic Analysis of Law* (Boston: Little, Brown, 3d. ed. 1986), pp. 134–37.

73. Compare Weitzman, *The Divorce Revolution*, with Heidi I. Hartmann, "Changes in Women's Economic and Family Roles in Post–World War II United States," in Catharine Stimpson and Lourdes Beneria, eds., *Women, Households, and the Economy* (New Brunswick, N.J.: Rutgers University Press, 1987), pp. 33–64.

74. See Weitzman, *The Divorce Revolution;* Saul Hoffman and Greg Duncan, "What Are the Economic Consequences of Divorce?" 25 *Demography* 641 (1988). See also the studies cited in Okin, *Justice, Gender, and the Family*, pp. 206–8, and Mary Ann Glendon, *Abortion and Divorce in Western Law* (Cambridge: Harvard University Press, 1987), p. 180 n. 67.

eration in deciding how firm a stand to take on, or even whether to raise, important issues that are likely to be conflictual."[75] This asymmetrical power affects daily life in a variety of ways. In most cases, it means that women who are saddled with the double duty of domestic responsibilities and paid work, while their husbands provide little or no assistance with the former, are in no position to renegotiate these arrangements.[76] Sometimes it takes more severe forms, as when women stay with men who batter them and sexually abuse their children. In short, we continue to live in a society in which different people have different degrees of power, prestige, and wealth on the basis of a status of birth. This state of affairs can hardly be called the triumph of equality.

Solutions

Suppose we took it as axiomatic that the purpose of antidiscrimination law is to help destroy the cultural processes by which certain groups are constituted as having an inferior status. What follows for sex discrimination law? Our previous analysis suggests a need for action on three fronts, corresponding to the injuries of biased decision making, stigma, and group disadvantage. The law should try to purge decision-making processes of sexism; it should avoid stigmatizing women, and should discourage private actors from doing so; and it should try to end women's material disadvantages.

Let us begin with group disadvantage. Sex discrimination resembles race discrimination in that one of the most important means of combating it, albeit

75. Okin, *Justice, Gender, and the Family,* p. 168.

76. Hochschild has calculated that women on average work roughly fifteen hours longer each week than men. *The Second Shift,* pp. 3, 271–73. This lopsided division of labor is observed and internalized by children, with ominous implications for the future. One study found that in households in which fathers are wage workers and mothers are housewives, boys and girls do approximately the same amount of household work, though what they do is divided along gendered lines: boys mow lawns, girls wash dishes. In households in which mothers and fathers both work full-time, by contrast, girls do almost four times as much household work as their brothers. Mary Holland Benin and Debra A. Edwards, "Adolescents' Chores: The Difference between Dual- and Single-Earner Families," 52 *J. Marriage & Family* 361 (1990). Susan Okin argues that the most plausible interpretation of these statistics is that "the boys are learning the pattern of family injustice established by their own fathers and, like them, getting away with as little as possible. And the daughters are falling, at a young age, into an even more exaggerated version of the 'drudge-wife' model established by their mothers." Susan Moller Okin, "Political Liberalism, Justice, and Gender," 105 *Ethics* 23, 36 (1994).

one of the most difficult politically, is to remedy the material inequalities that are its product. Stigma and material disadvantage are mutually reinforcing; amelioration of either tends to ameliorate the other. Women's disadvantages manifest themselves in both the workplace and the home. I will begin with what can be done about the workplace.

Perhaps most important, measures should be taken to increase working women's wages. Many "women's jobs" do not pay a subsistence wage, and the consequence of this is the impoverishment of children as well as their mothers. Comparable worth is a strategy with notorious difficulties, but the basic problem it addresses cannot be ignored: most working women are economically disadvantaged because they are segregated in low-paid jobs. Comparable worth seems radical, but it does not attempt to end the segregation of the workplace; any effective strategy for doing that would probably require equally strong legal measures.

The single measure that would do the most to make more jobs accommodate women's needs, and thus to desegregate the workforce, would be to make jobs available on a part-time basis, with pay and benefits proportionate to full-time ones. Most women who work are part-time workers; most of these would not choose the jobs they have, and work part-time because they must balance work with family obligations, or because they cannot find adequate child care.[77] "Surveys of working women regularly verify that full-time working mothers believe a work week of twenty to thirty hours would greatly improve the frantic quality of their everyday lives, but they simply cannot afford the drastic cut in pay or they often cannot bear the kind of work that is available to them."[78] The division of the job market into high-paying full-time work and low-paying part-time work also creates powerful incentives for couples to follow the traditionally gendered division of labor even when they would prefer not to, since at least one of them *must* take a full-time job (which means a job that does not accommodate responsibility for small children) if they are to avoid poverty. The full-time nature of many jobs is, as Mason observes, "a tradition rather than a necessity";[79] many jobs involve piecework of the sort that could be done as efficiently by part-time as by full-time work-

---

77. Mason, *The Equality Trap*, p. 205.
78. Ibid., p. 225.
79. Ibid.

ers. The law could address these problems in a number of ways, ranging from direct regulation to tax incentives or laws that facilitate the formation of unions.

Another approach, one that would make full-time work more feasible for mothers and equal sharing of responsibilities more feasible for couples, would be for government to subsidize day care for children. "National surveys have revealed that between a quarter and a third of interviewed mothers express dissatisfaction with their childcare arrangements or cite inadequate childcare as a major barrier to employment."[80]

Some obstacles to women's economic opportunities probably cannot be solved by gentler means than outright hiring quotas. Trades that have traditionally been all-male are particularly inhospitable to women workers, who must often contend with the overt hostility of their coworkers. The obstacles to entry that this situation creates are subtle ones, of a kind not easily perceived or remedied by courts on a case-by-case basis.[81] In these jobs, equality of opportunity does not seem possible until those workplaces include enough women to form a common defense against the inhospitable environment that male resistance creates. Many women stay away from such jobs, despite their attractive salaries, because they know what the sole woman in such a workplace is likely to face.[82] The special problem that quotas raise in this context is that

80. Rhode, *Justice and Gender*, p. 130.

81. See, e.g., Kath Weston, "Production as Means, Production as Metaphor: Women's Struggle to Enter the Trades," in Faye Ginsburg and Anna Lowenhaupt Tsing, eds., *Uncertain Terms: Negotiating Gender in American Culture* (Boston: Beacon Press, 1990), pp. 137–51; Vicki Schultz, "Telling Stories About Women and Work: Judicial Interpretations of Sex Segregation in the Workplace in Title VII Cases Raising the Lack of Interest Argument," 103 *Harv. L. Rev.* 1749, 1832–39 (1990).

82. A good example of this kind of situation is presented in *Johnson v. Transportation Agency*, 480 U.S. 616 (1987), which involved a constitutional challenge to an affirmative action plan for women in promotions to positions previously held only by men. In the agency involved, no woman had ever held any of 238 skilled craft positions. When one finally was promoted to such a position, despite the many hurdles in the evelution process, a man who was passed over brought suit. When the case was tried in the district court, after a two-day trial the court found that the agency had never discriminated against women in hiring skilled craftsmen (as the workers doubtless were originally called). As Mary Becker has observed, this finding is "incredible," given the complete absence of women from such positions in the past. Even after the 1964 Civil Rights Act was passed, unions and employers continued routinely and overtly to exclude women from skilled positions. "Prince Charming: Abstract Equality," 1987 *Sup. Ct. Rev.* 201, 210. The hazing and harassment that the woman involved in *Johnson v. Transportation Agency* experienced was also

there can be no confidence that the proportion of women in the workforce matches the proportion interested in *this* job. All that is certain is that *some* women would prefer to do this work. A quota should aim not at proportional representation but at an end to the almost total exclusion of women. The numbers of women in the trades should at least be sufficient to create a "critical mass"[83] that can make those jobs less forbidding to the next woman who thinks about applying for one.

If women's subordination in the workplace and the home are mutually reinforcing, then the law should address both. Family law, and in particular the catastrophe that is present-day divorce law, cries out for reform. Many commentators have recommended changes, most notably that child support payments should be adequate to equalize the two households' standard of living after divorce and that women's contributions to their husbands' earning power should be recognized and compensated.[84] (There is also much to be said for Susan Okin's proposal that nonworking spouses should be entitled to receive half the income of a working spouse.)[85] There is now virtual unanimity among legal scholars that the present state of affairs is a scandal, yet years after the problem was first brought to light, little has been done. This inaction is perhaps the strongest evidence yet of the failure of the political process to represent women's interests.

The core of the problem, the source of women's numerous disadvantages, is the culture that devalues them. It is a sociological commonplace that economic class and status are independent variables; although they may influence each other, neither necessarily determines the other. The argument of Chapters 1 and 2 is as applicable to sex as to race: the accumulation of material disadvantages, the injury of stigma, and the contamination of the decision-

---

evidence of the obstacles that women face in these jobs. Yet none of this was noticed or given any weight by the trial court or either of the reviewing courts. (Not all of the sexist harassment she experienced found its way into the Supreme Court's account of the facts. See Susan Faludi, *Backlash: The Undeclared War Against American Women* [New York: Crown, 1991], pp. 388–93.) The characterization of the case (by *all* of the justices, majority and dissenters alike) as one of preferential treatment is revealing. It suggests that the courts cannot recognize discrimination when they see it, and that the only way to reliably police the decision-making process is to police its results.

83. Rhode, *Justice and Gender*, p. 188.

84. See ibid.; Glendon, *Abortion and Divorce in Western Law*; Weitzman, *The Divorce Revolution*.

85. See Okin, *Justice, Gender, and the Family*, pp. 180–82.

making process are all rooted in the culture that makes these things normal and acceptable. Here, too, the problem cannot be remedied unless the culture itself is transformed.

We are finally in a position to answer Richard Epstein's question, discussed in the Introduction: Why should airlines not be permitted to have exclusively female flight attendants if that is what their customers prefer? The answer is that customers' preferences, whether for female flight attendants or for male doctors, lawyers, and managers, are likely to reflect assumptions of male superiority and female inferiority. The idea that women are particularly well suited for the task of flight attendant, for example, is closely associated with the idea of separate, ascriptive spheres for men and women, and *that* idea, we have seen, is closely associated with the devaluation of women. The customers' preferences thus have a component that is malign, that denies respect for persons. If we respect preferences only because we respect persons, then we must withhold our respect from *these* preferences. It is likely that intervention in the market will eventually produce a transformation of the preferences of customers, who in time will (if they do not already) take male flight attendants for granted. The end of sex-specific hiring has already brought about some expansion of women's employment opportunities, and this contributes, in the long run, to an improvement in women's material conditions and thereby in their social status. Customers' preferences are being frustrated for the sake of a project whose worthy goal is the transformation of preferences.

If antidiscrimination law is to be defended as a means of public education, then it would be foolish to neglect the usefulness for the project of the educational system itself. As it happens, there is now voluminous evidence that the state is already busily shaping children's ideas about the status of men and women, but it is doing much of this work in ways that reinforce, rather than help to change, women's subordinate status. The inferiority of girls to boys has been implicit in both the content of public school curricula and the ways in which those curricula have been taught. Typically, in the instructional materials used in schools, females appear as main characters in stories and in illustrations far less often than males, females and males are usually presented in sex-stereotypical roles, females appear more often than males in derogatory roles, and male generic language is used.[86] Sexist lessons are also implicit in

86. See Kathryn P. Scott and Candace Garrett Schau, "Sex Equity and Sex Bias in Instructional

the composition of the typical faculty: almost all elementary school teachers are female, while almost all school superintendents and principals are male. "[A]s long as women are hired as elementary-school teachers in far greater proportions than men, and men are hired as school administrators in far greater proportions than women, schools will teach children that 'men rule women and women rule children.' "[87] Moreover, girls in elementary and secondary schools receive less attention from teachers than boys do, are asked less difficult and abstract questions, receive less praise and constructive feedback, and are given less instruction on how to do things for themselves.[88] "When teachers criticized boys, they tended to attribute boys' academic inadequacies to lack of effort; however, when teachers criticized girls, they seldom attributed intellectual inadequacy to lack of effort."[89]

Efforts should be made to stop this sexism in education, for the same reason that racism in the content and manner of education should be ended. But educational reform should have positive as well as negative goals. As Okin argues, children should be taught about "the present inequalities, ambiguities, and uncertainties of marriage, the facts of workplace discrimination and segregation, and the likely consequences of making life choices based on assumptions about gender."[90] The sexism of the culture they inherit will have profound effects on their lives, and they are entitled to be informed about this. As I argued in Chapter 2, to the extent that "sensitivity" describes an intellectual virtue, it is one that the schools ought to cultivate. Sander Gilman notes that although the tendency to stereotype people may be ineradicable, "education and study can expose the ideologies with which we structure our world, and perhaps help put us in the habit of self-reflection."[91]

Education as an instrument of social change is less troubling when applied

Materials," in Susan S. Klein, ed., *Handbook for Achieving Sex Equity Through Education* (Baltimore and London: Johns Hopkins University Press, 1985), pp. 218–32.

87. Amy Gutmann, *Democratic Education* (Princeton: Princeton University Press, 1987), p. 113. For statistics on the disproportion, see citations therein.

88. David Sadker and Myra Sadker, "Sexism in American Education: The Hidden Curriculum," in Leslie R. Wolfe, ed., *Women, Work, and School: Occupational Segregation and the Role of Education* (Boulder, Colo.: Westview Press, 1991), pp. 58–59.

89. Ibid., p. 60.

90. *Justice, Gender, and the Family*, p. 177.

91. Sander L. Gilman, *Difference and Pathology: Stereotypes of Sexuality, Race, and Madness* (Ithaca and London: Cornell University Press, 1985), p. 12.

to children than when it is used to change the beliefs of sometimes unwilling adults. Direct reeducation of adults is usually unnecessary. In most cases, there will be mediating structures between the cultural apparatus and women's injuries, so that law can prevent those injuries by attacking the structures rather than the ideas. Sometimes, however, there will be no such mediating structures. In cases in which the relevant decision maker stands in a sufficiently direct relation to his (and it generally is *his*) victim, mandatory reeducation appears to be the only way to prevent him from abusing his power.

Sexual harassment is one of the clearest manifestations of the way in which traditional notions of women's inferior status continue to handicap them at work: women, more than men, have traditionally been thought of as essentially sexual beings, and this status seems to exclude the possibility of women fulfilling the asexual work-related ideals of competence and rationality.[92] The result is that many men, who are typically found in positions of authority over the women with whom they work, appear to feel authorized to treat those women as sexual objects. The only way to make the job opportunities of women equal to those of men appears to be to reeducate the potential harassers about what behavior is normal and acceptable. Since sexual harassment was recognized as actionable discrimination, this step has in fact been taken: many employers, fearing liability, have instituted sensitivity training for their employees.[93] Similar measures have been adopted to deal with the sexism of husbands who feel entitled to batter their wives: prosecution is often suspended on the condition that they attend batterers' workshops. (Such training may also be necessary to reduce gender bias in judicial decision making.)[94] The coercive reshaping of workplace norms, which sometimes extends to the

92. See Barbara A. Gutek, "Understanding Sexual Harassment at Work," 6 *Notre Dame J. L. & Pub. Pol'y* 335, 352–57 (1992).

93. Employers' willingness to do so appears to increase as the rules of law become more favorable to plaintiffs. See Jay Romano, "Sex Harassment on the Job Now Easier to Prove," *New York Times*, Sept. 12, 1993, sec. 13 (New Jersey Weekly), p. 1; Kingsley R. Browne, "Title VII as Censorship: Hostile-Environment Harassment and the First Amendment," 52 *Ohio St. L. J.* 481 (1991). Note, once again, the ambiguity of the word "sensitivity": whether or not people can be taught to be morally virtuous, they surely can be taught to behave appropriately.

94. See, e.g., Lynn Hecht Schafran, "Women in the Courts Today: How Much Has Changed," 6 *Law & Inequality* 27 (1988). The Ninth Circuit Gender Bias Task Force, after finding pervasive problems of gender bias in the courts, recommended that educational programs on the effects of gender be instituted as a regular and routine part of conferences, workshops, and seminars for lawyers, judges, and court personnel. See *The Effects of Gender in the Courts: The Final Report of the Ninth Circuit Gender Bias Task Force* (July 1993), Executive Summary, p. 26.

suppression of certain speech, raises important liberal objections that I discuss in Chapters 5 and 6.

Women should be free to choose traditional roles if they wish to do so, but care must be taken that they actually *choose* them rather than being pressured into them. This is why "liberal" solutions that disfavor interventions into the culture in fact fail to be liberal: they fail to see the nature of the obstacles to free choice.[95] There is no reason to expect an end anytime soon to the old debate whether the cure for women's subordination is to erase separate spheres or to valorize traditional femininity. In light of the ways in which women's powerlessness and devaluation reinforce one another, however, neither solution appears to be workable without the other. "If [domestic] work is despised, it will be performed by someone whose sex, class, or race—perhaps all three— consign her to an inferior status."[96] Full-time mothers will continue to be vulnerable unless courts stop assigning zero value to the work they do. Women with paying jobs will continue to be second-class workers unless those jobs accommodate, and men assume their fair share of, traditional female tasks. These things will not happen unless those tasks are thought of more highly than they are now. Yet women cannot valorize their activities, traditional or otherwise, unless they are empowered. "We may not be sure about the role gender ought to play in the good society, but we can share a sense of the role gender ought not to play."[97] Working women and full-time housewives ought to be able to unite to change a culture that devalues, disempowers, and ignores the needs of both.

The project's egalitarian goals are, as a general matter, best attained by

95. This is the trouble with David L. Kirp, Mark G. Yudof, and Marlene Strong Franks, *Gender Justice* (Chicago: University of Chicago Press, 1986). See Lucinda M. Finley, "Choice and Freedom: Elusive Issues in the Search for Gender Justice," 96 *Yale L. J.* 914 (1987) (reviewing *Gender Justice*). Another work that purports to be concerned with liberty, Michael Levin, *Feminism and Freedom* (New Brunswick and Oxford: Transaction, 1987), acknowledges the cultural obstacles to free choice but approves of them and so is less liberal than it claims to be. Levin thinks that men and women are biologically predisposed to (and are therefore happiest in) traditional roles, and that norms steering women into those roles therefore do them no real harm. However, he gives no consideration to the alternative hypothesis, that women's revealed preferences are adaptations to a limited set of opportunities—limited by no choice of the women themselves—and would change in response to a broader set of opportunities. The weight of the evidence supports the latter hypothesis. When nontraditional careers are genuine options for women, many women pursue those options. See Schultz, "Telling Stories About Women and Work," pp. 1815–43.

96. Matthews, *"Just a Housewife,"* p. xiv.

97. Rhode, *Justice and Gender*, p. 276.

liberal means: if people have the power freely to shape their lives as they see fit, they will do away with the cultural system that subordinates them without needing much direct help from the state. This, however, brings us to the one realm in which courts should have an unconstrained authority to intervene when they detect invidious social meanings at work. As I argued in Chapter 2, invidious cultural meaning may or may not be sufficient reason to outlaw a practice, but it is ample reason for invalidating a statute. Whatever else the law should do about the devaluation of women, it should not itself contribute to that devaluation. The fact that a meaning that is arguably stigmatizing is *imposed* on women should heighten suspicion: if this role were really valorizing and not stigmatizing, why would it be necessary to force it on people? One of the best indicators of what roles are stigmatized in a culture is the revealed preferences of those who live in it: if most people are anxious to avoid a role, it is likely that the occupants of that role are not particularly highly thought of.[98]

The Court has been surprisingly deferential toward coercive statutes whose stigmatizing cultural meaning should have been obvious. *Michael M. v. Superior Court*[99] involved a constitutional challenge to California's statutory rape law, which criminalized sexual intercourse with a female (but not with a male) under the age of eighteen. The seventeen-year-old male plaintiff had been convicted under the statute after having sexual relations with a sixteen-year-old female. The Court upheld the statute, because it served the important state interest of preventing illegitimate teenage pregnancy.[100] Justice Rehnquist's majority opinion concluded that because the harmful consequences of teenage pregnancy fall exclusively on the female, the legislature acted within its authority by punishing only the participant who, by nature, suffers few of the

---

98. Some people do evidently believe that restricting women's options will contribute to their valorization. Many pro-lifers, for example, feel that abortion is wrong "because *by giving women control over their fertility,* it breaks up an intricate set of social relationships between men and women that has traditionally surrounded (and in the ideal case protected) women and children." Kristin Luker, *Abortion and the Politics of Motherhood* (Berkeley: University of California Press, 1984), p. 162; emphasis in original. It is true, as we have seen, that the liberalization of sex roles has occurred simultaneously with the devaluation of women, but it is not true that liberalization has caused devaluation. Whatever causal relationship exists appears to work in the other direction: women have left the home in an effort to improve their status. Under these circumstances, forcibly returning women to their traditional roles will just make things worse.

99. 450 U.S. 464 (1981).

100. Ibid., at 468–69.

consequences of his conduct. This is at best a "post hoc rationalization"[101] for a law whose real purpose was to protect the chastity of young females. The law's likely effect was "legitimating stereotypes of male aggressiveness and female vulnerability, as well as double standards of morality that traditionally have served to repress women's sexual expression."[102] It fails both versions of Lawrence's cultural meaning test—that which scrutinizes decision-making inputs and that which scrutinizes outputs. When an arguably subordinating practice is enforced by coercion, the statute imposing such coercion should, absent powerful justification, be found unconstitutional.[103]

The symmetrical treatment of discrimination against both sexes should be preserved at least this far: neither should be coerced into the behavior traditionally deemed appropriate for that sex. Men should not be punished for "effeminate" activity; efforts by the state to maintain traditional masculinity are the functional equivalent of state efforts to foster racial pride among whites. The same restriction should apply to patterns of private action, at least when they are so pervasive as to be inescapable. And this is the way to think about the hotly contested issue of gay rights, to which I now turn.

101. Colker, "Anti-Subordination Above All," p. 1044.

102. Rhode, *Justice and Gender*, p. 102.

103. For similar reasons, there should be grave doubt, on sex equality grounds, of the constitutionality of restrictions on abortion. See my "Forced Labor: A Thirteenth Amendment Defense of Abortion," 84 *Nw. U. L. Rev.* 480 (1990).

4

Lesbians and Gay Men

It was a fairly straightforward task, in the last chapter, to show that discrimination based on sex was within the ambit of the antidiscrimination project. The major moves from the argument for the elimination of racism had only to be repeated. Sex, like race, is an ascribed characteristic, therefore unrelated to desert, so that once it was shown that American culture pervasively devalues women, the conclusion readily followed that this devaluation was unjustified. Because this unjustified devaluation biased government decision making and the distribution of goods—in each case to women's disadvantage—the extension of the project to women could be justified on grounds similar to those that are relevant in the core case of blacks. The case of lesbians and gay men[1] is more complicated.

It has become routine in discussions of invidious discrimination to speak of race, sex, and sexual orientation in the same breath, as if the same considerations weighed against discrimination based on any of these characteristics. This elides the objection that homosexuality is not a visible and immutable characteristic, but a desire that persons are free to hide; a desire, moreover, for behavior that persons are free to engage in or not. Because the Supreme Court has sometimes suggested that the immutability of a characteristic is

---

1. For the sake of brevity, I shall sometimes refer simply to "homosexuals" or "gays," but when I do this I mean to describe persons of both sexes who engage in or desire to engage in sexual intercourse with persons of the same sex. Except in those few passages where I discuss the immutability of exclusively homosexual orientation, the term includes bisexuals, who are typically stigmatized indiscriminately with those whose orientation is exclusively homosexual. As I noted in the Introduction, I have nothing to say about what "really" constitutes gay identity. My inquiry is focused rather on the false, unjustifiably stigmatizing meanings that have attached to gay identity.

relevant to the question of whether it should be deemed a suspect classification,[2] some writers have attempted to prove that homosexuality is as immutable as race or sex.[3] This is a vulnerable argument. The etiology of sexual desire remains uncertain, and the mutability of heterosexuality or homosexuality varies from one person to another.[4] More important is the fact that sexual activity, unlike desire, is a behavior that human beings are free to control.[5] There are many impulses that society properly requires people to control, even if they cannot help feeling those impulses. It may be true that it is difficult and uncomfortable to refrain from the kind of sexual activity that one finds satisfying, but this argument is hardly conclusive. We are not persuaded when it is made on behalf of rape or pedophilia.[6] By contrast, if a type of behavior

2. See, e.g., *Lyng v. Castillo,* 477 U.S. 635, 638 (1986); *Frontiero v. Richardson,* 411 U.S. 677, 686 (1972) (plurality opinion). See also chapter 2, notes 22 and 26.

3. See, e.g., Richard Delgado, "Fact, Norm, and Standard of Review—The Case of Homosexuality," 10 *U. Dayton L. Rev.* 575, 583–85 (1985); Kenneth Lasson, "Civil Liberties for Homosexuals: The Law in Limbo," 10 *U. Dayton L. Rev.* 645, 656–57 (1985); Harris M. Miller II, "An Argument for the Application of Equal Protection Heightened Scrutiny to Classifications Based on Homosexuality," 57 *S. Cal. L. Rev.* 797, 817–21 (1984).

4. See Janet Halley, "The Politics of the Closet: Towards Equal Protection for Gay, Lesbian, and Bisexual Identity," 36 *U.C.L.A. L. Rev.* 915, 932–46 (1989); Janet Halley, "Sexual Orientation andthe Politics of Biology: A Critique of the Argument from Immutability," 46 *Stan. L. Rev.* 503 (1994).

5. See, e.g., *Jacobson v. Jacobson,* 314 N.W.2d 78, 81 (N.D. 1981) ("Sandra's homosexuality may, indeed, be something which is beyond her control. However, living with another person of the same sex is not").

6. Richard Mohr emphasizes that people do not ordinarily set out to become gay and then do so. "Typically, gay persons-to-be simply find themselves having homosexual encounters and yet at least initially resisting quite strongly the identification of being a homosexual. Such a person even very likely resists having such encounters, but ends up having them anyway. Only with time, luck, and great personal effort does the person gradually come, if she does, to accept her orientation, to view it as a given material condition of life, coming as materials do with certain capacities and limitations. The person then begins to act in accordance with her orientation and its capacities, seeing its actualization as a requisite for an integrated personality and as a central component of personal well-being. As a result, the experience of coming out *to oneself* has for gays the basic structure of a discovery, not the structure of a choice." *Gays/Justice: A Study of Ethics, Society, and Law* (New York: Columbia University Press, 1988), p. 40. The trouble with this argument is that even if "one does not choose the gender (or genders) which excite one" (ibid., p. 41), one is responsible for the actions one takes. Sexual intercourse is not a reflex matter, like blinking at bright lights. One doesn't "end up having" sexual encounters without at some point deciding to do so, and to "act in accordance with her orientation and its capacities" is a deliberate project undertaken in conscious pursuit of "integrated personality" and "personal well-being."

is morally permissible and harmless, and a person wants to engage in that behavior, interference needs greater justification than the mere fact that she could choose to act otherwise. Why should she have to?

Yet immutability is not entirely irrelevant. In the first place, what is stigmatized is not only homosexual activity but homosexual desire. The stigma cannot simply be explained in terms of the immorality of the desire. In 1976, presidential candidate Jimmy Carter told an interviewer, "I've looked on a lot of women with lust. I've committed adultery in my heart many times. This is something God recognizes I will do—and I have done it—and God forgives me for it."[7] The statement caused a minor flap at the time, but Carter went on to win the election. Imagine the reaction if he had said that he had looked on a lot of men with lust.

Moreover, unless there is some good reason for thinking homosexual conduct to be wrong, then the immutability of homosexuality, at least for those persons who are attracted solely to persons of the same sex, makes the analogy with race and sex a persuasive one. If sexual gratification is important to happiness, and if some persons can only get such gratification from persons of their own sex, then the prohibition or stigmatization of homosexual intercourse imposes a significant burden on those people. If, as much evidence indicates, sexual orientation is already established in early childhood,[8] then like blacks and women, gays face severe disadvantages that they have done nothing to deserve. The penalization of harmless behaviors is an arbitrary infringement on liberty, but in most cases no equality issue is involved, because no one group is singled out to bear the cost of that infringement. Homosexuality appears to be different. This, perhaps, is why so many people think that immutability is relevant to the question whether the stigmatization of homosexuality is justifiable.[9]

The question of relevant reasons is central to the case of lesbians and gay men. To show that gays are stigmatized is easy: unlike sexism or racism,

7. Quoted in Jules Witcover, *Marathon: The Pursuit of the Presidency, 1972–1976* (New York: Signet, 1978), p. 603.

8. See Alan P. Bell, Martin S. Weinberg, and Sue Kiefer Hammersmith, *Sexual Preference: Its Development in Men and Women* (Bloomington: Indiana University Press, 1981).

9. One *New York Times*/CBS News poll found a strong split on the question of the acceptability of homosexuality between those who view homosexuality as a choice and those who do not. "Of those who consider it a choice, only 18 percent rated it as acceptable, compared with 57 percent of those who regard it as something gay men and lesbians cannot change." Jeffrey Schmalz, "Poll Finds an Even Split on Homosexuality's Cause," *New York Times*, March 5, 1993, p. A14.

there is no serious dispute about whether prejudice against gays is pervasive in the United States. This prejudice is often reflected quite overtly in political decisions affecting them, as when legislation to monitor hate crimes against gays, or to reduce the spread of AIDS through education about safe sex, has been opposed on the grounds that these measures might misleadingly imply approval of homosexuality. Unlike blacks or women, gays do not disproportionately suffer poverty. Their material disadvantages are subtler, but numerous: exposure to random violence of a particularly sadistic kind,[10] discrimination, exclusion from the economic benefits that are accorded to married heterosexuals.[11] But the principal disadvantage of which gays complain is stigma, and this stigma has different effects than it does in the cases of race and sex. Although it is possible to remain celibate and hide one's homosexuality, there remain ways in which this stigma, like racial and sexual ones, is inescapable. The stigmatization of homosexuality typically has destructive effects on even the closeted gay's self-respect that are probably more severe than the analogous damage done by racism and sexism. Both blacks and women know their status at birth, and their parents typically begin teaching them to cope with that status early in childhood. For gays it is different: one typically does not discover one's sexual orientation until adolescence, by which time one is likely to have deeply internalized the prevailing stigmatization of homosexuality. Internalized self-hatred appears to be a much more profound problem for homosexuals than for blacks or women. A federal task force on youth suicide noted that because "gay youth face a hostile and condemning environment, verbal and physical abuse, and rejection and isolation from families and peers," young gays are two to three times more likely than other young people to attempt and to commit suicide.[12]

Nonetheless, the oppression of gays differs from that of blacks or women in that the characteristic form of gay oppression has been the closet. The main effect of extending the employment discrimination laws to protect gays would

10. See Kendall Thomas, "Beyond the Privacy Principle," 92 *Colum. L. Rev.* 1431, 1462–69 (1992).

11. See Note, "The Legality of Homosexual Marriage," 82 *Yale L. J.* 573, 578–80 (1973).

12. "Report of the Secretary's Task Force on Youth Suicide," U.S. Department of Health and Human Services, 1989, quoted in Eve Sedgwick, *Tendencies* (Durham, N.C.: Duke University Press, 1993), p. 154. The report recommended an "end [to] discrimination against youths on the basis of such characteristics as sexual orientation." A few months after the report was published, Dr. Louis Sullivan, secretary of the Department of Health and Human Services, repudiated this section of the report.

not be to give them jobs and housing from which they have been excluded—they are already everywhere—but to allow them to stop hiding their sexuality, as they often must in order to keep their jobs and housing.

The availability of the closet does not diminish the demand for justification.[13] The closet is equally available for religious dissenters,[14] but it is clear that government may not take actions that, even indirectly, stigmatize certain religions. Justice O'Connor relies on something like Lawrence's cultural meaning test, which we discussed in Chapter 2, to decide whether government actions violate the First Amendment. "The Establishment Clause prohibits government from making adherence to a religion relevant in any way to a person's status in the community."[15] For this reason, the government may not take actions that send a symbolic message that nonadherents to any particular religion are "outsiders, not members of the political community."[16] This criterion recognizes a prima facie right to recognition as a full member of the community. If that right is violated because of the victim's religion, is the violation based on something unchosen? There is reason to believe that it is. A person's religion is ordinarily discovered rather than chosen; if a choice is made at all, it is usually made by one's parents. The

13. The Vatican's Congregation for the Doctrine of the Faith, for example, has argued the contrary. "As a rule, the majority of homosexually oriented persons who seek to lead chaste lives do not publicize their sexual orientation. Hence the problem of discrimination in terms of employment, housing, etc., does not usually arise." "Some Considerations Concerning the Response to Legislative Proposals on the Non-Discrimination of Homosexual Persons," 22 *Origins: CNS Documentary Service*, Aug. 6, 1992, p. 176.

14. Striking parallels between the ways in which religious identity and sexual identity have been managed and policed are implicit in Janet E. Halley's similar approaches to the history of repression of both kinds of identity. Compare "Equivocation and the Legal Conflict Over Religious Identity in Early Modern England," 3 *Yale J. L. & Hum.* 33 (1991), and "Heresy, Orthodoxy, and the Politics of Religious Discourse: The Case of the English Family of Love," 15 *Representations* 98 (Summer, 1986), with "Misreading Sodomy: A Critique of the Classification of 'Homosexuals' in Federal Equal Protection Law," in Julia Epstein and Kristina Straub, eds., *Body Guards: The Cultural Politics of Gender Ambiguity* (New York and London: Routledge, 1991), pp. 351–77.

15. *Lynch v. Donnelly,* 465 U.S. 668, 687 (1984) (O'Connor, J., concurring); see also p. 692.

16. Ibid., p. 688. Curiously, the context in which Justice O'Connor has advocated the use of this test may be the one in which it is least promising, since the cultural meaning of arguably religious messages is especially likely to be ambiguous and contested. See Steven D. Smith, "Symbols, Perceptions, and Doctrinal Illusions: Establishment Neutrality and the 'No Endorsement' Test," 86 *Mich. L. Rev.* 266 (1987). There are, however, unambiguous cases in which the stigmatizing meaning is widely understood. Laws that disadvantage gays generally fall into that category.

individual can still choose not to practice that religion, but religious practice may be quite important to the individual's sense of well-being and even sense of identity.[17] To force one group of citizens, solely on the basis of their unchosen religious beliefs, to choose between abandoning these important practices and being branded as outsiders seems as arbitrary as to stigmatize them because of their race or sex. The argument we have just made will work equally well with sexual orientation: in both cases, one class of persons is required, on the basis of unchosen desires, to choose between giving up or hiding activities that are very important to them or being outcasts in the community.

This is not the place to refute the various justifications for the stigmatization of homosexuality that are on offer. That has been done elsewhere.[18] If the stigma is unjustified but widespread, then it is morally equivalent to racism or sexism. The only arguments for the stigma that seem unanswerable are the religious ones, and by their terms they are not open to philosophical critique. For example, many Americans are Christians or Jews who interpret the Bible as forbidding homosexual conduct, and that settles the issue for them.[19]

It should not be surprising that the project conflicts with some people's religious beliefs. Slavery was once defended by ministers who taught that blacks had inherited the curse of Ham, and that their enslavement was therefore the will of God. As a practical matter today, religious objections to the antidiscrimination project's application to gays matter more than such objections to its application to blacks, because the former are more widely held. The conflict of principle between the free exercise of religion and the antidiscrimination project is, however, the same in both cases.[20] The problem is the same as that which arises whenever any secular project of social reform arouses religious objections. The project of seeing to it that all children get

17. A religious person would probably describe the benefits of religion quite differently, but I am trying to articulate those benefits in terms cognizable by a secular state.

18. See, e.g., Michael Ruse, *Homosexuality: A Philosophical Inquiry* (Oxford: Basil Blackwell, 1988); Stephen Macedo, "Homosexuality and the Conservative Mind," 84 *Georgetown L. J.* (forthcoming 1996); Andrew Sullivan, *Virtually Normal: An Argument About Homosexuality* (New York: Knopf, 1995); Gregory M. Herek, "Myths About Sexual Orientation: A Lawyer's Guide to Social Science Research," 1 *L. & Sexuality* 133 (1991); Andrew Koppelman, "Homosexuality, Natural Law, and Morality," in Robert P. George and Andrew Koppleman, eds., *Homosexuality and Natural Law*, forthcoming.

19. See, e.g., Anita Bryant, *The Anita Bryant Story* (Old Tappan, N.J.: Revell, 1977), pp. 16–18; Jerry Falwell, *Listen, America!* (Garden City, N.Y.: Doubleday, 1980), pp. 181–86.

20. This conflict is explored by Robert Cover, "Foreword: Nomos and Narrative," 97 *Harv. L. Rev.* 4 (1983).

decent medical care is a purely secular one that does not seem to entail any particular religious view; but if a family of Christian Scientists are commanded by the state to allow a life-saving medical operation to be performed on their child although their religion forbids it, they are in effect being told that their religious beliefs are false. If religious belief can justify injury here, it can justify it in many other places. It remains possible, of course, to say that while religion cannot justify *conduct*, the individual has a right to hold whatever *beliefs* she finds persuasive, even if these unjustly stigmatize others. But if the antidiscrimination project seeks to eradicate or marginalize the meanings, practices, and institutions that unjustifiably stigmatize and disadvantage some persons, then the project must try to change racist religious beliefs if these are held by a substantial part of the population. This is one illustration of a broader liberal objection to the project. The antidiscrimination project is centrally concerned with changing certain beliefs that are held by the citizens, but liberals tend to think that the beliefs of the citizens, and especially their religious beliefs, are not a legitimate concern of the state. This objection is a weighty one, and will be considered in some detail in Chapter 5.[21] Here I will simply say that, although religious freedom is a limitation on what the state can do in furtherance of the project, the project must press fairly hard against certain religious beliefs. Inevitably, state efforts to reduce any kind of discrimination will implicitly tell those whose religious beliefs sanction such discrimination that their religious beliefs are false and that they ought to change them.

The problem is particularly apparent here because in order to determine whether the project is appropriately extended to sexual orientation, it is inescapably necessary to take a position on the religious question. Advocates of gay rights must, if they seek full social acceptance of lesbians and gay men, persuade most of those whose religious beliefs condemn homosexuality that those beliefs are false. Ample tools for such a job are available within religious discourse: alternative biblical exegeses, or a more general argument that God cannot be as cruel as the traditionalist view seems to indicate. Both have persuaded some. But these may not succeed. To the extent that they do not,

---

21. Too, if the antidiscrimination project seeks to marginalize stigma based both on religion and on sexual orientation, it will end up in a dilemma with respect to those religions that teach that homosexuality is sinful. This dilemma is a real one, which has no entirely satisfactory solution; proponents of the antidiscrimination project must therefore contemplate with some relief the tendencies within some religions to modify or relax traditional teachings with respect to homosexuality.

the overlapping consensus that supports the antidiscrimination project simply stops overlapping. Those for whom relevant reasons do support the stigmatization of homosexuality simply will not agree that the antidiscrimination project is appropriately extended to gays, and they will insist on their right to stigmatize gays. A liberal state cannot overtly suppress stigmatizing ideas, but there is much that it can do to discourage them and reduce their incidence.

Heterosexism and Sexism

In the remainder of this chapter, I will develop a somewhat unfamiliar argument for including lesbians and gay men within the antidiscrimination project. Gay rights is typically thought of as involving either the right of privacy or the right of a historically disadvantaged group to be free of discrimination. Both of these ways of viewing the issue point to serious injustices that deserve to be remedied, but they capture only part of the picture. A satisfactory account of the stigmatization of gays would "record and respond to the question, 'In whose lives is homo/heterosexual definition an issue of continuing centrality and difficulty?' "[22] The case for gay rights is a powerful one for reasons that go well beyond the interests of gays themselves. The effort to end discrimination against gays should be understood as a necessary part of the larger effort to end the subordinate status of women, because the function of the stigmatization of homosexuality is to preserve the hierarchy of males over females.[23]

My claim is that the taboo against homosexuality is not irrational but serves a function similar to that of the taboo against miscegenation.[24] Both taboos

22. Eve Kosofsky Sedgwick, *Epistemology of the Closet* (Berkeley: University of California Press, 1990), p. 40.

23. This argument has aroused concern insofar as it "conveys the unfortunate suggestion that [the prohibition of homosexuality is] important only insofar as it bears upon the relations between men and women, or upon women's rights to the control of her body. By collapsing questions of sexuality into the 'more important' realms of gender, homosexuality is allowed salience insofar as it seems assimilable to heterosexuality, insofar as same-sex relations are taken to be no different from cross-sex ones." Jonathan Goldberg, *Sodometries: Renaissance Texts, Modern Sexualities* (Stanford: Stanford University Press, 1992), pp. 14–15. The point of the present argument is, however, not "to seek to hierarchize oppressions" (ibid., p. 14), but to map the ways in which they are related.

24. I have developed this analogy at greater length in two articles, "Why Discrimination Against Lesbians and Gay Men Is Sex Discrimination," 69 *N.Y.U. Law Review* 197 (1994), and "The

police the boundary that separates the dominant from the dominated in a social hierarchy that rests on a condition of birth. In the same way that the prohibition of miscegenation preserved the polarities of race on which white supremacy rested, the prohibition of homosexuality preserves the polarities of gender on which rests the subordination of women.

One might have attacked miscegenation laws by asserting that they infringe the right to privacy, or that they impermissibly "legislate morality," or that "miscegenosexuals"[25] are a special group, born into that class and unable to change their preferences, who therefore do not deserve the social and legal disadvantages that have traditionally been heaped upon them. But these approaches miss an important dimension of miscegenation laws: that, as the Supreme Court recognized in 1967, they are "measures designed to maintain White Supremacy." My claim is that the notion that discrimination against gays only involves the rights of gays is similarly shallow; it fails to recognize that the stigmatization of gays functions as part of a larger system of social control.

The Miscegenation Analogy

Let us begin by examining why discrimination against gays must, as a purely analytical matter, be recognized as a kind of sex discrimination. As a matter of definition, if the same conduct is prohibited or stigmatized when engaged in by a person of one sex, while it is tolerated when engaged in by a person of the other sex, then the party imposing the prohibition or stigma is discriminating on the basis of sex. That is what happens when gays are discriminated against. If a business fires Ricky, or if the state prosecutes him, because of his sexual activities with Fred, while these actions would not be taken against Lucy if she did exactly the same things with Fred, then Ricky is being disadvantaged solely because of his sex. If Lucy is permitted to marry Fred, but Ricky may not marry Fred, then Ricky is being disadvantaged because of his sex. It is sex discrimination when an option is expressly made available only to one sex but not the other.

Miscegenation Analogy: Sodomy Law as Sex Discrimination," 98 *Yale L.J.* 145 (1988). Further discussion and documentation of this chapter's argument may be found there.

25. This wonderfully awful neologism was invented by Samuel A. Marcosson. See his "Harassment on the Basis of Sexual Orientation: A Claim of Sex Discrimination Under Title VII," 81 *Georgetown L. J.* 1, 6 (1992).

This point has not persuaded most courts that have been presented with it. The only court that appears to have considered this question as a matter of Federal constitutional law has denied that a law that prohibits sexual intercourse between persons of the same sex imposes a quasi-suspect, sex-based classification.[26] In *State v. Walsh*,[27] the Supreme Court of Missouri reversed a lower court's declaration that a statute prohibiting "deviate sexual intercourse with another person of the same sex"[28] deprived the defendant of equal protection because "the statute would not be applicable to the defendant if he were a female."[29]

> The State concedes that the statute prohibits men from doing what women may do, namely, engage in sexual activity with men. However, the State argues that it likewise prohibits women from doing something that men can do: engage in sexual activity with women. We believe it applies equally to men and women because it prohibits both classes from engaging in sexual activity with members of their own sex. Thus, there is no denial of equal protection on that basis.[30]

The Missouri court's argument is essentially that of an 1883 Supreme Court decision, *Pace v. Alabama*,[31] in which the Court considered for the first time the constitutionality of the miscegenation laws. The statute in question in *Pace* prescribed penalties for interracial sex which were more severe than those imposed for adultery or fornication between persons of the same race. The Court unanimously rejected the equal protection challenge to the statute, and denied that the two sections discriminated on the basis of race:

> [The section prohibiting interracial sex] prescribes a punishment for an offence which can only be committed where the two sexes are of different races. There is in neither section any discrimination against either race. . . . Whatever discrimination is made in the punishment prescribed in the

26. More recently, however, a plurality of the Hawaii Supreme Court has held that a statute that denies marriage to same-sex couples discriminates on the basis of sex and so is subject to strict scrutiny under the equal protection clause of that state's constitution. *Baehr v. Lewin*, 852 P.2d 44 (1993).

27. 713 S.W.2d 508 (Mo. banc 1986).

28. *Mo. Rev. Stat.* § 566.090.1(3) (Vernon 1979).

29. 713 S.W.2d at 509.

30. Ibid., p. 510.

31. 106 U.S. (16 Otto) 583 (1883).

two sections is directed against the offence designated and not against the person of any particular color or race. The punishment of each offending person, whether white or black, is the same.[32]

The structure of *Walsh*'s reasoning is identical to that of *Pace*: the Missouri statute "prescribes a punishment for an offence which can only be committed where the two [participants] are of [the same sex]," and it is directed "against the offence designated and not against the person of any particular [sex]."

But the argument of *Pace* is a poor one, as the Supreme Court recognized in the next miscegenation case it considered, *McLaughlin v. Florida*.[33] In the wake of *Brown v. Board of Education*, the *McLaughlin* Court, again unanimously, invalidated a criminal statute prohibiting an unmarried interracial couple from habitually living in and occupying the same room at night. "It is readily apparent," wrote Justice White for the Court, that the statute "treats the interracial couple made up of a white person and a Negro differently than it does any other couple."[34] In response to the state's reliance on *Pace*, White declared that "*Pace* represents a limited view of the Equal Protection Clause which has not withstood analysis in the subsequent decisions of this Court."[35] Racial classifications, he concluded, can only be sustained by a compelling state interest. Since the state had failed to establish that the statute served "some overriding statutory purpose requiring the proscription of the specified conduct when engaged in by a white person and a Negro, but not otherwise,"[36] the statute must fall as "an invidious discrimination forbidden by the Equal Protection Clause."[37]

McLaughlin stands for the proposition (which should be obvious even without judicial support) that if prohibited conduct is defined by reference to a characteristic, the prohibition is not neutral with reference to that characteristic. Thus, the appropriate rejoinder to arguments like that of the Missouri court might be that if the defendant had been a woman, he could not have been prosecuted for having sex with a man. Indeed, the sexes of the participants would appear to be one of the essential elements of the crime that the

---

32. Ibid., p. 585.
33. 379 U.S. 184 (1964).
34. Ibid., p. 188.
35. Ibid.
36. Ibid., p. 192.
37. Ibid., pp. 192–93.

prosecution must prove.[38] To paraphrase *McLaughlin*, it is readily apparent that the law treats the same-sex couple differently than it does any other couple. "Such a practice does not pass the simple test of whether the evidence shows 'treatment of a person in a manner which but for the person's sex would be different.' "[39]

The seeming puzzle of whether the man who has sex with a man is engaging in "the same conduct" as the woman who has sex with a man is an artifact of the reification of a category: "homosexual sex." The *Walsh* court's confusion rests on its view that the man and the woman are not really engaging in the same conduct: one is engaged in "homosexual sex," while the other is engaged in "heterosexual sex." A similar argument could have been made in the miscegenation cases: the same-race couple was not "miscegenating," while the mixed-race couple was. Both of these arguments, however, require us to abstract from the actual, physical conduct that is occurring. (Although the reproductive potential of "heterosexual sex" is often invoked as a basis for distinguishing it from "homosexual sex," that approach is unavailable when any activity other than uncontracepted vaginal intercourse is permitted for different-sex couples and forbidden for same-sex couples.) Cunnilingus, for example, is conduct that both homosexual and heterosexual couples can engage in. The man who is engaged in cunnilingus is doing exactly the same things with exactly the same part of his body, and doing them to the same body parts of the woman, as the lesbian. The genitalia of the person performing an act of oral sex are simply not involved in that act, except to the extent that someone's insistence makes them so. And what is sex discrimination but the insistence on the salience of genitalia always, in every context—so that a woman who seeks to practice law, for example, is seen as engaging in a fundamentally different kind of activity from a male lawyer (because she is rebelling against her essential nature, forsaking her proper maternal role, etc.)?[40]

---

38. Compare *Jones v. Commonwealth*, 80 Va. 538, 542 (1885): "To be a negro is not a crime; to marry a white woman is not a crime; but to be a negro, and being a negro, to marry a white woman is a felony; therefore it is essential to the crime that the accused shall be a negro—unless he is a negro he is guilty of no offense."

39. *City of Los Angeles, Dept. of Power and Water v. Manhart*, 435 U.S. 702, 711 (1978) (Title VII prohibits assessment of larger pension fund contributions from female than from male employees, even though as a class women do live longer than men), quoting "Developments in the Law, Employment Discrimination and Title VII of the Civil Rights Act of 1964," 84 *Harv. L. Rev.* 1109, 1170 (1971).

40. See, e.g., *Bradwell v. Illinois*, 83 U.S. (16 Wall.) 130, 141 (1872) (Bradley, J., concurring).

The kind of argument necessary to make the sex of the performer relevant in this context, in order to define the heterosexual man and the lesbian as "dissimilarly situated," is in principle equally available in every other context in which one might desire to defeat a claim of sex discrimination. If claims of sex discrimination could thus be defined away, the prohibition of sex discrimination would be eviscerated.

Sexism and the Homosexuality Taboo

I argued in Chapter 3 that the core evil of sex discrimination is not gender classification, but gender hierarchy. Now, therefore, I want to show that the gender classification imposed by discrimination against gays does in fact reinforce gender hierarchy.

To begin with, let me note how much of the connection between sexism and the homosexuality taboo lies in social meanings that are accessible to everyone. The reader can confirm from ordinary experience that the stigmatization of the homosexual has *something* to do with the homosexual's deviance from traditional sex roles. "Our society," Joseph Pleck observes, "uses the male heterosexual-homosexual dichotomy as a central symbol for *all* the rankings of masculinity, for the division on *any* grounds between males who are 'real men' and have power and males who are not. Any kind of powerlessness or refusal to compete becomes imbued with the imagery of homosexuality."[41] Similarly, the denunciation of feminism as tantamount to lesbianism is depressingly familiar. While, as we shall see, the connection between sexism and the homosexuality taboo has been extensively documented by psychologists and historians, it should be obvious even without scholarly support.[42] Most Americans learn no later than high school that one of the

41. "Men's Power with Women, Other Men, and Society: A Men's Movement Analysis," in Elizabeth H. Pleck and Joseph H. Pleck, eds., *The American Man* (Englewood Cliffs, N.J.: Prentice-Hall, 1980), p. 424.

42. It has been obvious to many of the theorists of gay liberation. See Dennis Altman, *Homosexual: Oppression and Liberation* (New York: Avon, 1971), pp. 79–84; Phyllis Birkby, Bertha Harris, Jill Johnston, Esther Newton, and Jane O'Wyatt, eds., *Amazon Expedition: A Lesbian Feminist Anthology* (Washington, N.J.: Times Change Press, 1973); David Fernbach, *The Spiral Path: A Gay Contribution to Human Survival* (London: Gay Men's Press, 1981), pp. 69–112, 197–208; Suzanne Pharr, *Homophobia: A Weapon of Sexism* (Inverness, Calif.: Chardon Press, 1988); John Stoltenberg, "Pornography, Homophobia and Male Supremacy," in Catherine Itzin, ed., *Pornography: Women, Violence, and Civil Liberties* (Oxford: Oxford University Press, 1992), pp. 145–65.

nastier sanctions that one will suffer if one deviates from the behavior traditionally deemed appropriate for one's sex is the imputation of homosexuality. The recognition that in our society homosexuality is generally understood as a metaphor for failure to live up to the norms of one's gender resembles the recognition that segregation stigmatizes blacks, in that both are "matters of common notoriety, matters not so much for judicial notice as for the background knowledge of educated men who live in the world."[43]

This commonsense meaning shares certain implicit, rather ugly assumptions with the miscegenation taboo. Both assume the hierarchical significance of sexual intercourse and the polluted status of the penetrated person. The central outrage of sodomy is that a man is reduced to the status of a woman, and that is understood to be degrading. Just as miscegenation was threatening because it called into question the distinctive and superior status of being white, homosexuality is threatening because it calls into question the distinctive and superior status of being male. Male homosexuals and lesbians, respectively, are understood to be guilty of one aspect of the dual crime of the miscegenating white woman: self-degradation and insubordination. By analogy with miscegenation, a member of the superior caste who allows his body to be penetrated is thereby polluted and degraded, and he assumes the status of the subordinate caste: he becomes womanlike. "[M]en cannot simultaneously be used 'as women' and stay powerful because they are men."[44] Just as miscegenation became the central symbol of the necessity of racial segregation, so today homosexuality stands as *the* signifier of the importance of maintaining male status. Lesbianism, on the other hand, is a form of insubordination: It denies that female sexuality exists, or should exist, only for the sake of male gratification. The prohibition of lesbianism is, however, less central to the taboo. In the same way that black male–white female was the paradigmatic act that the miscegenation taboo prohibited, male sodomy is the paradigmatic act that the homosexuality taboo prohibits.[45]

43. Charles Black, "The Lawfulness of the Segregation Decisions," 69 *Yale L. J.* 421, 426 (1960). Any reader unable to think of anecdotal evidence that supports this claim should consult Marc Fajer's useful compilation in "Can Two Real Men Eat Quiche Together? Storytelling, Gender-Role Stereotypes, and Legal Protection for Lesbians and Gay Men," 46 *U. Miami L. Rev.* 511, 620–24, 631–32 (1992).

44. Andrea Dworkin, *Right-Wing Women* (New York: Perigee, 1983), p. 129.

45. Lesbians are often invisible in discussions of homosexuality. Respondents in surveys appear generally to equate "homosexuality" with "male homosexuality." Kathryn N. Black and Michael R. Stevenson, "The Relationship of Self-Reported Sex-Role Characteristics and Attitudes Toward

Thus the requirements of the stigma theory, described in Chapter 2, can easily be satisfied. As in the case of miscegenation, where the taboo notoriously connoted a narrative in which black males represented a dangerous, predatory sexuality that threatened pure and fragile white women, the meaning of the homosexuality taboo is well known. The basic objections to both taboos are similar. Implicit in both are premises incompatible with equal concern and respect for all citizens, namely that sexual penetration is a nasty, degrading violation of the self, and that there are some people (in the case of the homosexuality taboo, women) to whom, because of their inferior social status, it is acceptable to do it, and others (men) who, because of their superior social status, must be rescued (or, if necessary, forcibly prevented) from having it done to them.

What about the process theory? Can it be shown that laws that discriminate against gays are the products of a legislative process tainted by sexism? As I noted earlier, pervasive stigma in itself always gives some reason to suspect process defect. But less impressionistic evidence also exists.

Social psychologists have documented that hostility toward homosexuals is linked to other traditional, restrictive attitudes about sex roles. For example, one study found that "[h]igher support for equality between the sexes is associated with more positive attitudes toward male homosexuality and lesbianism," and concluded that "a major determinant of negative attitudes toward homosexuality is the need to keep males masculine and females feminine, that is, to avoid sex-role confusion."[46] In line with this reasoning, other studies have shown that subjects' dislike of, or unwillingness to interact with, a homosexual person is associated with that person's perceived incongruent sex-role behavior.[47] Another study concluded that "the best single predictor of

Homosexuality," 10 *J. Homosexuality* 83 (1984). In the recent political turmoil over the proposed lifting of the ban on gays in the military, there was almost no discussion of lesbians, even though women have been discharged from the armed forces on grounds of homosexuality at a rate far exceeding the rate for men. For the statistics, see sources collected in Kenneth L. Karst, "The Pursuit of Manhood and the Desegregation of the Armed Forces," 38 *U.C.L.A. L. Rev.* 499, 551 n. 200 (1991).

46. A. P. MacDonald and Richard G. Games, "Some Characteristics of Those who Hold Positive and Negative Attitudes Toward Homosexuals," 1 *J. Homosexuality* 9, 19 (1974).

47. Mary Riege Laner and Roy H. Laner, "Personal Style or Sexual Preference? Why Gay Men are Disliked," 9 *Int'l Rev. Modern Sociology* 215 (1979); Mary Riege Laner and Roy H. Laner, "Sexual Preference or Personal Style? Why Lesbians are Disliked," 5 *J. Homosexuality* 339 (1980); Jim Millham and Linda E. Weinberger, "Sexual Preference, Sex Role Appropriateness, and Restriction of Social Access," 2 *J. Homosexuality* 343 (1977).

homophobia is a belief in the traditional family ideology, i.e., dominant father, submissive mother, and obedient children. The second best predictor was found to be agreement with traditional beliefs about women, e.g., that it is worse for a woman to tell dirty jokes than a man."[48] Still another found that research subjects who were most prejudiced against homosexuals "held stronger stereotypes of masculinity and femininity and were more willing on the basis of those stereotypes to label a male as homosexual when he exhibited what they thought of as a single feminine characteristic."[49] Other studies using a wide variety of measures of sex-role attitudes and attitudes toward homosexuals have consistently found correlations between conventional expectations about gender roles and hostility toward homosexuals.[50] (Hostility toward homosexuals has also been shown to correlate with the belief that most homosexuals do, in fact, behave like members of the opposite sex—a belief that has been shown to be false.)[51] Correlation, of course, does not demonstrate the direction of causation, but it suggests that a causal connection may exist that deserves exploration.

There are significant differences between men's and women's attitudes toward homosexuality. Women's intolerance seems less profound and deeply rooted than that of men.[52] Moreover, laws that discriminate against gays, like most other laws, are produced by an overwhelmingly male population of officials. For this reason, the following discussion will focus first, and at greater

48. Stephen F. Morin and Ellen M. Garfinkle, "Male Homophobia," 34 *J. Soc. Issues* 29, 31 (Winter 1978).

49. John Dunbar, Marvin Brown, and Donald M. Amoroso, "Some Correlates of Attitudes Toward Homosexuality," 89 *J. Soc. Psychology* 271, 278 (1973).

50. These studies are listed in my "Why Discrimination Against Lesbians and Gay Men Is Sex Discrimination," pp. 238 n. 157, 249–50 n. 201, 270 n. 274.

51. See Alan Taylor, "Conceptions of Masculinity and Femininity as a Basis for Stereotypes of Male and Female Homosexuals," 9 *J. Homosexuality* 37 (1983).

52. "National opinion polls typically find no significant difference between males' and females' responses to questions about homosexuality. Smaller-scale experimental and questionnaire studies, in contrast, have generally found more negative attitudes among males than among females, especially with attitudes toward gay men. Both sets of data are revealing. Males and females probably hold roughly similar positions on general questions of morality and civil liberties, but males are more homophobic in their emotional reactions to homosexuality." Gregory M. Herek, "On Heterosexual Masculinity: Some Psychical Consequences of the Social Construction of Gender and Sexuality," 29 *Am. Behav. Sci.* 563, 564–65 (1986). See also Bernie S. Newman, "The Relative Importance of Gender Role Attitudes to Male and Female Attitudes Toward Lesbians," 21 *Sex Roles* 451 (1989); Lawrence A. Kurdek, "Correlates of Negative Attitudes Toward Homosexuals in Heterosexual College Students," 18 *Sex Roles* 727 (1988).

length, on the psychic roots of *male* attitudes toward homosexuals. It will then turn to the somewhat different roots of women's hostility toward lesbians and gay men.

Correlations between sexism and heterosexism, similar to those found by social psychologists, have been noted by historians who have investigated the origins of the modern condemnation of "homosexuality." These scholars, studying historical attitudes in a variety of different times and places, have converged on the hypothesis that the modern homosexuality taboo is linked with sexism.

The modern stigmatization of homosexuals as violators of gender norms—gay men as effeminate, lesbians as "mannish"—developed simultaneously with widespread anxieties about gender identity in the face of an emerging ideology of gender equality. It happened to male homosexuals first. Before about 1700, Randolph Trumbach has found, although homosexual behavior was illegitimate, it was not the preserve of any distinct subclass of society. Homosexual acts "were usually between an active adult male and a passive adolescent."[53] The adult male usually also had sexual relations with women, and such men "who took the active role probably actually increased their standing as dominant males."[54] The boy, "provided that he switched to an active role as manhood came on, did not suffer any loss of gender status."[55] The only males who suffered a loss of status were adults who took the passive role. "After 1700, it seems to make little difference whether a man takes the active or the passive role, or whether his partner is an adult male or a boy—any sexual desire by one male for another leads to categorization as an effeminate sodomite."[56] This transformation appears to be rooted in the major cultural shift that was taking place at that time, in which "a patriarchal morality that allowed adult men to own and dominate their wives, children, servants and slaves, was gradually challenged and partially replaced by an egalitarian morality which proposed that all men were created equal, that

53. Randolph Trumbach, "Gender and the Homosexual Role in Modern Western Culture: The 18th and 19th Centuries Compared," in Dennis Altman et al., *Which Homosexuality?* (Amsterdam: Uitgeverij An Dekker, 1989), p. 152. See also Randolph Trumbach, "The Birth of the Queen: Sodomy and the Emergence of Gender Equality in Modern Culture, 1660–1750," in Martin Bauml Duberman, Martha Vicinius, and George Chauncey Jr., eds, *Hidden From History: Reclaiming the Gay and Lesbian Past* (New York: New American Library, 1989), pp. 129–40.

54. Trumbach, "Gender and the Homosexual Role," p. 152.

55. Ibid.

56. Ibid., p. 153.

slavery must therefore be abolished, democracy achieved, women made equal with men, and children with their parents."[57] This egalitarianism, Trumbach contends, "raised profound anxiety in both men and women" that "resulted in a compromise with full equality that historians have called domesticity. Men and women were equal, but they were supposed to live in separate spheres, he dominant in the economy, she in the home."[58] This distinction between the sexes was reinforced by the idea of the homosexual as a deviant from his whole gender role. "All women in societies with transvestites experienced sexual domination all their lives, but only the transvestite minority of males ever did so."[59]

The rise of domesticity produced changes in child-rearing arrangements that may have contributed to this anxiety about the boundaries of gender. Men's work was increasingly relocated outside the home. The father was therefore away from home during most of a child's waking hours, while the mother's prime responsibility was child-rearing, she was excluded from other prestigious activities, and she therefore was likely to make the children the focus of her emotional life.[60] Recent explorations of the way gender identity is formed in such nuclear families help to clarify the nature of the psychological link between sexism and heterosexism that develops in such a context.[61] Doubtless heterosexism takes many forms, and develops differently in different individuals, but the following pattern seems typical.[62]

Because child-rearing is primarily a woman's task, children identify first with their mothers. For girls, this primary attachment continues uninterrupted through adulthood, because girls are taught that to become adults, they need only become increasingly like their mothers. Boys, by contrast, learn that to

57. Ibid., p. 154.

58. Ibid., p. 155.

59. Ibid.

60. David F. Greenberg, *The Construction of Homosexuality* (Chicago and London: University of Chicago Press, 1988), p. 388.

61. See Nancy Chodorow, *The Reproduction of Mothering* (Berkeley: University of California Press, 1978); Dorothy Dinnerstein, *The Mermaid and the Minotaur: Sexual Arrangements and Human Malaise* (New York: Harper Colophon, 1977); Jessica Benjamin, *The Bonds of Love: Psychoanalysis, Feminism, and the Problem of Domination* (New York: Pantheon, 1988).

62. This pattern is sometimes offered as a transcultural explanation for gender hierarchy, but as some critics have noted, it is dependent on modern Western society's gendered public/domestic separation. See, e.g., Linda J. Nicholson, *Gender and History* (New York: Columbia University Press, 1986), pp. 84–88. The historicization of Chodorow's thesis would help to explain why the modern stigmatization of the effeminate gay man emerged at the time it did.

become adults they must renounce this primary attachment and identify with their fathers, whose love is more distant and conditional. Their identity is not discovered but fashioned, and the materials that constitute it are achievement, competition, hierarchy, and control over their own feminine tendencies. In short, a man must prove his masculinity, over and over again, and continually resist the temptation to identify with his lost mother. That early renunciation must be continually reaffirmed. At the same time, this renunciation produces an intense guilt and sense of loss for the abandoned mother, and a hopeless yearning to return to her.

As noted earlier, prejudice often functions as the external projection of hated aspects of the prejudiced person's own self. The racist projects outward his own impulses toward lechery, laziness, aggression, and slovenliness, accusing blacks of possessing these traits; the anti-Semite does the same with pride, deceit, overambition, and sly achievement, personifying these evils in the Jew.[63] In modern society, the male homosexual often serves a similar projective function. If the argument of the previous paragraph is correct, he symbolizes the failure to individuate adequately from the mother. Whether it is correct or not, it is clear that in the community of males, the gay man is regarded as a slacker, one who has failed in or given up the difficult quest for masculinity.[64]

It should therefore be unsurprising that adolescent males, who tend to be most troubled by the conflict between their need to be dependent on their parents and the cultural expectation that they will separate from them, are the ones who carry heterosexism to the extreme of violent gay-bashing. Violence is, of course, itself regarded as a badge of masculinity.[65] The hypothesis that

63. Charles R. Lawrence III, "The Id, the Ego, and Equal Protection: Reckoning With Unconscious Racism," 39 *Stanford L. Rev.* 317, 333–34 (1987); Gordon W. Allport, *The Nature of Prejudice* (Reading, Mass.: Addison-Wesley, 1979), p. 199.

64. Marilyn Frye observes that for some men, the connection of heterosexuality with male supremacy is even starker than this. "A great deal of fucking is presumed to preserve and maintain women's belief in their own essential heterosexuality, which in turn (for women as not for men) connects with and reinforces female hetero-eroticism, that is, man-loving in women. It is very important to the maintenance of male-supremacy that men fuck women, a lot. So it is required; it is compulsory. Doing it is both one's duty and an expression of solidarity. A man who does not or will not fuck women is not pulling his share of the load. He is not a loyal and dependable member of the team." Marilyn Frye, *The Politics of Reality: Essays in Feminist Theory* (Freedom, Calif.: Crossing Press, 1983), p. 140.

65. See Richard Isay, *Being Homosexual: Gay Men and Their Development* (New York: Farrar, Straus and Giroux, 1989), pp. 77–78.

some defensive mechanism is at work in heterosexism is supported by the extraordinary brutality with which gay-bashers attack their targets. Violence against gays frequently involves torture and mutilation. Homophobic murders typically involve mutilation of the victim. The coordinator of one hospital's victim assistance program reported that "attacks against gay men were the most heinous and brutal I encountered."[66] A physician reported that injuries suffered by the victims of homophobic violence he had treated were so "vicious" as to make clear that "the intent is to kill and maim":

> Weapons include knives, guns, brass knuckles, tire irons, baseball bats, broken bottles, metal chains, and metal pipes. Injuries include severe lacerations requiring extensive plastic surgery; head injuries, at times requiring surgery; puncture wounds of the chest, requiring insertion of chest tubes; removal of the spleen for traumatic rupture; multiple fractures of the extremities, jaws, ribs, and facial bones; severe eye injuries, in two cases resulting in permanent loss of vision; as well as severe psychological trauma the level of which would be difficult to measure.[67]

This kind of behavior cannot intelligibly be attributed to the perpetrators' desire to uphold Judeo-Christian moral standards. That morality does not require—indeed, it does not permit—the torture, mutilation, or murder of strangers. Nor is it attributable to the typically violent propensities of many young men. Outside of war, violence of this degree of savagery is so unusual that the only parallel that comes to mind is the Southern lynch mob's treatment of a black man thought to have raped a white woman. Some extraordinary passion appears to be at work, such that the homosexual appears to the perpetrator to call for an extraordinarily violent response. If the homosexual's very existence threatens the security of the perpetrator's valued sense of gender identity, then the vehemence of the perpetrator's response becomes at least somewhat more intelligible.

In short, it appears that male hostility toward "effeminate" men has been a psychological defense against gender-identity conflict since at least the eighteenth century. "In early eighteenth-century England this hostility took the form of diatribes against fops and beaux—men who wore fancy clothes, paid excessive attention to their appearance, and spent too much time courting

---

66. Quoted in Thomas, "Beyond the Privacy Principle," p. 1463.
67. Quoted in ibid., p. 1466. Other illustrations may be found on pp. 1462–70.

women. . . . Men's clothing, which had been frilly in the Elizabethan age, became more sharply differentiated from women's from the 1770s on."[68] And since then, any failure to conform to the norms of masculinity has become imbued with the stigma associated with same-sex sexuality. "[T]he most salient characteristic of the homosexual role from about 1700 to the present day has been the presumption that all men who engage in sexual relations with other men are effeminate members of a third or intermediate gender, who surrender their rights to be treated as dominant males, and are exposed instead to a merited contempt as a species of male whore."[69]

There was no such dynamic at work with respect to lesbianism, which did not so directly challenge male supremacy.

> Though it may have challenged men's presumption that all women were placed on earth to gratify men's sexual desires and, when coupled with transvestism and financial independence, male supremacy in other spheres, it did not threaten male identity as such. . . . Nor did it threaten women's gender identity, at least not to any great extent. Whereas a boy had to relinquish his early identification with his mother to become an adult, a girl did not; her sexual identity was thus more secure. As an adult she was not threatened by masculine women as men were by feminine males: she had never been forced to give up a strong childhood identification with her father. His absence from the home did not permit a strong identification with him to develop.[70]

The contemporary notion of the "mannish lesbian," who now seems to be the mirror image of the "effeminate queen," took on that mirror-image status only in the late nineteenth century, the same time that medical writers created the idea of a "homosexual," a person (male or female) whose very being is constituted by his or her sexual orientation.[71] This was the period in which there first arose widespread concern over the "new woman," who preferred education and career to the traditional roles of wife and mother.[72] Investiga-

68. Greenberg, *The Construction of Homosexuality*, p. 390.
69. Trumbach, "Gender and the Homosexual Role," p. 153.
70. Greenberg, *The Construction of Homosexuality*, p. 390.
71. The role began to appear a century earlier, in the late eighteenth century, but did not become relevant to most women's status until much later. See Randolph Trumbach, "London's Sapphists: From Three Sexes to Four Genders in the Making of Modern Culture," in Julia Epstein and Kristina Straub, eds., *Body Guards*, pp. 112–41.
72. See Susan Bell and Karen Offen, eds., *Women, the Family and Freedom: The Debate in*

tions into the medical literature of that time have confirmed the hypothesis that "[t]he distinguishing of a 'same-sex' from an 'opposite-sex' eroticism reflected an increasing social emphasis . . . on the differentiation of females and males" and was "an effort to contain the contemporary movement of women out of the traditional women's sphere."[73] One illustration comes from the *New York Medical Journal* of 1900:

> The female possessed of masculine ideas of independence, the virago who would sit in the public highways and lift up her pseudo-virile voice, proclaiming her sole right to decide questions of war or religion, or the value of celibacy and the curse of women's impurity, and that disgusting antisocial being, the female sexual pervert, are simply different degrees of the same class—degenerates.[74]

The idea of homosexuality was a late development of this period, developing out of an earlier, distinct conception called "sexual inversion." " 'Sexual inversion' referred to a broad range of deviant gender behavior, of which homosexual desire was only a logical but indistinct aspect, while 'homosexuality' focused on the narrower issue of sexual object choice."[75] Since during the Victorian period women were typically thought to be naturally passionless and asexual, any woman who showed any interest in sexuality was thought to have become manlike in her sexual desire, and thereby to have abjured femininity generally. "[A] woman could not invert any aspect of her gender role without inverting her complete role."[76] Moreover, doctors writing about lesbian couples did not regard the women who took passive, "feminine" roles as particularly worthy of study, since these roles seemed to be appropriate for them.[77] On the other hand, as Carroll Smith-Rosenberg observes, medical writings of

---

Documents (Stanford: Stanford University Press, 1983), vol. 2, pp. 17–72 (excerpting writings on this issue by Ibsen, Strindberg, Shaw, Nietzsche, and others).

73. Jonathan Katz, *Gay/Lesbian Almanac* (New York: Harper & Row, 1983), p. 149. See also Sylvia Law, "Homosexuality and the Social Meaning of Gender," 1988 *Wis. L. Rev.* 187, 197–206.

74. William Lee Howard, "Effeminate Men and Masculine Women," 77 *N.Y. Med. J.* 686, 687 (May 5, 1900), quoted in Carroll Smith-Rosenberg, *Disorderly Conduct: Visions of Gender in Victorian America* (New York: Alfred A. Knopf, 1985), p. 280.

75. George Chauncey Jr., "From Sexual Inversion to Homosexuality: Medicine and the Changing Conceptualization of Female Deviance," 58–59 *Salmagundi* 114, 116 (1982–83).

76. Ibid., p. 121.

77. Ibid., p. 125.

this period reveal profound concern about the medical implications of higher education for women.

> The woman who favored her mind at the expense of her ovaries—especially the woman who spent her adolescence and early adulthood in college and graduate school—would disorder a delicate physiological balance. Her overstimulated brain would become morbidly introspective. Neurasthenia, hysteria, insanity would follow. Her ovaries, robbed of energy rightfully theirs, would shrivel. . . . Her breasts might shrivel, her menses become irregular or cease altogether. Sterility could ensue, facial hair might develop.[78]

This strategy for repressing women's ambitions failed. As gender roles in American society became increasingly complex, with the number of employed women steadily increasing, the binary division implicit in the inversion theory simply stopped making sense to people.[79] It was easily shown that deviation from traditional female roles did not destroy women's health.[80]

By the turn of the century, sexual object became more important than passive or aggressive sexual behavior in the medical classification of sexuality.[81] Doctors, psychologists, and academics "shifted the definition of female deviance from the New Woman's rejection of motherhood to their rejection of men."[82] The idea of female passionlessness was replaced by an ideology that sought to use women's sexual desires to bond them more tightly to men: the

78. Smith-Rosenberg, *Disorderly Conduct*, pp. 258, 260.

79. Chauncey, "From Sexual Inversion to Homosexuality," p. 143.

80. Smith-Rosenberg, *Disorderly Conduct*, pp. 262–64.

81. Lillian Faderman notes, however, that such a distinction is not "to be found in the work of many sexologists well into the twentieth century or in the popular imagination, which often assumes, even today, that lesbians are necessarily masculine and that female 'masculinity' is a sure sign of lesbianism." *Odd Girls and Twilight Lovers: A History of Lesbian Life in Twentieth-Century America* (New York: Penguin, 1991), p. 41. A similar tension may be noted in popular discourse about male homosexuality, which as late as World War I was still uncertain whether the essence of the identity stigmatized as sexually deviant was effeminacy or sexual activity with men. See George Chauncey Jr., "Christian Brotherhood or Sexual Perversion? Homosexual Identities and the Construction of Sexual Boundaries in the World War I Era," in Duberman et al., eds., *Hidden From History*, pp. 294–317. As Sedgwick has observed, "issues of modern homo/heterosexual definition are structured, not by the supersession of one model and the consequent withering away of another, but instead by the relations enabled by the unrationalized coexistence of different models during the times they do coexist." *Epistemology of the Closet*, p. 47.

82. Smith-Rosenberg, *Disorderly Conduct*, p. 265.

marriage manuals of the 1920s and 1930s stressed the need for men to develop "companionate marriages" in order to make marriage more attractive and satisfying to women.[83] "Linking orgasms to chic fashion and planned motherhood, male sex reformers, psychologists, and physicians promised a future of emotional support and sexual delights to women who accepted heterosexual marriage—and male economic hegemony. Only the 'unnatural' woman continued to struggle with men for economic independence and political power."[84] Thus J. F. W. Meagher wrote that "[t]he driving force in many agitators and militant women who are always after their rights is often an unsatisfied sex impulse, with a homosexual aim. Married women with a completely satisfied libido rarely take an active interest in militant movements." For Meagher, healthy female sexuality meant deference to men. "A homosexual woman often wants to possess the male and not to be possessed by him. . . . With them orgasm is often only possible in the superior position."[85]

If lesbians arouse bitterness on the part of males, it is of a different kind from that felt toward gay men, one predicated on the fear of being abandoned by the mother that one has oneself abandoned. A lesbian fails to provide the emotional nurturance and solace from the difficult world of maleness that many men feel women exist in order to provide; she signifies that there is no way back from that world. Compulsory heterosexuality's impact on women has an unmediated, direct relation to sex inequality: its effect is to guarantee that men will continue to have physical, economic, and emotional access to and control over women. The familiar insinuation that all feminists are lesbians[86] supports Adrienne Rich's speculation that "men really fear . . . that

83. Christina Simmons, "Companionate Marriage and the Lesbian Threat," 4 *Frontiers* 54–59 (Fall 1979).

84. Smith-Rosenberg, *Disorderly Conduct*, p. 283.

85. J. F. W. Meagher, "Homosexuality: Its Psychobiological and Pathological Significance," 33 *Urologic and Cutaneous Review* (1929), pp. 511, 513, quoted in Simmons, "Companionate Marriage," p. 57.

86. "In the early days of women's liberation the most hurtful accusation was that they were a bunch of lesbians, and feminists such as Betty Friedan took considerable pain to show that this was untrue and that they really were 'feminine' (i.e. liked men) after all." Altman, *Homosexual: Oppression and Liberation*, pp. 90–91. Such accusations continue to be potent weapons against feminists. See Pharr, *Homophobia*, pp. 27–43. Although lesbians have become prominent in the feminist movement, this kind of labeling precedes that development. Ti-Grace Atkinson reports that she first began to think about the connection between lesbianism and feminism as a consequence of this persistent accusation: "Since the beginning of the current Movement, feminist

women could be indifferent to them altogether, that men could be allowed sexual and emotional . . . access to women *only* on women's terms, otherwise being left on the periphery of the matrix."[87] This enraging fantasy of maternal abandonment helps to explain why the stigmatization of lesbians by heterosexual men typically takes the form of a rape fantasy: all she needs is a good fuck to straighten her out.

A final puzzle is a much more recent phenomenon, the stigmatization of the gay male top, the man who is not himself penetrated but who penetrates other men. There is nothing effeminate about him. He is perceived as, if anything, *too* masculine; all the socially destructive potentials of masculinity reach their maximal intensity in his person. To the heterosexual male, the gay top is essentially a *dangerous* man. He preys on other men and degrades them by turning them into women. No man is safe from him. No man's masculinity is secure against his assault. Like that other icon of unbridled male sexuality, the black rapist of white women, he defiles the temple and profanes what is most sacred, and he does this by penetrating the bodies of those who, because of their intrinsically superior status, are entitled to be assured that they will not be penetrated. With both sodomy and miscegenation, it is of little moment whether the person who is penetrated consents to the act. It is the caste to which that person belongs that is entitled not to be defiled; an individual who does not uphold the impenetrable character of the ruling caste is simply a traitor, whose consent does not excuse the crime committed by the penetrator.

We noted that one effect of the miscegenation taboo, intended or not, is the maintenance of the boundary between the races on which the system of racism depends. Similarly, compulsory heterosexuality keeps women in relationships in which men exert power over their lives. We also noted racism in the symbolic message of the taboo, which associated racial equality with sexual danger and endorsed the idea that the boundaries enforced by the taboo are terribly important. An analogous message can be seen in the homosexuality

---

activity has been labeled lesbianism. The first time I was called a lesbian was on my first picket line, in front of the New York Times, to desegregate the help-wanted ads. Generally speaking, the Movement has reacted defensively to the charge of lesbianism: 'no, I'm not'; 'yes, you are,' 'no, I'm not,' 'prove it.' For myself, I was so puzzled by the connection that I became curious. Whenever the enemy keeps lobbing bombs into some area you consider unrelated to your defense, it's worth investigating." Ti-Grace Atkinson, "Lesbianism and Feminism," in Birkby et al., eds., *Amazon Expedition: A Lesbian Feminist Anthology*, p. 11.

87. Adrienne Rich, "Compulsory Heterosexuality and Lesbian Existence," 5 *Signs* 631, 643 (1980).

taboo: sex equality is dangerous because it reduces men to the level of women; thus maintaining the boundary between the sexes is critical.

The reinforcement of sexism, then, is both a cause and an effect of the homosexuality taboo's survival. Note that my evidence is confined to contemporary American culture and its antecedents, and that my claim about the function of the taboo pertains only to this culture. I am not claiming that the stigmatization of homosexuality is indispensable to gender hierarchy. Such a claim would be unsustainable. Functional equivalents exist. Homosexuality has been tolerated and even institutionalized in cultures in which women are thoroughly subordinated, such as ancient Greece. (Revealingly, however, even those cultures tend to stigmatize the man who is penetrated, and this stigma arises out of the fact that he has allowed himself to be used like a woman.) Moreover, it is possible for male homosexuality (at least) to be associated with male privilege and the repudiation of women.[88] Rather, my claim is closer to Eve Sedgwick's argument that "homophobia directed by men against men is misogynistic, and perhaps transhistorically so."[89]

As with the miscegenation taboo and racism, some people support the homosexuality taboo for reasons unrelated to its connection to sexism. For some, it is simply part of the way they make sense of the world: there are certain ways one should not use one's body, for the same reasons of convention that there are certain ways one should not hold one's spoon when eating. For some, the taboo is simply an unexamined echo of attitudes they have unreflectively learned and internalized. But for a significant subset, the taboo is part of a defensive attitude that responds to a perceived threat to the boundaries of the self. It is a commonplace among political scientists that outcomes in democratic decision making are often determined by small groups with intense preferences. One of the groups most concerned about maintaining the homosexuality taboo evidently is men who are anxious about their own gender identity. The identity they are so eager to preserve is an identity based on sexual superiority, the superiority of men over women as manifested by the male's status as an impenetrable penetrator.[90] It should be clear that a law enacted on such a basis is unconstitutional. It stigmatizes women on the basis

88. See Frye, *The Politics of Reality*, pp. 128–51.

89. Eve Kosofsky Sedgwick, *Between Men: English Literature and Male Homosocial Desire* (New York: Columbia University Press, 1985), p. 20.

90. I owe this coinage to Richard Mohr, *A More Perfect Union: Why Straight Ameica Must Stand up for Gay Rights* (Boston: Beacon, 1994), p. 118.

of their sex, and it is hardly predicated on a lawmaking process that treats their interests with equal concern and respect.

In turning from considering the reasons for men's intolerance of gays to looking at women's attitudes, we may find it strange to think that women's attitudes can be sexist. It would be most surprising if women were to undertake, as a deliberate project, the perpetuation of their own subordination. Moreover, experimental social psychologists have found that among women who hold negative attitudes toward gays, sex role attitudes play a less important role than among men who hold such attitudes.[91] Gregory Herek has offered the following explanation of this effect:

> Because heterosexual females are less likely to perceive rejection of lesbians and gay men to be integral to their own gender-identity, they probably experience fewer social pressures to express hostile attitudes. Consequently, such women may have more opportunities for personal interaction with lesbians and gay men. However, where negative attitudes among heterosexual women exist, these presumably result from ideological concerns (religious beliefs, family-and gender-ideology) rather than gender-identity needs. . . . Gender-specific patterns such as these would help to explain why heterosexual males' attitudes are especially hostile toward gay men while heterosexual females' attitudes do not vary consistently according to the target's gender.[92]

When one examines the cluster of attitudes within which women's antipathy toward gays is typically embedded, however (Herek's "religious beliefs, family-and gender-ideology"), it turns out to be closely tied to traditional meanings of gender. The most important predictor of women's attitudes toward lesbians, one study found, was parents' attitude toward lesbians. Next in relative importance was gender role attitudes, authoritarian personality, and exposure to education and media regarding lesbians.[93] So although sex role attitudes are an important predictor of women's attitudes toward gays, these other factors are as well. Do we know enough about women who both hold traditional gender role attitudes and strongly repudiate homosexuality to

91. See Newman, "The Relative Importance of Gender Role Attitudes"; Gregory M. Herek, "Heterosexuals' Attitudes toward Lesbians and Gay Men: Correlates and Gender Differences," 25 *J. Sex Res.* 451, 470,73 (1988).

92. Herek, "Heterosexuals' Attitudes," p. 472.

93. See Newman, "The Relative Importance of Gender Role Attitudes," p. 461.

construct a persuasive hypothesis about the world view within which these attitudes are connected?

Political struggles over abortion and the Equal Rights Amendment, as well as over homosexuality, have produced many writings by and studies of antifeminist women, and these show a tight link between hostility toward gays and a desire to maintain traditional sex roles. On the most visceral level, this hostility seems to have something to do with the resentment that those with familial responsibilities that weigh heavily upon them feel toward those who seem free of such responsibilities. There is also an element of fear. The women who most strongly repudiate feminism do so because, as Jeffrey Weeks has written, "feminism may be seen as precisely a force that is undermining women's basic hold on social, economic, and sexual stability—marriage, family life and protection by men. In a culture where it is still relatively difficult for many women to become economically independent, and where status depends on the position of the male, women may see their very survival as dependent upon family life."[94] The well-grounded worry that underlies this resistance is "that the changes of the past generation have served to undermine the ties that bind men to women. A powerful force in the anti-ERA campaign, was a fear of the sexes mingling, of a breakdown of the traditional boundaries between the sexes, and of women losing traditional male support as a result."[95] From this perspective, homosexuality represents the culmination of the process, the ultimate disintegration of the gender order, with men and women entirely disconnected from one another. For women whose economic security depends on that order, homosexuality thus may carry connotations of personal threat.

When writers from this perspective address homosexuality, they overwhelmingly tend to condemn it as a threat to the family.[96] This is, at first blush, a curious argument. Most heterosexual family members do not appear to be so eager to become homosexual that only the fear of externally imposed sanctions prevents them from doing so. Many homosexual relationships are, except for the sex of the participants and the legal status of the union, indistinguishable from heterosexual marriages.[97] Adoption and new reproductive

94. Jeffrey Weeks, *Sexuality and Its Discontents* (London: Routledge, 1985), p. 37.
95. Ibid.
96. For numerous illustrations, see my "Why Discrimination Against Lesbians and Gay Men Is Sex Discrimination," p. 253 n. 212.
97. A study of San Francisco Bay Area gays found that 29 percent of the men, and almost

technologies have made it possible for increasing numbers of gay couples to raise children.[98] Moreover, there have been cultures in which homosexuality has been openly tolerated,[99] and in them families do not appear to have been less common or enduring than they are in contemporary America. How, then, can homosexuals be said to threaten the family?

The charge is intelligible only if "the family" is rigidly defined as an institution in which men, but not women, belong in the public world of work and are not so much members as owners of their families, while women, but not men, should rear children, manage homes, and obey their husbands.[100] Homosexuals are a threat to the family only if the survival of the family requires that men and women follow traditional sex roles.[101] Now it may be that traditional sex roles are the best ones for women. That claim becomes less persuasive, however, when its proponents find it necessary to force women into those roles. The constitutional guarantee of equality is not worth much if the law can force people into relationships of hierarchy and dependency.[102]

If these are the positions from which the homosexuality taboo now receives most of its support, then it is fair to conclude that that support is crucially

---

three-fourths of the women, were currently involved in a stable relationship. Alan P. Bell and Martin S. Weinberg, *Homosexualities: A Study of Diversity Among Men and Women* (New York: Simon & Schuster, 1978), pp. 91, 97. Many of these couples foster the same intimacy, caring, and enduring commitment that are valued in the most successful heterosexual marriages. See Kath Weston, *Families We Choose: Lesbians, Gays, Kinship* (New York: Columbia University Press, 1991); Letitia Anne Peplau, "Research on Homosexual Couples: An Overview," 8 *J. Homosexuality* 3 (Winter 1982), and citations in both of these works.

98. See Marjorie Maguire Shultz, "Reproductive Technology and Intent-Based Parenthood: An Opportunity for Gender Neutrality," 1990 *Wisc. L. Rev.* 297, 314–16. Indeed, gays have shown enough interest in nurturing children that legislation has been enacted in some states forbidding them from adopting.

99. See, e.g., John Boswell, *Christianity, Social Tolerance and Homosexuality: Gay People in Western Europe from the Beginning of the Christian Era to the Fourteenth Century* (Chicago and London: University of Chicago Press, 1980), which demonstrates that homosexuality was widely tolerated in Western Europe in the first centuries of Christianity and during the eleventh and twelfth centuries.

100. A description of this ideology, which focuses on its role in the anti-abortion movement but is also useful in the present context, appears in Kristin Luker, *Abortion and the Politics of Motherhood* (Berkeley: University of California Press, 1984), pp. 159–75.

101. See Law, "Homosexuality and the Social Meaning of Gender," pp. 218–21.

102. Some writers argue that the hierarchy of the sexes is inextricably linked with the stability of families, because families cannot endure unless women willingly subordinate themselves to men and children. I describe and address these arguments in "Sex Equality and/or the Family: From Bloom vs. Okin to Rousseau vs. Hegel," 4 *Yale J. L. & Humanities* 399 (1992).

dependent on sexism, without which it might well not exist. And when the state enforces that taboo, it is giving its imprimatur to sexism. As with the miscegenation taboo, the effect that the taboo against homosexuality has in modern American society is, in large part, the maintenance of hierarchy. The taboo accomplishes this by reinforcing the identity of the superior caste in the hierarchy, and this effect is at least in large part the reason why the taboo persists. Laws that discriminate against gays are thus the product of a political decision-making process that is biased by sexism, that implicitly stigmatizes women, and that reinforces the hierarchy of men over women.

What this conclusion requires of legal doctrine should be clear by analogy with the miscegenation cases. Just as interracial couples cannot be made to suffer any legal disadvantage that same-race couples are spared, gay couples cannot be made to suffer any legal disadvantage that heterosexual couples are spared. Nonmarital sex cannot be more heavily criminalized when it is homosexual than when it is heterosexual.[103] Gays must be permitted to marry.[104] Societal disapproval is not a permissible ground for denying custody of a child to a gay parent.[105] The military's exclusion of gays must end.[106] In short, any state action that disadvantages gays solely because they are gay is impermissible.

The obligations of ordinary citizens should be equally clear. Just as citizens' duty to purge their thinking of racism requires them to destigmatize miscegenation, so their duty to purge their thinking of sexism requires them to destigmatize homosexuality.

Juridical equality for gays is a step in the right direction. Destigmatization is what opponents of juridical gay rights most fear, and they are correct in thinking that this would be the consequence of legally recognizing such rights, for example gay marriage. As with impermissible stigma generally, government has, at a minimum, an obligation not to place its own imprimatur on such stigma. The denial of that imprimatur is, and will be understood as, a statement about the moral worth of homosexuality.

103. Cf. *McLaughlin v. Florida*, 379 U.S. 184 (1964) (invalidating statute prohibiting unmarried interracial couple from occupying same room at night).

104. Cf. *Loving v. Virginia*, 388 U.S. 1 (1967) (invalidating prohibition of interracial marriage).

105. Cf. *Palmore v. Sidoti*, 466 U.S. 429 (1984) (invalidating change in custody based on social stigmatization child would suffer because of mother's remarriage to a black man).

106. See my "Gaze in the Military: A Response to Professor Woodruff," 64 *UMKC L. Rev.* 179 (1995).

There are lingering civil liberties worries, raised by th
project in general, but at present particularly emphasized
extension of the project to lesbians and gay men. Enforce
nation laws deprives individuals of the liberty to choose
associate, and raises other liberal concerns as well. Thes
eral commitments are not peculiar to gay rights, but are
antidiscrimination project. They deserve separate consid   ., and I will try
to do them justice in Chapters 5 and 6.

5

Social Equality in Liberal Political Theory

I have argued thus far that our culture ought to be changed in ways that eliminate the stigmatization of blacks, women, and homosexuals, and I have maintained that the state has a useful role to play in this process. In this chapter I consider liberal objections to the latter claim, for liberalism characteristically tends to advocate a far more limited role for the state vis-à-vis culture than I have envisioned here.

In Chapters 1 and 2, I enumerated three kinds of injury that were traceable to aspects of culture: biased government decision making, unjustifiable social stigma, and the material disadvantaging of groups. In this chapter, I shall examine these injuries from the perspective of liberal political philosophy, taking up in turn the work of three major liberal thinkers: Robert Nozick, John Rawls, and Bruce Ackerman. More specifically, I shall examine each philosopher's answers to the following questions: Are any of these harms properly cognizable as injuries by a liberal state? If so, is action that seeks to bring about the reshaping of the culture or the character of the citizenry a legitimate response by the liberal state? Again if so, what limits are there to the means that the liberal state may use in pursuing these ends?

Efforts by the state to reshape culture will look deeply suspicious to a philosophy that seeks to maximize human freedom, even if that reshaping is animated by attractive moral ideals. In contemporary liberal theory, the objection to tutelary legislation is that the state, in order properly to respect citizens' freedom and dignity, must be neutral between different conceptions of the good. John Rawls writes that in the liberal state, "[s]ystems of ends are not ranked in value";[1] Ronald Dworkin interprets liberalism as holding that

1. John Rawls, *A Theory of Justice* (Cambridge: Harvard University Press, 1971), p. 19.

"political decisions must be, so far as is possible, independent of any particular conception of the good life, or of what gives values to life";[2] Bruce Ackerman holds that "[n]o reason [for exercising power] is a good reason if it requires the power holder to assert . . . that his conception of the good is better than that asserted by any of his fellows";[3] and Robert Nozick writes that in the liberal utopia, "people are at liberty to join together voluntarily to pursue and attempt to realize their own vision of the good life in the ideal community but . . . no one can *impose* his own utopian vision on others."[4] In recent liberal theory, there has been some movement away from this strong antiperfectionism. Most notably, Joseph Raz, William Galston, Rogers Smith, and Stephen Macedo have all developed accounts of liberalism that include liberal virtue and a liberal ideal of character.[5] None of these writers has had much to say about the relationship of liberalism to the effort to eradicate racism and sexism, however, and they do not say whether liberalism as they understand it would support or condemn the state's involvement in that effort.[6] This chapter builds on, and fills this gap in, their work, but it does not focus upon them. Since the neutralist version of liberalism is the one most plainly in tension

2. Ronald Dworkin, "Liberalism," in *A Matter of Principle* (Cambridge: Harvard University Press, 1985), p. 191.

3. Bruce Ackerman, *Social Justice in the Liberal State* (New Haven: Yale University Press, 1980), p. 11.

4. Robert Nozick, *Anarchy, State, and Utopia* (New York: Basic Books, 1974), p. 312, emphasis in original; cf. ibid., p. 33.

5. See Joseph Raz, *The Morality of Freedom* (Oxford: Clarendon Press, 1986); William Galston, *Liberal Purposes: Goods, Virtues, and Diversity in the Liberal State* (Cambridge: Cambridge University Press, 1991); Rogers M. Smith, *Liberalism and American Constitutional Law* (Cambridge and London: Harvard University Press, 1985); Stephen Macedo, *Liberal Virtues: Citizenship, Virtue, and Community in Liberal Constitutionalism* (Oxford: Clarendon Press, 1991).

6. A partial exception is Rogers Smith, whose recent work has emphasized the tension between American liberalism and America's traditions of ascriptive, unequal statuses. See Rogers M. Smith, "Beyond Tocqueville, Myrdal, and Hartz: The Multiple Traditions of America," 87 *Am. Pol. Sci. Rev.* 549 (1993); Rogers M. Smith, " 'One United People': Second-Class Female Citizenship and the American Quest for Community," 1 *Yale J. Law & Humanities* 229 (1989). Smith's approach "urges courts to focus on personal, not group [r]ights." Rogers M. Smith, "Equal Protection Remedies: The Errors of Liberal Ways and Means," 1 *J. Pol. Phil.* 185, 203 n. 53 (1993). Yet Smith often shifts his focus from individuals to groups. "We should ask . . . whether under existing conditions, whatever their source, there are persons, groups, races, or a gender who are effectively and corrigibly deficient in the legal, social, and material resources and opportunities the system aims to promote for everyone." "Equal Protection Remedies," p. 192. If the issue is *individuals'* liberty, then it is not clear why the inquiry goes beyond individuals to ask whether the relevant deprivation is disproportionately visited on "groups, races, or a gender." Smith has not yet synthesized his historical work on the status of groups with his normative individualism.

with the antidiscrimination project, and since I want in this chapter to address liberal objections in their strongest form, I shall concentrate my attention upon the proponents of liberal neutrality.

An account of liberalism that emphasizes the state's neutrality toward competing ideas of the good is obviously in tension with the antidiscrimination project. Antidiscrimination law violates neutrality inasmuch as it singles out certain conceptions of the good and selectively forbids their expression in private decision making. Herbert Wechsler's objection to *Brown* is silly with respect to public schools, which children are compelled to attend whether they are integrated or segregated (so that individual choice simply does not enter the picture), but it is quite to the point with respect to the civil rights statutes:

> [I]f the freedom of association is denied by segregation, integration forces an association upon those for whom it is unpleasant or repugnant. Is this not the heart of the issue involved, a conflict in human claims of high dimension, not unlike many others that involve the highest freedoms. . . . Given a situation where the state must practically choose between denying the association to those individuals who wish it or imposing association on those who would avoid it, is there a basis in neutral principles for holding that the Constitution demands that the claims for association should prevail? I should like to think there is, but I confess that I have not yet written the opinion.[7]

The same concern appears in a well-known early writing of Robert Bork, who argued in 1963 against the bill that became the Civil Rights Act of 1964 on the ground that it would mean "a loss in a vital area of personal liberty. . . . The principle of such legislation is that if I find your behavior ugly by my standards, moral or aesthetic, and if you prove stubborn about adopting my view of the situation, I am justified in having the state coerce you into more righteous paths. That is itself a principle of unsurpassed ugliness."[8]

7. Herbert Wechsler, "Toward Neutral Principles of Constitutional Law," 73 *Harv. L. Rev.* 1, 34 (1959).

8. Robert Bork, "Civil Rights—A Challenge," 149 *New Republic*, Aug. 31, 1963, p. 22. Bork recanted this position in 1973 because, as he more recently explained, "there are no general principles to decide competing principles of association and nonassociation. There being no correct general answer, the proper approach for the legislator is necessarily ad hoc, to ask whether the proposed law will do more good than harm. What do I mean by 'more good than harm'? I

Now it is perfectly consistent with, and indeed demanded by, neutrality to purge legislative decision making of the stigmatizing beliefs such as racism that the antidiscrimination project opposes.[9] Thus liberalism can easily be reconciled with the process defect theory. But when the law interferes with individuals' ability to act on their own racist preferences, then it seems that these individuals can themselves complain of a violation of neutrality. This apparent tension between liberalism and antidiscrimination law weakens the moral authority of both, since each seems less attractive when it appears to exclude the other. Antidiscrimination law becomes vulnerable to accusations that it interferes with freedom. Liberals' insistence on neutrality has left them vulnerable to the charge that liberalism is morally empty.[10] This vulnerability is particularly acute when liberalism opposes legislation based upon deeply felt moral convictions, as it does in the areas of gay rights and abortion: it becomes all too easy for conservatives to characterize the debate as one between morality and moral nihilism.[11] I shall argue, to the contrary, that the

---

mean that society itself will come to see the legislation as beneficial and will do so in the relatively short term." *The Tempting of America: The Political Seduction of the Law* (New York: Free Press, 1990), p. 80. Bork's revised position appears to be that the principle embodied in the Fourteenth Amendment has no bearing on the civil rights statutes, and no principle would be violated if it did not please Congress to pass such legislation. Bork has abandoned libertarianism for the crassest kind of utilitarianism. The libertarian objection to the civil rights statutes has been taken up by others. See, e.g., Richard Epstein, *Forbidden Grounds: The Case Against Employment Discrimination Laws* (Cambridge and London: Harvard University Press, 1992); Michael Levin, "Negative Liberty," 2 *Soc. Phil. & Pol'y* 84, 98–100 (1984).

9. This is true whether one adopts any of a number of different plausible interpretations of the idea of neutrality. See Raz, *The Morality of Freedom*, pp. 114–15; Galston, *Liberal Purposes*, pp. 100–101; John Rawls, *Political Liberalism* (New York: Columbia University Press, 1993), pp. 191–93. But for a survey of some pathological interpretations of neutrality that might produce a different result, see Bruce Ackerman, "Neutralities," in R. Bruce Douglass, Gerald M. Mara, and Henry S. Richardson, eds., *Liberalism and the Good* (New York and London: Routledge, 1990), pp. 29–43.

10. William Galston, "Defending Liberalism," 76 *Am. Pol. Sci. Rev.* 621, 629 (1982); see also Macedo, *Liberal Virtues*, pp. 9–38.

11. Thus, for example, one writer argues that "[t]he legitimization of homosexual relations . . . teaches and promotes an indifference [to marriage], where once there was an endorsement. Since that endorsement purported to be based upon knowledge of the objective good of marriage, it taught not only that marriage is good, but that we can know what is good. The latter is, in a way, a far more critical lesson." Robert Reilly, "Homosexual Rights and the Foundations of Human Rights," in Enrique Rueda, ed., *The Homosexual Network: Private Lives and Public Policy* (Old Greenwich, Conn.: Devin Adair, 1982), p. 538; quoted in Brief of Petitioner at 38, *Bowers v. Hardwick*, 478 U.S. 186 (1986) (No. 85–140).

new theorists of liberal virtue are correct that liberalism carries within it powerful moral ideals. I shall further argue that these ideals support, rather than contradict, the antidiscrimination project. These same ideals do limit what can be done in furtherance of the project, but those limits are dependent on context.

Nozick and Antidiscrimination

One way of describing the tension between liberalism and the antidiscrimination project is to note that a project of cultural transformation presses against the public/private distinction. Process theory, we noted in Chapter 1, need not make any particularly controversial moves when it claims that the *state* has an obligation to treat all citizens with equal concern and respect. In order to argue that citizens themselves have a similar obligation, however, it was necessary to invoke republican theories of citizenship that presuppose precisely what some liberal theorists would find objectionable about the project—the idea that the character and beliefs of citizens are a legitimate concern of the state. Liberalism clearly forbids the state from discriminating against one race or sex. But does it, in any degree, place the same injunction upon individuals? Even if it does, is that injunction enforceable by the state? Or does liberalism rather require that individuals be free to discriminate or not, as it pleases them? Traditionally, liberalism has chosen the second answer. It is in the public sphere that impersonality and neutrality are required; citizens may give expression to whatever preferences they happen to have in the private sphere, and it is none of the state's business what those preferences happen to be.[12]

A perennial problem is where the line that separates public from private is to be drawn. The simplest answer is the libertarian one, that citizens should be free to do as they like with their own property. The requirement of neutrality that forbids the state from discriminating also forbids it from interfering with private discrimination. This was the premise of Bork's 1963 position. The preeminent contemporary defender of this view is Nozick, for whom the only duty of the state is to protect all citizens equally from force and fraud. Beyond that, its functions, and the obligation of neutrality, stop. This conception pro-

12. This was the distinction that Justice Harlan relied upon in his *Plessy v. Ferguson* dissent, quoted at the beginning of the Introduction.

hibits some kinds of racist legislation, but it prohibits most civil rights legis-lation, too.[13] Libertarianism thus offers a clear answer to our question: the reshaping of culture is not a legitimate goal of the state. There are, however, reasons to doubt whether that answer is satisfactory, even given Nozick's premises.

The three harms enumerated in Chapters 1 and 2—process defect, stigma, and group disadvantage—are all cognizable even in Nozick's terms, although the latter two are so only to a limited extent. Nozick is as devoted to state impartiality as any of the process theorists, and so cannot tolerate racism, even unconscious racism, in government decision making. The state, in order to deserve allegiance, "scrupulously must be *neutral* between its citizens."[14] In a culture in which unconscious racism is pervasive, government decision makers who have internalized that racism will often be incapable of neutrality even with respect to the minimal range of government functions Nozick deems legitimate. Those functions must include criminal sanctions against private violence, but as we saw in Chapter 1 when we considered *McCleskey v. Kemp*, the Georgia death penalty case, the state today is unable to achieve neutrality in administering those sanctions.[15] Our conclusion, which was used there to criticize Ely, is equally applicable against Nozick: transformation of the culture is necessary if impartial government decision making is to be possible.

Nozick is extremely resistant to any conception of justice that focuses on

13. Thus Nozick's reasoning would support the Court's invalidation of legislation that imposes racist preferences on the market, as in *Buchanan v. Warley*, 245 U.S. 60 (1917) (invalidating a municipal ordinance forbidding persons of one race to occupy any house on a block inhabited mostly by persons of another race, because the Fourteenth Amendment forbids states from in-terfering with property rights on racial grounds, see ibid., pp. 75–79). See Epstein, *Forbidden Grounds*, pp. 112–15. The same reasoning would, however, also invalidate the Civil Rights Act of 1964, which interferes with individuals' freedom to express their own racist preferences in market transactions. See Epstein, *Forbidden Grounds*, pp. 130–43.

14. *Anarchy, State, and Utopia*, p. 33.

15. Daniel Ortiz thinks Nozick's argument supports the result in *McCleskey*, because state infringements on individual rights are easier to justify as the state's interest increases, and "pro-tecting citizens against violence, theft, and fraud represents the irreducible core of the state in classical liberal theory." "The Myth of Intent in Equal Protection," 41 *Stan. L. Rev.* 1105, 1148–49 (1989). But the state is also obligated to protect all its citizens equally, and this obligation is breached when the murderers of blacks are punished less severely than the murderers of whites. Nozick's argument therefore cuts the other way. This argument was suggested to me by Steven Winter.

results, as the stigma and group-disadvantage theories do. Nozick argues that any acceptable theory of justice must be a *historical* conception, rather than an *end-result* conception. According to end-result conceptions, "all that needs to be looked at, in judging the justice of a distribution, is who ends up with what; in comparing any two distributions one need look only at the matrix presenting the distributions." Such conceptions, Nozick observes, are rejected by most people, who "think it relevant in assessing the justice of a situation to consider not only the distribution it embodies, but also how that distribution came about." In contrast to end-result conceptions, historical conceptions "hold that past circumstances or actions of people can create differential entitlements or differential deserts to things." Instead of examining the overall pattern of distribution, a historical conception asks whether each individual is entitled to what he or she has. "If each person's holdings are just, then the total set (distribution) of holdings is just."[16] An important consideration that weighs in favor of historical principles, Nozick argues, is that

> no end-state or distributional patterned principle of justice can be continuously realized without continuous interference in people's lives. Any favored pattern would be transformed into one unfavored by the principle, by people choosing to act in various ways; for example, by people exchanging goods and services with other people, or giving things to other people, things the transferrers are entitled to under the favored distributional pattern. To maintain a pattern one must either continually interfere to stop people from transferring resources as they wish to, or continually (or periodically) interfere to take from some persons resources that others for some reason chose to transfer to them.[17]

Although Nozick thus purports to be indifferent to the results brought about by an unregulated market, he implicitly relies upon the premise that transactions between rational economic actors will bring about acceptable patterns. "[I]t must be granted that were people's reasons for transferring some of their holdings to others always irrational or arbitrary, we would find this disturbing. . . . Since in a capitalist society people often transfer holdings to others in accordance with how much they perceive these others benefiting

16. *Anarchy, State, and Utopia*, pp. 154, 155, 153.
17. Ibid., p. 163.

them, the fabric constituted by the individual transactions and transfers is largely reasonable and intelligible."[18] Part of the argument against stigma and group disadvantage is that these are morally repellent regardless of the process by which they came about. We shall shortly consider whether Nozick's indifference to results is justified. First, however, observe that the injuries of group disadvantage and stigma are cognizable, at least to some extent, even within Nozick's historical framework.

One might think that Nozick's relentlessly individualistic schema could not possibly recognize group disadvantage as a cognizable harm. No pattern of distribution is objectionable so long as it came about legitimately. Nozick, however, offers no reason for believing that the distribution of goods in *our* society did come about legitimately.[19] In one passage, moreover, Nozick acknowledges that there have been considerable past injustices against certain groups, and considers the possibility that the correction of these may require a larger and more intrusive state apparatus than would ordinarily be permissible.[20] George Kateb observes that if Nozick were to work out the implications of this idea, "he may take more money from whites than the welfare state ever has."[21] Thus, the disadvantages of blacks as a group may be cognizable after all. It is, however, hard to see how this argument could be extended to a less insular group, such as women. The material disadvantages of women as a group are not the result of their being born into families that in the past suffered gross injustice; they are much more the product of ongoing patterns of behavior that produce women's disadvantages anew in each generation. For gay men and lesbians the situation is even more difficult; their disadvantages are cognizable only if injuries arising out of culture are allowed to count.[22]

18. Ibid., p. 159. Ian Shapiro observes that Nozick frequently relies on "the belief that capitalist economies can be efficiently self-regulating, an empirical claim for which little evidence has ever been supplied." *The Evolution of Rights in Liberal Theory* (Cambridge: Cambridge University Press, 1986), p. 201.

19. Nozick's theory of entitlement is underdeveloped both in the abstract and as applied to our society. On the former, see Amy Gutmann, *Liberal Equality* (Cambridge: Cambridge University Press, 1980), pp. 156–67; Bruce Ackerman, "Why Dialogue?," 86 *J. Phil.* 5, 11–12 (1989). On the latter, see Ackerman, *Social Justice in the Liberal State*, pp. 185–86, 221–22.

20. *Anarchy, State, and Utopia*, pp. 152–53, citing with some approval Boris Bittker, *The Case for Black Reparations* (New York: Vintage, 1973). See also Michel Rosenfeld, *Affirmative Action and Justice* (New Haven and London: Yale University Press, 1991), pp. 61–64.

21. George Kateb, "The Night Watchman State" (review of *Anarchy, State, and Utopia*), 45 *American Scholar* 816, 825 (1975–76).

22. It appears that Nozick's insistence on state neutrality entails the condemnation of laws that

What, then, about stigma? Nozick appears to envision corrective justice as involving the transfer of resources rather than the changing of culture. It is not clear, however, that any such transfer could put the victims in the same position they would occupy had they not been injured. "Something fully compensates a person for a loss if and only if it makes him no worse off than he otherwise would have been."[23] If the effect of past injustices has been to restrict blacks' opportunities in the private sector, then some restructuring of the private sector may be a necessary part of any adequate remedy. Some versions of the stigma theory rely on the idea of reparations, such as the Supreme Court's extension of the Thirteenth Amendment to outlaw the "badges and incidents of slavery."[24] If culture is itself the product of injustice—if, for example, the present widespread bias against blacks, which imposes continuing economic costs on them, is a relic of the once-official view that blacks were "beings of an inferior order, and altogether unfit to associate with the white race, either in social or political relations; and so far inferior, that they had no rights which the white man was bound to respect"[25]—then perhaps this too ought to be an object of corrective justice.[26] And this argument, unlike the reparations claim considered in the last paragraph, can readily be extended to women, whose present subordination is the product of a culture that has developed on the basis of past deprivations of their rights. Women would not now find it so hard to make their way in the public sphere if they had not in the past been wrongly excluded from it.

These understandings of stigma and group disadvantage are, however, narrower than those explored in Chapter 2. The stigma and group-disadvantage

---

deny the right to marry to same-sex couples, but it is not clear that the registration of marriages is a function that Nozick's minimal state would be entitled to perform at all.

23. *Anarchy, State, and Utopia*, p. 57.

24. *Jones v. Alfred H. Mayer Co.*, 392 U.S. 409, 440 (1968).

25. *Dred Scott v. Sandford*, 60 U.S. (19 How.) 393, 407 (1857).

26. A Nozickian might reply that, while slavery did deprive blacks of certain rights, the right not to be stigmatized was not among them, because there is no such right. On this account, the stigma that is a relic of slavery is simply a misfortune for blacks, not something that they can justly ask the state to do anything about. But it is hard to tell what this argument would look like, since Nozick provides so little information about how he proposes to determine whether any given proposed entitlement should or should not be recognized as a right. It is clear that such an argument would be inconsistent with Nozick's own conception of corrective justice, which requires that the victim be fully compensated for his loss. In American law, there is no right to be free from pain and suffering, but there is a right to compensation for pain and suffering that results from another's tortious misconduct.

theorists of antidiscrimination law, such as Karst and Fiss, hold that these are injuries regardless of how they came about; if Nozick will recognize these injuries at all, he will do so only to the extent that they can be traced to historical wrongs. We shall shortly consider whether this narrowing can be justified. First, however, let us see whether the Nozickian state may permissibly concern itself with culture.

Nozick's theory does not logically require, and in fact probably cannot permit, state indifference to citizens' thoughts. Suppose that a group of contractors in a state of nature agreed to set up a libertarian state, but they knew that their culture did not include any particular respect for property rights. The newly established state would then have a choice of whether to (a) protect property by invasive, police-state methods, such as surveillance cameras in every room of every home and broad police powers to conduct warrantless searches, or (b) work to change the culture so that its members did have respect for property rights, thus lowering the rate of property crimes and eliminating the necessity for such a formidable police state. Which role for the state would the contractors agree to? Nozick's official position seems better able to accommodate the first option.[27] Much of the attractiveness of that position, however, lies in its valorization of freedom. His objection to any theory of justice that, like Rawls's, seeks to maintain any particular distributional pattern is that it will require "continuous interference in people's lives."[28] If a culture could be established in which such interference was no longer necessary in order to effectively protect property rights, then this would seem preferable. Nozick's social contractors are likely to agree with Rawls that "a scheme of just social cooperation advances citizens' determinate conceptions of the good; and a scheme made stable by an effective public sense of justice is a better means to this end than a scheme which requires a severe and costly apparatus of penal sanctions, particularly when this apparatus is dangerous to the basic liberties."[29] Without *some* degree of virtue among the citizens, moreover, even a Nozickian police state is simply unsustainable. Macedo observes that even the most minimal liberal state cannot dispense with

27. Kateb similarly argues that Nozick's principles "would not even exclude a vast state apparatus if it was required to repress a numerous discontented mass that felt itself neglected or exploited. This minimal state would be minimal only in the job it tried to do, not in the powers it exercised to do its job." "The Night Watchman State," p. 816.

28. Nozick, *Anarchy, State, and Utopia*, p. 163.

29. Rawls, *Political Liberalism*, p. 317.

liberal virtues. "If people are not prepared to accept the constraints and formalities implicit in the rule of law or the electoral process, for example (if bribery and other forms of corruption are rampant) these liberal institutions cannot survive."[30] Nozick pays little attention to the cultural preconditions of liberalism, but such attention seems indispensable. "Liberal institutions such as law and rights require the willing support of liberal citizens. For that support to be forthcoming and for a liberal state to flourish liberal values must be internalized by citizens."[31]

The virtue that Nozick's state requires is, however, quite minimal, consisting only in a willingness to obey the laws and a disposition to administer them impartially. As noted above, this virtue is incompatible with unconscious racism, and so the need to inculcate it already provides a Nozickian basis for the antidiscrimination project. Whether liberalism requires *only* this virtue depends upon whether it is as indifferent to patterns as Nozick thinks.

The deepest problem with Nozick is that the ultimate foundation of his theory is a doctrine of respect for persons,[32] and it is doubtful whether the system he erects adequately demonstrates such respect.[33] The same respect for persons that is the basis for property rights will, under some circumstances, demand overriding those rights. Persons are not reducible to their property-rights-bearing aspect, but that is the only aspect respected by a Nozickian society. An unemployed and starving person may be tempted to repeat Anatole France's jibe, that the law in its majestic equality forbids rich and poor alike from sleeping under bridges and stealing bread.[34] As an earlier and clearer-eyed generation of libertarians knew, it is not Kantianism, but social Darwinism, that is the most suitable tool for the formidable task of justifying such a person's predicament.[35]

---

30. Macedo, *Liberal Virtues*, p. 55.

31. Ibid.

32. Nozick, *Anarchy, State, and Utopia*, pp. 30–33.

33. For similar criticism, see Kateb, "The Night Watchman State," pp. 818–20; Thomas W. Pogge, *Realizing Rawls* (Ithaca and London: Cornell University Press, 1989), pp. 54–55.

34. Thus Ronald Dworkin argues that laissez-faire libertarianism "tries to win its position by fiat. It stipulates that treating people with equal concern means respecting economic rights that work to the benefit of those with talent and luck and against those with neither. That is hardly self-evident." "What is Equality? Part 3: The Place of Liberty," 73 *Iowa L. Rev.* 1, 15 (1987).

35. See, e.g., William Graham Sumner, *What Social Classes Owe to Each Other* (orig. ed. 1883; Caldwell, Idaho: Caxton Publishers, 1986). See generally Richard Hofstadter, *Social Darwinism in American Thought* (Boston: Beacon, rev. ed. 1955).

Nozick's public/private distinction is even more absolutist than that of the post–Civil War Supreme Court, which went to great lengths to defend private property and freedom of contract. For the Court did not identify the private realm as coextensive with the realm of private property: property could be privately owned and yet be part of the public sphere. Thus, for example, the Court held that businesses' constitutional immunity from regulation was attenuated if the business was "affected with a public interest."[36] More to the point, the Court observed in the *Civil Rights Cases* that innkeepers had a common-law duty to serve all who sought to patronize them, regardless of race[37]—reasoning that was relied on during the debate over the 1964 Civil Rights Act to rebut criticism like Bork's.[38]

It is revealing that even many libertarians lack the courage of their convictions on this issue. Libertarian writers have spilled a good deal of ink seeking to prove that in a minimal state that recognizes absolute liberty of property and contract, the lot of the poorest class will be better than under any other system, and that widespread racial discrimination is an artifact of state intervention in markets.[39] A principled Nozickian, by contrast, would have to insist that it makes no difference whether these or any other end-states are reached as long as the transactional process is just.[40] By arguing that libertarianism will redound to the benefit of the least advantaged, these writers reveal themselves to be closet Rawlsians.[41] Their libertarianism is contingent rather than principled, and they should abandon it if their factual arguments (which have been subjected to withering criticism) are false.[42]

Nozick claims that any theory of justice that seeks to maintain a particular

36. *Munn v. Illinois*, 94 U.S. 113, 130 (1877).

37. 109 U.S. 3, 25 (1883).

38. See Senate Report No. 872 accompanying S. 1732, Civil Rights Act of 1964, reprinted in *U.S. Code Cong. & Admin. News*, 88th Cong., 2d sess. 2355, 2363–65.

39. The fullest statement of this thesis is Epstein, *Forbidden Grounds.*

40. Nozick, *Anarchy, State, and Utopia*, pp. 153–64. Bernard Boxill notes this tension in the libertarian writings of Thomas Sowell and Walter E. Williams. See Boxill, *Blacks and Social Justice* (Lanham, Md.: Rowman and Littlefield, rev. ed. 1992), pp. 23–26. This criticism is not applicable to Epstein, who had shifted from natural rights libertarianism to limited government utilitarianism by the time he wrote *Forbidden Grounds.* See Richard Epstein, "Standing Firm, on Forbidden Grounds," 31 *San Diego L. Rev.* 1, 2–5 (1994).

41. Even John Locke, to whom libertarians look as their founding father, made such an argument. See *Two Treatises of Government*, ed. Peter Laslett (New York: Mentor, 1965), pp. 336, 338–39.

42. For examples of the criticism, see the reviews of Epstein cited in Chapter 1, footnote 131.

distributional pattern will violate people's rights, specifically their property rights. As already noted, however, he does not defend the institutional scheme by which people are assigned property rights. He treats property rights as if they were prepolitical, rather than being themselves the artifact of certain historical political decisions.[43] The same concern for the dignity of persons that animates Nozick's libertarianism might also require the allocation of rights in a way that prevents states of affairs in which some persons can exercise coercive power over others.[44]

Thomas Pogge observes that Nozick's theory rests on his belief in the moral salience of the distinction between established and engendered patterns of distribution. "Goods and ills are *established* when they are directly called for in the (written or unwritten) rules and procedures of the social system." *Engendered* pattern features are "ones that, like income differentials in a free-market system, are not directly called for in the relevant rules and procedures but merely foreseeably come about through them." Questions of justice, Nozick thinks, are raised only by established inequalities, not by engendered ones. Pogge argues, on the contrary, that this distinction cannot bear the moral weight that Nozick seeks to place upon it. The only plausible way to justify the ground rules of any institutional scheme is from the point of view of prospective participants. Those participants, however, have no reason to care whether a deprivation they are likely to face is established or engendered.[45]

If that is the case, then what issues of justice are raised by engendered racial or gender inequalities? Because Nozick excludes all engendered inequalities from his field of concern, we may safely infer that his state would regard inequalities arising from racial and gender patterns with the same indifference as those arising from social class. Nozick's implicit rejection of the antidiscrimination project is thus doubly unpersuasive: although his philosophy must condemn racism in public decision making, his indifference to engendered

---

43. "Nozick's belief that such self-regulating systems would emerge naturally has no basis in fact. A state would be (and in fact was) required to create the particular systems of property rights, contracts, torts, and other legal arrangements necessary to their preservation and reproduction. Once these are established the power of the state becomes latent and its inactivity will be sought by those desirous of preserving the broad socioeconomic status quo." Shapiro, *The Evolution of Rights,* pp. 201–2.

44. See G. A. Cohen, "Robert Nozick and Wilt Chamberlain: How Patterns Preserve Liberty," in John Arthur and William H. Shaw, eds., *Justice and Economic Distribution* (Englewood Cliffs, N.J.: Prentice-Hall, 1978), p. 246.

45. Pogge, *Realizing Rawls,* pp. 38, 55, emphasis in original.

inequalities is not adequately defended, and he offers no good argument for forbidding the state from attempting to shape culture. Nor does Nozick help us discern the limits of what the state legitimately may do in furtherance of the project. He offers a ringing declaration that the state may not violate people's rights, even when this is necessary to prevent a greater number of violations of rights,[46] but he has no persuasive account of what rights people do have. We must look elsewhere for a coherent account of liberal limits.

Rawls and Antidiscrimination

Rawls, who puts patterns of distribution into question, is somewhat misconstrued in Nozick's critique. He proposes not to violate anyone's rights but to raise the prior question of what rights ought to exist. To understand the dispute between Rawls and Nozick, writes Pogge,

> we must keep sharply distinct, as Nozick does not, *our* subject, *how the ground rules of a social system ought to be assessed/designed,* from the (secondary) subject of how actors (individuals, associations, the government) may and should act within an ongoing scheme whose terms are taken as fixed. The former of these subjects, *justice,* is concerned with the moral assessment and justification of social institutions; the latter, *morality,* with the assessment of conduct and character.[47]

Rawls thus argues that "the primary subject of justice is the basic structure of society, or more exactly, the way in which the major social institutions distribute fundamental rights and duties and determine the division of advantages from social cooperation."[48]

Rawls argues that the principles of justice regulating the basic institutions of society should be those that would be chosen by persons who deliberate in what he calls "the original position." In the original position, a "veil of ignorance" conceals from each party any knowledge of "his place in society, his class position or social status, ... his fortune in the distribution of natural assets or abilities, his intelligence and strength, and the like, ... his conception of the good, the particulars of his rational plan of life, even the special features

46. *Anarchy, State, and Utopia,* pp. 26–33.
47. Pogge, *Realizing Rawls,* p. 17, emphases in original; see also Rawls, *Political Liberalism,* pp. 262–69.
48. *A Theory of Justice,* p. 7.

of his psychology."[49] Because none of the parties knows which position in society he or she will end up occupying, any principles the parties reach will be fair ones.

Rawls concludes that two principles of justice will be chosen in the original position. First, "[e]ach person has an equal right to a fully adequate scheme of equal basic liberties which is compatible with a similar scheme of liberties for all."[50] Second, "[s]ocial and economic inequalities are to be arranged so that they are both: (a) to the greatest benefit of the least advantaged . . . and (b) attached to offices and positions open to all under conditions of fair equality of opportunity." The first principle takes priority over the second; basic liberties are not to be traded away for economic and social benefits, because "if the parties assume that their basic liberties can be effectively exercised, they will not exchange a lesser liberty for an improvement in well-being." The inequalities with which the parties are particularly concerned involve the distribution of "primary goods," defined as "things which it is supposed a rational man wants whatever else he wants." These include "liberty and opportunity, income and wealth, and the bases of self-respect." The parties in the original position do not know what their conception of the good is, but they do know that whatever it might be, it is better to have more rather than less of the primary goods. Since they do not know what social position they will end up occupying, it will be rational for them, in choosing a principle of distribution, "to adopt the alternative the worst outcome of which is superior to the worst outcomes of the others." They will choose the principle that maximizes the share of primary goods that go to the worst-off in society, and this will be the principle that primary goods "are to be distributed equally unless an unequal distribution of any or all of these goods is to the advantage of the least favored."[51]

How do things stand with the antidiscrimination project from this perspective? All of the disadvantages that flow from the stigmatized status of blacks or women evidently should have some weight in the parties' evaluation of social arrangements. Culture would itself appear to be part of the basic

49. Ibid., p. 137.

50. Rawls, *Political Liberalism*, p. 291. This formulation is somewhat modified from its original version: "Each person is to have an equal right to the most extensive total system of equal basic liberties compatible with a similar system of liberty for all." *A Theory of Justice*, p. 302. The reasons for the modification are discussed below, pp. 201–2.

51. *A Theory of Justice*, pp. 302, 151–52, 92, 303, 153, 303.

structure that is the subject of justice. The institutions that make up the basic structure include "the principal economic and social arrangements," and Rawls's examples of such arrangements include "the monogamous family."[52] These institutions

> define men's rights and duties and influence their life-prospects, what they can expect to be and how well they can hope to do. The basic structure is the primary subject of justice because its effects are so profound and present from the start. The intuitive notion here is that this structure contains various social positions and that men born into different positions have different expectations of life determined, in part, by the political system as well as by economic and social circumstances. In this way the institutions of society favor certain starting places over others. These are especially deep inequalities. Not only are they pervasive, but they affect men's initial chances in life; yet they cannot possibly be justified by an appeal to the notions of merit or desert. It is these inequalities, presumably inevitable in the basic structure of any society, to which the principles of social justice must in the first instance apply.[53]

Racism and sexism plainly are, if not part of the basic structure, then at least problems that the basic structure must address if it is to be just. Their effects are "profound and pervasive, and present from birth." They affect what people can expect to be or do. And they certainly favor certain starting places over others. Recall that Rawls's second principle of justice permits only those inequalities that are "to the greatest benefit of the least advantaged" and "attached to offices and positions open to all."[54] Susan Okin observes that this principle has major implications for the status of women:

> This means that if any roles or positions analogous to our current sex roles—including those of husband or wife, mother and father—were to survive the demands of the first requirement, the second requirement would prohibit any linkage between these roles and sex. Gender, with its ascriptive designation of positions and expectations of behavior in ac-

---

52. Ibid., p. 7. In his more recent writing, Rawls seems to offer a narrower definition of the basic structure than that set forth in *A Theory of Justice*, but this narrowing is not adequately defended and is inconsistent with his more fundamental commitments. See Pogge, *Realizing Rawls*, pp. 23–24; Susan Moller Okin, review of *Political Liberalism*, 87 Am. Pol. Sci. Rev. 1010 (1993).

53. *A Theory of Justice*, p. 7.

54. Ibid., pp. 96, 302.

cordance with the inborn characteristic of sex, could no longer form a legitimate part of the social structure, whether inside or outside the family.[55]

The same point can obviously be made about race. All three of the injuries we noted in Chapters 1 and 2 would be of concern to the parties in the original position. The parties would want to be treated impartially. They would not want to be subjected to material inequalities except to the extent that these benefit the worst-off. And they would not want to be unnecessarily stigmatized. Recall that we said, in Chapter 2, that if one enters a hospital ward of healthy newborn babies, one can predict their eventual positions in society on the basis of their social class. That is the kind of inequality that most concerns Rawls. We also said, however, that one can predict, on the basis of a baby's race or sex, whether it will be subjected to certain disadvantages and humiliations that others will not have to endure, or will have to endure far less often. This, too, should be a concern of Rawlsian justice.

The illegitimacy of racism and sexism from the perspective of Rawls's philosophy is clearest to the extent that these affect people's life chances, and thereby contradict the principle Rawls calls "fair equality of opportunity." This principle holds that "those who are at the same level of talent and ability, and have the same willingness to use them, should have the same prospects of success regardless of their initial place in the social system, that is, irrespective of the income class in which they are born."[56] This principle is more plausibly attainable if "race" or "sex" is substituted for "income class" in the sentence just quoted. History has not yet revealed a stratified society in which upper-class parents have not generally succeeded in passing on their status to their children, thereby largely excluding children of the lower classes.[57] The obstacles to "fair equal opportunity" imposed by racism and sexism may be less intractable.[58] But even if one is more hopeful about the prospects of abolishing inherited social class (or less hopeful about abolishing racism or sexism), the point remains that Rawls must condemn racism and sexism unless they can somehow be shown to benefit blacks or women. Like Dworkin, he must "pro-

---

55. Susan Moller Okin, *Justice, Gender, and the Family* (New York: Basic Books, 1989), p. 103.

56. *A Theory of Justice*, p. 73.

57. Pogge thinks that this fact makes Rawls's opportunity principle untenable. See *Realizing Rawls*, pp. 172–73.

58. But see Derrick Bell, *Faces at the Bottom of the Well: The Permanence of Racism* (New York: Basic Books, 1992).

tect people who are the objects of systematic prejudice from suffering any serious or pervasive disadvantage from that prejudice."[59] Rawls's theory must condemn patterned group disadvantage.

Explicating the significance of stigma in Rawls's theory is a more complicated matter than understanding the significance for him of biased decision making or group disadvantage, because the meaning of one of Rawls's key concepts, self-respect, is ambiguous and changes without announcement as his work develops. For this reason, we must look now at Rawls's arguments about self-respect in some detail.

In *A Theory of Justice*, stigma would be a central concern of the parties, because self-respect, there defined as "a person's sense of his own value, his conviction that his conception of the good, his plan of life, is worth carrying out," is a most important primary good. Self-respect, thus defined, is different from other primary goods, inasmuch as it is dependent on the thoughts of other people, specifically upon their holding the subject in esteem: "unless our endeavors are appreciated by our associates it is impossible for us to maintain the conviction that they are worthwhile." An extraordinarily strong version of the stigma theory would seem to follow from this argument, which implies (although Rawls does not say this) that we can bring to the bar of justice *all* the standards by which others judge us. If "the parties in the original position would wish to avoid at almost any cost the social conditions that undermine self-respect," then they would agree to state efforts to change the ideas in the better-off citizens' heads if the pervasiveness of those ideas undermined the self-respect of the worst-off citizens. Rawls's failure to appreciate the implications of his formulation may be the result of his inadequate understanding of stigma and shame: "It is our plan of life that determines what we feel ashamed of, and so feelings of shame are related to our aspirations, to what we try to do and with whom we wish to associate. Those with no musical ability do not strive to be musicians and feel no shame for this lack. Indeed it is no lack at all, *not at least if satisfying associations can be formed by doing other things.*"[60]

The final qualification is crucial. We do not simply choose the standards against which we judge ourselves. We are constituted as selves by the society in which we grow up, and its standards are part of what we are. Michael Sandel

59. Dworkin, "What is Equality? Part 3: The Place of Liberty," p. 37.
60. Rawls, *A Theory of Justice*, pp. 440, 441, 440, 444, emphasis added.

places great weight on this fact in his critique of Rawls, but he evades its disturbing implications by confining his discussion to the positive aspects of the thickly constituted self, particularly the fact that "we can know a good in common that we cannot know alone." It is not invariably a blessing for persons to "conceive their identity—the subject and not just the object of their feelings and aspirations—as defined to some extent by the community of which they are part."[61] A person's identity may be, in Erving Goffman's phrase, a "spoiled identity": "Those who have dealings with him fail to accord him the respect and regard which the uncontaminated aspects of his social identity have led them to anticipate extending, and have led him to anticipate receiving; he echoes this denial by finding that some of his own attributes warrant it."[62] My lack of musical ability may be a shameful matter if I am born into a family of virtuosi. If my family wishes to prevent this fact from injuring my self-respect, it may need to modify the standards by which it judges its members. We noted in Chapter 2 that stigma causes two kinds of intangible harm: internalized self-hatred and justified resentment at the injustice of being insulted with impunity. The first of these is the harm that does the most damage to self-respect, but the second also can severely impede people's ability "to pursue their conception of the good with zest and to delight in its fulfillment."[63]

It is not clear that the priority of liberty should override the need of the worst-off for amelioration of these stigmatic injuries. The priority of liberty, Rawls writes in *A Theory of Justice,* obtains only in certain societies; "when social conditions do not allow the effective establishment of these rights . . . one can allow their restriction." When the less favored still have urgent need of primary goods, their needs can override the interest in liberty; as their condition improves, "the marginal significance for our good of further economic and social advantages diminishes relative to the interests of liberty."[64] As Rawls's commentators have noted, however, the fact that social conditions *do* allow the effective establishment of these rights does not mean that there

---

61. Michael Sandel, *Liberalism and the Limits of Justice* (Cambridge: Cambridge University Press, 1982), pp. 183, 150.

62. Erving Goffman, *Stigma: Notes on the Management of Spoiled Identity* (Englewood Cliffs, N.J.: Prentice-Hall, 1963), pp. 8–9. Cf. ibid., p. 106: "Given that the stigmatized individual in our society acquires identity standards which he applies to himself in spite of failing to conform to them, it is inevitable that he will feel some ambivalence about his own self."

63. Rawls, *A Theory of Justice,* p. 178.

64. Ibid., p. 542.

is no group that lacks an adequate supply of primary goods. "Whatever the average per capita income there may be bag ladies living out of railway station lockers, and we might be them."[65] "A social system under truly favorable conditions is presumably advanced enough economically to *render feasible* economic institutions under which the most urgent needs are met, but the feasibility of such institutions hardly entails their existence."[66] What if the worst-off group in a society is so lacking in the primary good of self-respect that self-respect is more important to it than liberty?

Perhaps in response to these criticisms, Rawls has written a few sentences conceding, almost as an afterthought, that the basic rights and liberties may be overridden for the sake of citizens' basic needs,[67] because "below a certain level of material *and social* well-being . . . people simply cannot take part as citizens, much less equal citizens."[68] This would seem to imply that the state may disregard basic liberties altogether where this is necessary to provide for basic needs, a conclusion that has strong implications for the legitimacy of the antidiscrimination project. The processes by which some citizens are socially constructed as a stigmatized caste go beyond invidious state action. They extend into the soul of every citizen who thinks racist thoughts. Rawls acknowledges this when he writes that a liberal state would be entitled to take "steps to strengthen the virtues of toleration and mutual trust, say by discouraging various kinds of religious and racial discrimination (in ways consistent with liberty of conscience and freedom of speech)."[69] Moreover, given that the needs of members of a stigmatized caste must, if their self-respect is sufficiently damaged, overcome the priority of liberty, Rawls's parenthetical reservation

---

65. Shapiro, *The Evolution of Rights*, p. 219.

66. Pogge, *Realizing Rawls*, p. 140, emphasis in original; for a similar criticism, see Gutmann, *Liberal Equality*, p. 123. Rawls has since repudiated "the notion of the diminishing marginal significance of economic and social advantages relative to our interest in the basic liberties," because "the notion of marginal significance is incompatible with the notion of a hierarchy of interests . . . founded on a certain conception of the person as a free and equal person. . . ." Rawls, *Political Liberalism*, p. 371 n. 84. I shall argue below that this restricted conception of interests is too far removed from the interests that human beings actually have to be persuasive.

67. "[T]he first principle covering the equal basic rights and liberties may easily be preceded by a lexically prior principle requiring that citizens' basic needs be met, at least insofar as their being met is necessary for citizens to understand and to be able fruitfully to exercise those rights and liberties. Certainly any such principle must be assumed in applying the first principle. But I do not pursue these and other matters here." *Political Liberalism*, p. 7.

68. Ibid., p. 166, emphasis added.

69. Ibid., p. 195.

in the sentence just quoted seems too quick. Since what is most important is that every citizen have an adequate minimum of primary goods, and since "self-respect and a sure confidence in the sense of one's own worth is perhaps the most important primary good,"[70] the parties in the original position should not shrink from state programs of totalitarian reeducation where these would enhance the self-respect of the least advantaged.[71] For example, if the teachings of the church in a predominantly Catholic country are having the effect of damaging the self-respect of Jews or homosexuals, then the state should be entitled, and perhaps is required, to order the church to change its teachings.[72]

Can Rawls avoid this conclusion, which would destroy his theory's claim to be liberal? He does so in his later writings by redefining self-respect. Larry L. Thomas observes that A Theory of Justice does not adequately distinguish the conviction that one's plan of life is worthwhile from "the conviction that one deserves to be treated fairly in virtue of the fact that one is a person." Only the latter should be called self-respect; the former, which is what A Theory of Justice calls self-respect, is more properly called self-esteem. Thomas argues that "self-respect is a sense of worth which morality requires that the social institutions of society should be conducive to everyone having." But the same cannot be said of self-esteem. If people tend to place a comparatively greater value on those plans that display a greater number of well-trained abilities,

70. A Theory of Justice, p. 396.

71. See Allan Bloom, "Justice: John Rawls Vs. The Tradition of Political Philosophy," 69 Am. Pol. Sci. Rev. 648, 662 (1975): "What Rawls creates is an enormously active government whose goal is to provide the primary goods, including the sense of one's own worth, and therefore to encourage the attitudes that support the production and equal distribution of those goods. What can the future of liberty be in such a scheme? Liberty is, to be sure, Rawls's first principle of justice, but it is qualified by having to be 'compatible with a similar liberty for others.' Rawls does not elaborate the extent of that qualification."

72. Michael Walzer apparently thinks that this could never be necessary. "Domination is always mediated by some set of social goods. . . . Hence . . . equality as we have dreamed of it does not require the repression of persons. We have to understand and control social goods; we do not have to stretch or shrink human beings." Spheres of Justice: A Defense of Pluralism and Equality (New York: Basic Books, 1983), p. xiii. But he also says that one social good to which everyone is entitled is "some minimal respect" (ibid., p. 258), and that recognition "depends entirely upon individual acts of honoring and dishonoring, regarding and disregarding" (ibid., p. 255). He is correct that if other inequalities did not cumulate, for example if wealth (or race or sex) did not entail disproportionate shares of political power, education, physical security, and leisure, "it would certainly result in a distribution of honor and dishonor very different from the prevailing one" (ibid., p. 258). But the example in the text should suffice to show that stigma is not always the consequence of other inequalities, but can have a life of its own.

then this valuation will certainly be shared by those who are unable to attain such abilities. Therefore, "not all members of a well-ordered society will have equally high self-esteem, since some will undoubtedly have aspirations which are beyond their reach." Because ought implies can, Thomas concludes that a society cannot be morally required to provide everyone with equal self-esteem.[73]

Rawls has since acknowledged that *A Theory of Justice* does not adequately distinguish self-respect and self-esteem.[74] His understanding of self-respect now seems much closer to Thomas's. This shift is contemporaneous with a larger one in his theorizing toward a conception of justice that rests on a specific conception of moral personality.[75] The "fundamental idea" behind the theory, Rawls writes, is "that of society as a fair system of cooperation over time, from one generation to the next."[76] The theory adopts a conception of the person "to go with this idea."[77] Rawls's present position is that moral persons are "characterized by two powers and by two corresponding highest-order interests in realizing and exercising those powers. The first is the capacity for an effective sense of justice, that is, the capacity to understand, to apply, and to act from (and not merely in accordance with) the principles of justice. The second moral power is the capacity to form, to revise, and rationally to pursue a conception of the good."[78] These powers, Rawls claims, are "the necessary and sufficient condition for being counted a full and equal member of society in questions of political justice." They are what constitutes a person as "someone who can take part in, or who can play a role in, social life, and hence exercise and respect its various rights and duties." Persons are regarded as equal because they all have these powers "to the requisite minimum degree to be fully cooperating members of society." The parties regard their interests

73. Larry L. Thomas, "Morality and Our Self-Concept," 12 *J. Value Inquiry* 258, 265, 262 (1978). Nozick reaches substantially the same conclusion. See *Anarchy, State, and Utopia*, pp. 239–46. It is not clear that it is impossible for a society to guarantee everyone equal self-esteem. This could be accomplished by preventing anyone from developing greater abilities than the least able member of society. Such a cure would be worse than the disease. See Kurt Vonnegut Jr., "Harrison Bergeron," in *Welcome to the Monkey House* (New York: Dell, 1970), pp. 7–13.

74. John Rawls, "Justice as Fairness: Political Not Metaphysical," 14 *Phil. & Pub. Aff.* 223, 251 n. 33 (1985).

75. The shift in Rawls's conception of moral personality is briefly described in Galston, *Liberal Purposes*, pp. 119–20.

76. *Political Liberalism*, p. 14.

77. Ibid., p. 18.

78. John Rawls, "Kantian Constructivism in Moral Theory," 77 *J. Phil.* 515, 525 (1980).

in developing and exercising these powers as important for the sake of this cooperation. "Someone who has not developed and cannot exercise the moral powers to the minimum requisite degree cannot be a normal and fully co-operating member of society over a complete life. From this it follows that as citizens' representatives the parties [in the original position] adopt principles that guarantee conditions securing for those powers their adequate develop-ment and full exercise."[79]

Having thus redefined a person's highest-order interests, Rawls has revisited the definition of primary goods, which he now says are of concern to the parties because "these goods are essential all-purpose means to realize the higher-order interests connected with citizens' moral powers and their deter-minate conceptions of the good."[80] William Galston finds it remarkable that "this alteration in the *basis* of primary goods effects no changes whatever in the *enumeration* of these goods."[81] Self-respect, however, has been subtly re-defined in a way that reduces the likelihood of a conflict between it and liberty. Self-respect, Rawls now argues, has two elements: first, "our self-confidence as a fully cooperating member of society rooted in the development and ex-ercise of the two moral powers (and so as possessing an effective sense of justice)," and second, "our secure sense of our own value rooted in the con-viction that we can carry out a worthwhile plan of life."[82] Both of these ele-ments are supported by the guarantee of basic liberties:

> The first element is supported by the basic liberties which guarantee the full and informed exercise of both moral powers. The second element is supported by the public nature of this guarantee and the affirmation of it by citizens generally, all in conjunction with the fair value of the basic liberties and the difference principle. . . . By publicly affirming the basic liberties citizens in a well-ordered society express their mutual respect for one another as reasonable and trustworthy, as well as their recognition of the worth all citizens attach to their way of life.[83]

There cannot be a conflict between liberty and the basic good of self-respect, because "self-respect is most effectively encouraged and supported by the two

79. *Political Liberalism*, pp. 302, 18, 19, 74.
80. Ibid., p. 76.
81. *Liberal Purposes*, p. 317.
82. *Political Liberalism*, p. 319.
83. Ibid.

principles of justice, again precisely because of the insistence on the equal basic liberties. . . ."[84]

This line of argument appears to follow Thomas's suggestion that "[t]he social institutions in which we live can either sustain or undermine the view that we have full moral status, that we are members of good standing in the moral community, in virtue of the fact that we are persons."[85] Thomas thinks that institutions can accomplish this by distributing basic rights and liberties equally, but he also observes that the Black Consciousness Movement of the 1960s and 1970s produced "a change in the way blacks came to view themselves as persons *qua* persons" by rejecting "a conception of persons according to which to have a certain pigmentation of the skin was *ipso facto* to be less worthy of the rights and liberties to which other members of the American society had been so long accustomed."[86] If, however, the necessary and sufficient condition of this change in consciousness was the equal distribution of basic rights and liberties, then it is hard to understand how the Black Consciousness Movement, rather than contemporaneous legal reforms, could have played any important role in the enhancement of blacks' self-respect. A similar point may be made about women, whose consciousness-raising movement arose many decades after they attained substantial legal equality with men. Cultural meaning seems to matter after all.

If the state may legitimately concern itself with cultural meaning, then there may well be some tension between the antidiscrimination project and basic liberties. Before exploring this tension, however, let us note the great extent to which Rawls's theory in its latest version can accommodate the project. Process defect and group disadvantage count for Rawls, and so does stigma—at least to the extent that it either contributes to the other injuries or dimin-

84. Ibid, p. 318. The basic liberties are not, however, the sole basis of self-respect. The sentence continues: ". . . and the priority assigned them, although self-respect is further strengthened and supported by the fair value of the political liberties and the difference principle." Ibid. If the basic liberties are not the sole basis of self-respect, and the other principles of justice can also help to strengthen self-respect, then the question arises again whether in some cases the other principles are more relevant to self-respect, so that self-respect will be maximized if the priority of liberty is relaxed in such cases.

85. Larry L. Thomas, "Rawlsian Self-Respect and the Black Consciousness Movement," 8 *Phil. Forum* 303, 311 (1977–78).

86. Ibid., p. 307; see also Laurence Thomas, "Self-Respect: Theory and Practice," in Leonard Harris, ed., *Philosophy Born of Struggle: Anthology of Afro-American Philosophy from 1917* (Dubuque, Iowa: Kendall/Hunt Publishing Co., 1983), pp. 174–89.

ishes self-respect. Moreover, it is clear that the Rawlsian state can legitimately concern itself with the character of its citizens. One of the reasons Rawls expects that a well-ordered society will be stable is that its institutions will "tend to encourage the cooperative virtues of political life: the virtue of reasonableness and a sense of fairness, a spirit of compromise and a willingness to meet others halfway, all of which are connected with the willingness to cooperate with others on political terms that everyone can publicly accept."[87] Galston observes that "a member of a well-ordered liberal society cannot object to state-governed tutelary practices designed to inculcate a sense of justice, for 'in agreeing to principles of right the parties in the original position consent to the arrangements necessary to make these principles effective in their conduct.' "[88] If, as I argued in Chapter 1, our society tends to acculturate people in ways conducive to the development of unconscious racism, so that blacks and women are treated as unfairly as if they were the objects of deliberate discrimination, then the liberal virtues we need include an awareness of the continuing effects of our racist and sexist traditions and a determination to end them. "In a well-ordered society in which citizens know they can count on each other's sense of justice, we may suppose that a person normally wants to act justly as well as to be recognized by others as someone who can be relied upon as a fully cooperating member of society over a complete life." If it is possible to commit injustice inadvertently, then citizens will want to develop the dispositions necessary to avoid such inadvertences. Commitment to the antidiscrimination project would then appear to be a political virtue, which can be "identified and justified by the need for certain qualities of character in the citizens of a just and stable constitutional regime."[89]

The basic liberties that limit the means by which the state can promote such virtue are themselves limited. As we shall see, Rawls endorses some restrictions on freedom of speech for the sake of racial and sexual equality. He has abandoned his formulation of the first principle of justice in *A Theory of Justice*, which required each person to have "the most extensive total system of equal basic liberties compatible with a similar system of liberty for all."[90] This formulation discusses liberty in quantitative terms, but he has since concluded that the scheme of liberties "is not drawn up so as to maximize anything."

87. Rawls, *Political Liberalism*, p. 163.
88. Galston, *Liberal Purposes*, p. 95, quoting Rawls, *A Theory of Justice*, p. 515.
89. Rawls, *Political Liberalism*, pp. 306, 195 n. 29.
90. *A Theory of Justice*, p. 302.

What is guaranteed is not the most extensive scheme, but (as he now puts it) "a fully adequate scheme of equal basic liberties which is compatible with a similar scheme of liberties for all."[91]

The liberties and their priority are "to guarantee equally for all citizens the social conditions essential for the adequate development and the full and informed exercise of [the moral powers] in what I shall call 'the two fundamental cases.' " "The first of these cases . . . concerns the application of the principles of justice to the basic structure of society and its social policies." "The equal political liberties and freedom of thought are to secure the free and informed application of the principles of justice, by means of the full and effective exercise of citizens' sense of justice, to the basic structure of society." Protections for "the freedom of political speech and press, freedom of assembly, and the like" fall under this heading. "The second fundamental case is connected with the capacity for a conception of the good and concerns the application of the principles of deliberative reason in guiding our conduct over a complete life. Liberty of conscience and freedom of association come in here."[92]

The protection of liberty in the two fundamental cases does limit what the state may do in furtherance of the project. The political liberties prevent the state from censoring all speech that leads people away from the political virtues, as racist speech does. It protects even racist organizations, such as the Nazi party and the Ku Klux Klan, so long as those organizations obey the laws. And the liberties of conscience and association prevent the state from regulating what religious groups may say about, for example, homosexuality. Rawls's fundamental cases delimit a sphere of privacy that the state cannot infringe. The exercise of the moral powers is necessary in order for one to be a fully cooperating member of society. Impairing the ability of some to exercise those powers *would* damage their self-respect. There is, therefore, a strong presumption against infringement of the basic rights in the fundamental cases. (We shall see whether it is as absolute as Rawls tries to make it.) But, it must be noted, Rawls's sphere of privacy is a good deal narrower than was Nozick's. Speech that does not involve one of the fundamental cases of liberty, for example, is not entitled to special protection, and may be restricted in furtherance of racial or sexual equality: "Thus, announcements of jobs and positions can be forbidden to contain statements which exclude applicants of

91. *Political Liberalism*, pp. 332, 291.
92. Ibid., pp. 332, 334–35, 332.

certain designated ethnic and racial groups, or of either sex, when these limitations are contrary to fair equality of opportunity. . . . Observe here that the restrictions in question, in contrast with the basic liberties, may be restrictions on content."[93]

More generally, the scope of the override of basic liberties for the sake of basic needs remains unclear, because Rawls has not altogether succeeded in eliminating from his theory the dangerous idea that self-esteem is a primary good. It is far from clear that self-esteem is not a good that would concern the parties in the original position. Whether or not it was mislabeled as self-respect, all the arguments in *A Theory of Justice* for self-esteem as a primary good remain persuasive. The parties in the original position will not take lightly the prospect of a stigmatized social status. Although Thomas thinks that equal self-esteem is impossible, he does acknowledge that "morality condemns any arrangement of social institutions which systematically undermines the self-esteem of persons."[94] This connects with a more general problem, that Rawls's scheme of cooperation ignores any wants of citizens that are not connected with his political conception. "Citizens' needs are objective in a way that desires are not: that is, they express requirements of persons with certain higher-order interests who have a certain role or status. . . . A citizen's claim that something is a need can be denied when it is not a requirement."[95] But what Rawls calls "higher-order interests" cannot persuasively be assigned the preeminence he gives them. "If the account of social primary goods is to reflect a plausible notion of human needs," Pogge objects, "then it cannot deny the fundamental role basic social and economic needs actually play in a human life. But insistence on the preeminence of the basic (civil and political) rights and liberties constitutes just such a denial."[96] Rawls's override for the basic needs is limited in this political way; its rationale is that "below a certain level of material and social well-being . . . people simply cannot take part as citizens, much less equal citizens."[97] The parties in the original position, by contrast, are likely to be concerned about deprivation of basic needs for reasons that are less political and more, well, basic.

The narrowing of the list of primary goods, we have seen, follows from

93. Ibid., pp. 363–64.
94. "Morality and Our Self-Concept," p. 258.
95. Rawls, *Political Liberalism*, p. 189 n. 20.
96. Pogge, *Realizing Rawls*, p. 133.
97. Rawls, *Political Liberalism*, p. 166.

Rawls's move toward a conception of justice that is "political not meta-physical."[98] But it is not clear that the resulting scheme preserves the concern about fairness that animates *A Theory of Justice.* "One would be reluctant to employ Rawls's account of social primary goods, with its heavy emphasis on civil and political freedoms, as a guide for choosing 'a society in which his enemy is to assign him his place.' "[99] An interpretation of *A Theory of Justice* that seems different from, and in some respects more attractive than, Rawls's own has been offered by Okin, who argues that the moral power of the original position is best captured if the parties try to reason "from the point of view of everybody, of every 'concrete other' whom one might turn out to be." Rawls's ethic of justice, she argues, is also an ethic of care and concern. "Especially for those accustomed by class position, race, and sex to privilege, wealth, and power, a real appreciation of the point of view of the worst-off is likely to require considerable empathy and capacity to listen to others."[100]

If indeed it is rational in the original position to look to "the worst that can happen under any proposed course of action, and to decide in the light of that,"[101] then one cannot reasonably ignore the sheer pain that can be caused by the exercise, in some cases, of the basic liberties. Thus, for example, it is clear that a political message is being conveyed when skinheads burn a cross in front of the home of the only black family in a white neighborhood. Nonetheless, it is plain that the cost to the skinheads of restricting their political liberties—even taking into account the indignity of having a basic liberty restricted—is considerably less than the cost to the family of being captive in their own home and being compelled to watch this visible symbol of their stigma and exclusion. Which of these places in society would the parties in the original position find more unacceptable?[102] The uncertainty that this question produces brings us to the limits of Rawls's usefulness for our inquiry. The priority of liberty is sometimes, but by no means always, enough to trump

98. John Rawls, "Justice as Fairness: Political not Metaphysical," 14 *Phil. & Pub. Aff.* 223 (1985).

99. Pogge, *Realizing Rawls,* p. 134, quoting Rawls, *A Theory of Justice,* p. 152.

100. Susan Moller Okin, "Reason and Feeling in Thinking About Justice," 99 *Ethics* 229, 248, 245 (1989).

101. *A Theory of Justice,* p. 154.

102. There may be considerations of prudence that weigh against giving the state the power to repress hate speech, as I discuss in the next chapter, but these are very different from the kinds of reasons that Rawls gives for the protection of the basic liberties.

the values pursued by the antidiscrimination project. There seems to be no alternative to balancing these values directly.

Ackerman and Antidiscrimination

If the pain of those who are stigmatized should be counted by the Rawlsian state, perhaps this means that the most persuasive reading of Rawls remains too consequentialist to be genuinely liberal. The question we began with was whether the antidiscrimination project could be reconciled with liberal neutrality. We saw that for Rawls, the value of liberty is not great enough to consistently override the demands of the project. Sometimes, however, this is the consequence of the great weight that the parties in the original position would give to self-respect or self-esteem. The pain caused by stigma, we saw, carries so much weight under the original formulation of Rawls's theory that it could entirely swamp concerns about liberty. The more recent formulation of the theory largely avoided this difficulty, but as Galston has observed, "Rawls's new theory and perfectionism differ, not generically, but rather as species within a single genus. In each case, philosophical reflection must somehow pick out normatively favored individual ends and interests."[103] Rawls's credentials as a neutralist would appear to have become jeopardized.

For this reason, I shall conclude with a consideration of Bruce Ackerman, who, though as committed to neutrality as Nozick, avoids the worst of Nozick's pitfalls by recognizing that the basic structure of society is a proper subject of justice. One of Ackerman's greatest strengths—and the most striking difference between him and Nozick—is his relentless determination to question every aspect of our inherited social structure. "None of these power structures can be afforded the immense privilege of invisibility; *each* person must be prepared to answer the question of legitimacy when *any* of his powers is challenged by *anyone* disadvantaged by their exercise." At the same time, like Nozick, Ackerman is committed to historical rather than end-result conceptions of justice. The ultimate ambition of *Social Justice in the Liberal State* is to show that "commitment to a particular procedure of dispute resolution— here, the process of constrained conversation—can be transformed into a commitment to particular substantive outcomes."[104]

103. Galston, *Liberal Purposes*, p. 122.
104. Ackerman, *Social Justice in the Liberal State*, pp. 4–5, 14, emphases in original.

Liberalism, Ackerman argues, is "a way of talking about power, a form of political culture." "Whenever anybody questions the legitimacy of another's power, the power holder must respond not by suppressing the questioner but by giving a reason that explains why he is more entitled to the resource than the questioner is." What is distinctive about the liberal way of talking about power, Ackerman thinks, is the constraint he calls Neutrality: "No reason [for exercising power] is a good reason if it requires the power holder to assert: (a) that his conception of the good is better than that asserted by any of his fellows, *or* (b) that, regardless of his conception of the good, he is intrinsically superior to one or more of his fellow citizens." Ackerman thinks that this understanding of liberalism is an improvement on utilitarianism and contractarianism, both of which "require us to suppress our own identities as social beings—whose identities and objectives are defined through interaction with other concrete individuals—so that we may catch a fleeting glimpse of some transcendent individual who may sit as higher judge of our social conflicts."[105] Idealized perspectives such as that of the utilitarian ideal observer or the parties in the original position bear little resemblance to the perspectives we have here and now, and it is not clear why we ought to defer to the (purely hypothetical and therefore eminently contestable) judgments of imaginary beings.

Since the state may not exercise its power on the basis of the idea that some citizens are intrinsically superior to others, Ackerman, too, must endorse the process defect theory. If, as I have argued, cases like *McCleskey* compel Nozick to be concerned about the culture from which decision makers are drawn, Ackerman has to share this concern. But Ackerman's endorsement of the antidiscrimination project will be a limited one unless the harms of group-disadvantage and stigma also count.

Utilitarian considerations are entirely discarded by Ackerman. He has no use for Rawls's "abstract and ambiguous" notion of self-respect, and adopts an even thinner theory of the good. Distributive justice applies to four basic powers: genetic endowment, education, material resources, and the transactional framework within which these other resources can be traded. Citizens of the liberal state have a right to equal shares of these resources, not to any particular psychological state. "While no one can be guaranteed success in

105. Ibid., pp. 6, 4, 11, 331. Ackerman uses the word Neutrality, thus capitalized, as a term of art to signify the particular rule of conversational constraint stated here.

life, everybody is guaranteed an equal right to the material endowments he thinks his success requires." Some citizens may still be desperately unhappy, but "given scarce resources, the bare fact of frustration can *never* serve as a sufficient reason for gaining additional resources."[106]

Nor can a citizen complain if no one else is willing to associate with him on terms he finds acceptable. To illustrate this point, Ackerman offers a dialogue with Michelangelo Crusoe, who wants to devote his life to artistic creation but finds that none of his fellow citizens has any interest in his art. While they are prepared to employ him in other ways, he thinks those options entirely worthless and rejects them. Facing starvation and early death, he complains to the Commander (who adjudicates disputes in Ackerman's idealized model) that he has been abused. The Commander, noting that Crusoe is not the victim of censorship, monopoly, or force, suggests that he could live longer if he accepted some of the transactional offers that he *is* receiving.

CRUSOE: Absolutely not; life on those terms is not worth living.

COMMANDER: You said it. I didn't.

CRUSOE: How can you be so heartless and unfeeling? I am in pain. Why won't you help me?

COMMANDER: Because helping you requires hurting somebody else. And you have yet to explain to me why you think this step is justified. Do you, for example, think you are entitled to more manna than the next fellow or that your offers of association are entitled to a privileged position in the transactional network?

CRUSOE: Enough of this quibbling. Isn't there *anybody* out there who will help me?[107]

Crusoe's predicament, Ackerman writes, "may fairly symbolize the tragic aspect of the liberal vision." His suffering cannot state a claim for resources, because adjudicating that claim would require the Commander "to judge the intrinsic merit of Michelangelo's vision compared to those pursued by others." He concludes, "So long as relative scarcity remains a feature of social existence, there can be no hope of a political solution that will end frustration and disappointment."[108]

---

106. Ibid., pp. 137 n. 18, 63, 64, emphasis in original.
107. Ibid., p. 184.
108. Ibid.

This logic would appear equally to forbid legislation such as the Civil Rights Act of 1964, which forces some people to enter into transactions against their wishes. Blacks may have been dissatisfied with the transactional offers they received, which tended to be restricted to employment as laborers, janitors, housekeepers, and the like, but Crusoe's example teaches that dissatisfaction with one's options does not state a claim. Nozick writes: "A person's choice among differing degrees of unpalatable alternatives is not rendered nonvoluntary by the fact that others voluntarily chose and acted within their rights in ways that did not provide him with a more palatable alternative."[109] Ackerman does not, however, endorse Nozick's libertarianism, because it ignores the background injustices in the world. "Our political problem is far more difficult than Nozick imagines; rather than a single-minded defense of absolute transactional freedom, the task is to defend the principle of free exchange while taking effective steps to remedy injustice in genetic, educational, and material endowments that have been unearthed by liberal dialogue."[110]

If a group of citizens is cumulatively disadvantaged in a number of different power domains, then Ackerman thinks the group has a claim to redistribution. Blacks, for example,[111] "not only receive a smaller share of material resources but are shunted into an authoritarian educational system that prepares them to accept a limited number of subordinate roles, later to confront a transactional network that drastically limits a black's access to the means of communication and transaction."[112] Thus Ackerman can recognize group disadvantage. Moreover, though he is vague about *how* the market contributes to blacks' disadvantage,[113] it is clear that in light of these injustices, efforts to improve the status of the group are justified. Such efforts presumably include the Civil Rights Act of 1964.

Here, however, as with the group-disadvantage theorists we examined in

109. *Anarchy, State, and Utopia*, pp. 263–64.

110. *Social Justice in the Liberal State*, p. 186.

111. In a description of an "imaginary" society that bears a non-coincidental resemblance to our own.

112. *Social Justice*, p. 242.

113. He writes that blacks "confront a transactional system where whites use race as a proxy for individualized data on personal abilities." Ibid., p. 265. Participants in a market, however, ordinarily use all sorts of proxies to judge whether to enter into proposed transactions. This is an intrinsic feature of markets, because it is a rational response to the high cost of information. More must be said before blacks' disadvantages can be blamed on an unfair transactional system, even if the participants in that system discriminate against them.

Chapter 2, culture inevitably comes in. It is in the cultural dimension of power that the most serious damage would appear to be done: the worst-off blacks' inferior education prepares them for subordinate roles, because it limits their access to such cultural tools as literacy that are necessary to pursue larger ends, and also *psychologically* "prepares" them by the way it shapes their very ambitions themselves. This kind of acculturation is intolerable to Ackerman. "For example, I take it to be pretty obvious that women, as a group, have been the victims of pervasive forms of cultural domination. They have been socialized into a very narrow range of cultural ideals, and have confronted a broad range of coercive sanctions if they departed from socially approved models during their formative years."[114] He rejects utilitarianism, in part, because its demands could be satisfied if "a group of exploited blacks could be cheaply taught to be happy with their lot."[115] The power that must be called to account, then, is the power to shape worldviews, "the power processes behind the social construction of meanings and patterns that serve to get B to act and believe in a manner in which B otherwise might not, to A's benefit and B's detriment."[116] The socialization of people in such a way that they do not question the exercise of power over them is itself an illegitimate exercise of power. "It is only when people forget the meaning of the question of legitimacy that the liberal spirit will have been dealt a mortal blow."[117]

Now it must be noted that the same cultural process that can produce blacks acculturated to subordination can also produce whites unwilling to enter into transactions that are not stigmatizing and degrading to blacks. Does the majority culture's tendency to stigmatize blacks count as an exercise of power over them requiring justification? That Ackerman is willing to forbid stigmatizing actions by the state is evident from his discussion of the segregation decisions, which he plainly regards as just:

> Rather than standing passively to one side, the activist state was now intimately involved in the way children—both black and white—would

114. Ackerman, "Neutralities," p. 41.

115. *Social Justice in the Liberal State*, p. 265.

116. John Gaventa, *Power and Powerlessness: Quiescence and Rebellion in an Appalachian Valley* (Urbana: University of Illinois Press, 1980), pp. 15–16. *Social Justice in the Liberal State* does not discuss any of the theorists of this "hidden face of power," but the more recent "Neutralities," p. 42 n. 3, includes a sympathetic citation to Peter Bachrach and Morton S. Baratz, "Two Faces of Power," 56 *Am. Pol. Sci. Rev.* 947 (1962).

117. *Social Justice*, p. 324.

interpret the fact that they were being bussed to different schools on the basis of race. . . . The state, not the children, must bear responsibility for the fact that school segregation "generates a feeling of inferiority as to their status . . . in a way unlikely ever to be undone."[118]

Is there any corresponding obligation on the part of private citizens not to impose unwelcome meanings on others?

Ackerman thinks that in an ideal liberal world, a perfect technology of justice would permit each citizen to transmit whatever transactional offers she likes to all the others, while shielding herself from any messages, noises, or other effects of other citizens' activities that she does not wish to be exposed to. Ackerman's science-fictional "transmitter-shields" model a world in which no one can censor others' communications, and no one can punish others for dealing with competitors. This model "permits us to fulfill [John Stuart] Mill's promise by locating an important category of self-regarding actions that are, in principle, immune from state suppression." Such actions, Ackerman concludes, are those that are done "without anyone's committing an offense against the ideal transactional process," actions "that do not require censorship or monopolization before they can be effected."[119]

In an ideal liberal world, then, persons would be able to shield themselves from unwelcome messages from others. The absence of such leakproof transmitter-shields, however, means that second-best solutions must be considered. "Suppose that Manic and Depressive would prefer to conduct their public, as well as their private, dealings in the nude, while Noble is of the clothed persuasion. How, then, to manage the conflict that ensues when, thanks to imperfect shielding, both find themselves riding the same bus to work?" Here, one or the other regime must hold sway, at least in any given region. (Different regions may choose different regimes, and those unhappy with the regime under which they live must be free to emigrate.) As long as the nudists' privacy is respected in those contexts where they can shield others

118. Bruce Ackerman, "Constitutional Politics / Constitutional Law," 99 *Yale L.J.* 453, 533, 535 (1989), quoting *Brown v. Board of Educ.*, 347 U.S. 483, 494 (1954). Philosophy is not law, of course, but he also suggests that the two principles of neutrality of *Social Justice* "are rooted in" the First and Fourteenth amendments. Bruce Ackerman, *Reconstructing American Law* (Cambridge: Harvard University Press, 1984), p. 99.

119. *Social Justice in the Liberal State*, pp. 174–77, 178, 179.

out, it is legitimate for a clothed regime to be established, because it is "very costly to shield Nobles when they confront Nudist on the bus."[120]

If persons may legitimately be protected from having to look at unwanted nudity, then they may legitimately be protected from having to endure unwanted messages of stigma. As I noted in Chapter 2, one objection to the stigma theory is that people should be thicker-skinned, and the answer to this objection is that, in some cases, the stigmatizing meanings are so ubiquitous as to be inescapable. I concluded that one goal of the antidiscrimination project was to marginalize unjustifiable stigma so that it no longer causes those who are its objects from thereby suffering any serious or pervasive disadvantage.

If the absence of effective transmitter-shields means that the public display of racist ideas will cause stigmatic harm to blacks, then the "second-best" solution may be to confine the expression of those ideas. Thus Ackerman's liberalism should support the restriction, in certain contexts, of racist speech. Such speech must be allowed in the public forum; political dialogue must be unrestricted if the whole scheme is to work, and willing listeners must be free to hear whatever they want.[121] Unwilling listeners, on the other hand, must be equally free to retreat behind their transmitter-shields. In the private sphere—consider again the black family watching the skinheads burning a cross outside their window—people should be free from insulting messages that are *designed* to leak through their shields.

Laws against malicious stigmatization will not suffice, however. State power alone cannot guarantee that people will be free from this kind of humiliation. Citizens must learn to moderate their behavior so that they do not, even inadvertently, inflict stigmatic injuries on blacks. (Nudist must put clothes on before boarding the bus even if he never intended to offend Noble.) This implies a more substantial tutelary function for the state than Neutrality would at first seem to suggest. What the state must teach is a peculiar kind of virtue. Power in actually existing liberal societies (as opposed to the heuristic construct of *Social Justice in the Liberal State*) is diffuse. There is no Commander present to adjudicate local disputes. In order for the theory to regulate the deployment of power, then, it is necessary for each citizen to have a Com-

120. Ibid., pp. 193, 194.
121. See ibid., pp. 153, 177–78, 309.

mander of sorts within her own mind. The ability to follow this Commander's constraints can itself be understood as a kind of excellence or civic virtue to which one may aspire.[122]

> Each social role can be understood as a set of conventional constraints upon acceptable symbolic behavior. . . . Some role definitions allow for a broader range of symbolic behavior than others; but all roles are constraining, placing vast domains of conversation off the agenda so long as the participants are acting within a particular role framework. . . . Thus, in calling upon people to exercise conversational self-restraint in public life, I am asking them to exercise a fundamental competence that all socialized human beings possess (to one or another degree).[123]

If cultural symbols pertaining to race and gender are among the forms of power that citizens can abuse, then liberal virtue entails restraint in the use of these forms of power. If the racial insult, whether malicious or thoughtless, is an injury, then Ackermanian "conversational restraint" entails conversational restraint.

The antidiscrimination project goes further than this, however. Part of what is complained of is whites' unwillingness to enter into certain advantageous transactions with blacks. Should ostracism count as an illegitimate exercise of power? If so, then the ideas that produce it must be driven out of private spaces as well as the public space. Suppose that a filmmaker—let's call him D. W. Goebbels—produces movies that are spectacularly effective and entertaining racist propaganda. He disseminates them via the transmitter-shield network, so that only those who wish to see them do so. They are, however, enormously popular and influential. One of the effects of the movies is that those who view them repeatedly (as many white people do, because the movies are so entertaining) develop an aversion toward blacks, and cease to engage in any social or economic transactions with them. As a result, blacks become outcasts in the community, impoverished and despised. Has Goebbels exercised unjust power over blacks?

Like the good of initial equality, the good of recognition is a relational good: its realization depends on the relation between me and the other members of

122. See Bruce Ackerman, "Robert Bork's Grand Inquisition," 99 *Yale L.J.* 1419, 1436 (1990) (liberalism is a "tradition" in the sense used by Alasdair MacIntyre).
123. Ackerman, "Why Dialogue?," p. 20.

my society. Its relational nature does not make it any less a good, or its deprivation any less an injury. Still, Nozick is correct that the only way for *government* to prevent such end-states from coming about is to interfere with liberty—here, the liberty of Goebbels to distribute his films and of his audience to watch them. To be sure, government is not the only relevant decision maker here. The repugnant pattern could also be prevented if Goebbels or his customers could be persuaded to stop their activity because of its bad effects. As G. A. Cohen has observed, "[h]ow much equality would conflict with liberty in given circumstances depends on how much people would value equality in those circumstances."[124] And if equality is indeed a good, then it should not be impossible to persuade people to want it. But if Goebbels is, as it turns out, doing a brisk business with his films, may the state interfere? (May it not?)

Ackerman's objection to Rawls is that it is far from clear that self-respect or self-esteem is something that one is entitled to. Ackerman's own argument supporting this objection is not transparent,[125] but he could put it in terms similar to Dworkin's argument against the ideal of equality of welfare. Dworkin contends that any such ideal must be vacuous, because it must already presuppose some other, independent theory of what persons are entitled to. Equality of welfare can most reasonably be understood as meaning equality of success in the pursuit of goals. "People have lives of less overall success if they have more reasonably to regret that they do not have or have not done."[126] The idea of reasonableness necessarily carries much weight here. One is not entitled to compensation for the frustration of one's unreasonable expectations. (That is the premise behind Ackerman's answer to Michelangelo Crusoe.) A cannot complain of less welfare than B if (unlike B) A wishes for supernatural powers or desires an unfairly large share of the world's resources. These frustrated desires, even if they diminish A's welfare, are not good reasons for B to compensate A. But if the idea of equality includes a notion of reasonable regret, then that notion of reasonableness will already imply assumptions about what a fair distribution would be. So equality of success cannot justify or constitute a theory of fair distribution. Similarly with equality of

---

124. Cohen, "Robert Nozick and Wilt Chamberlain," p. 254.

125. He says only that "Rawls' comments about self-respect are sufficiently abstract and ambiguous to permit any number of (very different) interpretations in hard cases of the kind we are imagining." *Social Justice*, p. 137 n. 18.

126. Ronald Dworkin, "What is Equality? Part 1: Equality of Welfare," 10 *Phil. & Pub. Aff.* 185, 216 (1981).

self-respect or self-esteem, one can imagine cases in which a person's sense of self-respect demands more esteem from others than it is reasonable to expect. There is a scene in Mark Twain's novel *The Prince and the Pauper* in which the young king, having been mistakenly expelled from the palace in beggar's clothes and fallen among tramps who do not know his true identity, suffers terrible shame and indignation because they think he is no better than they and refuse to bow down and honor him. His plight is pitiful, but modern liberalism must say that they are right and he is wrong: he is not entitled to self-respect on such terms. To what esteem, then, is he entitled (if any)?

The case of the ex-convict's ostracized daughter, which we considered in Chapter 2, suggests that the liberal theories of Ackerman and even Rawls do not exhaust society's obligations to its members. Even if this girl's ability rationally to pursue a conception of the good or to question the power that is exerted over her is in no way impaired, and even if no one is exercising power over her in a way that cannot be justified by Neutral dialogue, she still appears to have a valid complaint. Unlike Michelangelo Crusoe, her plight is not the product of her own unreasonable expectations, and she has no reasonable option that would improve her lot. The community has a prima facie duty to value and respect her, which is being violated for arbitrary (because insufficient) and invidious (because contradictory to liberalism) reasons.

This notion of communal obligation obviously goes beyond what Ackerman's theory demands. It does not sound particularly Neutral. Still, Ackerman does not deny the existence of such obligations. Benjamin Barber's critique of Ackerman argues that justice can never be attained on the basis of constrained conversation; a decent politics requires some degree of fellow-feeling or patriotism.[127] Ackerman's reply does not disagree, but points out that any community has borders, and that communal obligations cannot be invoked between strangers.

> After all the familiar forms of communitarian rhetoric have played themselves out, Neutrality permits a polis-like community to find a voice when dealing with outsiders beyond the gates who will inevitably challenge their status as outcasts. By respecting the liberal principle of conversational priority, people on both sides of the communal frontier can continue to talk to one another in the accents of self-respect. Setting aside, for a time,

127. "Unconstrained Conversations: A Play on Words, Neutral and Otherwise," 93 *Ethics* 330, 334–35 (1983).

their ultimate disagreements, they may build a larger political community through the art of constrained conversation.[128]

The reason Ackerman's theory of justice finds it difficult to accommodate the inclusionary ambitions of the antidiscrimination project is that the dialogues that constitute it, the demands that the stigmatized make upon their stigmatizers, take place inside the walls of the city, where Neutrality does not constrain conversation. The fact that the claim of the ex-convict's daughter cannot be expressed in Neutral terms shows only that Neutral dialogue is too thin a language to express the obligation her neighbors owe her. It does not show that no such obligation exists. This obligation is not directly enforceable by the state, but it is an appropriate one for the girl's neighbors to feel. If they have inherited a custom of ostracizing the children of convicts, they have an obligation to change that custom. That effort deserves at least the moral support of the state, and it would clearly be unacceptable for the state to take the other side. Most obviously, the public school administrators and teachers could tell the children in no uncertain terms that what they are doing is wrong, and that they should ignore what their mothers tell them.

Such a solution would be unsatisfactory to Ackerman. Liberal education is supposed not to indoctrinate children—and the liberal state is supposed not to indoctrinate citizens—into any particular orthodox point of view, but rather to make a broad range of perspectives available to everyone. Ackerman would maintain that the person who believes children of convicts ought to be ostracized should be entitled to have his say as a guest lecturer in the school classrooms, as should the racist.[129]

In order for this argument to be persuasive, it will be necessary for us to be persuaded that the free expression of all viewpoints in the schools will produce the virtues that citizens require. It is not enough for a liberal to reply that even if people make bad choices, they still have a right to choose, and that "even if overwhelming numbers opted for lives that I consider mean and narrow, we should at last learn what human freedom amounts to."[130] If that is what freedom amounts to, then surely we want less of it. Dworkin is correct that "a political and economic system that allows prejudice to destroy some people's lives does not treat all members of the community with equal con-

128. Bruce Ackerman, "What is Neutral about Neutrality?," 93 *Ethics* 372, 375 (1983).
129. See *Social Justice*, pp. 154–63.
130. Ibid., p. 375.

cern."[131] The trouble with Ackerman's theory of liberty is, in the end, the same one we found in Nozick's.[132] A doctrine that is committed to recognizing the equal value of each individual cannot be indifferent to the effects that an unregulated social process may have on some.

The Liberal Dilemma

In each of the liberal theorists we have examined, we have seen that the antidiscrimination project can conflict with important liberties, and that this kind of conflict can be adjudicated persuasively not by the invocation of any abstract principle, but only by weighing the harm done by the cultural practice in question, on the one hand, against the importance of the liberty, on the other. This is, I think, one of the tensions between absolute claims that is inescapably part of the human condition. As Isaiah Berlin has argued:

> The world that we encounter in ordinary experience is one in which we are faced with choices between ends equally ultimate, and claims equally absolute, the realization of some of which must inevitably involve the sacrifice of others. Indeed, it is because this is their situation that men place such immense value upon the freedom to choose; for if they had assurance that in some perfect state, realizable by men on earth, no ends pursued by them would ever be in conflict, the necessity and agony of choice would disappear, and with it the central importance of the freedom to choose.[133]

131. Ronald Dworkin, "What is Equality? Part 3: The Place of Liberty," 73 *Iowa L. Rev.* 1, 36 (1987).

132. The resemblance between Ackerman's indifference to outcomes and that of the libertarian right has been emphasized by Dworkin. See Ronald Dworkin, "What Liberalism Isn't," *N.Y. Rev. of Books,* Jan. 20, 1983, pp. 49–50. Dworkin himself, however, is sometimes indifferent to outcomes, as in his defense of pornography. See Ronald Dworkin, "Women and Pornography," *N.Y. Rev. of Books,* Oct. 21, 1993, p. 41 (refusing to count among protectible interests "a right not to be insulted or damaged just by the fact that others have hostile or uncongenial tastes, or that they are free to express or indulge them in private"). Dworkin has not considered the problems raised by our hypothetical filmmaker D. W. Goebbels. His own arguments can be used against him here. See generally Rae Langton, "Whose Right? Ronald Dworkin, Women, and Pornographers," 19 *Phil. & Pub. Aff.* 311 (1990).

133. "Two Concepts of Liberty," in *Four Essays on Liberty* (Oxford: Oxford University Press, 1969), p. 168. Rawls, who obviously admires Berlin, suggests that his own theory, by showing "how the values and their weights are arrived at in the way they are specified by the deliberations of the parties in the original position," provides "a clearer conception of how weights may be

Berlin is careful to add that while this argument weighs in favor of liberty, it does not make it an absolute. "The extent of a man's, or a people's, liberty to choose to live as they desire must be weighed against the claims of many other values, of which equality, or justice, or happiness, or security, or public order are perhaps the most obvious examples. For this reason, it cannot be unlimited."[134] Because we must choose between absolute ends, the freedom to choose is a very high thing; but because that freedom itself conflicts with other absolute ends, the decision of how much freedom to allow must be made on a societal rather than an individual level.

The dilemma that liberalism faces is this. The autonomy to which persons are entitled includes, at a minimum, the freedom to form and pursue their own conceptions of the good. In the aggregate, however, such conceptions may form patterns that have damaging effects on some people, including in some cases the impairment of *their* ability to form and pursue *their own* conceptions of the good. These conceptions may thus be intolerable to liberalism, yet presumptively immunized from state intervention by liberal principles.

As Eugene Genovese has observed, political philosophy alone cannot determine the appropriate limits upon the powers of the liberal state.

> We neither have nor should expect to have a formula that could satisfactorily divide the public from the private sphere.... [H]istorical experience offers the safest guide, but the interpretation of historical experience will always be ideologically charged. Indeed ... the very distinction between the spheres makes an ideological statement. But it remains difficult to imagine any degree of individual freedom worthy of the name without a wide swath for privacy and the institutional autonomy upon which freedom and privacy often depend. The problem concerns the bias brought to bear on the large and unavoidable gray area between the claims of privacy and the necessity for intervention to curb atrocities.[135]

The question, then, is how much intrusion into traditionally private spheres is necessary in order to curb the atrocities of racism and sexism. The antidis-

---

determined" for the competing values than Berlin's. "The Idea of an Overlapping Consensus," 7 *Oxford J. Legal Stud.* 1, 7 n. 13 (1987). As we have seen, however, some ambiguity persists, and at the margins intuitive weighing cannot be avoided.

134. Berlin, "Two Concepts of Liberty," p. 170.

135. Eugene D. Genovese, "Critical Legal Studies as Radical Politics and World View," 3 *Yale J. L. & Hum.* 131, 147 (1991).

crimination project and the values of liberty and privacy bias us in different (sometimes opposite) directions, and the best resolution of the tension between them will be different in different contexts.

In one sense, any interference with liberty by the state is a compromise of liberal ideals. The ideal of the liberal state presupposes a critical mass of convinced liberals among its citizens; absent such a mass, the liberal state will sometimes be forced to take precisely the kind of measures that in any other circumstance it is most committed to resist. In an imperfect world, a liberal state needs to create liberals and to prevent illiberal ideologies from doing severe harm to citizens. There are a variety of ways to do this, some more unappetizing than others to liberals. If the more congenial approaches are incapable of doing the job, then the less attractive ones cannot be ruled out.

Most congenial of all, of course, is the possibility that a liberal regime will promote liberal dispositions among the citizens automatically, without anyone trying to make this happen. By virtue of the sheer fact of living in a society of a certain kind, people tend to internalize as norms the way of life of that society, and this is as true of a liberal society as any other. The liberal state cannot be faulted for socializing citizens in this way, because this kind of socialization is in any case unavoidable.

Somewhat more suspect, perhaps, is the liberal state's forthrightly proclaiming its partisanship for liberal dispositions and views. Here the state uses such moral authority as it has for ends that, as between competing conceptions of the good, are partisan rather than neutral. It takes sides. The state may, for example, declare that racism is intrinsically wrong, and condemn it even as it tolerates it. This approach is perhaps less congenial to neutralist conceptions of liberalism than the first, but it is not *very* incongenial, since it does not violate anyone's liberty. The infringement is an infringement of principle rather than a harm to any particular person, somewhat like a state endorsement of a particular religious view that does not infringe on anyone's free exercise. On about the same footing is the state's use of its coercive power to design public education in a way that inculcates liberal ideals into children, for example by teaching them that racism and sexism are wrong. Since public education is coercive in any case, the troubling element here remains the state's partisanship.

More suspect still is for the state to use its coercive power over adults in order to inculcate liberal ideals in *them*, for example by regulating conduct in a way intended to encourage certain tastes and discourage others. This is what happened in *Diaz v. Pan American World Airways, Inc.,* in which airline passengers' taste for exclusively female flight attendants was denied gratification in the hope that it would eventually change.

Still worse, from a liberal perspective, is for the state to censor speech on the basis of its viewpoint, even if such censorship is undertaken only in those places, such as the workplace, where it is doing the most harm. As I shall show in the next chapter, this is a frequent effect of the law of sexual harassment.

Finally, a state dedicated to the eradication of illiberal ideologies could simply prohibit their dissemination altogether. Thus, for example, racist speech could simply be banned. There are, of course, stronger medicines than this; one could imagine Montagnard inquisitions into individuals' sincerity in espousing the antidiscrimination cause. But this is as far as I will go here. Speech is the realm in which the tension between liberalism and the antidiscrimination project is most obvious. It is precisely the kind of conception of antidiscrimination law I have advocated here, as a project of cultural transformation, that has been invoked by those who would suppress hate speech and pornography.

Liberalism must regard the progression from each of these steps to the next with increasing sadness and resistance. It cannot rule out a priori any one of the steps, but at each point it must be persuaded of the necessity of the next step. In the cases of hate speech and pornography, then, the key question is whether the necessity of suppression has been shown. I shall take up this question in the next chapter.

6

Racist Speech and Pornography

Recall from the last chapter Robert Nozick's distinction between historical and end-result conceptions of justice. According to some theorists of justice, such as Nozick, any result is legitimate as long as it comes about through a process of free individual choices. According to others, the legitimacy of any process must be judged according to the results it generates. The antidiscrimination project has roots in both approaches: it values freedom, but for that very reason it emphasizes that a certain state of affairs—specifically, the existence of a dominant culture that unjustifiably stigmatizes and disadvantages certain groups of people, and that thereby tends to bias political decisions against those groups—is a massive impediment to the freedom of members of those groups. It therefore must condemn, and try to change, any process that predictably permits that result to come about, even if that process consists of a sequence of free individual choices. Racism is wrong even if people freely choose to be racist. One of the central freedoms that liberalism has traditionally been concerned to protect is freedom of communication, but racism, which is deeply inimical to liberalism, is perpetuated by communicative means. This is why racist speech, sexist speech, and pornography pose such a difficult problem.

Freedom of speech is one of the most important basic liberties. The arguments for strong protection of speech are familiar. Free and open debate advances the search for truth. Citizens of a democracy must be able to freely communicate their opinions if they are to participate in government decision making. Free expression is necessary for free thought; thus it is argued that "suppression of belief, opinion, or other expression is an affront to the dignity of man, a negation of man's essential nature."[1] Free expression produces a

1. Thomas I. Emerson, *The System of Freedom of Expression* (New York: Random House, 1970), p. 6.

more adaptable community, facilitating adjustment to changing circumstances and new ideas. Finally, this limitation on government power helps remind the citizens of their status as free and equal. George Kateb argues that even worthless and harmful speech ought to be protected, because "unless there is almost unrestricted freedom of expression, in a supposedly free society, the people develop, in the face of government and of all authorities in all spheres of life, the mentality of dependence, while thinking themselves free. They come to learn to speak and perhaps to think and feel by permission."[2] While free speech helps to realize all these values, its privileged place is also based, in large part, on the faith that the practice of protecting speech will produce decent outcomes. Indeed, some of the rationales just mentioned implicitly rest on predictions about outcomes: democracy will in fact flourish, rather than be destroyed by demagogues; truth will in fact be advanced; and so on.[3]

But the pervasiveness of the ideas that the antidiscrimination project seeks to eliminate give us reason to be apprehensive about the consequences of unrestrained communication. This is emphasized by Catharine MacKinnon: "Social inequality is substantially created and enforced—that is, *done*— through words and images. Social hierarchy cannot and does not exist without being embodied in meanings and expressed in communication."[4] Speech and symbolic communication are the stuff of which racism, sexism, and prejudice against gays are made. "Blacks and other people of color are . . . skeptical about the absolutist argument that even the most injurious speech must remain unregulated because in an unregulated marketplace of ideas the best ideas will rise to the top and gain acceptance," writes Charles Lawrence. "Our experience tells us the opposite. . . . The American marketplace of ideas was founded with the idea of the racial inferiority of non-whites as one of its chief commodities, and ever since the market opened, racism has remained its

---

2. George Kateb, "The Freedom of Worthless and Harmful Speech," in Bernard Yack, ed., *Liberalism Without Illusions: Essays on Liberal Theory and the Political Vision of Judith N. Shklar* (Chicago and London: University of Chicago Press, forthcoming). This appears to overstate a basically valid point. As I shall argue below, speech is already properly restricted in many ways when it is low in value and harmful. Kateb's concern is legitimate, but it can be outweighed by other concerns, most importantly the degree of harm caused by the speech.

3. Emerson acknowledges the unprovable character of these premises. See *The System of Freedom of Expression*, pp. 7–8.

4. Catharine MacKinnon, *Only Words* (Cambridge: Harvard University Press, 1993), p. 13.

most active item in trade."[5] We have seen, in the last chapter, that liberalism, although it is devoted to the principle that people should, to the greatest possible extent, be left free to live their lives as they see fit without the interference of the state, cannot be wholly indifferent to the character and beliefs of the citizens. The puzzle is how the necessary character and beliefs are to be cultivated in a way that is consistent with the near-absolute prohibition of government intervention in certain areas of life, such as religion, speech, press, and assembly. The problem is posed most sharply by recent proposals to restrict racist speech and pornography. If, as this book has argued, stigmatizing ideas are precisely what the antidiscrimination project must eliminate, then does the project not demand that we enact laws penalizing the spread of those ideas?[6]

High Value and Low Value Speech

The freedom of speech is not, in fact, and cannot be, unlimited. "Some people purport to be free speech 'absolutists,' advocating constitutional protection for every form of speech; but no one really thinks this way. The government can prevent many forms of speech, including perjury, attempted bribes, threats, private libel, false advertising, unlicensed medical and legal advice, conspiracies, and criminal solicitation. It can do this even if the only target of regulation is 'speech' rather than conduct."[7] As Frederick Schauer has observed, absolute protection of expression would render unconstitutional "all of contract law, most of antitrust law, and much of criminal law."[8] It is probably inevitable that any system of free expression will distinguish among different kinds of speech by reference to their relation to the purposes of the First Amendment guarantee. Some kinds of speech, such as political speech,

5. Charles R. Lawrence III, "If He Hollers Let Him Go: Regulating Racist Speech on Campus," 1990 *Duke L. J.* 431, 467–68.

6. Some arguments for regulation of hate speech and pornography advocate criminal penalties, while others propose civil laws enforced by private citizens. For my purposes, nothing turns on this distinction, because either type of penalty can effectively suppress the speech that it targets. See Nadine Strossen, *Defending Pornography: Free Speech, Sex, and the Fight for Women's Rights* (New York: Scribner, 1995), pp. 63–69.

7. Cass R. Sunstein, *Democracy and the Problem of Free Speech* (New York: Free Press, 1993), pp. 121–22.

8. Frederick Schauer, "Categories and the First Amendment: A Play in Three Acts," 34 *Vand. L. Rev.* 265, 270 (1981).

scientific speech, art, and literature, cannot be suppressed unless government meets an unusually heavy burden of justification, because they advance the central purposes of the amendment. Other kinds of speech, such as bribery and false advertising, do little to advance those purposes, so a lesser showing of harm is necessary in order for the state to restrict them. Unless free speech doctrine distinguished high value speech from low value speech in this way, it would either afford too little protection to the former or too much protection to the latter.[9]

Part of the case against racist speech and pornography is that these are low value speech. Speech that does not advance the core purposes of the First Amendment, and that causes great harm, is the kind properly afforded the smallest degree of First Amendment protection. The claim of the proponents of suppression is that racist speech and pornography are in fact of very low value, and that they cause considerable harm.

The purposes of the First Amendment are not confined to the protection of the most valuable kinds of speech, however. The amendment also reflects a fear of overweening government power. For this reason, even low value speech may be protected when there is good reason to be suspicious of government's reasons for wanting to regulate it. "In general, government cannot regulate speech of any sort on the basis of (1) its own disagreement with the ideas that have been expressed, (2) its perception of the government's (as opposed to the public's) self-interest, (3) its fear that people will be persuaded or influenced by ideas, and (4) its desire to ensure that people are not offended by the ideas that the speech contains."[10] These justifications ordinarily cannot count, because they corrode the democratic and expressive processes that the amendment serves. Democracy is diminished if, and to the extent that, the state is free to decide what it is suitable for the people to know or to think. Censorship may reflect the corrupt desire of those in power to prevent the spread of truthful information that would cause voters to lose confidence in them. People must be free to try to persuade others, even if their views are offensive to many, so that the search for truth may be advanced. If speech could be suppressed because the ideas it expressed are offensive to some, then people would not be exposed to contending ideas of the right and the good,

9. See ibid.; Frederick Schauer, "Codifying the First Amendment: New York v. Ferber," 1982 *Sup. Ct. Rev.* 285; Sunstein, *Democracy and the Problem of Free Speech*, pp. 124–29.

10. Sunstein, *Democracy and the Problem of Free Speech*, p. 155.

as they must be in order to deliberate intelligently. Even when low value speech is the target of regulation, then, the state must show that the regulation is not based on an impermissible motive. Restrictions of speech on the basis of its viewpoint are regarded with great distrust by the courts, even when the speech is low value. Nonetheless, Cass Sunstein argues that the presumption that viewpoint-based restrictions on speech are invalid can be overcome "when there is no serious risk of illegitimate government motivation, when low-value or unprotected speech is at issue, when the skewing effect on the system of free expression is minimal, and when the government is able to make a powerful showing of harm."[11] The presence of these factors makes permissible such viewpoint-discriminatory measures as "the bans on advertising for casino gambling, cigarette smoking, and alcohol; the SEC's regulation of proxy statements; the controls on what employers may say during a union election; the prohibition of advertising for illegal products."[12]

We must therefore ask two questions about racist speech and pornography. First, are these kinds of expression high value speech or low value speech? Second, can these kinds of expression be shown to be sufficiently harmful that (in light of whatever their value is determined to be) their suppression is justified? I shall argue here that though these kinds of speech cannot be regarded as low value for First Amendment purposes, since they are closely tied to the core purposes of the amendment, sometimes the harms they cause are so great that diminished First Amendment protection is justified.

There is some ambiguity about whether racist and sexist speech is high or low value. Much racist and sexist speech neither reflects nor promotes rational deliberation. Yet what is objectionable about such speech is precisely the political content of the message that it conveys. The basis for wanting to repress it is precisely that it induces people to believe that message.

Let us begin with pornography. Sunstein argues that "much pornographic material lies far from the center of the First Amendment concern."[13] MacKinnon similarly thinks that pornography is not the kind of expression that the amendment protects, because "pornography does not engage the conscious mind in the chosen way the model of 'content,' in terms of which it is largely defended, envisions and requires."[14] The classification of pornography

11. Ibid., p. 177.
12. Ibid., p. 223; see also pp. 175–77.
13. Ibid., p. 215.
14. *Only Words*, p. 16.

as low value speech rests on an understanding of high value speech as appealing to the intellect, not the emotions. "The effect and intent of pornography . . . are to produce sexual arousal, not in any sense to affect the course of self-government. Though comprised of words and pictures, pornography does not have the special properties that single out speech for special protection; it is more akin to a sexual aid than a communicative expression."[15]

This argument presupposes that appeals to the emotions are no important part of political speech, and that norms of decorum therefore can be enforced without restricting the range of possible political expression. Yet, when subordinated groups have sought emancipation, their protests have often been most effective in precisely those cases in which they challenged established norms of decorum: the sit-ins and freedom rides of the 1960s, women's presence in places from which they have traditionally been excluded, or the act of attending a gay bar or two men dancing together.[16]

The argument that pornography deserves no First Amendment protection because it contains no ideas has been elaborated by Frederick Schauer, who writes that "a refusal to treat hard core pornography as speech in the technical sense at issue is grounded in the belief that the prototypical pornographic item shares more of the characteristics of sexual activity than of communication."[17] He illustrates the point with a hypothetical extreme example:

> Imagine a motion picture of ten minutes' duration whose entire content consists of a close-up colour depiction of the sexual organs of a male and a female who are engaged in sexual intercourse. The film contains no variety, no dialogue, no music, no attempt at artistic depiction, and not even any view of the faces of the participants. The film is shown to paying customers who, observing the film, either reach orgasm instantly or are led to masturbate while the film is being shown.[18]

This film is a sexual surrogate, like a plastic or vibrating sex aid; it takes pictorial form only because that is another way of helping individuals achieve

---

15. Cass R. Sunstein, "Pornography and the First Amendment," 1986 *Duke L. J.* 589, 606.

16. See Robert C. Post, "Cultural Heterogeneity and Law: Pornography, Blasphemy, and the First Amendment," 76 *Calif. L. Rev.* 297, 309 (1988); Kenneth L. Karst, "Boundaries and Reasons: Freedom of Expression and the Subordination of Groups," 1990 *U. of Ill. L. Rev.* 95.

17. Frederick Schauer, *Free Speech: A Philosophical Enquiry* (Cambridge: Cambridge University Press, 1982), p. 181.

18. Ibid.

sexual gratification. "The mere fact that in pornography the stimulating experience is initiated by visual rather than tactile means is irrelevant if every other aspect of the experience is the same."[19] It is true that some serious literature can also produce sexual arousal, but that literature has other elements that entitle it to protection. The reason such protection is not appropriately extended to hard core pornography "is not that it has a physical effect, *but that it has nothing else.*"[20] Schauer's argument may be sound, but it cannot be brought to bear on the pornography that MacKinnon and Sunstein want to target. That pornography has something else: a message that women are an inferior class of people, appropriately treated as commodities to be consumed and discarded. The message is horrible, but it is a message.

In his more recent writing on the subject, Sunstein continues to rely on the basic point, but with important caveats and qualifications. He argues that, like many kinds of speech that are not entitled to protection, much pornography "do[es] not amount to part of social deliberation about public matters, or about matters at all—even if this category is construed quite broadly, as it should be, and even if we insist, as we should, that emotive and cognitive capacities are frequently intertwined in deliberative processes, and that any sharp split between 'emotion' and 'cognition' would be untrue to political and social discussion."[21] The claim that precedes the dash in the sentence just quoted is, however, drained of its force by the concessions that follow it.[22] If it is recognized that sexuality is one of the most fiercely debated political issues of our time, then all pornography can convey a message about political matters. Some pornography even effectively conveys ideas that the antidiscrimination project needs to *promote.* Sara Diamond writes that "feminism and porn have something in common. Both insist that women are sexual beings. Both have made sex an experience open to public examination and . . . de-

---

19. Ibid., p. 182.

20. Ibid.

21. *Democracy and the Problem of Free Speech,* p. 215.

22. The part after the dash has also gotten longer the more Sunstein has thought about the issue. Compare Cass R. Sunstein, *The Partial Constitution* (Cambridge and London: Harvard University Press, 1993), p. 265; in this work, published earlier in 1993 than *Democracy and the Problem of Free Speech,* the same sentence lacks the final clause. The same is true of Cass R. Sunstein, "Neutrality in Constitutional Law (With Special Reference to Pornography, Abortion, and Surrogacy)," 92 *Columb. L. Rev.* 1, 23 (1992). In his 1986 article "Pornography and the First Amendment," Sunstein sharply distinguished cognitive from noncognitive speech, and argued that pornography should not be protected because it is nonpolitical and noncognitive (pp. 602–8).

bate."[23] Even the pornography MacKinnon and Sunstein regard as most worthless, that associated with violence and coercion, appears to have political value, and not just for opponents of sex equality.

> [M]any women . . . fantasize about being ravished. It is not surprising that women daydream about being uncontrollably desired in a culture in which our value as human beings is based on our attractiveness, and in which we are constantly prevented from acting out our desires. If we fantasize a partner taking complete control of a sexual encounter, then we are absolved of responsibility for our abandoned behavior. In this way we can mentally break sexual taboos that still remain in place in practice.[24]

Although much pornography contains an extraordinarily degrading and insulting message about women, even this pornography can sometimes be deployed for feminist ends. Nadine Strossen observes that, ironically, "an essential element of the anti-pornography feminists' message is conveyed by publicly displaying sexually explicit work that is graphic, violent, and misogynistic."[25] The revulsion that this kind of pornography induces can have great political effectiveness.[26]

23. Sara Diamond, "Pornography: Image and Reality," in Varda Burstyn, ed., *Women Against Censorship* (Vancouver and Toronto: Douglas and McIntyre, 1985), p. 40; quoted in Nadine Strossen, "A Feminist Critique of 'the' Feminist Critique of Pornography," 79 *Va. L. Rev.* 1099, 1133 (1993).

24. Diamond, "Pornography," p. 51, quoted in Strossen, "A Feminist Critique," p. 1134. Strossen also quotes Nancy Friday, who has collected thousands of women's sexual fantasies from interviews and letters: "The most popular guilt-avoiding device [in these fantasies] was the so-called rape fantasy—'so-called' because no rape, bodily harm, or humiliation took place in the fantasy. It simply had to be understood that what went on was against the woman's will. Saying she was 'raped' was the most expedient way of getting past the big No to sex that had been imprinted on her mind since early childhood." Nancy Friday, *Women on Top: How Real Life Has Changed Women's Sexual Fantasies* (New York: Simon and Schuster, 1991), pp. 16–17, quoted in Strossen, "A Feminist Critique," p. 1134 n. 144.

25. Strossen, "A Feminist Critique," p. 1135. In New York City, a group called Feminists Fighting Pornography was compelled to enlist the aid of the New York Civil Liberties Union after it was ordered to remove its display of pornography from Grand Central Terminal. The NYCLU succeeded in establishing FFP's right to display pornography for the purpose of persuading the public that pornography should not be protected speech. Ibid., p. 1136.

26. Catharine MacKinnon, the most prominent feminist proponent of pornography regulation, occasionally acknowledges that the recent widespread availability of pornography may aid the cause of sex equality by making it possible for women to inspect it. "This central mechanism of

The claim that racist speech is low value speech is similarly unsustainable. Such speech, unlike pornography, is overtly political. The claim that it is low value speech must rest on the obvious wrongness of its content, as well as (raising the separate issue of its harmfulness) the disastrous consequences that would ensue should it succeed in persuading its audience.[27] Thus Mari Matsuda argues that racist speech presents "an idea so historically untenable, so dangerous, and so tied to perpetuation of violence and degradation of the very classes of human beings who are least equipped to respond that it is properly treated as outside the realm of protected discourse."[28] For Matsuda, racist speech is objectionable not because it is irrelevant to political debate but because its persuasive power may influence political debate in a catastrophic direction.

Even those arguments that concern only demeaning epithets, rather than racist speech in general, tend to invoke rather than to deny their political meaning. Richard Delgado argues that racist epithets should not be protected by the First Amendment, because they do not "advance political dialogue, further the search for truth, or help society strike a balance between stability and orderly change,"[29] but he also writes that those epithets are "harmful in themselves,"[30] because they "constitute 'badges and incidents of slavery' and contribute to a stratified society in which political power is possessed by some and denied to others."[31] These words "injure the dignity and self-regard of the person to whom they are addressed, communicating the message that distinctions of race are distinctions of merit, dignity, status, and personhood."[32] Kingsley R. Browne observes that Delgado's argument "suffers from

---

sexual subordination, this means of systematizing the definition of women as a sexual class, has now become available to its victims for scrutiny and analysis as an open public system, not just as a private secret abuse. Hopefully, this was a mistake." Catharine MacKinnon, *Feminism Unmodified: Discourses on Life and Law* (Cambridge and London: Harvard University Press, 1987), p. 151 (footnote omitted).

27. See, e.g., David Kretzmer, "Freedom of Speech and Racism," 8 *Cardozo L. Rev.* 445, 462 (1987).

28. Mari Matsuda, "Public Response to Racist Speech: Considering the Victim's Story," 87 *Mich. L. Rev.* 2320, 2359 (1989).

29. Richard Delgado, "Professor Delgado Replies," 18 *Harv. Civ. Rts.–Civ. Liberties L. Rev.* 593, 594 (1983).

30. Richard Delgado, "Words That Wound: A Tort Action for Racial Insults, Epithets, and Name-Calling," 17 *Harv. Civ. Rts.–Civ. Liberties L. Rev.* 133, 173 (1982).

31. Ibid, p. 178 (footnotes omitted), quoting Civil Rights Cases, 109 U.S. 3, 20 (1883).

32. Delgado, "Words That Wound," pp. 135–36.

a substantial internal inconsistency."[33] If the words cause harm because of their political message, then it cannot be said that the words are unprotected because they convey no political message. The trouble with them is the loathsomeness of the message, and the suffering of those who are subjected to it. Both of those considerations are relevant to the weighing of the harm against the value of the speech; neither shows that the speech itself is low value speech for First Amendment purposes.

Epithets are, of course, generally tangential to the purposes of free speech. The Court has held that "the lewd and obscene, the profane, the libelous, and the insulting or 'fighting' words" are unprotected by the First Amendment, because "such utterances are no essential part of any exposition of ideas, and are of such slight social value as a step to the truth that any benefit that may be derived from them is clearly outweighed by the social interest in order and morality."[34] Racist fighting words, by contrast, are distinguished from other fighting words precisely by their political content. Racial epithets may be thought of as low value speech containing a tiny grain of high value. The problem with regulations targeting such epithets is that they make that grain of value the basis of regulation.

Another argument for deeming racist speech "low value" is that the political ideas it is conceded to contain are so clearly wrong that there seems little danger that suppressing them will inhibit the search for truth or prevent the people from discovering the wisest political course.[35] The premise of this argument is sound. As we noted in Chapter 1, the absence of a diversity of views on the equal humanity of blacks, women, or gays would be a great social good. To carve out an exception to the First Amendment on this basis, however, would give the state the power directly to censor political opinions on the basis of their erroneous content. Such a power would be difficult to contain. A restriction on racist speech, Browne observes, "would cause a major chilling effect on all speech dealing with racial matters."[36] Matsuda would allow as-

33. Kingsley R. Browne, "Title VII as Censorship: Hostile-Environment Harassment and the First Amendment," 52 *Ohio St. L. J.* 481, 533 (1991).

34. *Chaplinsky v. New Hampshire,* 315 U.S. 568, 572 (1942).

35. See, e.g., Alon Harel, "Bigotry, Pornography, and the First Amendment: A Theory of Unprotected Speech," 65 *S. Cal. L. Rev.* 1887 (1992). For a critique, see Larry Alexander, "Trouble on Track Two: Incidental Regulations of Speech and Free Speech Theory," 44 *Hastings L. J.* 921, 952 (1993).

36. Browne, "Title VII as Censorship," p. 534.

sertions of social scientific fact that have racist implications, such as "theories of genetic predisposition to violence, cultural lag, and race/intelligence correlation," only if the theory is "free of any message of hatred and persecution."[37] It would not be easy for a speaker to predict how this standard would be applied. "For example, some would no doubt argue that statements urging the elimination of affirmative action are hateful and advocate persecution, yet such statements seem to be the kind of speech that is at the core of First Amendment protection."[38] Racist speech may be substantively worthless, but outlawing it would give the state the power to decide *which* political views are worthless because racist. Such a power is so easily abused that it can be justified only if the speech in question is also exceedingly harmful.

How Courts Have Addressed the Dilemma

Thus, it cannot be said that either racist speech or pornography is low value speech for First Amendment purposes. What is proposed is precisely the kind of restriction that most worries First Amendment theorists: restriction of speech on the basis of the viewpoint it expresses.[39] Now one reading of the First Amendment—a more contained sort of First Amendment absolutism—holds that such viewpoint-based restrictions are *never* permissible, regardless of the harm sought to be prevented. This is the view that the Supreme Court took in *R.A.V. v. City of St. Paul,* in which the Court invalidated an ordinance that had been construed to outlaw only unprotected "fighting words" when such speech "arouses anger, alarm, or resentment in others on the basis of race, color, creed, religion or gender."[40] Although conceding that fighting words are ordinarily unprotected (in our terms, low value) speech, Justice Scalia held that this statute impermissibly discriminated on the basis of viewpoint by proscribing "fighting words of whatever manner that communicate messages of racial, gender, or religious intolerance."[41] Scalia rejected as "word-

37. Matsuda, "Public Response to Racist Speech," p. 2364–65. Matsuda would criminalize speech when "1. The message is of racial inferiority; 2. The message is directed against a historically oppressed group; and 3. The message is persecutorial, hateful, or degrading." Ibid., p. 2357.

38. Browne, "Title VII as Censorship," p. 535.

39. Schauer acknowledges that "the decision not to allow first amendment protection to turn on the point of view adopted by the speaker goes to both the epistemological and political cores of free speech theory." "Categories and the First Amendment," p. 284.

40. *R.A.V. v. City of St. Paul,* 505 U.S 377, 380 (1992).

41. Ibid., p. 393–94.

play" Justice Stevens' claim, in his separate opinion, that the viewpoint discrimination is justified by the fact that racist fighting words cause injuries that are "qualitatively different from that caused by other fighting words."[42] "What makes the anger, fear, sense of dishonor, etc. produced by violation of this ordinance distinct from the anger, fear, sense of dishonor, etc. produced by other fighting words," Scalia wrote, "is nothing other than the fact that it is caused by a distinctive idea, conveyed by a distinctive message."[43] This argument does not establish, however, that the distinctive idea conveyed by the speech is not more hurtful than the idea conveyed by other fighting words.[44] Sunstein observes that "[i]t is only obtuseness—a failure of perception or empathetic identification—that would enable someone to say that the word 'fascist' or 'pig' or even 'honky' produces the same feelings as the word 'nigger.' In view of our history, invective directed against minority groups, and racist speech in general, creates fears of physical violence, exclusion, and subordination that are not plausibly described as mere 'offense.' "[45] If a classification is viewpoint-based, Scalia appears to be claiming, it is unconstitutional regardless of the severity of the harm sought to be prevented; no amount of harm can *ever* justify viewpoint-based prohibitions of speech. That implies that Oliver Wendell Holmes was wrong when he wrote that free speech does not protect "a man in falsely shouting fire in a theatre and causing a panic."[46] Censoring such speech would almost certainly be viewpoint-based: it would be surprising if the man were punished, or punished as severely, for shouting "All is well!" in the theater.

An even more implausible reading of the First Amendment has guided the courts' treatment of attempts to regulate pornography on an antidiscrimination basis. Some feminists allege that pornography promotes violence against women and more generally exacerbates their subordinate status in society. In 1984 Indianapolis enacted an ordinance written by Catharine MacKinnon and Andrea Dworkin, the most prominent proponents of this view, defining "pornography" as a practice that discriminates against women and offering the

42. Ibid., pp. 392 (majority opinion), 424 (Stevens, J., concurring in the judgment); see also p. 415–16 (Blackmun, J., concurring in the judgment).

43. Ibid., p. 392–93.

44. See ibid., p. 433 n. 9 (Stevens, J., concurring in the judgment).

45. Sunstein, *Democracy and the Problem of Free Speech*, p. 186. For a critical discussion of this issue in the *R.A.V.* case, see ibid., pp. 190–93.

46. *Schenck v. United States*, 249 U.S. 47, 52 (1919).

same administrative and judicial methods of redress used for other discrimination.[47] A group of booksellers challenged the ordinance on First Amendment grounds. The federal courts invalidated the ordinance, essentially by the talismanic invocation of freedom of speech.

Both the district court and the court of appeals in *American Booksellers Association v. Hudnut* agreed that there was a significant state interest in preventing sex discrimination, but both also held that this interest was not, and could never be shown to be, sufficient to overcome the prohibition of interference with free speech. The district court thought that giving compelling weight to this interest invited a parade of horribles:

> If this Court were to accept defendants' argument—that the State's interest in protecting women from the humiliation and degradation which comes from being depicted in a sexually subordinate context is so compelling as to warrant the regulation of otherwise free speech to accomplish that end—one wonders what would prevent the City-County Council (or any other legislative body) from enacting protections for other equally compelling claims against exploitation and discrimination as are presented here.[48]

The court thought that the state's argument would also permit the outlawing of racist, ethnic, and religious slurs, and therefore "would signal so great a potential encroachment upon First Amendment freedoms that the precious liberties reposed within those guarantees would not survive."[49] No amount of

---

47. "Pornography" was defined as "the graphic sexually explicit subordination of women, whether in pictures or in words, that also includes one or more of the following: (1) Women are presented as sexual objects who enjoy pain or humiliation; or (2) Women are presented as sexual objects who experience sexual pleasure in being raped; or (3) Women are presented as sexual objects tied up or cut up or mutilated or bruised or physically hurt, or as dismembered or truncated or fragmented or severed into body parts; or (4) Women are presented as being penetrated by objects or animals; or (5) Women are presented in scenarios of degradation, injury, abasement, torture, shown as filthy or inferior, bleeding, bruised, or hurt in a context that makes these conditions sexual; or (6) Women are presented as sexual objects for domination, conquest, violation, exploitation, possession, or use, or through postures or positions of servility or submission or display." *Indianapolis Code* 16-3(q), quoted in Andrea Dworkin and Catharine MacKinnon, *Pornography and Civil Rights: A New Day for Women's Equality* (Minneapolis: Organizing Against Pornography, 1988), pp. 113–14.

48. *American Booksellers Ass'n v. Hudnut*, 598 F. Supp. 1316, 1335 (S.D. Ind. 1984), aff'd, 771 F. 2d 323 (7th Cir. 1985), aff'd mem., 475 U.S. 1001 (1986).

49. 598 F. Supp. at 1336.

evidence supporting the state's case could change that conclusion. "To permit every interest group, especially those who claim to be victimized by unfair expression, their own legislative exceptions to the First Amendment so long as they succeed in obtaining a majority of legislative votes in their favor demonstrates the potentially predatory nature of what defendants seek through this Ordinance and defend in this lawsuit."[50]

This argument assumes that the court would have to accept the "claim to be victimized by unfair expression" at face value, without independently considering the weight of the asserted state interest, the evidence of the asserted harms to the victim class, or the evidence that regulation will diminish those harms. But that assumption is nowhere defended. The claim that pornography injures women is doubtless a controversial one, but its difficulty could weigh against restriction as easily as in its favor, depending on which party has the burden of proof. The dangers invoked by the court suggest that the state should be required to support its claims. This option, strangely, does not appear to have been considered. Instead, the court reduced the question to one of which side ought to receive the benefit of an irrebuttable presumption.

On appeal, the Seventh Circuit, in an opinion by Judge Frank Easterbrook, similarly evaded the question of the strength of the state's claims, this time by assuming the correctness of those claims because "as judges we must accept the legislative resolution of such disputed empirical questions."[51] The court therefore conceded that "[d]epictions of subordination tend to perpetuate subordination. The subordinate status of women in turn leads to affront and lower pay at work, insult and injury at home, battery and rape on the streets."[52] But, the court held, "this simply demonstrates the power of por-

50. Ibid., p. 1337.

51. 771 F. 2d at 329 n. 2. Given that this acceptance rests on the Seventh Circuit's peculiar conception of its institutional role rather than any evaluation of the evidence, it is misleading to say, as the authors of the ordinance do, that it was "conceded by the court" that pornographic materials "cause assaults." Dworkin and MacKinnon, *Pornography and Civil Rights*, p. 59. It is true that the court found that "the legislative finding of a causal link was judicially adequate," MacKinnon, *Only Words*, p. 92, but this concession was meaningless, since the court would similarly have accepted *any* empirical finding of the legislature. Such "acceptance" was irrelevant to the outcome of the case. The logic of the opinion implies that the court, without reaching a different result, would have "accepted" a legislative finding that unregulated pornography would bring about the speedy extermination of the human race.

52. 771 F. 2d at 329.

nography as speech. All of these unhappy effects depend on mental interme-diation."[53] All speech affects the world, the court reasoned; relying on such effects to justify suppression of speech would give government a frightening degree of power:

> Racial bigotry, anti-semitism, violence on television, reporters' biases—these and many more influence the culture and shape our socialization. None is directly answerable by more speech, unless that speech too finds its place in the popular culture. Yet all is protected as speech, however insidious. Any other answer leaves the government in control of all the institutions of culture, the great censor and director of which thoughts are good for us.[54]

The trouble with this ringing defense of free speech is that it proves far too much. On this account, none of the traditional exceptions to the First Amendment could stand. Conspiracy, bribery, and the fraudulent sale of adulterated food "depend on mental intermediation." Libel law, or a law against false advertising or perjury, "implies the power to declare truth."[55] Moreover, the court's argument that the asserted injury "simply demon-strates the power of pornography as speech" carries the astonishing impli-cation that the greater the harm that speech causes, the greater its protection under the First Amendment.[56] If a person falsely shouts fire in a crowded theater and causes a panic, do not the broken bodies of those who are tram-pled (an unhappy effect that results from mental intermediation) demon-strate the power of the shout as speech? If it is indeed the case that the dissemination of this speech results in acts of discrimination and even phys-ical violence against women, and that repression of this speech would pre-vent those harms, as the Seventh Circuit purports to stipulate, then the case for repression is exceedingly strong. It is not unfair to conclude that the court's reasoning implies that "whatever the value of pornography is[,] . . . the value of women is lower."[57]

Outside the context of racist and sexist speech, First Amendment law has

---

53. Ibid.

54. Ibid., p. 330.

55. Ibid.

56. The extraordinary brutality of the court's reasoning is noted by MacKinnon. See *Feminism Unmodified*, pp. 210–11; *Only Words*, pp. 92–93.

57. MacKinnon, *Feminism Unmodified*, p. 211.

not, in fact, been indifferent to the harms that speech can cause. When the connection between the speech and the harms is sufficiently clear, the law is not helpless to prevent the harms, even where high value speech is involved. Speech that criticizes government officials must be regarded as speech of the very highest value for First Amendment purposes, yet it is not immune to regulation: a public official may recover damages for a defamatory falsehood, so long as the official proves that the statement was made with knowledge of its falsity or with reckless disregard of whether it was false or not.[58] The proper question to ask, then, is whether speech that disseminates the meanings that the antidiscrimination project seeks to eliminate or marginalize is sufficiently harmful, and whether legal intervention would be sufficiently effective, to justify outlawing it.

The harms that the proponents of censorship have attributed to racist and sexist speech fall into three categories: physical harm, psychic harm, and damage to a group's status.[59] The case for suppression must rest on a showing, first, that these harms are remediable in a liberal state; second, that the speech in question is closely linked to these harms; and third, that suppression of the speech will end or diminish the incidence of these harms. How strong these showings must be will depend on whether the speech in question is deemed high value or low value. For the reasons already stated, I shall consider racist speech and pornography to be high value speech. I shall argue that some regulation of that speech is nonetheless justified.

58. See *New York Times v. Sullivan*, 376 U.S. 254 (1964).

59. A fourth kind of harm, which I shall not take up here in any detail, is that many women are coerced in the making of pornography. See MacKinnon, *Feminism Unmodified*, pp. 179–83; MacKinnon, *Only Words*, p. 15; Sunstein, *Democracy and the Problem of Free Speech*, pp. 216–17. MacKinnon and Sunstein both argue that repression of pornography, by eliminating the financial benefits of such coercion, may be the only realistically effective way to eliminate such coercive practices. (The Supreme Court has been persuaded by a similar argument for the repression of child pornography. See *New York v. Ferber*, 458 U.S. 747 [1982].) It is far from clear, however, that the most effective remedy would be suppression of pornography rather than the elimination of obscenity laws. Richard Posner argues, just as plausibly, that the mistreatment of models that now occurs "is exactly what one expects in an illegal market. We know from Prohibition, prostitution, the campaign against drugs, and the employment of illegal immigrants that when an economic activity is placed outside the protection of the law, the participants will resort to threats and violence in lieu of the contractual and other legal remedies denied them. The pimp is an artifact of the illegality of prostitution, and the exploitation of pornographic actresses and models by their employers is parallel to the exploitation of illegal immigrant labor by its employers. These women would be better off if all pornography were legal." Richard Posner, "Obsessed with Pornography," in *Overcoming Law* (Cambridge and London: Harvard University Press, 1995), p. 363.

Speech and Violence

Let us begin with physical harm. It is alleged that hate speech and pornography incite violence against blacks and women. If this is true, the patterned nature of this violence makes it a matter of concern for the antidiscrimination project. Violence, as Iris Young notes, is one of the major forms that oppression of groups takes, and one of the means by which other oppressions are enforced.[60] Blacks, women, and gays have all been targets of violence for many years, and fear of violent harm remains a daily concern for many of them. This is why enhanced penalties for hate crimes are appropriate: such crimes harm not only their immediate victims but all members of the targeted group. They are part of a socially coordinated offensive against an already unjustly subordinated group, and they help to perpetuate that subordination in the face of state efforts to ameliorate it. For this reason it is appropriate for the state to treat perpetrators of such crimes not on a par with ordinary criminals but as if they were soldiers in an invading army or members of a huge conspiracy. Though they may not be members of a terrorist organization, they are as dangerous to society as if they were. If certain speech can be shown to induce this kind of patterned violence, then arguably it should be subject to regulation for the same reason that criminal solicitation is.

The argument linking expression with violence is most prominently made by MacKinnon with reference to pornography: "Pornography sexualizes rape, battery, sexual harassment, prostitution, and child sexual abuse; it thereby celebrates, promotes, authorizes, and legitimates them."[61] She points out that pornography "is a specific and compelling behavioral stimulus, conditioner, and reinforcer."[62] A similar argument has sometimes been made with reference to racist speech, but it has been neither well developed nor heavily relied upon in making the case for suppressing such speech.[63] I shall, therefore, concentrate on the question of the relation between pornography and violence.

60. See Iris Marion Young, *Justice and the Politics of Difference* (Princeton: Princeton University Press, 1990), pp. 61–63.

61. MacKinnon, *Feminism Unmodified*, p. 171.

62. Ibid., p. 200.

63. Thus, for example, Matsuda claims that "escalating racist speech always accompanies racist violence," but she does this in a short footnote, does not explain what she thinks is cause and what is effect, and offers no evidence that repression of racist speech is more effective in diminishing the incidence of violence than official condemnation of the speech and punishment of the violence. See Matsuda, "Public Response to Racist Speech," p. 2352 n. 166. MacKinnon reports

Three categories of evidence have been cited as linking pornography to sexual violence: laboratory studies, longitudinal studies of the experience of states and countries that have changed their practices with respect to pornography, and victim accounts. The laboratory findings are most disturbing when they involve pornography that includes violence against women. Exposure to violent pornography in laboratory tests

> increases normal men's willingness to aggress against women under laboratory conditions; makes both women and men substantially less able to perceive accounts of rape as accounts of rape; makes normal men more closely resemble convicted rapists psychologically; increases all the attitudinal measures that are known to correlate with rape, such as hostility toward women, propensity to rape, condoning rape, and predicting that one would rape or force sex on a woman if one knew one would not get caught; and produces other attitude changes in men like increasing the extent of their trivialization, dehumanization, and objectification of women.[64]

These studies, however, only showed short-term attitudinal changes; they did not purport to show that exposure to violent pornography would change the viewers' behavior. Moreover, when men who had been exposed to these misogynistic materials were later given debriefing sessions that included materials dispelling rape myths and detailing the harms women suffer as a consequence of rape, the net effect was striking. After these men were exposed *both* to violent pornography *and* to profeminist material, they had more positive, less discriminatory, and less stereotyped attitudes toward women than they did before the experiment. Moreover, negative attitudes toward women

---

that "I was surprised to discover, at the end of an extensive literature search, that no laboratory or experimental research on racist hate literature exists parallel to that on the effects of pornography." *Only Words*, p. 134 n. 53. MacKinnon adds: "This is not to suggest that the Holocaust or the U.S. experience with lynching or with racism in general, provides an insufficient body of evidence on its effects." Ibid. This argument is concerned, not with direct incitement, but with the effect of racism on the propensity of a target group to violence. Through the mediation of culture, *all* racist and sexist violence is ultimately traceable to speech. This implies that even racist speech that does not directly incite violence should be suppressed because of its effect on the social construction of blacks, which in turn creates a climate in which violence is more likely. The harm directly caused by this kind of speech is not violence, but harm to the group's status. The case for suppression on the basis of this kind of harm is considered below.

64. Catharine MacKinnon, *Toward a Feminist Theory of the State* (Cambridge and London: Harvard University Press, 1989), p. 304 n. 6; see sources cited therein.

were more effectively reduced by exposure to both violent pornography and feminist materials than by exposure only to the latter.[65] Nadine Strossen observes that these findings are "completely consistent with a central tenet of U.S. free speech jurisprudence: that the appropriate antidote to speech with which we disagree, or which offends us, is more speech."[66] Moreover, even the negative attitudinal effects associated with violent pornography seem to have less to do with their sexual content than with their violence. Nonviolent sexual materials do not produce any increase in negative attitudes toward women, much less aggressive behavior.[67] Some studies have even found that exposure to nonviolent, sexually explicit materials actually *reduces* aggression in laboratory settings.[68] Moreover, exposure to violent but nonsexual films, particularly those that show violence against women, produce attitudinal and behavioral responses in experimental subjects similar to those that exposure to violent pornography produces.[69] The real problem, then, appears to be depictions of violence, with or without sexual content. Censoring such expressions would, of course, require a much larger censorial apparatus than even MacKinnon contemplates. If the antidiscrimination project seeks to change the culture, then speech is indispensable to that enterprise: the ultimate goal is to persuade people to look at the world differently, and that can only be done by transmitting different thoughts to them than the ones they have habitually been exposed to. Violent pornography may, as we have seen, play a useful part in that undertaking. As antipornography activists are well aware, its existence is powerful evidence of women's inferior social status, and it may be useful in persuading skeptics that sex equality remains an unachieved goal.

The second kind of evidence that has been cited as linking pornography to violence is research suggesting that the greater or lesser availability of pornography in particular geographic areas is associated with increases or decreases in rape and other forms of sexual violence. The largest such study,

65. See Edward Donnerstein, Daniel Linz, and Steven Penrod, *The Question of Pornography: Research Findings and Policy Implications* (New York: Free Press, 1987), pp. 180–85, and citations therein.

66. Strossen, "A Feminist Critique," p. 1168.

67. See Donnerstein, Linz, and Penrod, *The Question of Pornography*, p. 72.

68. Strossen, "A Feminist Critique," p. 1182, and sources cited.

69. See Donnerstein, Linz, and Penrod, *The Question of Pornography*, pp. 108–36; Edward I. Donnerstein and Daniel G. Linz, "The Question of Pornography: It Is Not Sex, But Violence, That Is an Obscenity in Our Society," *Psychology Today*, Dec. 1986, pp. 56–59.

comparing the experience of different American states, has found that "the higher the circulation rate of sex magazines, the higher the rape rate."[70] The authors of this study were "extremely hesitant to interpret our findings as reflecting a cause-effect relationship,"[71] however, citing another longitudinal study that compared the United States, Denmark, Sweden, and West Germany and which found either no increase or a decrease in the rape rate following the legalization and wide increase in the circulation of pornographic materials.[72] They hypothesized that both sexual violence and pornography consumption might be caused by a third variable, "the presence of a hyper-masculine or macho culture pattern" that includes "such traits as normative support for violence, the use of physical force to settle quarrels, belief in male supremacy, endorsement of rape myths, and approval of sexual coercion."[73] They tested this proposition by introducing into the regression analysis the results of survey questions that measured social approval of violence.[74] When this factor is introduced, "the relationship between sex magazine circulation and rape vanishes."[75] In sum, this type of evidence is far from proving a causal link between pornography and violence.

There is also a large amount of anecdotal evidence by victims of sexual violence, who report that the perpetrators often read pornography beforehand and sometimes used it as a kind of "how-to" manual. The stories these women (they usually are women) tell are horrifying, but they do not show which, if any, of the rapes would not have occurred had the pornography not been available, nor do they "indicate the importance of pornographic materials in causing sexual aggression, as distinguished from shaping the forms that aggression takes."[76] Other evidence of this kind comes from perpetrators of sexual violence, who sometimes report that pornography induced them to

70. Larry Baron and Murray A. Straus, *Four Theories of Rape in American Society: A State-Level Analysis* (New Haven and London: Yale University Press, 1989), p. 185.

71. Ibid., p. 186.

72. Ibid.; see Berl Kuchinsky, "The Politics of Pornography Research," 26 *Law & Society* 447 (1992), and other studies by Kuchinsky cited therein. For citations to similar evidence from other countries, see Strossen, "A Feminist Critique," p. 1184.

73. Baron and Straus, *Four Theories of Rape*, p. 186.

74. The index used is described in ibid., pp. 165–68.

75. Ibid., p. 186.

76. Deborah L. Rhode, *Justice and Gender* (Cambridge and London: Harvard University Press, 1989), p. 268.

commit their crimes. The self-serving and unreliable character of these claims should be obvious.[77] Even if some rapes did occur because of the impact of the pornography, this tells us little about pornography's overall effect: perhaps these harms are balanced by an overall lowering of the incidence of sexual violence as a consequence of pornography's availability, as some clinical and cross-cultural evidence suggests.[78] Anecdotal evidence is a notoriously poor measure of aggregate phenomena.[79]

The weakness of the evidence connecting pornography with sexual violence may be highlighted by comparing it with the evidence that smoking causes lung cancer, or that drunk driving causes accidents. MacKinnon has pressed the analogy with the evidence in these other cases in order to argue that the opponents of pornography have been held to an unreasonably strict standard of causation.[80] To the extent that defenders of pornography have not acknowledged the validity of a probabilistic *concept* of causation, the analogy is sound.[81] In the tobacco and alcohol cases, however, the *evidence* of probabilistic causation is far stronger than in the case of pornography. Laboratory studies consistently show that exposure to tobacco smoke causes cancer in laboratory animals, and that ingestion of alcohol diminishes reaction time and coordination.[82] Correlational studies show that populations who smoke are ten times as likely to develop lung cancer as those who do not.[83] Half of all fatal

77. See Strossen, "A Feminist Critique," pp. 1156–59. MacKinnon is remarkably credulous of these claims, as when she writes that "pornography makes rapists unaware that their victims are not consenting." *Only Words,* p. 96. This statement appears in the context of a discussion of a death penalty case in which a sex murderer claimed that he could not be held responsible for his actions because he was a lifelong consumer of pornography.

78. See Strossen, "A Feminist Critique," pp. 1176–85, and sources cited therein.

79. Scientific studies of convicted rapists have similarly failed to establish any causal connection between consumption of pornography and propensity to rape. See Mary R. Murrin and D. R. Laws, "The Influence of Pornography on Sexual Crimes," in W. L. Marshall, D. R. Laws, and H. E. Barbaree, eds., *Handbook of Sexual Assault: Issues, Theories, and Treatment of the Offender* (New York: Plenum Press, 1990), pp. 73–91.

80. See MacKinnon, *Toward a Feminist Theory of the State,* p. 207.

81. See Frederick Schauer, "Causation Theory and the Causes of Sexual Violence," 1987 *Am. Bar Found. Res. J.* 737.

82. See *Smoking and Health: A Report of the Surgeon General* (Washington, D.C.: U.S. Dept. of Health, Education, and Welfare, 1979), ch. 5, pp. 29–31; Henrik Wallgren and Herbert Barry III, *Actions of Alcohol, v. 1: Biochemical, Physiological and Psychological Aspects* (Amsterdam: Elsevier Publishing Co., 1970), pp. 295–317.

83. See *Smoking and Health: A Report of the Surgeon General,* p. 5–11.

car accidents involve, and at least half of those are caused by, drunk drivers.[84] There is anecdotal evidence in these cases, too, but the cases against smoking and drunk driving do not need to rely upon such evidence.

Thus Sunstein appears to be overreading the evidence when he reports that "the real question is not the existence of a causal connection [between violent pornography and real-world violence] but its degree."[85] "In light of current information," he concludes, "it is at least reasonable to think that there would be significant benefits from regulation of violent pornography."[86] This conclusion is sustainable only if one thinks (as Sunstein does) that such pornography is wholly worthless, so that nothing important is lost if it is censored on the basis of evidence that is merely suggestive.[87] Moreover, even if the evidence is believed, it does not support targeting violent *pornography,* rather than all violent expression. (MacKinnon and Dworkin's ordinance covers all pornography, violent or not, and so is overinclusive as well as underinclusive.) Targeting sexual materials has unfortunate cultural effects of its own, which I shall consider below. Unless one thinks that sexuality is somehow particularly distant from First Amendment concerns, it is a mistake to use sexual explicitness as the basis for distinguishing high value speech from low value speech.[88]

84. H. Laurence Ross, *Confronting Drunk Driving: Social Policy for Saving Lives* (New Haven and London: Yale University Press, 1992), pp. 36–37.

85. Sunstein, *Democracy and the Problem of Free Speech,* p. 218.

86. Ibid.

87. Sunstein argues that, in other contexts, such as that involving regulation of toxic chemicals, "suggestive evidence might well, in the face of potentially severe harm, justify immediate governmental action. . . . Inaction pending the accumulation of definitive proof has costs of its own. The question, a familiar one in the regulatory context, is who should bear the burden of uncertainty: the pornography industry or the potential victims of sexual violence." "Pornography and the First Amendment," p. 601. The problem with this argument is that the production of toxic chemicals is not a constitutionally protected activity. The discredited "bad tendency" cases of the early-twentieth-century Supreme Court, which held that speech could be suppressed when its "natural tendency and reasonably probable effect" was to induce illegal behavior, *Debs v. United States,* 249 U.S. 211, 216 (1919), are ample illustration that "the government would acquire enormous and intolerable powers of censorship if it were to be given the authority to penalize any speech that would tend to induce in an audience disagreeable attitudinal changes with respect to future conduct." Post, "Cultural Heterogeneity and Law," p. 325.

88. The Supreme Court has, of course, drawn the line in precisely this way, but it has done so on the basis of a judgment that sexually explicit materials per se cause a particularly severe kind of offense that may legitimately be the basis of repression. See *Miller v. California,* 413 U.S. 15 (1973). That judgment has no relevance to an effort to repress pornography because it is thought to induce violence.

If there is a case for repressing pornography, it must rest on more than its alleged link to violence. I turn, then, to other kinds of harm that have been linked to pornography and to other kinds of racist and sexist speech.

Words That Wound

The second kind of harm attributed to racist and sexist speech is psychic harm. When assessing the injuries of stigma, we noted that these were twofold: stigma not only affects a group's treatment by the state, its opportunities for employment, and its share of goods, but also hurts directly. When a black customer returns merchandise to a store, and is required to sign a slip on the top of which is written, "Arrogant Nigger refuses exchange—says he doesn't like products," the experience is not that different from being struck.[89] Moreover, taken in context, such insults typically have connotations of physical threat. The effect is sometimes similar when women are forced to look at pornography. The offenses associated with racist and sexist insults are due directly to the stigma historically associated with the victim group. As David Kretzmer writes, "a derogatory remark about the ethnic group to which an individual belongs, in a society with no history of antagonism towards that group, and when the individual himself has no experience of antagonism towards his own ethnic group, may cause no harm at all."[90] But being directly targeted for insult causes pain, and the pain is greater when the insult is a racist insult directed at a member of a traditionally oppressed group. Antidiscrimination law has long recognized this kind of pain. Lawrence observes that *Brown v. Board of Education* "speaks directly to the psychic injury inflicted by racist speech in noting that the symbolic message of segregation affected 'the hearts and minds' of Negro children 'in a way unlikely ever to be undone.' "[91]

In the case of psychic harm, unlike the case of violence, there is no question of a link between the speech and the harm. Nor is there any question of any

89. See *Irving v. J. L. Marsh, Inc.,* 46 Ill. App. 3d 162, 164, 360 N.E. 2d 983, 985 (1977). The court held that such conduct was not "sufficiently severe" to support a suit for intentional infliction of emotional distress. 46 Ill. App. 3d at 167, 360 N.E. 2d at 986. The case is discussed in Delgado, "Words That Wound," pp. 155–58.

90. Kretzmer, "Freedom of Speech and Racism," p. 465.

91. Lawrence, "If He Hollers Let Him Go," p. 462, quoting *Brown v. Board of Educ.,* 347 U.S. 483, 494 (1954).

means other than censorship that could prevent the harm. The speech causes harm in a wholly unmediated way. Just as the only way to keep your fist from breaking my nose is to restrain your fist, the only way to prevent this speech from wounding its victims is to restrain it. Moreover, as in the case of racist violence, the patterned nature of these psychic harms makes them a matter of concern for the antidiscrimination project. The subjection of blacks and women to this kind of insult, like their disproportionate poverty, is a badge of their inferiority that worsens their subordinate status.

Now one does not always have a right to be free from offense and insult. If one did, then the state could censor as "harmful" any political speech that offended or insulted enough people, or that offended or insulted even a few people severely enough. The problem here, as already noted, is that even high value speech can cause psychic harm, and the psychic harm can sometimes even be directly linked to the political message of the speech. Censorship of political ideas is precisely what the First Amendment primarily forbids. We noted in the last chapter that a propensity to be aware of and to resist racism is a liberal virtue, which a substantial proportion of the citizens must have if liberal ideals are to be realized. Another liberal virtue is the thickness of skin that enables one to tolerate even hateful speech, recognizing that exposure to it is the price that one pays for living in a free society.[92] The law's refusal to prohibit most insulting or offensive language has the effect of forcing citizens to cultivate this virtue.

Even so, however, the public good of an environment in which debate is "uninhibited, robust, and wide-open"[93] should not be purchased wholly at the expense of the least advantaged citizens. "Tolerance of hate speech," Matsuda writes, "is not tolerance borne by the community at large. Rather, it is a psychic tax imposed on those least able to pay."[94] Even if racist speech must be protected, it may still be permissible to regulate its time, place, and manner so that it is not inflicted upon unwilling victims.[95] The First Amendment

92. See generally Lee Bollinger, *The Tolerant Society: Freedom of Speech and Extremist Speech in America* (New York: Oxford University Press, 1986).

93. *New York Times v. Sullivan,* 376 U.S. at 270.

94. Matsuda, "Public Response to Racist Speech," p. 2323. See also Lawrence, "If He Hollers Let Him Go," pp. 472–76; Frederick Schauer, "Uncoupling Free Speech," 92 *Colum. L. Rev.* 1321 (1992).

95. The argument here is not that such a restriction is like other restrictions on the "time,

should not protect an employer who subjects his black employees to the repeated use of the word "nigger" in the workplace. The federal court that held that this did not constitute employment discrimination (in a decision that probably is no longer good law)[96] invoked the liberal virtue of tolerance: " 'Against a large part of the frictions and irritations and clashing of temperaments incident to participation in a community life, a certain toughening of the mental hide is a better protection than the law ever could be.' "[97] The trouble with this argument is that society has already done quite a lot to make members of certain groups thin-skinned, with a fragile and easily damaged sense of self-worth. An "eggshell skull" defense is doubly unjust if the perpetrator has deliberately taken advantage of the fragile condition of the defendant's skull.[98] There comes a point at which it becomes unreasonable to ask citizens to endure certain kinds of verbal assault. The difference between this kind of speech and other kinds of offensive expression is a difference in kind, not just in degree. "There is a great difference between the offensiveness of words that you would rather not hear—because they are labeled dirty, impolite, or personally demeaning—and the *injury* inflicted by words that remind the world that you are fair game for physical attack, evoke in you all of the millions of cultural lessons regarding your inferiority that you have so painstakingly repressed, and imprint upon you a badge of servitude for all the world to see."[99] Part of the harm in this kind of epithet, as Lawrence observes, is that it carries connotations of physical threat, a kind of speech that the law has never protected. But the psychic harm is not limited to fear for physical safety. The greatest vulnerability of the liberal argument, as Toni Massaro notes, is that it "tends to assume away human pain in order to preserve its

---

place, and manner" of expression that the Court has upheld. Unlike those restrictions, the one considered here is neither content-neutral nor viewpoint-neutral. See Browne, "Title VII as Censorship," pp. 520–25; Eugene Volokh, "Freedom of Speech and Workplace Harassment," 39 *U.C.L.A. L. Rev.* 1791, 1826–28 (1992).

96. See *Bailey v. Binion*, 583 F. Supp. 923, 931–34 (N.D. Ill. 1984); see generally Browne, "Title VII as Censorship," and Volokh, "Freedom of Speech."

97. *Howard v. National Cash Register Co.*, 388 F. Supp. 603, 606 (S.D. Ohio 1975), quoting Calvert Magruder, "Mental and Emotional Disturbance in the Law of Torts," 49 *Harv. L. Rev.* 1033, 1053 (1936).

98. The so-called "eggshell skull" defense, that the victim's injuries would have been less severe if he had not been frailer than the ordinary person, has long been rejected in tort law. See W. Page Keeton, Dan B. Dobbs, Robert E. Keeton, and David G. Owen, *Prosser and Keeton on the Law of Torts*, 5th ed. (St. Paul, Minn.: West, 1984), § 43, p. 292.

99. Lawrence, "If He Hollers Let Him Go," p. 461 (emphasis in original).

basic formula that the answer to bad speech is counterspeech."[100] We saw in the last chapter that the same liberal conceptions of justice that support freedom of speech cannot be indifferent to its costs. Direct racial insult, in which "the perpetrator's intention is not to discover truth or initiate dialogue but to injure the victim,"[101] may therefore be regulable.

Thus a case can be made for a speech code like the one Thomas Grey drafted for Stanford University, which prohibits only insulting expression that conveys "visceral hatred and contempt" for people on the basis of their sex, race, color, handicap, religion, sexual orientation, or national and ethnic origin, and "is addressed directly to the individual or individuals whom it insults or stigmatizes."[102] The speech prohibited by this code is precisely the speech designed to function as a kind of assault. The reasons for banning such speech have nothing to do with universities as such. They support not only a campus regulation but a legal prohibition.[103] The code is nonetheless underinclusive, to the extent that it only focuses on low value speech, while high value speech can be even more hurtful.[104] Henry Louis Gates illustrates this point by offering two statements addressed to a black freshman at Stanford:

(A) LeVon, if you find yourself struggling in your classes here, you should realize it isn't your fault. It's simply that you're the beneficiary of a disruptive policy of affirmative action that places underqualified, underprepared, and often undertalented black students in demanding educational environments like this one. The policy's egalitarian aims may be well-intentioned, but given the fact that aptitude tests place African-Americans

100. Toni M. Massaro, "Equality and Freedom of Expression: The Hate Speech Dilemma," 32 *William and Mary L. Rev.* 211, 230 (1991). The idea that the harms caused by speech are necessarily lesser in degree than other harms has been persuasively refuted by Schauer. See Frederick Schauer, "The Phenomenology of Speech and Harm," 103 *Ethics* 635 (1993).

101. Lawrence, "If He Hollers Let Him Go," p. 452.

102. Thomas C. Grey, "Responding to Abusive Speech on Campus: A Model Statute," *Reconstruction*, Winter 1990, p. 51; see also Thomas C. Grey, "Civil Rights vs. Civil Liberties: The Case of Discriminatory Verbal Harassment," 8 *Soc. Phil. & Pol'y* 81 (1991).

103. "The verbal harassment deemed punishable is that which triggers a 'fight or flight' response—a form of assault. Given the limited nature of the identified harm, no good reason exists to declare that the speech is worse on campus than elsewhere. Just as geographical location per se tends not to change the nature of a battery, this location has little bearing on the nature of hate speech." Massaro, "Equality and Freedom of Expression," p. 262.

104. As I argued earlier in this chapter, racist epithets are not entirely low value speech, but they are decidedly lower in value than more sophisticated forms of racial insult.

almost a full standard deviation below the mean, even controlling for so-cioeconomic disparities, they are also profoundly misguided. The truth is, you probably don't belong here, and your college experience will be a long downhill slide.

(B) Out of my face, jungle bunny.

"Surely there is no doubt which is likely to be more 'wounding' and alienating to its intended audience."[105] The first statement is harder to use as a verbal missile than the second, if only because it takes so long to say it. But the first statement is so plainly high value speech under the First Amendment that it could not be repressed without doing severe harm to free speech values.

The second statement is both severely harmful and nearly worthless, and it is therefore permissible in principle to suppress it. Nonetheless, there is reason for caution. It is not easy to write a regulation that bans the second statement without at least having some chilling effect on the first, and regulations that are badly written or badly enforced or both have sometimes produced an atmosphere of forbidden ideas and blacklisting. Laws against hate speech have historically had a distressing tendency to be deployed disproportionately against the very groups they were intended to protect.[106] We have already noted that fighting words are unprotected, low value speech, but the question of whether they should be outlawed is not thereby settled. One survey concludes that "it is virtually impossible to find fighting words cases that do not involve either the expression of opinion on issues of public policy or words directed toward a government official, usually a police officer."[107] Moreover, blacks are often prosecuted and convicted for the use of fighting words.[108] This tendency has been reflected in the application of the new wave of campus speech codes. Thus, for example, during the year that the University of Michigan had a rule against discriminatory harassment, there were more than twenty cases of whites charging blacks with racist speech, and the only speech

105. Henry Louis Gates Jr., "War of Words: Critical Race Theory and the First Amendment," in Henry Louis Gates Jr., et al., *Speaking of Race, Speaking of Sex: Hate Speech, Civil Rights, and Civil Liberties* (New York and London: NYU Press, 1994), pp. 46–47.

106. See Jonathan Rauch, *Kindly Inquisitors: The New Attacks on Free Thought* (Chicago: University of Chicago Press, 1993), pp. 111–54; Nadine Strossen, "Regulating Racist Speech on Campus: A Modest Proposal?", 1990 *Duke L. J.* 484, 512, 556–58 (1990).

107. Stephen W. Gard, "Fighting Words as Free Speech," 58 *Wash. U. L. Q.* 531, 548 (1980).

108. Strossen, "Regulating Racist Speech," p. 512 and n. 139.

that was punished as racist was that by or on behalf of black students.[109] These episodes reflect a more general problem with censorship in the name of the antidiscrimination project. Because unconscious racism and sexism are so pervasive as to make powerful decision makers untrustworthy, we should be exceedingly cautious about giving those decision makers new powers to regulate speech in the name of the project.[110] The debate over repressing racist epithets is finally unresolvable, because it turns on the balance between two unmeasurable chilling effects: some worthless and harmful speech is deterred but so is some valuable speech about important matters. In each case, something is *prevented* from occurring, so both effects are unmeasurable. No wonder reasonable people disagree about whether the costs of such regulation outweigh the benefits.

The worst harms caused by racist insults cannot, in any case, be remedied by suppression. One of the most powerful passages in Lawrence's article on hate speech describes an incident in which four students, at the mostly white school where Lawrence's sister is one of the few black faculty members, painted a large mural there one night containing racist and anti-Semitic slogans, swastikas, drawings of hooded Klansmen, and threats of violence against one clearly identified black student. When Lawrence visited his sister soon thereafter, she was clearly in great pain as a result of the incident.

> And when I talked to my sister, I realized the greatest part of her pain came not from the incident itself but rather from the reaction of white parents who had come to the school in unprecedented numbers to protest the offending students' expulsion. "It was only a prank." "No one was physically attacked." "How can you punish these kids for mere words, mere drawings." Paula's pain was compounded by the failure of these people, with whom she had lived and worked, to recognize that she had been hurt, to understand in even the most limited way the reality of her pain and that of her family.[111]

109. See ibid., pp. 557–58; for the text of the Michigan code, see ibid., p. 526 n. 203.

110. This difficulty might be avoided by adopting an asymmetric speech code, which only prohibits epithets against members of oppressed groups. See Matsuda, "Public Response to Racist Speech," p. 2357; Lawrence, "If He Hollers Let Him Go," p. 450 n. 82. Such an approach, however, raises a fearsome array of practical as well as political problems. See Strossen, "Regulating Racist Speech on Campus," pp. 558–59; Massaro, "Equality and Freedom of Expression," pp. 241–44.

111. Lawrence, "If He Hollers Let Him Go," pp. 460–61.

In the situation that Lawrence describes, punishment of the speech accomplishes little. The students were expelled, but the pain persists. What is wanted is the community's sympathetic understanding of the plight of the victims. Had the whites reacted differently, it might not have mattered so much whether the students were officially punished. Ostracism and disgrace might have been all the punishment that was needed. For hurts of this kind, the only remedy that can work is more speech, to persuade the community that what the students did was evil and harmful. The law can be a useful tool for educating citizens about the harms of racism, but it cannot ameliorate the pain that racist speech causes. Law is the wrong tool for that job.

The case for repression of high value racist speech becomes persuasive only in those cases where the speech can be shown to contribute directly to the subordinate status of women or blacks, *and* where it can be shown that suppressing the speech is *necessary* to an effort to ameliorate that status. That turns out to be the case primarily in contexts in which hateful expression is used to keep disadvantaged groups out of places and positions from which they have been traditionally excluded, and in which integration is necessary in order to ameliorate their disadvantaged status.

The case for viewpoint-based repression of hate speech and pornography is strongest in the context of workplace harassment. The law is now well settled that racial or sexual harassment in the workplace violates antidiscrimination law, even where the harassment consists entirely of speech that is offensive solely because of its political content. This raises difficult First Amendment issues. In this context, however, the restriction even of high value speech is indispensable if the goals of the antidiscrimination project are to be realized.

Title VII of the Civil Rights Act of 1964 provides that it is an unlawful employment practice for an employer "to discriminate against any individual with respect to his compensation, conditions, or privileges of employment because of such individual's race, color, religion, sex, or national origin."[112] The courts have interpreted this language as prohibiting racial or sexual harassment, because such harassment is inherently discriminatory. Sexual harassment, for example, creates a "discriminatorily hostile or abusive environment"[113] for members of one sex, but not the other. As Justice Ginsburg observes, the statute is violated when "members of one sex are exposed to

112. 42 *U.S.C.* § 2000e–2(a)(1).
113. *Harris v. Forklift Systems,* 114 S. Ct. 367, 370 (1993).

disadvantageous terms or conditions of employment to which members of the other sex are not exposed."[114] Actionable sexual harassment may be of the "quid pro quo" variety, in which an employee is required to submit to sexual advances as a condition of getting or keeping a job, but it may also be "hostile work environment" harassment, in which the employee is subjected to " 'discriminatory intimidation, ridicule, and insult' that is 'sufficiently severe or pervasive to alter the conditions of the victim's employment and create an abusive working environment.' "[115] Equal opportunity does not exist, the Court held, when members of one sex must " 'run a gauntlet of sexual abuse in return for the privilege of being allowed to work and make a living.' "[116] Racial harassment is prohibited for similar reasons.

Hostile environment harassment is more likely to be actionable the plainer its message of hatred and inferiority. Racial slurs and epithets are often cited in racial harassment cases. In one case, a Title VII violation was found based on a pattern of offensive writings: signs posted with such comments as "Ray Wells is a nigger," "The only good nigger is a dead nigger," "Ray Wells is a mother," "Send all blacks back to Africa," and "Niggers are a living example that Indians screwed buffalo."[117] Sexual harassment cases, too, often involve words of hostility such as "broad," "bitch," or "cunt," which convey a message that women are unwelcome and do not belong in the workplace, and sexual words such as "honey" and "sweetie," which often indicate that the harasser views the addressee or women in general in a primarily sexual light.[118]

Some of the regulated speech is unquestionably high value speech for First Amendment purposes: it conveys a political message. Indeed, one survey of the cases found that

courts have suggested that they have the power to impose liability, not just because the message was expressed in a particularly offensive manner

---

114. Ibid., p. 372 (Ginsburg, J., concurring). Justice Ginsburg made the same point more pithily in the oral argument, suggesting that the law is violated if "one sex has to put up with something that the other sex doesn't have to put up with." Quoted in Linda Greenhouse, "Ginsburg at Fore in Court's Give-and-Take," *New York Times*, Oct. 14, 1993, p. A1.

115. *Harris*, p. 370, quoting *Meritor Savings Bank v. Vinson*, 477 U.S. 57, 67 (1986).

116. *Meritor*, p. 67, quoting *Henson v. Dundee*, 682 F. 2d 897, 902 (11th Cir. 1982).

117. *EEOC v. Murphy Motor Freight Lines, Inc.*, 488 F. Supp. 381, 384 (D. Minn. 1980), quoted in Browne, "Title VII as Censorship," p. 499.

118. See Browne, "Title VII as Censorship," pp. 491–92; Volokh, "Freedom of Speech," pp. 1800–1816.

but because of the offensiveness of the idea conveyed. The closer the expression came to statements such as "blacks don't belong here, because they are fit only to be slaves" or "women belong in the bedroom and not the factory," the more likely the courts were to uphold the claim. In other words, the more "political" the message, the more offensive it was found to be.[119]

Thus, for example, a picture of a nude woman posted in a police station is more harassing, and more likely to be actionable, when the words "Do women make good cops?—No—No—No" are posted next to it.[120] The poster is obviously conveying a political message about sex equality, and it is equally obvious that the presence of the poster creates for women police officers "an objectively hostile or abusive work environment—an environment that a reasonable person would find hostile or abusive."[121] The restriction of political speech is particularly apparent in another police station case, in which the court imposed liability in part on the basis of posters stating "The KKK is still alive" and the wearing of "Wallace for President" buttons by on-duty police officers.[122] Browne notes that the issue was not "the employer enforcing an even-handed ban on the wearing of political buttons by uniformed police officers, but imposition of liability against the employer because the officers wore *certain* political buttons. That is, liability would not have been imposed based upon the wearing of Humphrey or McGovern buttons."[123]

Ordinarily, offense at the political content of another's expression is the worst possible reason for repressing speech. "The standard for hostile-environment harassment cases is strongly viewpoint-based and can be upheld only by a showing of a government interest of the highest order."[124] Moreover, the law, by subjecting employers to liability if they do not adequately censor their employees' speech, creates a strong incentive for them to overregulate their employees' speech by prohibiting all expression that is even arguably

119. Browne, "Title VII as Censorship," p. 501.

120. See *Arnold v. City of Seminole*, 614 F. Supp. 853, 862–63 (N.D. Okla. 1985), cited in Browne, "Title VII as Censorship," p. 493 n. 75.

121. *Harris v. Forklift Systems*, p. 370.

122. *United States v. City of Buffalo*, 457 F. Supp. 612, 633 (W.D.N.Y. 1978), modified and aff'd, 633 F. 2d 643 (2d Cir. 1980), cited in Browne, "Title VII as Censorship," p. 499.

123. Browne, "Title VII as Censorship," p. 499 n. 123.

124. Ibid., pp. 512–13.

actionable.[125] The restriction thereby imposed on employees' speech is severe. "[F]or most citizens—who are not political activists—the great bulk of their discussion of political and social issues probably occurs in the home and the workplace. For example, there are probably very few workers in the United States who did not discuss the Gulf War while at work."[126]

Browne therefore concludes that "evidence of protected speech should not be admitted at trial to support a claim of hostile environment."[127] The trouble with this solution to the problem is that it will permit the use of hostile environments to keep blacks and women out of workplaces from which they have traditionally been excluded. "A discriminatorily abusive work environment, even one that does not seriously affect employees' psychological well-being, can and often will detract from employees' job performance, discourage employees from remaining on the job, or keep them from advancing in their careers."[128] The effect, most persuasively documented in the case of sexual harassment, is to maintain the segregated status quo. Vicki Schultz observes that harassment "creates a serious disincentive for women to enter and remain in nontraditional jobs."[129] Women who consider moving into blue-collar, male-dominated professions tend to anticipate—accurately—that they will be harassed if they do so. Women are far more likely to be sexually harassed in male-dominated occupations, and women in nontraditional jobs quit because of sexual harassment at least twice as often as women in traditional jobs.[130] The result is a vicious circle. "Women are disempowered from pursuing or staying in higher-paid nontraditional jobs because of the hostile work cultures.

125. See ibid., pp. 504–10.

126. Ibid., pp. 515–16. Browne suggests that the neglect of workers' free speech rights in Title VII jurisprudence, at a time when speech issues on campus receive obsessive attention, reflects "an elitist perspective" that simply values the speech of students and faculty more than that of workers. "The lack of value of the speech of workers seems to be based on one or more of the following opinions: (1) when workers speak they do not convey ideas; (2) ideas are not important to workers; (3) the ideas of workers are not important to us. These judgments can form no part of a first amendment jurisprudence." Ibid., p. 482.

127. Ibid., p. 484.

128. *Harris v. Forklift Systems*, pp. 370–71.

129. Vicki Schultz, "Telling Stories About Women and Work: Judicial Interpretations of Sex Segregation in the Workplace in Title VII Cases Raising the Lack of Interest Argument," 103 *Harv. L. Rev.* 1749, 1833 (1990).

130. See ibid., p. 1834, and sources cited therein.

The only real hope for making those work cultures more hospitable to women lies in dramatically increasing the proportion of women in those jobs."[131]

We noted in Chapter 3 that women's disadvantaged status is largely the consequence of the fact that most women do low-paid work that mostly women do. The goal of integrating the sexes in the workplace is therefore an indispensable one for the antidiscrimination project. If free speech impedes the realization of that goal in a major way, and if antidiscrimination values could be realized by means of a significant, but limited, infringement on free speech, then it is not unreasonable to strike the balance in favor of antidiscrimination. The workers whose speech is thus chilled are (or should be— some courts go further) required merely to keep (the offensive parts of) that speech out of the sight or hearing of the protected group; the impact on women as a class of the kind of laissez-faire rule that Browne proposes would be far more severe. Thus, for example, the hostile environment cases that have been thought to raise the most severe First Amendment issues, those involving the pervasive display of pornography in the workplace, should not be seen as particularly hard ones. As the court held in the leading case finding that such display could be the basis of a Title VII violation, "[t]he sexualization of the workplace imposes burdens on women that are not borne by men."[132] The effects of such a sexualized environment "encompass emotional upset, reduced job satisfaction, the deterrence of women from seeking jobs or promotions, and an increase of women quitting jobs, getting transferred, or being fired because of the sexualization of the workplace. By contrast, the effect of the sexualization of the workplace is 'vanishingly small' for men."[133] It has been argued that a woman who does not want to look at the pornography in such a sexualized workplace should not "thrust[] herself into harm's way" by starting work there.[134] Such an argument, according to Samuel Marcossen, "effectively embraces the idea that women simply do not belong in some workplaces, or, if they belong, acceptable behavior must be defined on male

131. Ibid., p. 1839.

132. *Robinson v. Jacksonville Shipyards,* 760 F. Supp. 1486, 1505 (M.D. Fla. 1991).

133. Ibid.

134. Jules B. Gerard, "The First Amendment in a Hostile Environment: A Primer on Free Speech and Sexual Harassment," 68 *Notre Dame L. Rev.* 1003, 1032 (1993). See also *Rabidue v. Osceola Refining Co.,* 805 F. 2d 611, 621 (6th Cir. 1986), cert. denied, 481 U.S. 1041 (1987) (arguing that "Title VII was not meant to—or can—change" the sexual vulgarity in some work environments, because the statute was not "designed to bring about a magical transformation in the social mores of American workers").

terms."[135] As Marcossen notes, "[w]hat has come to be considered appropriate, or at least acceptable, behavior in such places is due, at least in part, to the fact that women have traditionally been excluded from what has been considered 'male only' positions. The very discrimination that Title VII was designed to eliminate thus created the conditions which define the workplace—what is 'reasonable' in the workplace—and provided the basis for maintaining those conditions."[136]

Browne rejects the distinction, offered by Marcy Strauss,[137] between speech that merely advocates discrimination (which she argues should be protected) and speech that discriminates by causing women to leave their jobs or suffer worsened work conditions (which she would prohibit). "The distinction for Strauss is simply that 'discriminatory speech' has an unattractive effect, but that is not a basis for treating it as an unprotected class of expression."[138] The unattractive effect is, however, a basis for finding that the harm it causes is sufficiently severe to justify prohibition of even protected speech. Browne claims that Title VII regulation is not "narrowly tailored to serve a significant governmental interest,"[139] but he does not explain how a narrower regulation could adequately promote the goal of workplace equality.[140]

Thickness of the mental hide may be a liberal virtue that is enhanced by the constitutional protection of offensive speech, but if the liberal state seriously wants to increase the number of blacks and women in jobs from which they have traditionally been excluded, it must take blacks and women as it finds them. If harassment raises the cost of being in those workplaces to a point at which almost all blacks and women decline to take those jobs, then

---

135. Samuel A. Marcossen, "Harassment on the Basis of Sexual Orientation: A Claim of Sex Discrimination Under Title VII," 81 *Georgetown L. J.* 1, 22–23 (1992).

136. Ibid., p. 22.

137. See Marcy Strauss, "Sexist Speech in the Workplace," 25 *Harv. Civ. Rts.–Civ. Liberties L. Rev.* 1, 37–41 (1990).

138. Browne, "Title VII as Censorship," p. 524.

139. Ibid., p. 521; see also ibid., pp. 539–40.

140. Eugene Volokh does better when he proposes that liability be imposed for offensive speech directed at an unwilling listener, but not for any speech that is not so directed; sexist and racist words and pictures that are posted on walls and bulletin boards would fall into the protected category. He emphasizes that "the great majority of harassment cases, especially the most egregious ones, involve directed harassment." If this standard is able to "provide a remedy for all but a few hostile work environments," as he claims, then his proposed standard, which still allows viewpoint-based regulation of directed speech, may be sufficient to promote workplace equality. "Freedom of Speech," p. 1871.

it does no good for liberals to wish that people were not so sensitive. If verbal harassment has the effect of maintaining segregation, then it must be stopped.[141]

The most important thing the state can do, in the long run, is to get blacks and women into these workplaces. The most effective way to raise the consciousness of their coworkers is to force those coworkers to get used to the idea that blacks and women have a right to be there. At the same time, the law of workplace harassment will inevitably force employers to conduct some reeducation of their workers, in order to prevent those workers from engaging in the kinds of behavior that produces liability. And some of that behavior is high value speech. The law of workplace harassment today infringes quite severely on workers' First Amendment rights. For that reason, while it is now necessary, it should, like racial and gender preference, be regarded as a temporary measure, to be modified or discarded as soon as that can be done without abandoning the goals of the antidiscrimination project.

Similar considerations may support special speech codes in traditionally white colleges, but the case here is weaker. Universities have a special duty to be open forums of free discussion and expression, but in recent years they have also been the location of an epidemic of racist incidents.[142] Whether the speech component of these incidents is anything the university has a duty to do anything about depends on whether such speech impairs the functioning of the university. There is some evidence that it does. Many college students are away from home for the first time and at a vulnerable stage of their psychological development. At predominantly white schools, minority students are often particularly at risk. Matsuda argues that for these students, subjection to officially tolerated slurs can have devastating effects, including withdrawal from campus activities, obsession with racism, feelings of conspicuousness in classes, defensiveness, anger, shame, and helplessness.[143] A school that tolerates such effects is not providing equal educational opportunity to its black stu-

141. This is not, of course, to declare open season on male workers' liberty and privacy, only to prohibit that speech which has the direct effect of creating a hostile environment for protected workers. See Strossen, "A Feminist Critique," pp. 1122–26; Nadine Strossen, "Regulating Workplace Sexual Harassment and Upholding the First Amendment—Avoiding a Collision," 37 *Villanova L. Rev.* 757 (1992).

142. See Matsuda, "Public Response to Racist Speech," p. 2333 n. 71.

143. Ibid., pp. 2370–71.

dents. On the other hand, it is not clear to what extent the repression of overtly racist speech will help the situation.

As I argued above, repression of direct, face-to-face insult may be justifiable whether or not it occurs on campus. The question here is whether it makes sense to go further in the context of the university. It is arguable that in residence halls, students subjected to hateful displays are captive audiences, like a person forced to endure a cross-burning in front of her home, so that hate speech may be regulated there for the same reasons that persons are protected from harassment in their homes.[144] But some campus hate speech regulations go much further, to prohibit *any* racially insulting speech *anywhere* on the campus.[145] This begins to look like the degree of regulation that has developed in workplaces. Such regulation appears to be better justified in the workplace than on the campus. It has been well documented that sexual harassment is a major reason women leave traditionally male jobs; there is less evidence that racial harassment is a major reason blacks leave traditionally white colleges.[146] As in the case of Lawrence's sister, legislative prohibition of hate speech is only a step, and perhaps a trivial step, toward full inclusion in the community. White students need to be made aware of the ways they tend to create a racially exclusionary environment, sometimes without even meaning to do so. Such awareness will be of benefit not only to the black students; it will make the white students into better liberal citizens. Campus speech codes may, on balance, make sense, but much more is needed.

Social Construction Redux

The third kind of harm that those who would suppress racist and sexist speech complain of is harm to a group's status in society. Here we return to the core

144. See Calvin R. Massey, "Hate Speech, Cultural Diversity, and the Foundational Paradigms of Free Expression," 40 *U.C.L.A. L. Rev.* 103, 176–77 (1992).

145. One example is the University of Connecticut's first regulation specifically addressing hate speech. See Beverly Weinberg [Garofalo], Note, "Treating the Symptom Instead of the Cause: Regulating Student Speech at the University of Connecticut," 23 *Conn. L. Rev.* 743, 746, 802 (1991).

146. In fact, black students graduate from the best traditionally white colleges at higher rates than they do from the best traditionally black colleges. See Theodore L. Cross, "The Myth That Preferential College Admissions Create High Black Student Dropout Rates," *J. of Blacks in Higher Ed.*, Autumn 1993, pp. 71–74.

of the antidiscrimination project. Cultural construction as inferior, this book has argued, is a harm that the liberal state must care about and can appropriately take at least some steps to remedy. MacKinnon argues that this is one of the harms that is caused by pornography: "It institutionalizes the sexuality of male supremacy, fusing the erotization of dominance and submission with the social construction of male and female. To the extent that gender is sexual, pornography is part of constituting the meaning of that sexuality. Men treat women as who they see women as being. Pornography constructs who that is. Men's power over women means that the way men see women defines who women can be. Pornography is that way."[147] Similarly, Charles Lawrence, on whose explorations of the cultural dimensions of the antidiscrimination project I have relied heavily, argues that racist speech is one of the core evils that the Fourteenth Amendment prohibits. *Brown v. Board of Education*, Lawrence argues, is best understood as a case about speech. "*Brown* held that segregated schools were unconstitutional primarily because of the *message* segregation conveys—the message that black children were an untouchable caste, unfit to be educated with white children."[148] He continues, "[i]f segregation's primary goal is to convey the message of white supremacy, then *Brown*'s declaration that segregation is unconstitutional amounts to a regulation of the message of white supremacy. Properly understood, *Brown* and its progeny require that the systematic group defamation of segregation be disestablished."[149] *Brown* involved invective by government, but Lawrence thinks that its gravamen is also applicable to private speech. The stigmatic harm that the state was inflicting by segregation, Lawrence argues, is inflicted equally by private racist speech. "The injury to blacks is hardly redressed by deciding the government must no longer injure our reputation if one then invokes the first amendment to ensure that racist speech continues to thrive in an unregulated private

147. MacKinnon, *Feminism Unmodified*, p. 172. See also *Toward a Feminist Theory of the State*, p. 197; *Only Words*, p. 25.

148. Lawrence, "If He Hollers Let Him Go," p. 439 (emphasis in original).

149. Ibid., p. 441. This is a straightforward, and hardly novel, application of the stigma theory, discussed in Chapter 2. See Charles Black, "The Lawfulness of the Segregation Decisions," 69 *Yale L. J.* 421 (1960). Some commentators have criticized Lawrence's argument that *Brown* was about speech, claiming that the restriction of the message of segregation was an incidental effect of the Court's decision rather than its central point, but these commentators have extraordinary difficulty in explaining what, then, the central point of *Brown* in fact was. See Strossen, "Regulating Racist Speech on Campus," pp. 542–44; Gates, "War of Words," pp. 53–54.

market."[150] The state's obligation is rather one of "disestablishing the system of signs and symbols that signal blacks' inferiority."[151]

If the argument of Chapters 1 and 2 was sound, MacKinnon and Lawrence are on to something profoundly important. The struggle against racist and sexist oppression cannot succeed as long as racism and sexism thrive. The core of these oppressions, from which all the other injuries flow, is the social construction of blacks and women as inferior, less worthy of concern and respect than white men. "Words and images are how people are placed in hierarchies, how social stratification is made to seem inevitable and right, how feelings of inferiority and superiority are engendered, and how indifference to violence against those on the bottom is rationalized and normalized. Social supremacy is made, inside and between people, through making meanings."[152] If it is the case (and it plainly is) that racist and sexist speech are causes of the social construction of blacks and women as subordinate classes, *and* if (it's this second "if" that matters) repression of that speech is necessary in order to end that subordinating construction, then we are faced with a dilemma. The speech is alleged to cause harm precisely by means of its political message, the thing that entitles the speech to First Amendment protection. To protect the speech, if it does cause the harm, would bring about a result that is even more repugnant to democracy than political censorship: the perpetuation of an unjustifiably stigmatized and disadvantaged caste of persons, who because of their devalued status do not have their interests equally represented in the political process.[153]

When speech corrodes the very foundations of democracy, repression is the only acceptable option. Thus, for example, the following constitutional provision cannot, in light of history, be said to be a departure from sound principles of government: "Parties which, by reason of their aims or the behavior of their adherents, seek to impair or abolish the free democratic basic order

150. Lawrence, "If He Hollers Let Him Go," p. 447.
151. Ibid., p. 449.
152. MacKinnon, *Only Words*, p. 31.
153. This is why Frank Michelman, for example, thinks that regulation of pornography may be the most effective way for the state to minimize infringements of both liberty and equal protection. See Frank Michelman, "Conceptions of Democracy in American Constitutional Argument: The Case of Pornography," 56 *Tenn. L. Rev.* 291, 307–9 (1989). This "silencing" argument is a more specific version of the argument, considered in Chapter 2, that stigma can infect and thereby distort the decision-making process.

or to endanger the existence of the Federal Republic of Germany, shall be unconstitutional."[154] Democracy was probably strengthened rather than weakened when the West German government shut down a neo-Nazi party.[155] Would that the government had been so resolute in the 1930s! Walter Murphy argues that such a restriction on electoral choice "is compatible with the basic tenets of democratic theory. Although the people's decision to move to a totalitarian system might be the result of free choice resulting from open political processes, that decision will inevitably deny most citizens in the polity the right to further meaningful participation in self-government. Thus, a democratic government may validly protect its people's basic right to self-rule."[156] MacKinnon and Lawrence might reasonably argue that democracy is equally subverted when some citizens are habitually treated, privately and by the political system, as if they are not fully human and their interests do not count. When that happens, the result is a twisted caricature of democracy. If repression of some liberties is necessary in order to bring the real thing into being, then democracy demands that that be done. Repression on this basis is not contemplated by any of the present exceptions in First Amendment law, but that cannot settle the matter; part of the trouble with the structure of existing law is that it was constructed almost entirely by white heterosexual men who were oblivious to the concerns of disadvantaged groups.[157]

The very pervasiveness of the views sought to be extirpated, however, is a reason to be wary of censorship. Any effective cure by censorship would have to be far worse than the disease. When considering the link between pornography and violence, we observed that censorship as a remedy for the cultural causes of violence against women could not be limited to pornography, but would have to extend to *all* violent expression. More generally, any effort to eliminate racism and sexism would have to call into existence a massive regime of censorship, as Thomas Emerson noted in his critique of MacKinnon:

154. Basic Law, Federal Republic of Germany, Article 21, par. 2, quoted in Walter F. Murphy, "Excluding Political Parties: Problems for Democratic and Constitutional Theory," in Paul Kirchhof and Donald P. Kommers, eds., *Germany and Its Basic Law: Past, Present and Future—A German-American Symposium* (Baden-Baden: Nomos Verlagsgesellschaft, 1993), p. 181.

155. See Murphy, "Excluding Political Parties." The only other target of the constitutional provision, the Communist party, presents a harder case. See ibid., pp. 181–82.

156. Ibid., p. 191.

157. See MacKinnon, *Toward A Feminist Theory of the State*, p. 238; Frederick Schauer, "Exceptions," 58 *U. Chi. L. Rev.* 871 (1993).

As Professor MacKinnon emphasizes, male domination has deep, pervasive and ancient roots in our society, so it is not surprising that our literature, art, entertainment and commercial practices are permeated by attitudes and behavior that create and reflect the inferior status of women. If the answer to the problem, as Professor MacKinnon describes it, is government suppression of sexual expression that contributes to female subordination, then the net of restraint must be cast on a nearly limitless scale. Even narrowing the proscribed area to depictions of sexual activities involving violence would outlaw a large segment of the world's literature and art.[158]

The same point can be made about racist speech. Because racism is everywhere, a censorial apparatus that sought to stamp out its expression would have to be everywhere, too.[159]

The MacKinnon-Dworkin ordinance reaches a narrower category of speech, but a solution that only targets *sexual* speech probably does the antidiscrimination project more harm than good. This was emphasized by an amicus brief filed in the *Hudnut* case by a group of prominent feminists, which the Seventh Circuit ignored. The brief argued that the ordinance "will have precisely the opposite effect" from that intended.[160] The statute, they argued, "would reinvigorate those discriminatory moral standards which have limited women's equality in the past,"[161] because it "implies that sexually explicit images of women necessarily subordinate and degrade women and perpetuates stereotypes of women as helpless victims and people who could not seek or enjoy sex."[162] Any attempt to regulate the production of sexual meanings is fraught with danger, because "[i]n the sexual realm, perhaps more so than in

158. Thomas Emerson, "Pornography and the First Amendment: A Reply to Professor MacKinnon," 3 *Yale L. and Pol'y Rev.* 130, 132 (1984).

159. Narrower laws, such as those that prohibit racist defamation, appear to be wholly inadequate for the task of fighting racism. Britain has had such a law since 1965, but racism in that country is arguably worse than in the United States. See Strossen, "Regulating Racist Speech on Campus," pp. 554–55.

160. Nan D. Hunter and Sylvia A. Law, "Brief Amici Curiae of Feminist Anti-Censorship Task Force, et al., in *American Booksellers Association v. Hudnut*," 21 *U. Mich. J. L. Ref.* 69, 89 (1987–88).

161. Ibid., p. 105.
162. Ibid., p. 126.

any other, messages and their impact on the viewer or reader are often multiple, contradictory, layered and highly contextual."[163]

The difficulties raised by the ambiguous meanings of sexual speech are exacerbated by the fact that prosecutors, judges, and politicians tend to have fairly conventional values. (If they did not, they probably would not have gotten those jobs.) Many of these values are precisely what the antidiscrimination project seeks to call into question. Under MacKinnon's ordinance, women rather than the state would have the power to bring suit, but it would still be the state that would decide, on the basis of the pornography's content, which claims of injury to remedy. Any standard for determining which images subordinate women "would require the judiciary to impose its views of correct sexuality on a diverse community. The inevitable result would be to disapprove those images that are least conventional and privilege those that are closest to majoritarian beliefs about proper sexuality."[164] Thus the ordinance "can as readily be used to curtail feminist speech about sexuality, or to target the speech of sexual minorities, as to halt hateful speech about women."[165]

This worry has been borne out. In Canada, where goverment officials had already been harassing lesbian and gay bookstores for some years, government censorship was given renewed authority by a Canadian Supreme Court decision interpreting existing obscenity law in accordance with the MacKinnon-Dworkin rationale. The first obscenity conviction after the decision was imposed on a small lesbian and gay bookstore in Toronto. While it is unfair to blame MacKinnon and Dworkin for a pattern of repression that was virtually unaffected by their victory, Canada's experience does show that a prohibition of "degrading" material can be interpreted to serve purposes that are very far from what they had in mind.[166] Laws against hate speech, we have already noted, similarly tend to be deployed disproportionately against the very groups they are intended to protect. In short, even if censorship is permissible in theory, there is plenty of reason to worry about it going dreadfully wrong in practice. Arguments like those that support Germany's Basic Law have often been invoked in the United States to support repression of subversives, but in this country that power has almost always been abused by

163. Ibid., p. 106.
164. Ibid., p. 109.
165. Ibid., p. 135.
166. See Jeffrey Toobin, "X-Rated," *The New Yorker*, Oct. 3, 1994, pp. 70–78.

repressing legitimate dissent, usually from the left, thereby depriving the electorate of legitimate political choices.[167]

Lawrence, by arguing that the Fourteenth Amendment requires the affirmative disestablishment of racist ideas, is essentially seeking to apply to the private sphere the "cultural meaning test" that he has proposed to determine which government actions should receive heightened judicial scrutiny under the Fourteenth Amendment: "This test would evaluate governmental conduct to see if it conveys a symbolic message to which the culture attaches racial significance."[168] Whether the racist message comes from the state or from a private person, the injury is the same, and so Lawrence concludes that both should be prohibited. In Chapter 2, I endorsed the "cultural meaning" test, but noted (as Lawrence does) that one of the problems with having courts apply the test is that the judges are products of the same racist culture that produces the suspicious decisions that the judges must monitor. I concluded that, in the Fourteenth Amendment context, there was no way to avoid this problem, because legislatures cannot be the final arbiters of whether their decisions have complied with the Constitution. Legislative power is already concentrated; the question posed for constitutional interpretation is what kind of judicial check should be imposed on that power. A judiciary that applies the cultural meaning test may be somewhat unreliable, but it is a good deal better than nothing (or what amounts to nearly nothing, the intent test that now prevails). The power to decide what ideas shall be expressed, by contrast, is diffuse rather than concentrated unless and until a regime of censorship is inaugurated. Distrust for the powers that be in a racist and sexist society is a reason for keeping the power to censor as far away from the hands of state officials as possible.

Certainly pornography is the most striking medium by which the erotici-

167. See Murphy, "Excluding Political Parties," pp. 182–90. Schauer observes that any slippery-slope argument depends for its persuasiveness on empirical evidence that the decision makers are in fact likely to make bad decisions if the proposed rule is adopted. Frederick Schauer, "Slippery Slopes," 99 *Harv. L. Rev.* 361, 381–82 (1985). My claim here is that this evidence is amply available in the United States. It may not be in other regimes that are less protective of hate speech. If distrust of the decision maker is sufficiently warranted, then the case for restraint need not rest on "a comparatively rosy view of the status quo," as Schauer has suggested elsewhere. Frederick Schauer, "The Calculus of Distrust," 77 *Va. L. Rev.* 653, 666 (1991).

168. Charles R. Lawrence III, "The Id, the Ego, and Equal Protection: Reckoning With Unconscious Racism," 39 *Stan. L. Rev.* 317, 356 (1987).

zation of domination and violence is encapsulated. And because symbolism is so important to the project, it is unsurprising that some feminists focus their energies on the symbol that seems most revealing. "Pornographic photographs, films, and videos are the starkest possible expression of the idea feminists most loathe: that women exist principally to provide sexual service to men."[169] As a causal force, however, pornography has less effect on the perception of women than other, more widely circulated media: Karst observes that these include "movies, romance novels, billboards, television (both the programming and the advertising), newspapers, song lyrics, magazines, rock videos, clothes fashions, the art on gallery walls, and the cosmetics on drugstore shelves."[170] If the antidiscrimination project were to embrace censorship, the rationale for such censorship would extend to these media, too. Such a solution is impossible, of course, because literally nothing would be left of the First Amendment: even speech that is at the center of the amendment's concerns would be subject to censorship. Instead, the antipornography feminists have concerned themselves exclusively with sexual representations, which traditionally have received a reduced degree of First Amendment protection.[171] The trouble with this strategy is that censorship confined solely to *sexual* representations has so many unfortunate connotations, and is so open to abuse against feminist speech, that it does more harm than good, even if "harm" is defined solely in terms of the project's own goals.

The case for censoring racist speech is subject to similar objections. Racism is transmitted in our culture through films, books, television, and ordinary conversation. Racist epithets are only racism's rawest and nastiest expression. There is little reason to think that the underlying problem will be ameliorated by the suppression of the worst racist symbols. Moreover, a state that is empowered to monitor speech for racism is easily turned against those who work against racism. The danger presented by the movement to suppress racist speech and pornography (a danger that is always immanent in the stigma theory, standing alone) is that it tends to promote an empty, symbolic politics that focuses only on the expressions of racism and sexism, while neglecting

169. Ronald Dworkin, "Women and Pornography," *N.Y. Rev. of Books*, Oct. 21, 1993, p. 36.
170. Karst, "Boundaries and Reasons," p. 137.
171. This is equally true of those who, unlike MacKinnon and Dworkin, would censor only *violent* pornography. See, e.g., Sunstein, *Democracy and the Problem of Free Speech*, pp. 212–13; Rhode, *Justice and Gender*, p. 271.

the underlying processes by which racism and sexism are reproduced.[172] As I have said, it is a mistake to attack one part of the elephant as if it were the whole thing.

Thus, even if the antidiscrimination project can theoretically support measures to restrict this kind of speech, it also supports caution in resorting to that option. The problem of the unintended and undesirable message is a familiar one from the case of affirmative action, which some argue stigmatizes blacks by suggesting that they cannot achieve the desired positions "on their own." In that case, the standoff between contested meanings is arguably resolved by the provision of tangible benefits to a traditionally disadvantaged class, benefits that may be expected to have the effect of ameliorating that class's inferior social status. If repression of hate speech stops violence or psychic injury, or if it is necessary to promote tangible equality (for example, in the workplace) then the problem may be similarly resolved, subject to prudential constraints based on concern about overweening state power. But with respect to the harm of inferiority as a cultural construction, all that repression can bring about is (at best) a tangle of mixed messages, and there is good reason to think that the wrong message will prevail. Such ambiguity does not—or does not to the same degree—plague efforts at private persuasion.[173] MacKinnon has been notably successful in changing the way many of her fellow citizens think about the connections between pornography, sex, and sexism, even though she has been unable to enlist the state on her behalf. Education is a strategy that holds real promise. There is reason to believe that the traditional, hierarchical relationship between the sexes is unsatisfying even to the males who are its beneficiaries.[174] And if that is so, then it may not be impossible to persuade men to

172. Lawrence's acknowledgement of this objection concedes that punishing hate speech may not be necessary at all, so long as the community makes it clear that it takes harassment seriously and recognizes its collective responsibility for it. See "If He Hollers Let Him Go," pp. 479–80 n. 166.

173. I acknowledge the speculative and intuitive elements in my judgment. Any resolution of the hate speech debate turns on contestable value judgments and unverifiable predictions. Less First Amendment protection for such speech would open the door to abuses, but it could remedy harms that are presently without a remedy. There are dangers in both the new proposals and the status quo, and reasonable people balance them in different ways. The acrimonious tone that has become typical on both sides of the debate is uncalled for.

174. See my "Sex Equality and/or the Family: From Bloom vs. Okin to Rousseau vs. Hegel," 4 *Yale J. L. & Hum* 399 (1992).

become less interested in the sensation of being patriarchal masters.[175] State action, once more, appears to be the wrong tool for the job.

A Final Reflection

Not only are there limits to the means that the law ought to employ in the service of the antidiscrimination project, but there are also limits to what it is even possible for the law to do. Countering racist and sexist speech with more speech is the best available remedy, but it is hardly a panacea. The social forces that perpetuate racism and sexism are enormously strong ones. There is no guarantee that the project will succeed, although it seems to be slowly advancing on many fronts. This is, of course, no comment on the worth of the project, any more than the value of the practice of medicine is weakened by the recognition that we will all die. The inevitable imperfection of the world is no reason not to do what we can to improve it.

The biggest frustration the antidiscrimination project faces is not one of principled or prudential limits, but one of a lack of political will. Our survey has shown much that can be done. If the project has limits, our present practice does not approach them. Schools can be genuinely integrated. The courts can abandon the confused notion that affirmative action programs violate the rights of whites. The requirement of discriminatory intent can be abandoned in equal protection cases where blacks or women are systematically disadvantaged. Other measures can be taken to ameliorate the second-class status of women. Parental leave can be made more readily available to workers, either by private action or by legislation. Working hours can be made more flexible. The distribution of assets in divorce cases can be changed. Gays can be brought within the protection of antidiscrimination statutes, and the law can sanction gay marriages. Perhaps most urgent and importantis the need for our society to decide that black poverty is a problem worth bothering about.

These are reforms that must be undertaken by large institutions, which as this is written are showing little interest in these tasks. Private citizens should organize and do what they can to bring pressure on these institutions to act. But this does not exhaust our responsibilities. We exert power every time we hear a racist or sexist or homophobic remark and let it pass in silence. The

175. For one such attempt, see John Stoltenberg's address to college students in *Refusing to Be a Man* (Portland, Ore.: Breitenbush, 1989), pp. 37–38.

lack of political will just noted is the product of the very problem that the project seeks to address: a culture that regards as trivial the troubles of blacks, women, and gays. Each of us has some ability, and therefore some obligation, to reshape the culture in which we live, because we, in our daily lives, *constitute* that culture. Day-to-day life and ordinary experience are precisely what need to be changed, and these are within everyone's control. Antidiscrimination is not just a matter for lawyers, judges, politicians, bureaucrats, academics, and other specialists. Without the active and committed participation of ordinary people, the project must become tyrannical or fail, or (most likely) both. It is therefore important that everyone understand the new and subtle forms of racism and sexism and know why they need to be eliminated. The antidiscrimination project can hope to succeed only to the extent that it is an antidiscrimination movement.

Index

Blacks (*continued*)
75–76, 79, 83, 84, 191, 204, 209, 211, 242–
43; violence against, 236; women, 9, 124.
See also Miscegenation; Race; Racism; Segregation; Slavery; Whites
Bloom, Allan, 197n
Bork, Robert, 179, 179–80n, 181, 188
Boxill, Bernard, 38n, 65n
Brennan, William J., 45n, 118, 131, 133n
Brest, Paul, 29, 40–41, 58, 63, 82, 83, 115,
132
Brown v. Board of Education: counter-
majoritarian, 19; and cultural transformation, 2, 3; and Fourteenth Amendment, 13,
119n, 156; implementation, 46–47; and
malign preferences, 40; and neutrality, 179;
and speech, 242–43, 256; and stigma, 57,
58, 59, 95, 104, 118, 242–43, 256. *See also*
School segregation
Browne, Kingsley R., 228–29, 230, 249–51 and
n, 252, 253
Buchanan v. Warley, 182n
Burke, Edmund, 109, 111, 114

Canada, obscenity law in, 260
Carolene Products. See *United States v. Carolene Products*
Carter, Jimmy, 148
Carter, Stephen, 102n
Caste. *See* Hierarchy
Child care, 2, 117, 124, 125, 127, 135, 137–38,
163
Choice: ascription and, 64, 65 and n, 71–72,
146; of employment, 137; of gender role,
133–34, 143 and n, 144, 145, 174; of
religion, 150–51; of sexual orientation,
146–48, 147n, 148n
City of Cleburne v. Cleburne Living Center,
65n, 116n
City of Richmond v. J. A. Croson Co., 32 and
n, 51–55 and n, 92n
Civil Rights Act of *1964,* 2, 3, 5, 25n, 110,
138n, 179, 180n, 182n, 188, 208, 248
Clark, Kenneth, 61
Class, social, 71–72, 83. *See also* Distribution,
patterns of; Group disadvantage; Hierarchy;
Poverty

Classification. *See* Scrutiny
Cohen, G. A., 213
Colleges: admissions, 33, 103, 107; black, 118;
speech codes, 245–47, 251n, 254–55
Community: of constrained conversation,
214–15; identity and, 66–71; obligations of,
214–15, 247–48; obligations toward, 70–71,
73; sense of, 66–70; stigmatizing, 70–71, 73,
214. *See also* Hierarchy
Connell, R. W., 133–34
Connolly, William, 68–69
Constitution, U.S. *See* First Amendment;
Fourteenth Amendment; Supreme Court,
U.S.
Contract law, 6
Counter-majoritarian difficulty, 19, 39
Craig v. Boren, 131
Crenshaw, Kimberle, 47–48
Croson. See *City of Richmond v. J. A. Croson
Co.*
Cultural imperialism, 86
Cultural meaning, 104–8, 117, 118n, 119,
133–34, 145, 200, 261
Cultural transformation: antidiscrimination
project goal, 2, 4–5, 7, 8, 10, 11, 25–26, 92,
100, 116, 264–65; community obligation,
215; conflicts with freedom, 177, 179, 181–
82; democracy requires, 47–51;
governmental role, 4, 46, 50, 53, 177, 215;
group-disadvantage theory requires, 89; judicial role, 46, 54–55, 111n, 130; individual
obligations, 111–14, 175, 264–65; justice
and, 184–86; as legal goal, 1–2, 6–7, 10;
libertarianism and, 181–82, 186, 190; nongovernmental, 25–26 and n; process
theories require, 45–47, 50, 51; public education, 112–13, 141–42; of religious beliefs,
152–53; and reparations, 90n, 91; social
construction theory requires, 99

Davis v. Bandemer, 65n
Death penalty, 43–46
Debs v. United States, 241n
Degler, Carl, 125
Delgado, Richard, 228–29
Democracy: and citizen virtue, 47–51; and ju-
dicial review, 19, 39, 46, 261; and malign

Ortiz, Daniel, 46, 108 and n, 182n
Ortner, Sherry, 121–22, 123

Pace v. Alabama, 155–56
Parsons, Talcott, 66 and n
Patterson, Orlando, 62
Personnel Adm'r v. Feeney, 40n
Piazza, Thomas, 36–37n
Pleck, Joseph, 158
Plessy v. Ferguson, 1–2, 3, 4, 57 and n, 181n
Pluralism, 49, 50, 75n, 106
Pogge, Thomas, 189, 190, 203, 204
Pornography: allegedly violence-provoking, 231, 233 and n, 234, 236–42, 258; feminist uses of, 226–27, 227–28nn, 259–60; legal efforts to penalize, 231–35, 241n, 259–60; production of, 235n; and sexism, 226, 227, 231–32, 233–34, 237, 239, 255–59, 261–62; value of, 223, 224–27, 234; violent, 227, 237–38; in the workplace, 252. *See also* Speech
Posner, Richard, 235n
Poverty: black, 47–49 and nn, 79, 83, 88–89, 93, 97, 99, 101, 264; discrimination against the poor, 41; distributive justice, 82–83; stigma of, 9, 47–48, 79, 88–89, 97, 101; women's, 134–35, 137–39, 184. *See also* Distribution, patterns of
Powell, Lewis F., 118–19
Preferences: cultural transformation of, 5–7, 140; customers', 5–7, 140; external, 19–22, 27, 42; malign, 20–27, 28, 31, 39–43 and n, 55–56, 63–64, 97, 98, 140; moral obligations in forming, 28; personal, 19, 22, 23, 27; for stereotypes, 140. *See also* Racism; Reverse discrimination
Prejudice, 40. *See also* Racism; Stereotyping
Private life. *See* Morality; Public versus private life
Process defects: discriminatory intent, 17, 42, 43; in distribution, 17, 98; error, 25n, 31, 41–42, 131, 133; factionalism, 51–55; hierarchy, 206; inequality of concern and respect, 25, 39, 42, 50, 58, 182n; judicial failure to recognize, 139n; lack of neutrality, 180; and preferences, 18–19, 21–22, 25–26, 28, 32, 39, 40–41; prejudice against

gays, 160, 171–72, 175; racism as, 31, 42–43, 55–56, 128; and segregation, 50–51; and sexism, 127–28, 130, 134, 139, 192–93; stereotyping, 32–34 and n, 41–42, 43, 131–34; and stigma, 59–60 and n, 84, 98, 107, 160
Process-based theories: reverse discrimination and, 32, 33, 35, 37, 51–55; and cultural meaning, 107, 118n, 145, 261; cultural transformation and, 24–31, 43–47, 51, 53, 130; and democracy, 39–43, 46, 47, 49–51; R. Dworkin, 18–26, 18n, 38–39, 55, 98; Ely, 17, 21–22, 38–43, 47, 49, 55, 98; equality of concern and respect, 18, 19, 29, 31, 32, 39, 42, 43–44, 50, 55; impartiality, 33, 43, 46, 59; incomplete, 46–47, 55–56, 77 and n, 96, 97, 98–99, 134; judiciary's role, 19, 39, 46–47, 109–10 and n; legal basis, 17
Property, private, 188–89 and n. *See also* Distribution, patterns of; Libertarianism
Public versus private life, 24, 30, 67, 181, 188, 211

Quotas, 138–39. *See also* Reverse discrimination

Race: as a category, 100, 170; factionalism, 32, 33, 49–50, 51–55; strict scrutiny requirement, 15–16, 17, 104, 106; unchosen, 65–66
Racism: causes of, 105, 185, 188; consensus on basic error of, 1, 3–4, 7, 23–24, 30–31, 72–73, 74, 229; definition, 29; pervasive, 2, 25–26, 29, 36, 36–37n, 38 and n, 53, 56, 73–74, 99–100, 111, 115, 182, 221, 247, 258–59, 262; socially constructed, 93, 98, 105; unconscious, 29, 36, 42, 43, 56, 67, 98, 100, 104, 105, 107, 112, 182, 187, 201, 247. *See also* Blacks; Equality; Stigma; Whites
Racist speech: epithets, 228–29, 230–31, 245, 247, 262; harm of, 228–29, 230, 236n, 242–49, 256–57, 262; increases racism, 212–13, 256; value of, 223, 224, 228–30, 243, 245–46. *See also* Harassment; Speech
Rape, 130 and n, 144, 227 and n, 237–38, 239–40 and nn
R.A.V. v. City of St. Paul, 230–31

Rawls, John, 23, 31, 72n, 120n, 132–33, 177, 186, 190–205, 206, 214
Raz, Joseph, 178
Reagan, Ronald, 48 and n, 53n
Redlining, racial, 108
Regents of Univ. of California v. Bakke, 57–58, 118–19
Rehnquist, William, 32n, 144
Religion: attitudes toward homosexuality, 150n, 151–53; cultural transformation of, 152–53 and n; stigmatizing of, 150–51 and nn; as unchosen, 150–51
Result-based theories. *See* Group-disadvantage theories; Stigma theories
Reverse discrimination: racial, 31–38, 51–55, 91–92, 99–103, 263; gender, 138–39
Reynolds, William Bradford, 3, 32n
Rhode, Deborah L., 145
Rich, Adrienne, 169–70
Rights: employment, 34–37; equal concern and respect, 18–19 and n, 24, 191; freedom from insult, 243; freedom from stigma, 185n; primary goods, 196–97 and n; property, 188–89 and n. *See also* Civil Rights Act of *1964;* Justice
Role models, 101n
Rosenblum, Nancy, 75n
Rosenfeld, Michel, 54 and n
Rousseau, Jean-Jacques, 67

Sandel, Michael, 71, 194–95
Scalia, Antonin J., 32n, 230–31
Schauer, Frederick, 222, 225–26, 230n, 261n
School segregation: desegregation effects, 50–51, 105–6; detrimental effects, 2, 209–10; Fourteenth Amendment and, 13; and malign preferences, 40; and process defect, 50–51. See also *Brown v. Board of Education*
Schultz, Vicki, 251
Scrutiny: cultural meaning test, 104, 118n, 145, 261; Fourteenth Amendment requirements, 15–16; judicial balancing, 109–10 and n, 261; minimal, 15, 108 and n, 261; of race, 15–16, 17, 104, 106; of sex, 16, 115; suspect classifications, 15–16, 115, 147, 155
Sedgwick, Eve Kosofsky, 168n, 171
Segregation: and freedom of association, 179

and n, 202; stigmatizing, 57, 58, 59, 74, 95, 104–5, 118, 159, 209–10, 256. *See also* Jim Crow laws; Racism; School segregation
Self-esteem and self-respect, 26, 35–36, 61–62, 194–201, 202, 203, 205, 206, 213–14. *See also* Identity
Sex, as a category: power and, 133, 136; scrutiny level, 16, 115, 133n; social construction of, 117, 119, 133–34; stereotyping, 131, 133. *See also* Men; Sexism; Women
Sex roles: in definition of the family, 174 and n; chosen or forced, 133–34, 143 and n, 144, 145, 174; historical changes in, 124–25, 135, 144n, 162–63, 165–68; homosexuality violates, 158–62, 163, 166–69; and justice, 192–93; separate spheres, 124–26, 143, 163; sexism and, 119–21, 143n; traditional female, 119, 120, 121, 127, 135n, 143 and n, 172–74; traditional male, 145, 158–59, 161, 166
Sexism: consensus on basic errors of, 1, 3, 122; cultural transformation necessary, 139–40, 143–44; in education, 140–42; education about, 141–42; in employment, 138–39; hierarchical, 153, 158; historical, 185; internalized, 128; judicial, 130, 144–45; pervasive, 80–82, 128–30, 247, 258–59, 261–62; prevalence or rarity, 122; as process defect, 127–28, 130, 134, 139, 192–93; social and political equality, 2–3; stereotyping, 131–34; and traditional roles, 119–21, 143n; unconscious, 129, 130, 247. *See also* Men; Women
Sexual harassment, 4, 248–49, 251, 255
Sexual intercourse, 123 and n, 157, 159, 160
Shakespeare, William, 121n
Shapiro, Ian, 37n, 184n, 189n
Shelley v. Kraemer, 95–96
Shils, Edward A., 66 and n
Shklar, Judith N., 120n
Simon, Robert, 32–33
Slavery, 3, 14, 25, 27, 59, 62–63, 91, 99, 151, 185
Smith, Rogers, 178 and n
Smith, Steven B., 71
Smith-Rosenberg, Carroll, 167–68
Sniderman, Paul, 36–37n

Social construction theory, 92–99; cultural meaning, 104–8, 117, 118n, 119, 133–34, 145, 200, 261; race, 93, 98, 105; sex, 117, 119, 133–34; speech, 255–57; stigma, 94–95, 96, 97–98, 104–8, 118–19, 118n, 255–57. *See also* Cultural transformation

Society. *See* Community; Cultural transformation; Hierarchy

Sodomy, 159, 162, 170, 171

Speech: arguments for its protection, 220–22; arguments for its restriction, 201, 202–3, 211, 213, 224, 233, 235–58; basic liberty, 202, 220–21; in colleges, 245–47, 251n, 254–55; criminal, 222 and n; cultural transformation through, 238; emotional, 225, 226 and n; "fighting words," 228–29, 230–31, 232, 246; government censorship, 223, 229–30, 232–34, 235, 241n, 259–61; harmful, 221 and n, 223, 229–30, 231, 234–36, 242–49, 245nn, 247; high-value, 222–23, 235, 236, 245–46, 249–50; individual obligations, 211, 212; insulation from painful, 210–11; laws against hate, 246–47; legal distinctions, 222–23, 235; low-value, 221 and n, 222–25, 230; and the marketplace of ideas, 220–21, 224, 238; pervasiveness of stigmatizing, 221, 258–59; private/public distinction, 211; results of, 221; social construction through, 255–57; tension between antidiscrimination project and liberalism, 219, 220; tolerance for, 243, 244, 253; value determination, 224–25; violence-provoking, 236, 236n, 244; workplace, 248–54. *See also* Harassment; Pornography; Racist speech

Stanton v. Stanton, 131

State v. Walsh, 155–56

Steelworkers v. Weber, 32n

Stereotyping: cognitive aspects, 33, 100, 129, 141; as error, 41–42, 131–32 and n, 133; gender, 122–27, 128, 131–34; internalized, 128; normative, 42, 87, 131, 132–33, 134; as process failure, 32–34 and n, 41–42, 43, 131–34; racial preferences and, 32–34 and n, 101–2; socially universal, 132–33, 141. *See also* Stigma

Stevens, John Paul, 231

Stigma: ascriptive or immutable characteristics, 64–67 and nn, 72 and n, 73; as central wrong of discrimination, 9, 10, 11, 57, 58, 61, 62, 79, 86–87, 97, 104; and communal obligations, 214; compound, 123–24, 127, 129; as cultural imperialism, 86–87; decreased by limiting freedom, 144n; definition, 56, 67–69, 72, 76, 84, 86, 118, 126; and distributive justice, 71–72, 191; and the Fourteenth Amendment, 57–58; individual obligation to avoid, 210–12; and inequality, 58–59, 65, 75, 197n; injuries of, 66–70, 75, 79, 84, 133, 204, 205, 242; insulation from, 210–11; internalized, 61–62, 67, 69, 95, 123, 127, 149, 195 and n; law as inflicting, 144–45, 209–10; as malign preference, 63, 73, 97, 98; material disadvantage and, 137; norms as source of, 68; permissible and impermissible, 64–65 and nn, 67, 72; of poverty, 9, 47–48, 79, 88–89, 97, 101; process defect and, 59–60 and n, 84, 98, 107, 160; reparations and, 90n, 185; and reverse discrimination, 36n, 263; right to be free from, 185n; and self-respect, 194–95 and n, 200–201; separation implies, 57, 58, 59, 74, 95, 104–5, 118, 159, 209–10, 256; slavery, 62–63; socially constructed, 94–95, 96, 97–98, 118–19, 255–57; toward women, 117. *See also* Racism; Stereotyping

Stigma theories: cultural transformation and, 59, 73–75; and equal citizenship, 58–59; incomplete, 75–76, 77 and n, 96, 97, 99; judicial application of, 118–19 and n; result-based, 183; and social construction, 104–8, 118n

Strauder v. West Virginia, 57 and n, 59–60

Strauss, David, 17–18, 33, 34, 109–10 and n

Strauss, Marcy, 253

Strossen, Nadine, 227, 238

Sunstein, Cass: anticaste principle, 83–84, 84n, 121; on free speech, 222, 224, 226 and n, 227, 231, 235n, 241 and n

Supreme Court, U.S.: antidiscrimination project role, 11, 108, 109; counter-majoritarian, 19; First Amendment rulings, 229, 230–31, 241n; Fourteenth Amendment

Supreme Court, U.S. (*continued*)
rulings, 1, 15–16, 57–58, 95–96, 146–47, 155–56; on miscegenation, 154; perpetrator perspective, 77, 91–92; on private property, 188; on sexism, 131–35, 144–45. *See also* Judiciary; Scrutiny; *specific cases and individual justices*

Thirteenth Amendment, 11n, 63, 185
Thomas, Larry L., 197–98, 200
Trumbach, Randolph, 162–63, 166

United Kingdom, racism in, 259n
United States v. Carolene Products, 17, 49
Utilitarianism, 18–23, 27, 38, 39, 42–43, 180n, 206, 209

Van Alstyne, William, 101n
Village of Arlington Heights v. Metropolitan Housing Development Corp., 104–5, 107, 108n
Violence: gays as targets of, 149, 164–65; group disadvantage, 236; pornography and, 227, 231, 233 and n, 234, 236–42, 258; rape, 130 and n, 144, 227 and n, 237–38, 239–40 and nn; speech and, 236 and n, 244. *See also* Harassment
Virtue. *See* Morality
Volokh, Eugene, 253n

Wald, Patricia, 81
Walzer, Michael, 29–30, 31, 34–35, 37, 38, 73n, 120n, 197n
Wards Cove Packing Co. v. Atonio, 110n
Warren, Earl, 57
Washington, Booker T., 38
Washington v. Davis, 16n, 107, 108n, 110–11
Wasserstrom, Richard, 29, 46–47
Watkins v. United States Army, 116n

Wechsler, Herbert, 79–80, 179
Weeks, Jeffrey, 173
Weitzman, Lenore, 135
White, Byron, 65n, 156
Whites: antidiscrimination project consequences for, 114; benefits of racism to, 62; cultural transformation to end racism, 2, 4, 26, 51, 74, 97; desegregation does not harm, 106; higher value placed on, 40, 43, 45, 48, 100; as norm, 8, 69, 77, 100–101 and n; poor, 48, 85n; preferences for racism, 22–23, 25, 26–28, 31, 40; racial factionalism, 52, 53–54; racist assumptions of, 36–38, 47–48, 112; reparations by, 89–90; reverse discrimination against, 31–38, 52; role in racism, 89. *See also* Blacks; Race; Racism
Williams, Bernard, 119–20
Williams, Patricia, 35–36, 111–12
Women: black, 9, 124; child-care responsibilities, 2, 117, 124, 125, 127, 135, 137–38, 163; coerced into traditional roles, 133–34, 143 and n, 144, 145, 174; devalued, 121–27; double duty of, 135n, 136 and n; historical change in roles, 124–25, 135, 166–68; identity development, 163, 166, 172; marriage and, 134–36, 139; need for paid employment, 117 and n; poverty of, 134–35, 137–39, 184; separate spheres, 124–26, 143, 163; stigmatization of gays among, 161 and n, 172–74; stigmatized, 117, 122, 123–24, 126–27, 143; support for traditional roles, 119, 120, 121, 127, 135n, 143 and n, 172–74. *See also* Lesbians; Men; Sex, as a category; Sexism
Work. *See* Employment

Young, Iris Marion, 5n, 8, 68, 85–88 and nn, 94–95, 98, 236